Environmental Virtue Ethics

Environmental Virtue Ethics

EDITED BY
RONALD SANDLER
AND
PHILIP CAFARO

ROWMAN & LITTLEFIELD PUBLISHERS, INC.
Lanham • Boulder • New York • Oxford

ROWMAN & LITTLEFIELD PUBLISHERS, INC.

Published in the United States of America
by Rowman & Littlefield Publishers, Inc.
A wholly owned subsidary of The Rowman & Littlefield Publishing Group, Inc.
4501 Forbes Boulevard, Suite 200, Lanham, Maryland 20706
www.rowmanlittlefield.com

PO Box 317
Oxford
OX2 9RU, UK

British Library Cataloguing in Publication Information Available

Library of Congress Cataloging-in-Publication Data

Environmental virtue ethics / edited by Philip Cafaro and Ronald Sandler.
        p. cm.
    Includes index.
    ISBN 0-7425-3389-1 (hardcover : alk. paper0—ISBN 0-7425-3390-5 (pbk. : alk. paper)
    1. Human ecology. 2. Environmental ethics. I. Cafaro, Philip, 1962-   II. Sandler,
Ronald D.

  GF21.E58 2004
  179'.1—dc22

                                        2004017328

Printed in the United States of America

♾™ The paper used in this publication meets the minimum requirements of American National Standard for Information Sciences—Permanence of Paper for Printed Library Materials, ANSI/NISO Z39.48-1992.

To Jerry Freilich and in memory of Eugene Odum, colleagues at the University of Georgia who taught me to appreciate nature and its many contributions to human flourishing, and to Mark Easter and Kelly Ohlson, working to preserve wild nature in northern Colorado and to create a society to match the scenery

—Phil Cafaro

To my grandparents, Sidney and Beatrice Motel and Louis and Elizabeth Sandler

—Ron Sandler

Contents

Acknowledgments   ix

Introduction: Environmental Virtue Ethics   1
   Ronald Sandler

PART 1: RECOGNIZING ENVIRONMENTAL VIRTUE ETHICS

1   The Emergence of Ecological Virtue Language   15
   Louke van Wensveen

2   Thoreau, Leopold, and Carson: Toward an Environmental Virtue Ethics   31
   Philip Cafaro

PART 2: ENVIRONMENTAL VIRTUE ETHICS THEORY

3   Ideals of Human Excellence and Preserving Natural Environments   47
   Thomas Hill Jr.

4   Environmental Virtue Ethics: Half the Truth but Dangerous as a Whole   61
   Holmes Rolston III

5   Virtue Ethics as Foundational for a Global Ethic   79
   Laura Westra

6   A Virtue Ethics Approach to Aldo Leopold's Land Ethic   93
   Bill Shaw

7   Virtue Ethics and Repugnant Conclusions   107
   David Schmidtz and Matt Zwolinski

PART 3: ENVIRONMENTAL VIRTUES AND VICES

8   Benevolence as an Environmental Virtue   121
   Geoffrey Frasz

9   Gluttony, Arrogance, Greed, and Apathy: An Exploration of
   Environmental Vice   135
   Philip Cafaro

10   Vices and Virtues in Religious Environmental Ethics   159
     Charles Taliaferro

11   Cardinal Environmental Virtues: A Neurobiological Perspective   173
     Louke van Wensveen

PART 4: APPLYING ENVIRONMENTAL VIRTUE ETHICS

12   Synergistic Environmental Virtues: Consumerism and
     Human Flourishing   197
     Peter Wenz

13   A Virtue Ethics Perspective on Genetically Modified Crops   215
     Ronald Sandler

Contributors   233

Index   237

Acknowledgments

Chapter 1, "The Emergence of Ecological Virtue Language," originally appeared as chapter 1 of Louke van Wensveen's *Dirty Virtues: The Emergence of Ecological Virtue Ethics* (Humanity Books, 2000). We thank both the author and Humanity Books for permission to reprint the chapter here.

Chapter 2, "Thoreau, Leopold, and Carson: Toward an Environmental Virtue Ethics," originally appeared in *Environmental Ethics* 23 (2001): 3–17. We thank *Environmental Ethics* for permission to reprint the article here.

Chapter 3, "Ideals of Human Excellence and Preserving Natural Environments," originally appeared in *Environmental Ethics* 5 (1983): 211–24. We thank both the author and *Environmental Ethics* for permission to reprint the article here.

Chapter 6, "A Virtue Ethics Approach to Aldo Leopold's Land Ethic," originally appeared in *Environmental Ethics* 19 (1997): 53–67. We thank both the author and *Environmental Ethics* for permission to reprint the article here.

Note: Each of the above articles has been slightly stylistically altered from the original.

Introduction: Environmental Virtue Ethics

Ronald Sandler

It is a wholesome and necessary thing for us to turn again to the earth and in the contemplation of her beauties to know of wonder and humility.

—Rachel Carson

When we see land as a community to which we belong, we may begin to use it with love and respect.

—Aldo Leopold

All the wild world is beautiful, and it matters but little where we go . . . everywhere and always we are in God's eternal beauty and love.

—John Muir

Those things of real worth in life are worth going to any length in love and respect to safeguard.

—Julia Butterfly Hill

There is at least one certainty regarding the human relationship with nature: there is no getting away from it. One simply cannot opt out of a relationship with the natural world. On some accounts this is because humans are themselves a part of nature. On others it is because we must breathe, eat, drink, and decompose, each of which involves an exchange with the natural world. But whereas a relationship with nature is given, the nature of that relationship is not. Both human history and the contemporary world are replete with diverse and contradictory ways of conceiving of and interacting with the natural environment. Environmental ethics as a field of inquiry is the attempt to understand the human relationship with the environment (including natural ecosystems, agricultural ecosystems, urban ecosystems, and the individuals that populate and constitute those systems) and determine the norms that should govern our interactions with it. These norms can be either norms of action or norms of character. The project of specifying the latter is *environmental virtue ethics*, and a particular account of the character dispositions that we ought to have regarding the environment is an *environmental virtue ethic*.

Why Is There a Need for an Environmental Virtue Ethic?

The central ethical question is, "How should one live?" Answering this question of course requires providing an account of what actions we ought and ought not to perform. But an account of right action—whether a set of rules, a general principle, or a decision-making procedure—does not answer it entirely. A complete answer will inform not only what we ought to do but also what kind of person we ought to be. An adequate ethical theory must provide an ethic of character, and our lived ethical experience belies the claim that one's character is merely the sum of one's actions. Environmental ethics is simply ethics as it pertains to human–environment interactions and relationships. So an adequate environmental ethic likewise requires not only an ethic of action—one that provides guidance regarding what we ought and ought not to do to the environment—but also an ethic of character—one that provides guidance on what attitudes and dispositions we ought and ought not to have regarding the environment.

Consider the four widely regarded environmental heroes quoted above: Rachel Carson (naturalist and author of *Silent Spring*), John Muir (naturalist and founder of the Sierra Club), Aldo Leopold (wildlife ecologist and author of *A Sand County Almanac*), and Julia Butterfly Hill (activist who lived two years atop a threatened redwood). Why do we admire these individuals? Is it their accomplishments in defense of the environment? Yes. The sacrifices they made for those accomplishments? Of course. Their capacity to motivate others to take action? To be sure. But it is not only what they have done and the legacy they have left that we admire. It is also them—the individuals who managed those accomplishments, made those sacrifices, and have left those legacies. That is, we admire them also for their character—their fortitude, compassion, wonder, sensitivity, respectfulness, courage, love, appreciation, tenacity, and gratitude.

It is not always easy to keep this dimension of environmentalism in mind. Public discourse regarding the environment tends to be framed almost exclusively in legislative and legal terms, so it is tempting to become fixated on what activities and behaviors regarding the environment are or ought to be legal. After all, we might restrict the use of off-road vehicles in an ecologically sensitive area and take legal action against those who fail to adhere to that boundary; but we will not legislate against ecological insensitivity or indifference itself, and no one will be called to court merely for possessing those attitudes. We legislate regarding behavior, not character; policy concerns actions, not attitudes; and the courts apply the standards accordingly.

But as our environmental heroes remind us—both by example and by word—we must not take so narrow a perspective of our relationship with the environment. It is always *people*—with character traits, attitudes, and dispositions—who perform actions, promote policies, and lobby for laws. So while we decry removing mountaintops, filling wetlands, and poisoning wolves and we make our case against these practices before lawmakers, the courts, and the public, we must also consider the character of persons responsible for them. Indeed, how one interacts with the environment is largely determined by one's disposition toward it, and it seems to many that the enabling cause of reckless environmental exploitation is the attitude that nature is merely a boundless resource for satisfying human wants and needs. In Muir's words, "No dogma taught by the present civilization seems to form so insuperable an obstacle in the way of a right understanding of the relations which culture sustains to wildness as that which regards the world as made especially for the uses of man." So it would seem that any significant change in our environmental practices and policies is going to require a substantial shift in our dispositions toward the environment. In this way proper character is indispensable for facilitating right action and behavior.

But as our environmental heroes also remind us—again, by example and by word—environmental virtue is not merely instrumentally valuable as the disposition to identify and then perform proper actions; it is also valuable in itself. It is life-affirming and life-enhancing. Those who possess it are better off than those who do not, for they are able to find reward, satisfaction, and comfort from their relationship with nature; and it is their character—their capacity to appreciate, respect, and love nature—that opens them to these benefits. "Those who dwell, as scientists or laymen, among the beauties and mysteries of the earth are never alone or weary of life," writes Carson; and according to Muir, "Everybody needs beauty as well as bread, places to play in and pray in, where nature may heal and give strength to body and soul alike." To those who are receptive to it, nature is a source of joy, peace, renewal, and self-knowledge.

Once the need for an environmental virtue ethic is recognized two questions immediately present themselves. First, what are the attitudes and dispositions that constitute environmental virtue? Second, what is the proper role of an ethic of character in an environmental ethic? These two issues—specifying environmental virtue and identifying the appropriate role of virtue in an environmental ethic—are central to environmental virtue ethics and largely orient the philosophical work that appears in this collection. The remainder of this introduction is intended to serve as a primer on these issues and to locate the contributions in this collection within these philosophical themes.

Specifying Environmental Virtue

The environmental virtues are the proper dispositions or character traits for human beings to have regarding their interactions and relationships with the environment. The environmentally virtuous person is disposed to respond—both emotionally and through action—to the environment and the nonhuman individuals (whether inanimate, living, or conscious) that populate it in an excellent or fine way. But although this formal account may be accurate, it does not provide any substantive description of what the environmentally virtuous person will actually be like. So how does one establish which dispositions regarding the environment are constitutive of virtue and which are constitutive of vice (and which are neither)? That is, how does one go about providing a substantive account of the environmental virtues and vices?

Perhaps the most common strategy for specifying environmental virtue is to argue by extension from standard interpersonal virtues, that is, from virtues that are typically applied to relationships among humans. Each interpersonal virtue is normative for a particular range of items, activities, or interactions, and that range is its sphere or field of applicability. For example, the field of honesty is the revealing or withholding of truth; the field of temperance is bodily pleasures and pains; and the field of generosity is the giving and withholding of material goods. Extensionists attempt to expand the range of certain interpersonal virtues to include nonhuman entities by arguing that the features that characterize their fields in interpersonal interaction or relationships also obtain in (at least some) environmental contexts. The virtues, they conclude, should therefore be normative in those environmental contexts as well. For example, if compassion is the appropriate disposition to have toward the suffering of other human beings and there is no relevant moral difference between human suffering and the suffering of nonhuman animals, then one should be compassionate toward the suffering of nonhuman animals. Or if gratitude is the appropriate disposition toward other human beings from whom one has benefited and one has similarly benefited from the natural environment, then gratitude is also an appropriate disposition to have toward the natural environment. Extension from the substance of the interpersonal virtues is thus one strategy for specifying the environmentally virtuous person.

A second strategy is to appeal to agent benefit. On this approach, what establishes a particular character trait as constitutive of environmental virtue is that it typically benefits its possessor. This is a wide-ranging approach bounded only by the limit to the ways in which the environment benefits moral agents. The environment provides not only material goods—such as clean water and air—but also aesthetic goods, recreational goods, and a location to exercise and develop physically, intellectually, morally, and aesthetically. That the environment can benefit individuals in such ways straightforwardly justifies a disposition to preserve these opportunities and goods. But it does not only justify a disposition toward conservation and preservation. It justifies cultivating the kind of character traits that allow one to enjoy those goods. The natural environmental provides the opportunity for aesthetic experience, but that benefit accrues only to those who possess the disposition to appreciate the natural environment in that way. It provides the opportunity for intellectual challenge and reward, but those benefits come only to those who are disposed first to wonder and then to try to understand nature. The natural environment provides plentiful opportunities for meaningful relationships with its denizens, but those relationships are only possible for those who are open to having them. So considerations of which environmental dispositions benefit their possessor (and allow their possessor to be benefited by the natural environment) are relevant to the substantive specification of environmental virtue. In this way environmental virtue ethics emphasizes the role that enlightened self-interest can play in promoting or motivating environmental consciousness and its corresponding behavior in a way that reinforces rather than undermines the other-regarding aspects of environmental ethics. It allows for environmental ethics to be self-interested without being egoistic.

A third strategy for the specification of environmental virtue is to argue from considerations of human excellence. On this approach what establishes a particular character trait as constitutive of environmental virtue is that it makes its possessor a good human being. What it means to be a good human being—to flourish as a human being—is typically understood naturalistically. That is, it is understood in terms of the characteristic features of the life of members of the human species. Human beings are, for example, social beings. Excellence as a human being therefore involves character dispositions that promote the good functioning of social groups and encourage one to maintain healthy relationships with members in the group. A human being who is disposed to undermine social cohesion, disrupt the conditions that make cooperation among individuals possible, and sour relationships with others is properly described as deviant. Such a person fails to be a good human being precisely in virtue of his or her antisocial disposition. Many environmental philosophers have argued that a proper naturalistic understanding of human beings will locate them not only socially (as members of the human community) but also ecologically (as members of the broader biotic community). If this is correct, then excellence as a human being would include dispositions to maintain and promote the well-being of the larger ecological community. Given that the well-being of the ecological community is threatened by further habitat fragmentation and biodiversity loss, a disposition to oppose these would thereby be constitutive of environmental virtue. A human being who lacked these dispositions would, from the perspective of human beings as members of the biotic community, be properly described as deviant. Considerations of human excellence need not, however, be confined to secular or naturalistic accounts of environmental virtue. Human excellence is often understood by religious traditions in a way that transcends the natural by connecting it with divine or cosmic purposes. For example, if it is the divinely proscribed role of human beings that they be stewards of the land, then the environmental virtues will be those character traits or dispositions that make human beings reliable and effective stewards.

A fourth strategy for specifying environmental virtue is to study the character traits of individuals who are recognized as environmental role models. By examining the life, work, and character of exemplars of environmental excellence we may be able to identify particular traits that are conducive to, or constitutive of, that excellence. The lives of John Muir, Rachel Carson, and Aldo Leopold, for example, are not just compelling narratives; they also instruct us on how to improve ourselves and our approach to the natural world. Environmental role models of course need not be such public or renowned figures as Carson, Muir, and Leopold. Exemplars of environmental excellence can be found in local communities and in many organizations working for environmental protection and improvement. No doubt many of us have been benefited by such people, not only by their accomplishments but also by the guidance, inspiration, and example they provide.

These four approaches to the specification of environmental virtue—extensionism, considerations of benefit to agent, considerations of human excellence, and the study of role models—are not mutually exclusive. A particular disposition might draw support from all four approaches. Indeed, in the contributions in this collection one often finds them working in concert. Collectively they provide a rich variety of resources for thinking about the substance of environmental virtue.

The Role of Environmental Virtue in Environmental Ethics

A complete environmental ethic will include both an account of how one ought to interact with the natural environment and an account of the character dispositions that one ought to have regarding the natural environment. But what is the proper relationship between these two? This is an instance of the more general (and very much live) question in moral philosophy: What is the appropriate role of virtue in ethical theory?

Some moral philosophers believe that the virtues are simply dispositions to do the right thing. In the context of environmental ethics this would imply that environmental virtue is merely the disposition to act according to the rules, principles, or norms of action of the correct environmental ethic. On this account the environmental virtues are strictly instrumental and subordinate to right action. First one determines what the right ways to act or behave regarding the environment are, and then one determines which character dispositions tend to produce that behavior. Those dispositions are the environmental virtues.

I argued earlier that environmental virtue is instrumental to promoting proper action. The environmentally virtuous person—precisely because of his or her virtue—will be disposed both to recognize the right thing and to do it for the right reasons. However, there is more to how one ought to be in the world than the rules, principles, or guidelines of moral action. For example, it might not be morally required that one appreciate the beauty or complexity of the natural environment, but those who are disposed to do so are benefited and so better off than those who are not. So although it is undoubtedly true that the environmental virtues are dispositions to act well regarding the environment, they are not only that. As we have seen, they can be excellences or beneficial to their possessor in their own right, not merely insofar as they tend to produce right action.

Moreover, environmental virtue might provide the sensitivity or wisdom necessary for the application of action-guiding rules and principles to concrete situations. At a minimum, this sensitivity is required to determine which rules or principles are applicable to which situations, as well as for determining what course of action they recommend in those situations where they are operative. But it may also be indispensable in adjudicating between conflicting demands of morality or resolving moral dilemmas that arise from a plurality of sources of value and justification. Indeed, many moral philosophers have argued that it is implausible and unreasonable to believe that there is some finite set of rules or principles that can be applied by any human moral agent in any situation to determine what the proper course of action is in that situation. If they are correct—if action guidance cannot always be accomplished by moral rules and principles alone—then the wisdom and sensitivity that are part of virtue (including environmental virtue) are in some situations indispensable for determining or identifying right action (including environmentally right action).

Some moral philosophers believe that virtue should play an even more prominent or fundamental role within ethical theory than it is afforded in the previous account. These virtue ethicists consider an ethic of character to be theoretically prior to an ethic of action. On this approach to moral philosophy an action is right if and only if it is the virtuous thing to do, it hits the target of virtue, or it is what the virtuous person would do under the circumstances. So a substantive account of the virtues and the virtuous person informs what actions one ought or ought not to perform. In the context of environmental ethics this would imply that reflections on the content of the virtues and studying the character traits and behavior of environmentally virtuous people are what ultimately inform how we ought to behave regarding the environment.

There is thus a range of roles—from instrumental to foundational—that environmental virtue might play within a complete environmental ethic. This is not, however, to claim that each position is equally defensible. I have, for example, argued that a merely instrumental role for environmental virtue is too narrow. But those arguments notwithstanding, it is very much an unsettled issue what the proper role (or roles) of virtue is in an adequate environmental ethic, and the reader will find a sampling of the range of possibilities in the selections in this collection.

The Selections

The selections—which consist of ten original contributions written specifically for this collection, as well as reprints of four key previously published works on the topic—are divided into four sections. In this first section, "Recognizing Environmental Virtue Ethics," Louke van Wensveen and Philip Cafaro reflect on the roles that considerations of virtue and character have traditionally played in environmental discourse. In "The Emergence of Ecological Virtue Language" Wensveen tracks this history by reviewing the language that environmentalists and environmental ethicists, both secular and religious, have used to characterize their environmental ethics. She finds virtue language ubiquitous in these articulations. Indeed, she writes that she is "yet to come across a piece of ecologically sensitive philosophy, theology, or ethics that does not in some way incorporate virtue language." Moreover, she finds the discourse to be integral, diverse, dialectic, dynamic, and visionary. Virtue language is not only everywhere in the discourse, it is indispensable to the discourse. Virtue language, Wensveen concludes, puts us in touch with a rich set of evaluative concepts and perspectives, and if afforded sufficient attention, it can expand and enhance our capacity to respond to environmental issues. As she says, "One more language is one more chance."

In "Thoreau, Leopold, and Carson: Toward an Environmental Virtue Ethics," Cafaro tracks the role of virtue and character in environmental discourse by reflecting on the lives and writings of three widely influential and respected environmental figures: Henry David Thoreau, Aldo Leopold, and Rachel Carson. Although these models of environmental excellence lived very different lives and expressed their virtue in diverse ways, we nonetheless find among them certain commonalities. These commonalities, Cafaro argues, are characteristic of environmental excellence and must be embraced by any environmental virtue ethic worth the name. They include putting economic life in its proper place, cultivating scientific knowledge, extending moral considerability beyond human beings, promoting wilderness protection, and believing in the goodness of life (both human and nonhuman). Cafaro also emphasizes the importance of these environmental heroes as examples of individuals who live well with nature. Their lives suggest that "greater attention to our true happiness would do as much to protect the environment as the acceptance of the intrinsic value of wild nature."

In the second section of the collection, "Environmental Virtue Ethics Theory," Thomas Hill Jr., Holmes Rolston III, Laura Westra, Bill Shaw, and David Schmidtz and Matt Zwolinski consider the proper role for environmental virtue ethics within environmental ethics. In "Ideals of Human Excellence and Preserving Natural Environments" Hill argues that there are cases of environmental behavior that are intuitively improper—for example, needlessly paving over a patch of natural landscape—whose impropriety is best understood in the context of an account of human excellence and the dispositions that we ought to express in our environmental interactions. Hill argues that such behavior, or "even [seeing nature's] value solely in cost/benefit terms," betrays the absence of traits that are the natural facilitators for developing proper humility and appreciation. If he is correct, then sometimes the answer to the question "What is wrong with treating the environment that way?" is intelligible only against the background of an answer to the question, "What is wrong with the kind of person who would do that?"

However, in "Environmental Virtue Ethics: Half the Truth but Dangerous as a Whole," Rolston warns against casting environmental virtue in too fundamental a role in environmental ethics. Although environmental virtue is an intrinsically good state, valuable to its possessor, and enables attunement to "the flow of nature," we must not identify human virtue or excellence as the source of natural value. Natural entities do not derive their value from their relationship to human virtue and flourishing; nature and natural entities have value in themselves. Indeed, environmental virtue is only intelligible as a responsiveness to the independent value of nature. After all, "it is hard to gain much excellence of character from appreciating an otherwise worthless thing." Rolston thus finds environmental virtue ethics dangerous to the extent that its focus on human flourishing distracts us from the intrinsic value of natural entities that makes environmental virtue possible. "Our deeper ethical achievement," he writes, "needs to focus on values as intrinsic achievements in wild nature. These virtues within us need to attend to values without us."

Westra, like Rolston, believes that natural value is not derived from the value of humans or human flourishing. However, in "Virtue Ethics as Foundational for a Global Ethic" she argues that virtue ethics has a foundational role nonetheless. It provides an account of flourishing—for humans, nonhumans, and natural systems—which it is the goal of a global ethic to promote. This foundation justifies the need for both ecological integrity and environmental or ecological rights because all individuals (human and nonhuman) depend on ecosystem services for their survival, health, and optimum functioning. This is true (in regard to humans) not only for Aristotelian accounts of human excellence but also for Kantian accounts that identify human functioning with moral agency, for the cultivation and exercise of moral agency depend on the capacity of natural ecosystems to provide their preconditions (e.g., food, clear air, and clean water). So both ecosystem integrity and human rights are supported by virtue ethics. But because international discourse is largely framed in terms of human rights, Westra urges that "we must emphasize the human rights dimension of this ethic and its implication for international law."

In "A Virtue Ethics Approach to Aldo Leopold's Land Ethic," Shaw examines Leopold's land ethic—that one ought to promote the integrity, beauty, and stability of the biotic community—from a virtue ethics perspective. He argues that operationalizing or enacting the land ethic requires cultivating certain virtues, which he calls "land virtues," that not only dispose individuals to act in ways that promote the integrity, stability, and beauty of natural systems but also mitigate some of the difficulties that arise when the land ethic is treated strictly as an account of right action. Shaw suggests three land virtues—respect (or ecological sensitivity), prudence, and practical judgment—each of which he considers to be an adaptation of a conventional interpersonal virtue. However, any character trait that contributes to an attitude of community with the land and promotes its integrity, stability, and beauty is properly a land virtue.

In the final contribution of this section, "Virtue Ethics and Repugnant Conclusions," Schmidtz and Zwolinski argue that virtue ethics offers indispensable resources for addressing Derek Parfit's "repugnant conclusions," the most notorious of which is that for any number of persons, all with lives well worth living, there is some much larger human population whose existence would be better, even though the lives of its members are only barely worth living. The repugnant conclusions have typically been thought to arise from (and thereby indict) only certain forms of utilitarianism, but Schmidtz and Zwolinski argue that they are considerably more insidious and "suggest problems for the whole idea that moral theorizing should culminate in a simple formula for right action." An appropriate response to the repugnant conclusions will therefore not be found by merely reformulating traditional principles of right action but, instead, must involve considerations of character and human excellence. In so arguing they both embrace and expand on Hill's claims that the impropriety of some environmental behaviors is best understood by reflecting on the kind of person who would do such a thing. One implication of this for moral theory is that no principle of right action is a replacement for moral wisdom, sensitivity, and experience. "The proper lesson," they write, "is not that act-centered theories are useless . . . but, rather, that we are better off treating act-centered theory as the sort of thing from which wise persons can gain insight that is useful, even if limited."

The third section of the collection, "Environmental Virtues and Vices," contains discussions of the substantive content of environmental virtue and vice by Geoffrey Frasz, Philip Cafaro, Charles Taliaferro, and Louke van Wensveen. Rather than focusing on a detailed account of any specific environmental virtue or vice, the authors aim to provide a general account or typology of environmental virtue and vice from which future work can proceed. In "Benevolence as an Environmental Virtue" Frasz employs an extensionist approach to articulate and defend benevolence as an environmental virtue. He considers benevolence to be a genus under which fall specific other-regarding environmental virtues such as compassion, friendship, kindness, and gratitude. Among the vices counter to benevolence he considers jealousy, selfishness, greed, and profligacy. Central to benevolence, in both interpersonal and environmental contexts, is a genuine concern for the welfare of another. This concern is made possible by what Frasz calls "an imaginative dwelling on the condition of the other," which requires understanding the interests of the other. There is thus "an important role for the biological and ecological sciences, for nature writing, and for personal accounts of encounters with wild creatures" in the cultivation and maintenance of environmental benevolence. Frasz concludes with a discussion of the ways in which environmental benevolence benefits its possessor. He argues that "in cultivating the environmental virtue of benevolence we can discover who we really are and what it will take to live in a joyous way with the nonhuman world of which we are a part."

If, as Frasz argues, environmental virtue benefits both its possessor and the natural environment, then perhaps the concept of environmental vice is best understood in terms of the frustration of human and environmental flourishing, as well as the connections between them. In "Gluttony, Arrogance, Greed, and Apathy: An Exploration of Environmental Vice," Cafaro develops such an account. According to Cafaro, "A vice harms the vicious person, those around him or her, or both." Judgments about the vices are thus derivative on particular conceptions of the "goods" that make up a good human life, a well-functioning society, and a healthy natural environment. Establishing that a particular disposition regarding the environment is a vice thus requires showing how the disposition is detrimental to its possessor, those around him or her, and nonhuman nature. Cafaro applies this standard in the course of elucidating four key environmental vices—gluttony, arrogance, greed, and apathy—each of which, he argues, harms its possessor, other people, and nature.

In "Vices and Virtues in Religious Environmental Ethics," Taliaferro discusses virtues and vices in both theistic (Jewish, Christian, and Islamic) and Buddhist environmental ethics. Taliaferro begins apologetically, arguing that there are several reasons why environmental ethicists should be attentive to religious ethical traditions, not least of which are that at least one religious tradition may be true. Moreover, the majority of the world's population subscribes to some religious tradition, so to be relevant to the actual world an environmental ethic must be able to engage those traditions. Taliaferro then demonstrates how environmental virtues such as gratitude, respect, solidarity, and caring (and the corresponding vices of ingratitude, vanity, and exploitiveness) emerge from the central tenets of theistic environmental ethics: creation, divine ownership, and the identification of natural goods with God's presence. Regarding the Buddhist traditions, Taliaferro focuses on the emergence of mindfulness and compassion as environmental virtues as part of the Buddhist goal of detachment. He concludes by examining how these religious virtues function both explicitly and implicitly in environmental contexts such as agriculture.

In the final contribution of this section, "Cardinal Environmental Virtues: A Neurobiological Perspective," Wensveen considers whether the traditional cardinal virtues—practical wisdom, justice, temperance, and courage—are sufficient for providing guidance in this age of ecological crises. She argues that we ought to neither cling to the traditional account of these virtues nor jettison them entirely. We should instead take a "middle course" and revamp them in light of our improved biological, ecological, and neurological vantage point. After all, we are "now in a better position than the ancients ever were to judge how well the traditional cardinals shape our emotions, allowing us to pursue the goals of our lives in ways that are appropriate within our particular environments." Wensveen thus advocates putting a contemporary ecological spin on the venerable tradition of the cardinal virtues. She argues that we should consider a particular virtue cardinal "if its cultivation consists of conditioning a particular type of neurobiological system that plays a pivotal role in processes of emotional fine-tuning by which agents are enabled to flourish and let flourish under changing circumstances." Using this definition she argues for several environmental virtues that are themselves cardinal (for example, sensitivity and tenacity), related to cardinals as constituents (for example, humility, respect, gratitude, benevolence, attentiveness, and loyalty), or particular instantiations of cardinals (for example, friendship, love, frugality, and simplicity).

In the final section of the collection, "The Application of Environmental Virtue," Peter Wenz and I apply environmental virtue ethics to concrete environmental issues and problems. These contributions belie the criticism that environmental virtue ethics is unable to provide guidance regarding actual environmental issues or decisions. In "Synergistic Environmental Virtues: Consumerism and Human Flourishing" Wenz considers the relationship among traditional anthropocentric virtues and vices, nonanthropocentric environmental ethics, and consumerism. He argues that for people in industrialized nations the traditional virtues foster both human and environmental flourishing, whereas the traditional vices diminish both. Anthropocentric and nonanthropocentric accounts of virtue and flourishing are thus synergistic— "each is stronger in combination with the other than alone." The key to this synergism is a shared repugnance to consumerism, which as practiced in industrialized countries is harmful to both humans and nature. Wenz therefore suggests that individuals in industrialized countries ought to adopt what he calls "the principle of anticipatory cooperation" when making consumer decisions. This principle "calls for actions that deviate from the social norm in the direction of the ideal that virtuous people aspire to for themselves and others but which do not deviate so much that virtue impairs instead of fosters flourishing."

In "A Virtue Ethics Perspective on Genetically Modified Crops," I propose a virtue ethics approach for assessing the acceptability of the use of genetically modified crops in agriculture. From a virtue ethics perspective, an environmental assessment of a particular genetically modified crop involves determining whether the technology will compromise the capacity of the environment to produce the goods essential to the development and maintenance of human virtue, as well as determining if the technology is contrary to any of the virtues applicable to human interactions with the natural environment. Using these criteria I defend a limited endorsement position regarding genetically modified crops. There is, I argue, a presumption, justified by humility, against the use of genetically modified crops in agriculture. However, if the external goods criterion is met, this presumption can be overcome by other virtue-based considerations. For example, in the case of golden rice (rice genetically modified to produce the precursor to vitamin A), the external goods criterion is met, and the presumption against the use of genetically modified crops is overcome by compassion for those suffering from vitamin A deficiency.

Although work on environmental virtue has become increasingly visible in recent years, environmental virtue ethics remains a relatively underappreciated and underdeveloped aspect of environmental ethics. Philip Cafaro and I hope that the work collected here will not only help establish the indispensability of this area of environmental ethics but also enhance the breadth and quality of the ongoing discussion of environmental virtue and vice and the role they should play in an adequate environmental ethic. This collection is thus not intended to settle the central issues of environmental virtue ethics but, rather, to provide an impetus and orientation for further work on them. We very much look forward to those discussions.

PART 1

RECOGNIZING ENVIRONMENTAL VIRTUE ETHICS

CHAPTER 1

The Emergence of Ecological Virtue Language

Louke van Wensveen

The word *virtue* has an old-fashioned ring to it. The word *vice* perhaps even more so. When as Westerners we hear these terms, we may think of professors belaboring the significance of the ancient four cardinal virtues or priests sermonizing on the perennial three theological virtues and the seven deadly sins. Even if we cannot exactly remember what they all are, we know these virtues and vices represent tradition, and so they inspire us with awe, or rather with resentment, or perhaps with an uneasy mixture of both. Then, of course, we may also think we have moved entirely beyond virtue and vice—either in skeptical rejection of tradition or for lack of familiarity with it. Even so, *virtue* and *vice* will sound old-fashioned and hardly relevant to a book on the future-oriented and somewhat counter-cultural topic of ecological ethics.

I will not retort with an apology on the surprising relevance of established Western virtue traditions in an ecological age. Yet I will draw attention to a particular type of moral language that pervades the writings of those who seek to respond to the environmental crisis. In this mushrooming ecological literature, we are encouraged to care for our bioregions, to respect trees, to show compassion for the suffering of animals, to be humble and wise in the use of technology, to be frugal and creative in the use of limited resources, and to have hope in the face of impending global disaster. Conversely, we are warned to avoid the arrogance of anthropocentrism, to stop being cruel in our treatment of animals, to admit that we habitually project our fears onto nature, and to put a halt on our greed and the resulting manipulative exploitation of natural resources.

What would be an appropriate name for this language? The term *virtue language* (which includes vices as well) does seem appropriate. But then somehow we must indicate that we are not simply dealing with a rehash of tradition. Perhaps *ecological virtue language* is most descriptive, if somewhat mundane. I will use this expression in the remainder of the chapter. Personally I like to think of the virtue language that ecologically minded people tend to use as "dirty virtues"—"dirty" because this language expresses a preoccupation with the earth (read: dirt = soil) and also because many ecological virtues would have been considered not particularly praiseworthy, or even vicious, during most of Western history (read: dirty = bad, taboo).

What does this dirty virtue language look like? The examples I have given immediately speak to the imagination. Respect for nature, caring, frugality, and hope clearly must be important attitudes in an ecological age. And arrogance, cruelty, and greed clearly must be avoided. Yet what exactly do we mean when we use these terms? Eco-literature contains many thoughtful passages that relay the flavor of ecological virtues and vices. We also discover in this literature a much wider range of virtues and vices than we might expect. To give an idea of this richness in flavor and range, let me share some passages that describe ecological virtues:

> Respecting nature literally involves "looking again." We cannot attend to the quality of relations that we engage in unless we know the details that surround our actions and relations.[1]
>
> The proper response to an emerging sense of the vastness and opacity of "wild connection" is not a (further) retreat into our own small realms of (supposed) transparency. Instead: fascination, interest, humility. Bowing before the mysteries of the world, entering a kind of wild etiquette.[2]
>
> Adherents to voluntary simplicity, those who content themselves with no more than they need, can now be found in significant numbers in most Western industrial societies and in some other societies as well. Deliberately abandoning the frenetic pursuit of material goods in favor of a simpler lifestyle, they are involved in recycling, home gardening, biking to work, and the rebellion against conspicuous consumption and planned obsolescence.[3]
>
> Awe and amazement are the results of a rich creation story, and the awe we feel should encompass our very selves, since every self is part of the unfolding creation story. We feel our interconnection with other creatures and peoples on this surprising planet in this amazing universe of one trillion galaxies, each with 200 billion stars.[4]
>
> I would define an ethical position most simply as this: acting to the best of one's ability from a sensibility that simultaneously knows and values oneself as an individual; is compassionate through identification with human and nonhuman others caring about others' lives and well-being; and is creative, undergoing self-transformation through cultivating a relation to collectives ranging from human families to the planetary community.[5]

The richness of this language, and the fact that it flows from so many mouths, has inspired me to compile a catalog of ecological virtues and vices—much as biologists record the variety of flora and fauna they encounter.[6]

I have yet to come across a piece of ecologically sensitive philosophy, theology, or ethics that does not in some way incorporate virtue language. Ecological virtue language turns up in the writings of social ecologists as well as deep ecologists, bioregionalists as well as animal rights activists, creation theologians as well as environmental philosophers, mainstream theologians as well as radical ecofeminists. Within these different strands, however, ecological virtue language seems to turn up especially when authors assume a hortatory, personal, reflection-filled mode of writing. This most often happens in their concluding statements. Conversely, if a source contains much technical language, whether scientific, philosophical, theological, or metaethical, virtue language tends to turn up much less frequently. Still, even though remnants remain of the once widespread attempt to avoid normative discourse in the context of "objective" discussions, virtues and vices often seem to elude such a ban, so that even in more technical pieces authors can unabashedly use terms such as *respect* and *manipulation*.

At this point we may well ask: If such a rich variety of ecological virtues and vices exists in such a wide range of literature, why is this moral language not better known? Why, in fact, have some commentators even lamented the low profile of virtues in environmental ethics?[7] This curious situation becomes understandable, I think, if we consider that those who have initiated key *methodological* discussions in the field of environmental ethics have generally not (or not primarily) been virtue ethicists.[8] Discussions in environmental ethics have largely focused on rights, values, duties, principles, and consequentialist arguments. This emphasis has created a blind spot for a segment of ecological moral language that, quietly living between the often heated debates about the rights of trees or the intrinsic values of rocks, actually flourishes quite profusely.

But, we might protest, choice of method is political, so the low profile of ecological virtue language cannot be seen as an innocent oversight! Val Plumwood, one of the few authors who has recently promoted a virtue-based ecological ethic, develops this argument based on a feminist analysis of the public/private distinction:

> Rights seem to have acquired an exaggerated importance in ethics as part of the prestige of the public sphere and the masculine, and the emphasis on separation and autonomy, on reason and abstraction. A more promising approach for an ethic of nature, and also one much more in line with the current directions in feminism, would be to remove rights from the centre of the moral stage and pay more attention to some other less universalistic moral concepts such as respect, sympathy, care, concern, compassion, gratitude, friendship and responsibility. . . . These more local moral concepts, because of their dualistic construal as feminine, and their consignment to the private sphere as subjective and emotional, have been treated as peripheral and given far less importance than they deserve.[9]

I find Plumwood's thesis quite plausible.

I also believe other factors have contributed to the methodological "virtue blindness" of environmental ethicists. For one thing, consider the context of litigation, an important focus of reform environmentalism. Here virtue language has much less bite than the language of rights. (I imagine that appealing to a chemical company's love of nature in a court of law would be as effective as appealing to an ex-spouse's love of his or her children in a child custody case.) No wonder then that in the midst of heated litigation involving toxic cleanup, pollution control, and the destiny of forests, virtues have not received much attention.

Another reason for the virtue blindness of environmental ethicists may be that recent interest in virtue ethics is about as old as the field of environmental ethics itself. Both represent nodes of great creativity in the field of ethics. We can imagine them as seeds that sprouted relatively independently and which only now, as plants, are beginning to cross-pollinate. Such a scenario is quite plausible given the specialized nature of much academic reflection and the limited ability of scholars to explore various new developments simultaneously. (This is the kind explanation. The more suspicious version states that the two seeds belong to different species, one conservative and the other progressive, which is the reason why they do not, nor should they be made to, interact much.)

Most of all, and here I return to my opening thought, I think the methodological virtue blindness of environmental ethicists is a result of the fact that the terms *virtue* and *vice* carry the stigma of sounding old-fashioned, preachy, and self-righteous. It is one thing to say, "We should respect nature!"; but it is another thing to reflect on this statement and happily conclude that one is uttering virtue language. Those of us who count themselves among the still largely counter-cultural activists who cultivate respect and love of nature in their daily lives—in other words, those who provide the practical base of environmental ethics—will more likely experience shock at this realization. (And vice versa, the theorists who have recently helped to revive interest in virtue ethics—i.e., those who would be made very happy by the realization that they too are, in fact, uttering virtue language—are generally not the ones who broadcast a personal interest in cultivating respect and love of nature.)

Instead, people who live ecologically responsible lives, and the academics who reflect on their lifestyles, tend to describe their ways of being and acting using the term *attitude*. They typically coin phrases such as: "an attitude of humility" or "a new attitude of caring for creation."[10] Conversely, they reject our "aggressive attitude towards the natural world" and "anthropocentric and greedy attitudes."[11] Occasionally, the term *habit* is used. For example, Joanna Macy identifies the "habits of suppression" that keep us from being honest with our feelings and hence from experiencing compassion. Macy also revives the idea of "practice" (a traditional synonym for the cultivation of virtue), by which she means "fortifying the mind and schooling its attitudes."[12]

In all of these passages, the air is thick with a consciousness of life as an effort to grow from vice into virtue. Yet the terms *virtue* and *vice* themselves are conspicuously absent. I can only explain this widespread absence as the result of a certain stigma that must be attached to the idea of using virtue language. Listen again, for example, to Joanna Macy: "Please note: virtue is not required for the emergence of the ecological self! This shift in identification is essential to our survival at this point in our history precisely because it can serve in lieu of 'ethics' and 'morality.' Moralizing is ineffective; sermons seldom hinder us from pursuing our self-interest as we construe it. Hence the need to be a little more enlightened about what our self-interest is."[13] Had this stigma of preachiness not existed (is Christian moralistic zeal to blame here?), and had popular ecoliterature used the labels "virtue" and vice" as freely as it explores new "attitudes," then surely academics would have noticed sooner what riches lie within this discourse.

At any rate, it may be perplexing that the riches of ecological virtue language are not better known, but it is even more perplexing to contemplate how this language emerged, with such a profusion of variations, in such a short time, and despite the stigma attached to the *idea* of virtue language. Although I have no certain answer, I would like to offer some conjectures on this point.

One reason for the flourishing of ecological virtue language may simply be that this is how, at least in the West, we tend to talk when we are worried and would like to see things change.[14] Virtue discourse, in Western languages, connotes a combination of intention and action that shows a seriousness about thorough and lasting change. It is the discourse we use when we are willing to make commitments and to express these publicly. (Think, for example, of the role of terms like *courage* and *loyalty* during wartime or terms like *responsibility* and *caring* in the family values debate.) Since ecologically minded people tend to perceive the current environmental crisis as extremely serious, it should not be surprising if they resort to those traditional linguistic constructions that connote active commitment, even if they do not call this language by its traditional name.

Second, I also believe that Lynn White's influential article, "The Historical Roots of Our Ecologic Crisis," has stimulated the use of virtue language among ecologically minded people. White, we may recall, argues that orthodox Christian doctrine has inspired harmful and arrogant "attitudes towards nature." As an antidote to this tradition of domination, and as the first step in a truly thoroughgoing social transformation, White recommends following St. Francis's "belief in the virtue of humility."[15] In response to White's article, a heated debate ensued about Christianity's degree of guilt in contributing to the environmental crisis. Many Christians sought to rectify what they perceived as a misrepresentation of the concept of stewardship. Others, Christians as well as non-Christians, accepted the criticism and went on to explore alternatives. But critics and supporters in this great debate had one thing in common: Since White's thesis hinges on the necessity of a change of *attitude*, they focused their investigations and energies on *attitudes*. This development, I believe, significantly stimulated the use of ecological virtue language—and it may also have stimulated the use of the term *attitude* as a substitute for both *virtue* and *vice*.

Still, neither of these conjectures seems to get to the heart of the matter. Linguistic traditions and fashionable topics of debate remain only external incentives for the development of a moral language. They may trigger trends, but they cannot fully account for the kind of proliferation and creativity we find in ecological virtue language. Such flourishing must ultimately be based on a good fit between a moral language and people's ways of experiencing and seeing the world.

Virtue language, in many ways, fits well with efforts to live out an ecological worldview.[16] The cultivation of virtues allows and encourages us to integrate emotions, thoughts, and actions. Thus it fits with the ideal of personal wholeness that many ecologically minded people espouse. The cultivation of virtues depends on narratives, vision, and the power of examples. It does not require external commands or force. This fits with the preference of many ecologically minded people for change through conviction rather than coercion. And, as the many synonyms and closely related concepts in Appendix A of *Dirty Virtues* illustrate, the cultivation of virtues provides rich expression to many different facets of human experience. This fits with an ecological appreciation for diversity. These may be some of the more substantive reasons explaining why ecologically minded people have discovered the language of virtue.

Whatever the reasons, however, the fact remains that ecological virtue language has emerged and is rapidly growing. In the remainder of this chapter I will outline five features that characterize dirty virtue language. Obviously, the picture that will emerge is an interpretation, a vision that carries the stamp of my own interests and way of perceiving.

Yet I like to think that the picture is not completely arbitrary, that others who pay attention to this emerging ecological virtue language would recognize similar features and patterns. (If not, at least we will have material for a good discussion!)

An Integral Discourse

Ecological virtue language represents a distinct moral discourse with an internal unity and logic—what I will call an integral discourse. This does not mean, of course, that it is entirely separate from other branches of moral discourse, particularly not other virtue discourses. The best way to understand ecological virtue language as an integral discourse is to see it as analogous to a bioregion, which has an integrity and unique character but which connects with other bioregions and participates in the larger cycles of the biosphere.

What makes ecological virtue language an integral discourse? Not, as one might expect, the presence of a single undergirding ecological worldview, for we find quite a variety of ecological worldviews. Rather, I would say that the integrity of ecological virtue language derives from its unique *practical* base in the environmental movement, a rootedness that is reflected in a particular moral vocabulary and its conventions.

Intuitively, it is easy to grasp the distinctiveness and inner logic of ecological virtue language when one compares it to a moral discourse that has sprouted from a rather different practical base. Take, for example, the virtue language generated by Western corporate cultures. If one needs to make a profit in business, it generally helps to be "tough," "efficient," and "shrewd."[17] It may also help to be caring and trustworthy, but usually these traits are redefined as being, in fact, tough—that is, they produce "hard" results.[18] Although the same combination of traits may aid in the achievement of environmental goals, ecologically minded people generally do not speak this way. First on their lips is not toughness but humility and sensitivity, not efficiency but sustainability, not shrewdness but wisdom. And caring is a basic way of being in the web of relations, not primarily a means to an end. Clearly, business practice and the practice of dedication to ecological well-being generate distinctive ways of using virtue language, each calibrated to the unique goals of the underlying practice.[19]

At this point an objection may well be raised. Can one accurately characterize the environmental movements as a single practical base? Are there not so many internal groups, each with its own approach, often disagreeing with each other, that the idea of a single practice giving rise to an integral moral discourse is no more than an artificial construct? One way to address this objection is to argue that, when push comes to shove, different environmental groups find themselves fighting for a common goal. In his book, *Toward Unity among Environmentalists*, Bryan Norton defends the thesis that anthropocentrists and nonanthropocentrists converge at the practical level of environmental management. Norton bases his claim on the observation that "no long-term human values can be protected without protecting the context in which they evolved."[20] One also hears the related view that seemingly incompatible approaches, such as seeking legislative change and using illegal tactics of radical resistance, complement each other strategically: The radical vanguard tends to increase the popularity of the moderate reformers, thus speeding up the process of gaining popular support for environmental causes.

Yet not everyone is comfortable with such irenic interpretations of the practical scene. For example, some nonanthropocentrists are not convinced that anthropocentrists go far enough in their efforts at species protection.[21] And some ecofeminists resist the idea that deep ecology can adequately subsume their practical concerns and the concerns of other justice-oriented ecologists.[22] As Don Marietta points out, the emphasis on differences may be a matter of principle: "Insistence on a unifying principle is seen [by some feminists] as causing the rejection of the voices of oppressed people. There is no clear denial of the possibility of there being a unifying principle yet to be discovered, but there is strong resistance to making this search the goal of ethical inquiry."[23] I very much resonate with these concerns. Therefore, I do not want to belabor too much the question of whether ecological virtue language is an integral discourse rooted in a distinct practice. Yet I do think that the sheer existence of debates and practical disagreements between ecologically minded people shows that there is a degree of common ground, an ecological culture, *that makes disagreement meaningful.* This point is underscored by the practical fact that these debates take place in shared forums such as journals and conferences.

As an integral discourse, ecological virtue language has a distinct vocabulary and operates according to a discrete set of conventions, just as a bioregion displays a distinct flora and fauna bound together by custom-made patterns of interaction. Thus certain virtues and vices occur across the board in environmental literature, typifying as it were the moral landscape.[24] For example, "respect for nature" is a commonly used expression. Different authors might mean somewhat different things by it, of course, but the expression seems to be universally accepted and used. The same applies to the virtues of adaptability, benevolence, care, compassion or solidarity, connectedness, creativity, cooperation, fostering, friendship, frugality, gratitude, healing, hope, inclusivity, joy, justice, moderation or restraint, openness, passion, perseverance, realism, self-examination, sensuousness, sharing, spontaneity, vulnerability, wisdom, and wonder. As for vices, ecological discourse is typified by terms such as *anthropocentrism, arrogance, carelessness, competitiveness, consumerism* or *greed, contempt, cruelty, denial, despair, domination* or *mastery, dualistic thinking, elitism, exploitation, (inexcusable) ignorance* or *thoughtlessness, indifference, insensitivity, manipulation, pride, otherworldliness, reductionism, romanticism,* and *wastefulness.*

Clearly, not all of these terms are unique to ecological virtue discourse, just as not all the plants and animals that typify a bioregion are unique to it. It is the particular combination of terms, as well as the distinctive ways in which these terms are interpreted and related to each other, that makes for a unique, integral moral discourse.

A Diverse Discourse

Having highlighted the integral character of ecological virtue language, I also want to highlight its internal diversity. By this I do not so much mean to say that we find here a highly diversified set of virtues and vices (though that is the case, as one can see from

Appendix A of *Dirty Virtues*) but, rather, that no two ecologically minded people speak and write in exactly the same way. To some extent the presence of such diversity is unremarkable, because variation occurs between the speakers of any language. Yet differences in virtue discourse can betray differences in the worldviews, backgrounds, and characters of ecowriters. Such variations are significant and must be highlighted if we are to honor and safeguard the inclusivity of ecological moral discourse.

For one thing, different authors employ different configurations of virtues and vices. One could say that their *catalogs* differ, as long as one remembers that these catalogs are never completely spelled out. Occasionally an author will even go so far as to exclude explicitly a virtue or vice that others deliberately include.[25]

Diversity also shows up in the form of different emphases. What may be a particularly important attitude to one author may be of little interest or even objectionable to another. To use a traditional expression: Different authors may identify different cardinal virtues. For example, poet and essayist Linda Hogan writes: "Caretaking is the utmost spiritual and physical responsibility of our time, and perhaps that stewardship is finally our place in the web of life, our work, the solution to the mystery of what we are."[26] Yet ecofeminist Elizabeth Dodson Gray finds such a view of stewardly care presumptuous, since "we still in our gut feel we're above and we do not have to fit in." Gray suggests that the key attitude we must cultivate is, rather, attunement:

> That means you've got to listen. It's like what I consider good parenting to be—cybernetic. It means being guided by information feedback: you do one thing tentatively and you wait to see what happens. You monitor it very carefully (which we do not bother to do). If it looks like it's not doing well, you pull back and you change your behavior, trying something else. Attunement means listening, it means adapting yourself. It means fitting in. And it will never be done by us as a culture unless we, as a culture, realize we are not above.[27]

Not surprisingly, as these examples illustrate, disagreements about key moral attitudes tend to parallel more basic differences within ecological thought, such as the difference between hierarchical and radically nonanthropocentric theories.

Generally, diversity in the area of cardinal virtues is not a topic of explicit debate. Yet one can identify variations between authors by comparing which virtues receive the most emphasis or turn up most frequently in their works. For example, the most-discussed virtue in Wendell Berry's *A Continuous Harmony* is discipline: We need discipline in focusing on details on the farm, in mending our ways for the sake of conservation, in carefully determining proper means to a desired end, in exercising self-criticism, and so on.[28] By contrast discipline only turns up once (as the discipline of prayer needed for ecological sensitivity) in Sean McDonagh's *To Care for the Earth*, despite the author's Roman Catholic heritage. This is not to say that these authors entirely diverge on what are the most crucial virtues in an ecological age. Both Berry and McDonagh often stress care, love, and respect or reverence. Still, the example of discipline reminds us that in speaking about dirty virtue language, we must remember that what is cardinal to one ecologically minded person may be minor to another.

Similarly, what may be a particularly worrisome vice to one author may seem like a small or misplaced concern to another. To use a traditional expression again, different authors may identify different capital vices. Hubris (pride), for example, is an important vice in James Nash's *Loving Nature*. It expresses itself in human attempts to "play God" in relation to nature.[29] In ecofeminist literature, one rarely finds this orthodox theological term, whereas psychological and sociological terms like *alienation, control, domination,* and *denial* resound like a familiar refrain. In a few extreme cases of variation, what is a most serious vice to one author represents a great good to another. Ecofeminists Marti Kheel and Chaia Heller, for example, argue that calls to "save" and "protect" nature are very harmful, since they diminish and objectify the nonhuman world. Rather than such hierarchical, heroic attitudes, we need holistic virtues of allied resistance and attentive care.[30] Yet *saving* and *protecting* are exactly the watchwords of popular environmentalism. "Save the Whales!" and "Protect the Forests!" are battle cries we have all heard (or seen on bumper stickers).

Diversity also shows up when particular virtues and vices are interpreted differently. John F. Haught, for example, highlights variations in the meanings of environmental abuse and care for nature. He correlates the variations with different theological visions: "In the sacramental view we condemn environmental abuse because it is a sacrilege. But in the eschatological perspective the sin of environmental abuse is one of despair. To destroy nature is to turn away from a promise. What makes nature deserve our care is not that it is divine but that it is pregnant with a mysterious future."[31] To find such an explicit articulation of diverse interpretations within ecolotal virtue language is actually rare. Most variations still remain to be uncovered. The question of whether there are recognizable patterns of variety, patterns that might be correlated with distinct branches of the environmental movement, contains much unexplored promise.

Finally, I want to highlight the diverse ways in which virtues and vices can be causally linked. Christian animal rights activist Andrew Linzey, for example, attributes our dominant abuse of animals to spiritual immaturity, which he interprets as a lack of Christian theocentrism.[32] Yet ecofeminist animal rights activist Lori Gruen sees Judeo-Christian religious belief exactly as causing our instrumentalist use of animals, since it would encourage the view of animals (and women) as "others" to be used and even sacrificed.[33] On the virtue side, mainstream Christian authors typically argue that respect for nature follows from faith in a transcendent Creator.[34] By contrast, deep ecologists trace our capacity for respect to the virtue of identification with the larger Self of the natural world. Causal relationships between vices and between virtues have long been of interest to ethicists and theologians, since these relationships affect our ability to change harmful habits and cultivate helpful ones. The diversity of relationships that emerges from ecoliterature calls for renewed reflection on this topic.

Differences between catalogs, cardinal virtues, capital vices, and causal relationships indicate that ecological virtue discourse is a lived language that has been neither logically constructed nor psychologically tested. In its current multifaceted form, we can treasure it as a discursive correlate of the diversity we find in the natural world, a diversity that carries with it the potential for creativity and regeneration. Still, a degree of systematic reflection on this lived language is needed to help distinguish between mere messiness and variations that are pregnant with significance and moral promise.

A Dialectical Discourse

The diverse ways in which different ecowriters use virtue discourse serve as a reminder that we must not too hastily draw general conclusions about this moral language. Nevertheless, we may notice patterns that, with appropriate reservation, help us understand the structure of ecological virtue discourse. In this section I will highlight a pattern of logical and psychological tensions. To the extent that these tensions are deliberate and produce desirable results that cannot be achieved otherwise, ecological virtue language can be called a dialectical discourse.

Not all tensions are deliberate, however. Some represent the kinds of inconsistencies one can expect to find in an ethic that is still in its infancy. For example, I am puzzled when I read the following: "Love is respect's strongest foundation, although it is often difficult to uncover because of our own desires and fears. Nevertheless, seeing value in another regardless of his/her/its utility to us is a crucial first step towards discovering that love. Without respect we cannot love."[35] In this passage I first read that love is the foundation for respect, but then I learn that the opposite is the case: Respect is a necessary condition for love. Such convoluted thinking (unless it is an intentional exploration of circularity) can only confuse those who are genuinely interested in cultivating these virtues.[36] Inconsistencies of this kind will need to be straightened out in the interest of moral clarity.

Other tensions within ecological virtue discourse seem to be deliberately maintained in the interest of securing a delicate balance of characteristics. Take, for example, the virtues of earthiness and attunement, both widely valued in ecoliterature. Each points us in a different direction. Earthiness demands practicality, a no-nonsense attitude, even a degree of bluntness. All of this is necessary if we are serious about offering down-to-earth solutions to urgent problems. Attunement, however, requires an opening up of all our senses to the greatest degree of sensibility. It demands gentleness, a dwelling on details, and personal vulnerability. One could say that as virtues, earthiness and attunement want different things for our hearts. Earthiness encourages a certain hardening of our hearts for the sake of justice; attunement encourages a softening of our hearts for the sake of love. Yet both are necessary to keep our hearts in the right place. If earthiness is not balanced by a tuning in to the other, it may turn into a crude form of instrumental reasoning that inflicts unnecessary harm. If attunement is not balanced by earthy commitment to justice, it may turn into a form of nature romanticism that provides an escape but not an ethic (and hence confirmation of the status quo). The tension between these ecological virtues is needed to avoid extremes that could lead ecologically minded people in dangerous directions.

Thus, whereas some tensions reflect the infancy of ecological virtue discourse and must be straightened out in due time, others reflect a dialectical richness that ensures flexibility and prevents harmful extremes. This feature challenges us to take another look at the Aristotelian image of a virtue as a mean between extremes of excess and deficiency. While ecological virtue discourse seems geared to avoid extremes as well, it does so in an innovatively relational way. We need not always rely on individual virtues to achieve balance. We can rely on a *network of virtue relations*. This view of the life of virtue nicely corresponds with the general emphasis in ecoliterature on relational or holistic modes of thinking, acting, and being.

A Dynamic Discourse

As a diverse and dialectical discourse, ecological virtue language is obviously hard to pin down. The fact that it is also a dynamic discourse further underscores the futility of such an effort. Ecological virtue language is *emerging*; its shape is not fixed, nor is it likely to become fixed in the near future. To some extent this dynamism can be attributed to the newness of the discourse, which has not yet settled or come to full fruition. But dynamism also belongs to ecological virtue discourse as an integral feature, since this discourse is connected with various evolving realities. Here we discover another recognizable pattern.

One connection involves the natural sciences. New insights from the natural sciences require constant reexamination of basic moral assumptions. For instance, recent discoveries about the importance of symbiosis in biological evolution have given rise to speculation about a possible natural basis for relational virtues such as cooperation, benevolence, and care.[37] Such a natural basis would imply that the life of virtue is less a matter of exercising control (a notion that had drawn support from the prior emphasis on competition in biology) and more a matter of fostering spontaneity. In fact, in a significant move away from established control-centered traditions, ecologically minded authors rarely portray the cultivation of virtues in terms of mastering unruly impulses.[38] Searching for a moral language that suits new biological (and psychological) emphases, they stress the need for a vulnerability that gives basic instincts a chance to be expressed. Their search in this key area, which cuts to the course of the moral life, illustrates how the connection between scientific discourse and ecological virtue language introduces a dynamism with far-reaching consequences.

Another source of dynamism is our changing understanding of the possibilities of human and nonhuman existence on this planet. When we still believed that the Earth could, with the right technology, produce enough food for all people, our moral focus was on technological creativity, redistribution, and development. Virtues like simplicity and responsibility predominated in environmental discourse (this ethic was primarily addressed to rich elites). Now that many of us can no longer support this belief, and now that we are developing a greater interest in the plight of nonhuman life as well, our moral focus is shifting to the challenges of fashioning integrated forms of existence. As a result, virtues like humility, vulnerability, and feeling kinship are becoming increasingly prevalent in ecoliterature. Clearly, such dynamism is necessary if our cultivation of virtues is to be attuned to realistic possibilities in an ecological age. Lack of such attunement could lead us to embrace "virtues" that, despite our good intentions, undercut rather than follow the options that are still open.

Because ecological virtue language has to be dynamic, it is unlikely that this discourse will ever become systematized to the extent that, for example, Thomas Aquinas systematized Christian virtue language. Ecowriters appreciate the ever changing and multifaceted structures of the world, an appreciation that contradicts efforts to build a closed intellectual system with strong claims to ultimacy. In fact, an ecological virtue theory that claimed to be *the* virtue theory would constitute an oxymoron.

It is one thing to value dynamism and quite another to engage in intellectual sloppiness. Insofar as ecological virtue discourse is still a new moral language, there is much room and need for development, for aiming at greater precision of expression, for better understanding conceptual connections and distinctions. As of yet, while the literature contains many virtues and vices, few have been thoroughly interpreted. And conversely, while some traditional virtues and vices receive no mention at all, the reasons for this silence are usually not spelled out, so that the reader is left to wonder whether the omission expresses the author's disapproval or, rather, the opposite, automatic acceptance. (The virtue of cleanliness, for example, comes to mind here.) Efforts to address these and other instances of incompleteness need not undercut the dynamism of ecological virtue ethics, as long as they flow from a desire to achieve greater moral clarity rather than from a desire to build the ultimate intellectual system.

A Visionary Discourse without a Social Ethic

By expressing themselves through dirty virtue languages, ecologically minded people express an interest in the cultivation and transformation of their own and other people's characters. Yet, unlike Aristotle and many of his followers, ecologically minded people are not interested in character development for the sake of achieving personal harmony within an existing social system. Rather, their dirty virtues are tied to a social vision for the future, a vision of ecologically sustainable societies. The change from present social structures to ecological societies is seen as necessary for the survival of diverse life-forms on Earth. And, in the viewpoint of many, the cultivation of appropriate attitudes can foster such change.[39]

Ecological virtue discourse thus derives much of its impetus from a social ideal. Ironically, however, most ecological virtue language does not display the features of a social ethic. Calls to respect nature, to change our dominating attitudes, to be frugal, careful, and wise, tend to remain just that: calls. Usually they are not followed by a detailed analysis of how heeding them will bring about the desired social change. Although much ecoliterature does address legal, communal, and institutional changes required to build sustainable societies, virtue discourse is rarely an explicitly integrated part of these specific discussions. Even if a single work contains much virtue language as well as a theory of social change, the two aspects tend to be in different chapters or sections of chapters. Thus we are confronted with the irony that the language of dirty virtues witnesses to a social vision without being connected to a social ethic.

Again, I believe Lynn White's article, "The Historical Roots of Our Ecologic Crisis," was instrumental in setting this pattern of "a social vision without a social ethic." White's thesis that attitudes must change if we are to avert further ecological disaster provides a clear image of ordered social progression, which puts a vice-to-virtue transformation at the start. At the end of the progression we find a vision, inspired by the teachings of St. Francis, of a harmonious, radically inclusive, and egalitarian world. Yet White does not indicate what, if anything, beyond the vice-to-virtue transformation would be necessary to get to this better world. His silence on this point was transmitted to the widespread debates that followed the publication of his article, debates about the core questions of the causes behind and possible solutions to the ecological crisis. Although virtue language flourishes profusely in these debates, social analysis is often thinly represented or totally absent, and the listener is expected to simply go along with the assumption that all will pan out as long as we change our basic attitudes (there are exceptions, most notably the work of social ecologists and of many ecofeminists).[40] The end result is the curious phenomenon of a discourse committed to social change without a developed theory of social change.

In my view, this phenomenon calls for critical reflection. I see the current situation as somewhat analogous to the case of the earliest Christians, who were energized by a vision of social transformation through the coming of God's Kingdom, who fervently called for people to practice virtues such as neighborly love, peacefulness, and long-suffering, but who did not develop a social ethic.[41] Hence the early churches did not present a real challenge to reigning powers or to practices such as war and slavery. Yet the history of Christianity also provides a different model. In the nineteenth and early twentieth centuries, the Social Gospel movement responded to widespread social problems by enriching early Christian eschatological teachings with the insights of contemporary social analysis (at that time especially socialist theory). By so doing the movement was empowered to bring about widespread changes, including legislative changes that ended the exploitation of child labor and limited the workweek to six days. A similar move could now provide more bite to the commitment to social change that characterizes ecological virtue language.[42] In effect, this means that this discourse needs to become more integrated with those sections of environmental literature where we do find the development of a social ethic.[43]

Conclusion

Ecological virtue discourse, as a distinct, diverse, dialectical, dynamic, and visionary moral language, deserves more attention than it has received so far. Many riches hide among the dirty virtues, as well as significant challenges to ancient traditions. While these facts may be sufficient to warrant academic interest, there should be a practical benefit as well. Rich moral discourse, rooted in transformative praxis, carries the promise of moral creativity. We are sorely in need of such creativity as we face the many ecological challenges ahead and as we increasingly find ourselves perplexed by the difficulties involved in adapting traditional moral languages to the needs of our age. One more language is one more chance. It would border on irresponsibility not to pay attention to the virtue discourse that emerges from the environmental movement.

In fact, with this new virtue language we may be given not just another chance but even a *good* chance at achieving moral breakthroughs, at finding fresh ways of looking at problems and dilemmas that are already getting stale (such as the question whether trees or rivers have rights). Virtue language has premodern roots, and although it comes to us sifted through the mazes of modernity, its internal consistency and comprehensibility are not dependent on the worldview that came into power with the scientific and industrial revolutions. Given that many critics see the modern worldview as an important factor in bringing about the ecological crisis, it will be helpful to have access to a form of moral discourse that is not too much in cahoots with this worldview. Even though virtue ethics may have acquired an image of conservatism, a virtue ethic based in the lived discourse of the environmental movement could have surprisingly radical effects.

Notes

1. Marti Kheel, "From Heroic to Holistic Ethics: The Ecofeminist Challenge," in *Ecofeminism: Women, Animals, Nature*, ed. Greta Gaard (Philadelphia: Temple University Press, 1994), 58.

2. Anthony Weston, *Back to Earth: Tomorrow's Environmentalism* (Philadelphia: Temple University Press, 1994), 58.

3. Lester R. Brown, *Building a Sustainable Society* (New York: W. W. Norton and Co., 1981), 354.

4. Matthew Fox, *Creation Spirituality: Liberating Gifts for the Peoples of the Earth* (San Francisco: HarperSanFrancisco, 1991), 28.

5. Stephanie Lahar, "Roots: Rejoining Natural and Social History," in *Ecofeminism: Women, Animals, and Nature*, ed. Greta Gaard (Philadelphia: Temple University Press), 111.

6. This catalog can be found in Louke van Wensveen, *Dirty Virtues: The Emergence of Ecological Virtue Ethics* (Amherst, NY: Prometheus Books, 2000), Appendix A.

7. See Geoffrey B. Frasz, "Environmental Virtue Ethics: A New Direction for Environmental Ethics," *Environmental Ethics* 15 (1993): 259–74; and Val Plumwood, *Feminism and the Mastery of Nature* (New York: Routledge, 1993).

8. Only a handful of ecological writers have deliberately called for, developed, or explored virtue-based approaches, often in response to what are perceived as more mainstream approaches. See Thomas E. Hill, "Ideals of Human Excellence and Preserving Natural Environments," *Environmental Ethics* 5 (fall 1983): 211–24; Eugene C. Hargrove, "The Role of Rules in Ethical Decision Making," *Inquiry* 28 (1985): 3–42; Paul W. Taylor, *Respect for Nature* (Princeton: Princeton University Press, 1986), especially 198–218; Jay B. McDaniel, *Of God and Pelicans* (Louisville, KY: Westminster/John Knox Press, 1989), especially 73–74; Plumwood, *Feminism and the Mastery of Nature*; Frasz, "Environmental Virtue Ethics"; Ron Erickson, "Comment on Environmental Virtue Ethics," *Environmental Ethics* 16 (1994): 334–36; James A. Nash, *Loving Nature* (Nashville: Abingdon Press, 1991); John Patterson, "Maori Environmental Virtues," *Environmental Ethics* 16 (1994): 397–409; Laura Westra, *An Environmental Proposal for Ethics: The Principle of Integrity* (Lanham, MD: Rowman and Littlefield, 1994); Jamie Schaefer, "Ethical Implications of Applying Aquinas's Notions of the Unity and Diversity of Creation to Human Functioning in Ecosystems" (Ph.D. dissertation, Marquette University, 1994); Pamela A. Smith, "Aquinas and Today's Environmental Ethics: An Exploration of How the Vision and the Virtue Ethic of 'Ecothomism' Might Inform a Viable Ecoethic" (Ph.D. dissertation, Duquesne University, 1995); Deborah D. Blake, "Toward a Sustainable Ethic: Virtue and the Environment," in *And God Saw That It Was Good*, ed. Drew Christiansen, S.J., and Walter Grazer (Washington, DC: U.S. Catholic Conference, 1996), 197–210; and Michael S. Northcott, *The Environment and Christian Ethics* (Cambridge: Cambridge University Press, 1996), especially 121–23, 314–17.

9. Plumwood, *Feminism and the Mastery of Nature*, 173.

10. David G. Hallman, *A Place in Creation: Ecological Visions in Science, Religion, and Economics* (Toronto: United Church Publishing House, 1992), 27; Sean McDonagh, *To Care for the Earth: A Call to a New Theology* (Santa Fe: Bear and Co., 1986), 49.

11. Thomas Berry, *The Dream of the Earth* (San Francisco: Sierra Club Books, 1988), 5; Bill Devall, *Simple in Means, Rich in Ends: Practicing Deep Ecology* (Salt Lake City: Gibbs Smith, 1988), 186.

12. Joanna Macy, "Faith, Power, and Ecology," in *This Sacred Earth: Religion, Nature, Environment*, ed. Roger S. Gottlieb (New York: Routledge, 1996), 417, 421.

13. Joanna Macy, "Awakening to the Ecological Self," in *Healing the Wounds: The Promise of Ecofeminism*, ed. Judith Plant (Philadelphia: New Society, 1989), 209. In this passage Macy elaborates on Arne Naess's criticism of the traditional notion of altruism.

14. Ecological virtue language also appears in non-Western texts. One thinks, for example, of the role of *ahimsa* and benevolence in Buddhist environmental literature. However, my expertise does not extend to these areas. I do hope that in the future comparative studies will be carried out.

15. Lynn White Jr., "The Historical Roots of Our Ecologic Crisis," *Science* 155 (10 March 1967): 1206–7.

16. For a description of the cluster of worldviews that can be designated as "ecological," see Wensveen, *Dirty Virtues*, chap. 2.

17. On toughness as a business virtue, see Robert Solomon, *Ethics and Excellence: Cooperation and Integrity in Business* (New York: Oxford University Press, 1992), 213–16.

18. See Louke M. van Wensveen, "Is Toughness a Business Virtue?" *International Journal of Applied Philosophy* (winter/spring 1995): 15–25.

19. I do not mean to imply here that either the corporate world or the environmental movement has a single goal or set of goals that is uniformly interpreted and accepted. I am thinking rather of two nodes of conglomerate goal-oriented behavior where each aggregate of goals is sufficiently distinctive to yield an identifiable practice and matching moral discourse.

20. Bryan Norton, *Toward Unity among Environmentalists* (New York: Oxford University Press, 1991), 240.

21. Brian K. Stevenson ("Contextualism and Norton's Convergence Hypothesis," *Environmental Ethics* 17 [1995]: 135–50), for example, criticizes Norton's model for not accommodating nonanthropocentrist requirements for species protection.

22. See Deborah Slicer, "Is There an Ecofeminism–Deep Ecology 'Debate'?" *Environmental Ethics* 17 (1995): 151–69.

23. Don E. Marietta Jr., "Pluralism in Environmental Ethics," *Topoi* 12 (1993): 70.

24. I make these claims very hesitantly, since I am wary of attempts to seek or construct a unified environmental ethic. My observation that ecological virtue language (still) forms a single discourse represents what I see as the most fitting interpretation of my findings; it does not represent a program. My own position of pluralism resembles Don Marietta's statement above.

25. For catalogs, based on the work of Murray Bookchin and Thomas Berry, illustrating the level of variety on this point, see Wensveen, *Dirty Virtues*, chaps. 2–3.

26. Linda Hogan, "The Kill Hole," in *This Sacred Earth: Religion, Nature, Environment*, ed. Roger S. Gottlieb (New York: Routledge, 1996), 40.

27. Elizabeth Dodson Gray, "A Critique of Dominion Theology," in *For Creation's Sake: Preaching, Ecology, and Justice,* ed. Dieter Hessel (Philadelphia: Geneva Press, 1985), 80.

28. Wendell Berry, *A Continuous Harmony: Essays Cultural and Agricultural* (San Diego: Harcourt Brace Jovanovich, [1970] 1972), 53, 81, 86, 108.

29. Nash, *Loving Nature*, 104.

30. Chaia Heller, "For the Love of Nature: Ecology and the Cult of the Romantic," in *Ecofeminism: Women, Animals, Nature*, ed. Greta Gaard (Philadelphia: Temple University Press, 1994), 235; Kheel, "From Heroic to Holistic Ethics," 248.

31. John F. Haught, *The Promise of Nature* (New York: Paulist Press, 1993), 110.

32. Andrew Linzey, *Christianity and the Rights of Animals* (New York: Crossroad, 1987), 15ff.

33. Lori Gruen, "Dismantling Oppression: An Analysis of the Connection between Women and Animals," in *Ecofeminism: Women, Animals, Nature*, ed. Greta Gaard (Philadelphia: Temple University Press, 1994), 64.

34. See, for example, Nash, *Loving Nature*, 100.

35. Gus diZerega, "Individuality, Human and Natural Communities, and the Foundation of Ethics," *Environmental Ethics* 17 (1995): 37.

36. There may be instances, of course, in which two or more virtues need to be cultivated simultaneously because they depend on each other. Perhaps diZerega would say this is the case for love and respect also. Yet in that case it is important to clarify how such simultaneous cultivation can be achieved.

37. Many ecological authors, especially ecofeminists, in fact already treat the natural basis of these virtues as a given. Cf. "Our children need to be sustained in their natural empathy with and compassion for animals" ("Liberating Life: A Report to the World Council of Churches," in *Liberating Life: Contemporary Approaches to Ecological Theology*, ed. Charles Birch, William Eakin, and Jay B. McDaniel [Maryknoll, NY: Orbis, 1990], 287).

38. For a critique of "ethics as restraint," see Kheel, "From Heroic to Holistic Ethics."

39. Not all hold this view, however. Christopher Stone, for example, writes: "If the world is going to be changed, it is going to be changed by people who can get past talking up a reform of the human spirit and lessons to be learned from Buddhism, and put in the effort to understand fisheries quotas, pollution taxes, trade barriers, and what the International Court of Justice can and cannot do" (*The Gnat Is Older than Man: Global Environment and Human Agenda* [Princeton: Princeton University Press, 1993], xiv).

40. Many ecofeminists draw on general feminist social theory. Analytical concepts such as patriarchy, oppression, and ideology play an important role in their work.

41. See J. Philip Wogaman, *Christian Ethics: A Historical Introduction* (Louisville, KY: Westminster/John Knox Press, 1993), 30.

42. Such a move would also benefit the development of virtue theory in general, much of which fails to deal with larger questions of social change.

43. One promising step in this direction can be found in Max Oelschlaeger's book *Caring for Creation: An Ecumenical Approach to the Environmental Crisis* (New Haven: Yale University Press, 1994). Oelschlaeger sees the virtue of caring for creation as a metaphor embedded in various religious narratives. Such narratives are crucial for social change in democratic societies, he argues, since they inspire discourse on the public good and they challenge the idea that the state as such is already moral. Although social change requires more than religious narratives (i.e., "politically coordinated, scientifically informed, and institutionally empowered actions that are consistent with our basic democratic freedoms and diversity of ultimate commitments"), Oelschlaeger's narrative ethic explicitly integrates the dynamics of social change with the cultivation of virtue (*Caring for Creation*, 10, 76–77).

Elsewhere, Oelschlaeger (with Michael Bruner) also argues for the importance of rhetoric in bringing about social change ("Rhetoric, Environmentalism, and Environmental Ethics," *Environmental Ethics* 16 [1994]: 377–96). Since virtue discourse is highly suitable for rhetorical purposes, this argument could also be used to construct a theory of the role of virtue in social transformation.

CHAPTER 2

Thoreau, Leopold, and Carson: Toward an Environmental Virtue Ethics

Philip Cafaro

Environmental Virtue Ethics

Over the past twenty-five years, much scholarship in environmental ethics has focused on the intrinsic value or moral considerability of nonhuman nature. This valuable work has clearly formulated many environmentalists' intuitions that the destruction, overuse, or excessive appropriation of nature is morally wrong. It has given us plausible reasons for extending moral considerability beyond our own species and limiting our conduct accordingly.[1]

In contrast, little has been written in environmental ethics from a virtue ethics perspective that focuses on human excellence and flourishing. While individual authors such as Arne Naess and Erazim Kohak have discussed the joy and fulfillment to be found in a more environmentally conscious life, this theme has not been central within academic environmental ethics.[2] However, recent years have seen increased interest in developing an environmental virtue ethics, one that incorporates a respect for nature, conceives "human interests" broadly, and presents environmental protection as being in our *enlightened* self-interest.[3] I believe that further development of such an environmental virtue ethics is timely and useful for two main reasons.

First, in the absence of an environmental virtue ethics, environmental ethics itself is incomplete and unbalanced. Recent virtue ethics proponents have made the (general) case forcefully.[4] An ethics that concentrates exclusively on rights and responsibilities, and judges our actions solely on whether they violate or uphold moral duty, ignores further, crucial ethical questions: What is the best life for a person, and how can I go about living it? What is a good society, and how can we move closer to achieving it? These questions are just as important within environmental ethics as within ethics generally, because actions that affect the environment rebound and affect us, opening up or closing off possibilities. Our environmental decisions make us better or worse people and create better or worse societies: healthier or sicker, richer or poorer, more knowledgeable or more ignorant. Any complete valuation of our actions and lives must include a virtue ethics component, and any complete environmental ethics must include an environmental virtue ethics.

Second, there is a practical need to develop positive arguments for environmental protection. Often, the general public views environmentalists as killjoys, willing to countenance any trade-offs of human freedom or happiness in pursuit of their aims.[5] Partly this view is unavoidable. In defending wild nature and asserting its intrinsic value, environmentalists are necessarily proscriptive. Yet the writings of the great naturalists, and our own experiences, tell a story of joyful interrelation with nature. Just as classical virtue ethics provided strong self-interested reasons for treating others with respect—reasons based on a person's concern for his own virtue and flourishing—so an environmental virtue ethics can provide strong grounds for environmental protection. Above all, it can move us beyond our initial ethical response to environmental destruction—contrite self-abnegation—and toward a more positive, sustainable position of respectful dwelling in nature.[6]

Thoreau, Leopold, and Carson

While professional philosophers have largely neglected the subject, some of our greatest environmental writers can plausibly be seen as environmental virtue ethicists. In this section, I briefly discuss three of them: Henry David Thoreau, Aldo Leopold, and Rachel Carson.

"I went to the woods because I wished to live deliberately," Thoreau writes in a central passage in *Walden*, "to front only the essential facts of life, and see if I could not learn what it had to teach, and not, when I came to die, discover that I had not lived. . . . I wanted to live deep and suck all the marrow out of life . . . to know it by experience, and be able to give a true account of it in my next excursion."[7] *Walden* describes a life of personal development and enriched experience, centered on the pursuit of knowledge of self and nature. It advocates ethical, intellectual, and creative striving. Thoreau alternately harangues his readers for their inertia and failure to demand more from life and entices them onward with fair possibilities, noble ideals, and accounts of his own successes: Thoreau snug and secure in his well-built cabin, facing winter's blasts; Thoreau floating on the calm summer waters of Walden Pond, fishing pole in hand, a symbol of personal equilibrium and harmony with his surroundings. Interestingly, Thoreau uses the terms *flourishing*, *living well*, and *chief end* to describe his overall goal: words and phrases employed by recent scholars to translate and resurrect the proper ancient Greek understanding of *eudaimonia*, in place of our more subjective and trivial "happiness."[8]

Taking *Walden* as a whole, a clear picture of Thoreau's view of the good life emerges, which includes health, freedom, pleasure, friendship, a rich experience, knowledge (of self, nature, God), self-culture, and personal achievement.[9] He specifies his pursuit of these "goods" in detail, often in terms of his relationship to nature. Freedom, for Thoreau, includes not just the absence of physical coercion but also having the time to explore his surroundings and the privilege to saunter through the local landscape without being arrested for trespassing. Perhaps some readers will define freedom similarly! He finds great physical pleasure and sensual stimulation in living and working in the woods, comparing his life favorably to the indoor lives of so many of his contemporaries: poor factory girls driven by necessity but also wealthy Concord burghers who are free to live otherwise. Dwelling solitary and apart from people awakened him to possibilities for friendship and connection to the rest of nature, he reports. Thoreau makes it clear that he is not setting up rules that all must follow. But his experiment by the pond suggests possibilities for living well in nature, for those inclined to make the attempt. It also suggests what we may give up in living a more urbanized existence.

Thoreau tries, in *Walden*, to recover the ancient sense of virtue as personal excellence, asserting that nowadays, "philanthropy is almost the only virtue which is sufficiently appreciated by mankind. Nay, it is greatly overrated."[10] His catalog of virtues includes moral virtues such as sympathy, honesty, justice, and generosity, but also intellectual virtues such as curiosity, imagination, intelligence, and alertness, and even physical virtues such as health, beauty, and hardiness. Thoreauvian virtues crucial for the construction of an environmental virtue ethics include temperance, integrity, sensibility to beauty, and, perhaps most important, simplicity.

Thoreau's "simplicity" is not simplicity of thought or experience, which he seeks to complicate and enrich. It is, rather, a limited use of external goods, combined with a focus on the task at hand. Simplicity, to borrow a concept from ecology, is a "keystone" virtue for Thoreau. It plays an important role in stabilizing and focusing our lives and allows the development of a rich character manifesting diverse virtues. In a complicated world, such simplicity allows us to understand the effects of our actions and act with integrity.[11] Simplicity is also one key to freedom, for if we live simply, we need not trade most of our time to an employer and can spend it as we wish.[12] Simplicity will be an important virtue for any environmental virtue ethics, for the obvious reason that living simply decreases our impact on other living things; but Thoreau, along with many environmentalists, also claims that living simply will improve our own lives.

Aldo Leopold can also be interpreted as an environmental virtue ethicist, as Bill Shaw recently argued in *Environmental Ethics*.[13] While Leopold's classic essay "The Land Ethic" makes a moving plea for moral extensionism and human self-restraint, he devotes much of *A Sand County Almanac* to showing the opportunities for knowledge and self-development made possible by a greater attentiveness to nature. "We abuse land because we regard it as a commodity belonging to us," he writes in the foreword: "When we see land as a community to which we belong, we may begin to use it with love and respect. There is no other way for land to survive the impact of mechanized man, *nor for us to reap from it the esthetic harvest it is capable, under science, of contributing to culture.*"[14] Along with ethical extensionism, then, Leopold describes a parallel aesthetic and intellectual extensionism, in which "our ability to perceive quality in nature begins . . . with the pretty, [and] expands through successive stages of the beautiful to ['higher'] values as yet uncaptured by language."[15] Capturing such values improves our lives. "To promote perception is the only truly creative part" of recreation management, he writes further on. "This fact is important, and its potential power for bettering 'the good life' only dimly understood."[16] Here, and elsewhere, Leopold puts "the good life" in ironic quotation marks, suggesting that the *truly* good life is not defined solely or even mainly in material terms.

Leopold might appear to undermine this interpretation, when he writes of a "formula" for conservation that is "too easy to accomplish anything worthwhile," continuing: "It defines no right or wrong, assigns no obligation, calls for no sacrifice, implies no change in the current philosophy of values. In respect of land-use, it urges only enlightened self-interest."[17] Here Leopold accepts the modern dichotomy of altruistic moral action, as defined by moral philosophy, versus selfish, hedonistic action, as dealt with by the economists. This acceptance clarifies his moral extensionism but obscures his environmental virtue ethics. In fact, *A Sand County Almanac* explicitly and repeatedly asks us to recognize our "enlightened self-interest," contrasting it with a benighted, economistic, and *mistaken* definition of self-interest.[18]

Wealthy Americans have reached the point, Leopold believes, where they cannot better their lives through increased wealth or possessions. Instead, building on a foundation of material sufficiency, they should strive to live lives that are rich in perception and knowledge of their surroundings. Along these lines Leopold makes a pioneering plea for a more environmentally informed understanding of human history. He praises and—more importantly—demonstrates an aesthetic appreciation of plants, animals, and places.[19] Reading the many dramas written in the animal tracks on his farm or wading half a day in a marsh for a closer view of a family of grebes, he exhibits the peculiar virtues of the naturalist: patience, eagerness, physical endurance, persistence, a keen perception, skill in making fine distinctions, precise description. Such activities make us happier and better people, he suggests.[20] They allow us to pursue knowledge and enrich our experience, without diminishing nature. Leopold asks us to conceive our own flourishing in ways that sustain—indeed, depend on—the flourishing of the natural communities of which we are part.

Reading *A Sand County Almanac*, it is striking how often Leopold praises the virtues of the nonhuman world: the "grace" of a plover, the "valor" of a chickadee, the "accumulated wisdom" of a stand of pine trees—a natural wisdom that silences the people who walk below—the "harmony" of a river ecosystem.[21] These expressions are more than metaphors. Human and nonhuman beings may share some virtues because we are in some respects similar. "How like fish we are," Leopold muses in an interval between casts, "ready, nay eager, to seize upon whatever new thing some wind of circumstance shakes down upon the river of time! And how we rue our haste, finding the gilded morsel to contain a hook. Even so, I think there is some virtue in eagerness, whether its object prove true or false. How utterly dull would be a wholly prudent man, or trout, or world!"[22] Henry David Thoreau, fellow angler, concurs, adding that other species may exhibit virtues quite different from the human, which are no less genuine for all that: "Away with the superficial and selfish phil-*anthropy* of men,—who knows what admirable virtue of fishes may be below low-watermark, bearing up against a hard destiny, not admired by that fellow creature who alone can appreciate it!"[23]

Environmental ethics here takes us back to philosophy's prehistory, beyond the reach of the army of philosophers who, from Aristotle onward, have patiently explained that only human beings have virtue—back to Homer, who could speak of the *arête* of a horse and have all Greece understand him.[24] This naturalizing of virtue is no mere literary conceit but, rather, the very foundation of Leopold's land ethic. "A thing is right when it tends to preserve the integrity, stability, and beauty of the biotic community," he writes. "It is wrong when it tends otherwise."[25] Leopold identifies these three qualities as key virtues of natural and mixed human/natural communities; in a sense, they are "supervirtues," which promote the continuous generation of virtue in individual species and organisms, including us. Recognizing nature's excellence and ability to generate excellence gives us strong reasons to preserve it, for nature's sake and for our own.[26]

Rachel Carson has been called the founder of the modern environmental movement, which some date, plausibly, to the publication of *Silent Spring* in 1962. *Silent Spring*'s case rests above all on numerous factual and scientific accounts of the use and abuse of agricultural and industrial chemicals. Ethically, its plea for restraint rests on the triple foundation of human health considerations, the moral considerability of nonhuman beings, and the value to humans of preserving wild nature.

Doubtless, most important for many readers were Carson's chapters on acute pesticide poisoning and these chemicals' potential to cause cancer and human birth defects. For these readers, Carson states the moral clearly: "Man, however much he may like to pretend the contrary, is part of nature. [He cannot] escape a pollution that is now so thoroughly distributed throughout the world."[27] Carson herself seems to have been equally if not more concerned with the destruction of wild nature and its resultant human loss. "I wrote [*Silent Spring*]," Carson told *Life* magazine, "because I think there is a great danger that the next generation will have no chance to know nature as we do."[28] As she finished *Silent Spring*, she was planning her next book, a guide to nature for parents and children, tentatively titled *Help Your Child to Wonder*.

Silent Spring clearly shows Rachel Carson's concern for all of life, human and nonhuman. Many of its arguments explicitly assert or implicitly rely on the moral considerability of nonhuman organisms:

> These creatures [birds, rabbits, domestic pets] are innocent of any harm to man. Indeed, by their very existence they and their fellows make his life more pleasant. Yet he rewards them with a death that is not only sudden but horrible. . . .
>
> These insects [honeybees, wild bees, and other pollinators], so essential to our agriculture and indeed to our landscape as we know it, *deserve something better from us* than the senseless destruction of their habitat.[29]

Silent Spring also expresses Carson's belief that preserving wild nature helps promote human happiness and flourishing. She approvingly quotes Paul Shepard and William O. Douglas on the aesthetic value and intellectual stimulation provided by wildlife and wild places and adds her own arguments:

> To the bird watcher, the suburbanite who derives joy from birds in his garden, the hunter, the fisherman or the explorer of wild regions, anything that destroys the wildlife of an area for even a single year has deprived him of pleasure to which he has a legitimate right. . . .
>
> Over increasingly large areas of the United States, spring now comes unheralded by the return of the birds, and the early mornings are strangely silent where once they were filled with the beauty of bird song. . . . Can

anyone imagine anything so cheerless and dreary as a springtime without a robin's song? . . .

Who has decided—who has the *right* to decide—for the countless legions of people who were not consulted that the supreme value is a world without insects, even though it be also a sterile world ungraced by the curving wing of a bird in flight. The decision is that of the authoritarian temporarily entrusted with power; he has made it during a moment of inattention by millions to whom beauty and the ordered world of nature still have a meaning that is deep and imperative.[30]

Before we can appreciate such ethical arguments, however, we must appreciate wild nature, and we cannot appreciate what we have not seen, experienced, or at least imagined. Carson's best-selling natural history writings—she once had two books on the *New York Times* best-seller list at the same time—took readers to places wilder and harder to imagine than any visited by Thoreau or Leopold: arctic tundra in the grip of winter; the weird, dark depths of the ocean; microscopic planktonic worlds. Just as surely, Carson uncovered the many details of nature close to hand: the fishing techniques of herons and skimmers, the fine structures and hidden beauties of jellyfish. Moreover, she was a great explainer of relationships and connections. "It is now clear that in the sea nothing lives to itself," she writes, and what holds true in the sea holds true throughout the biosphere.[31]

This oft-repeated message resounds somewhat ominously in *Silent Spring*, but even here Carson's clear message is that life's complexity and interconnections are cause for appreciation and celebration, if also for restraint. "One might easily suppose," she writes in an earlier book, "that nothing at all lived in or on or under these waters of the sea's edge," but by its end we know differently, and we come to the edge of the sea with new eyes, a better sense of "the spectacle of life in all its varied manifestations," and a desire to learn more.[32] Carson never doubted that increased knowledge was more precious than increased material wealth or that a more widespread knowledge of nature would motivate people to protect it.[33] Knowledge, for her, was not simply learned but lived and experienced, engaging and developing the senses and emotions as well as the mind, our imaginations as much as our analytic skills.

Carson saw humility as, perhaps, the cardinal environmental virtue. She concluded in *Silent Spring* that "the 'control of nature' is a phrase conceived in arrogance, born of the Neanderthal age of biology and philosophy, when it was supposed that nature exists for the convenience of man. . . . [The] extraordinary capacities of life have been ignored by the practitioners of chemical control who have brought to their task . . . no humility before the vast forces with which they tamper."[34] Speaking directly to millions of Americans on *CBS Reports* a few months before her death, she repeated the message: "We still talk in terms of conquest. . . . I think we're challenged, as mankind has never been challenged before, to prove our maturity and our mastery, not of nature but of ourselves."[35]

Carson's own genuine humility was no meek quiescence, however. She had a strong sense of her own abilities and responsibilities, shown in all areas of her life: personal, professional, and, when the need arose, political. No one else, she realized, had the combination of literary skill and scientific knowledge to write *Silent Spring*. Her determination to publish her book and defend its conclusions publicly, in the face of declining health and a well-financed, personal smear campaign by the chemical and agribusiness industries, is one of the heroic chapters in conservation history. In her final years as earlier, Carson epitomized the virtues that environmentalists will need in order to fight, and win, future battles: tenacity, intelligence, courage, and a passionate commitment to nature.

Common Themes

Consideration of the very different careers of these three conservation giants suggests that there will be much variety as individuals live their own good lives in nature.[36] Nevertheless, certain common positions emerge in their writings that I believe any environmental virtue ethics worthy of the name must also include:

1. *A desire to put economic life in its proper place—that is, as a support for comfortable and decent human lives, rather than as an engine powering endlessly more acquisition and consumption.* Thoreau focuses on our personal economies, Carson, on whole sectors of the modern industrial economy; both approaches are necessary. All three reject a purely economic view of nature: this is the essence of Leopold's A/B cleavage. All three express, not just disagreement, but contempt for people who fail to acknowledge higher, noneconomic values. Yet all three acknowledge the centrality of economic problems and the need for conservationists (and others) to meet them head-on: "Economy is a subject which admits of being treated with levity," Thoreau writes, "but it cannot so be disposed of."[37] In seeking to subordinate economic life to life as a whole, environmental virtue ethics sounds an ancient and very necessary ethical theme.

2. *A commitment to science, combined with an appreciation of its limits.* Thoreau, Leopold, and Carson were not just interested bystanders but active participants in the science of their day, striving to learn as much as they could about those aspects of nature that intrigued them. At the same time, they resisted a cold objectivity and insisted that science be supplemented by personal acquaintance, appreciation, and celebration of wild things and wild places. They cultivated strong ties to particular places and worked to protect them. Carson was in some ways the first and greatest conservation biologist, deploying her knowledge and eloquence in service to nature, in contrast to the Baconian technicians who sought to dominate and radically transform nature for human benefit (and profits). As Linda Lear documents in her recent Carson biography, *Silent Spring* sparked a vigorous debate among scientists on the nature and purpose of science.[38] An environmental virtue ethics—concerned to know and protect nature—must take up this debate.

3. *Nonanthropocentrism.* As shown above, Thoreau, Leopold, and Carson are all resolutely nonanthropocentric: their early love and continuing interest in the nonhuman world led them to recognize its moral considerability. Leopold states this memorably when he asserts that "a land ethic changes the role of *Homo sapiens* from conqueror of the land-community to plain member and citizen of it."[39] Thus, an

environmental virtue ethics is not an alternative to environmental ethics that focus on the moral considerability of wild nature but, rather, completes them. This clarification should answer an objection some readers might have, that an environmental virtue ethics is necessarily anthropocentric, since it focuses on *human beings'* enlightened self-interest. An environmental virtue ethics may start from a concern for human interests, but it cannot remain there, since it says it is in our interest to explore and experience the world, and in doing so we discover intrinsically valuable nonhuman beings. Furthermore, an environmental virtue ethics does not assume that our self-interest—even our enlightened self-interest—always coincides with the interests of other nonhuman beings or that human interests should always prevail when there is a conflict of interests.[40]

Thoreau, Leopold, and Carson also remind us that nonanthropocentrism is both an ethical position and an intellectual task, and the latter demands as much from us as the former. In particular, it demands repeated attention to the nonhuman world: the setting aside of our works and purposes and a concentration on nature's own stories and realities.[41] Experienced often enough and set within the proper intellectual frameworks, we may, we hope, see ourselves truly as parts of a more-than-human whole. Our naturalists are convinced that such nonanthropocentrism is a part of wisdom. Here again, an environmental virtue ethics touches on venerable themes.

4. *An appreciation of the wild and support for wilderness protection.* Thoreau, Leopold, and Carson all seek out wild nature close to home, and all three argue eloquently for the protection of wilderness areas farther afield. Protecting such areas is the key to preserving individual species and organisms, as contemporary conservation biology reminds us. But wilderness preservation also preserves human possibilities. While Leopold emphasizes the contribution of wilderness to human freedom and self-reliance, Carson emphasizes its role in stretching our imaginations and teaching us humility.[42] She repeatedly invokes the ocean's radical nonhumanity in *The Sea around Us*, asking readers to imagine underwater "tides so vast they are invisible and uncomprehended by the senses of man" or lights traveling over the water "that flash and fade away, lights that come and go for reasons meaningless to man," though "man, in his vanity, subconsciously attributes a human origin" to them.[43] This ocean wilderness teaches humility and wisdom, she believes, for modern man "cannot control or change the ocean as, in his brief tenancy on earth, he has subdued and plundered the continents. In the artificial world of his cities and towns, he often forgets the true nature of his planet and the long vistas of its history, in which the existence of the race of men has occupied a mere moment of time."[44] Wildness must be known and experienced, on pain of ignorance, arrogance, and impoverishment.[45]

5. *A bedrock belief that life is good: both human and nonhuman.* "Joy!" Thoreau shouts from his perch along the shores of Walden Pond, and we feel it too with Leopold along the Rio Gavilan and with Carson at dawn by the edge of the sea. All three are great lovers of spring, searching for its earliest signs in Concord marshes, on Wisconsin hills, and in the depths of winter in the mid-Atlantic.[46] All three are early risers. Indeed, Thoreau asks, "Who would not be early to rise, and rise earlier and

earlier every successive day of his life, till he became unspeakably healthy, wealthy, and wise?"[47]

These are some of the commonalities in these environmental philosophers' visions of human flourishing; visions that are securely grounded in their own experiences and which they worked to realize in their own lives.

Conclusion

Thoreau, Leopold, and Carson provide inspiring accounts of human beings living well in nature. They suggest to me the rudiments of an environmental virtue ethics that is noble and challenging and makes room for the rest of creation. To arguments for preserving nature in our own materialistic self-interest and arguments for preserving nature for its intrinsic value, they add arguments for preserving nature in order to preserve human possibilities and help us become better people. That such arguments may convince and inspire is proven by these authors' enduring popularity and by their roles in shaping modern environmental consciousness.

There remains, of course, much to be said, and even more to be done, in furthering an environmental virtue ethics. Some of the challenges to the creation of an environmental virtue ethics are common to virtue ethics generally: Is it possible to specify objective, unchanging standards of human excellence, or is excellence largely a matter of fitting in well to particular, historically contingent situations? Are the virtues unified or sometimes in conflict? Is a single, unitary, and objective account of human virtue possible or desirable? Philosophers' faith in reason and our desire for theoretical simplicity lead us to choose the first options noted, but there might be limits to the possibility of finding such all-encompassing answers, and to their value if we did find them.

There are also issues more specific to an environmental virtue ethics. Perhaps the most important is the "artificial alternatives" argument: that when we have specified the good human life, we will find that it can be lived just as well in a largely artificial world, so that we do not need wild nature. The answer here, I believe, must build on an appreciation of diversity and of the radical otherness of nonhuman nature; and on defending an account of the good life focused on developing our higher capabilities, against accounts focused on status seeking or increased consumption. For such an appreciation and defense, one need not argue the absolute superiority of the wild over the tame but should, rather, try to specify an optimal mix of wildness and culture in individuals and landscapes. Given human dominance over so much of the biosphere, such considerations should strongly support the preservation of what wild nature remains, as well as extensive ecological restoration and "rewilding."

These and other complications exist; yet the need for an environmental virtue ethics remains, for a strong case can be made that greater attention to our true happiness would do as much to protect the environment as the acceptance of the intrinsic value of wild nature for which so many environmental ethicists have argued. Both, if taken to heart, would result in less consumption and a more conscious production and hence in less environmental damage.[48]

Furthermore, issues of self-interest play an important part in environmental conflicts; if only for this reason, they compel our attention. When the dam builders and the river lovers argue before a town council or national parliament, they often clash over whether a free-flowing river and its wild inhabitants have an intrinsic value that must be respected. But they also clash over what sort of society is better: one with cheaper electricity and more factories or one where it is still possible to walk along a natural river and see and study its wild inhabitants. Economists rightly point out that decisions concerning use or preservation always involve "opportunity costs." I believe a full accounting must also tote up these "costs and benefits." It would be a mistake to dismiss such considerations and arguments as anthropocentric. They are important for the protagonists and for coming to correct ethical judgments.

Notes

1. Strong arguments for the intrinsic value of wild nature are found in Holmes Rolston III, *Environmental Ethics* (Philadelphia: Temple University Press, 1988); and Keekok Lee, "The Source and Locus of Intrinsic Value," *Environmental Ethics* 18 (1996): 297–309. Influential works denying such intrinsic value are John Passmore, *Man's Responsibility for Nature*, 2d ed. (London: Duckworth, 1980); and Luc Ferry, *The New Ecological Order* (Chicago: University of Chicago Press, 1995).

2. This situation has partly been due to the commendable desire of most environmental ethicists to develop a nonanthropocentric ethical position. Arne Naess, *Ecology, Community and Lifestyle: Outline of an Ecosophy* (Cambridge: Cambridge University Press, 1989); Erazim Kohak, *The Embers and the Stars* (Chicago: University of Chicago Press, 1984).

3. See Bill Shaw, "A Virtue Ethics Approach to Aldo Leopold's Land Ethic," *Environmental Ethics* 19 (1997): 53–67; Stephen Kellert, *The Value of Life: Biological Diversity and Human Society* (Washington, DC: Island Press, 1996), 3–34; John Patterson, "Maori Environmental Virtues," *Environmental Ethics* 16 (1994): 397–409; John O'Neill, *Ecology, Policy and Politics: Human Well-Being and the Natural World* (London: Routledge, 1993), 159–62; Geoffrey Frasz, "Environmental Virtue Ethics: A New Direction for Environmental Ethics," *Environmental Ethics* 15 (1993): 259–74; Thomas Hill Jr., "Ideals of Human Excellence and Preserving Natural Environments," *Environmental Ethics* 5 (1983): 211–24. Recently Louke van Wensveen published the first book-length study of environmental virtue ethics, her excellent *Dirty Virtues: The Emergence of Ecological Virtue Ethics* (Amherst, NY: Humanity Books, 2000).

4. See Alasdair Macintyre, *After Virtue*, 2d ed. (Notre Dame: University of Notre Dame Press, 1984), 118–19; and chapters by Sarah Conly, R. Z. Friedman, and David Norton in Peter French et al., eds., *Ethical Theory: Character and Virtue* (Notre Dame: Notre Dame University Press, 1988). The best short introduction to virtue ethics is Richard Taylor, *Virtue Ethics* (Amherst, NY: Humanity Books, 2002).

5. "Without a change in consciousness, the ecological movement is experienced as a never-ending list of reminders: 'shame, you mustn't do that' and 'remember, you're not allowed to. . . .' With a change in mentality we can say 'think how wonderful it will be, if and when look there! what a pity that we haven't enjoyed that before. . . .' If we can clean up a little internally as well as externally, we can hope that the *ecological movement will be more of a renewing and joy-creating movement*" (Naess, *Ecology, Community and Lifestyle*, 91). I cannot follow Naess (*Ecology, Community and Lifestyle*, 8–9) in his ultimate synthesis of deontological and eudaemonistic judgments, as self-interest is eclipsed by self-interest. The important point remains that

recognition of our enlightened self-interest gives us further incentive to respect wild nature's intrinsic value. This recognition can make doing our duty less onerous. Moreover, Naess is correct that it can help us lead better, more joyful lives.

6. See Kohak, *The Embers and the Stars*, 90–91. This is not to say that self-interested arguments should supplant appeals to duty or to the intrinsic value of wild nature. Rather, they should supplement them. As I see it, deontology and virtue ethics are the two necessary halves of a complete ethics.

7. Henry Thoreau, *Walden* (Princeton: Princeton University Press, 1989), 90–91. For a discussion of Thoreau as a virtue ethicist, see Philip Cafaro, *Thoreau's Living Ethics: Walden and the Pursuit of Virtue* (Athens: University of Georgia Press, 2004).

8. *Living well*: Thoreau, *Walden*, 51; and J. L. Akrill, "Aristotle on Eudaimonia," in *Essays on Aristotle's Ethics*, ed. Amelie Rorty (Berkeley: University of California Press, 1980), 17. *Flourishing*: Thoreau, *Walden*, 79; and Martha Nussbaum, "Non-relative Virtues: An Aristotelian Approach," in *The Quality of Life*, ed. Martha Nussbaum and Amartya Sen (Oxford: Oxford University Press, 1993), 243. *Chief end*: Thoreau, *Walden*, 9, 90–91; and Julia Armas, *The Morality of Happiness* (Oxford: Oxford University Press, 1993), 46.

9. *Health* is often referred to as "hardiness." Thoreau several times speaks of his willingness to sacrifice health for higher goods (*Walden*, 27, 60–61). *Pleasure* is occasionally mentioned favorably in a fairly direct way, as on p. 240. More often it is assumed to be good, and more specific pleasures are noted. *Rich experience*: 42, 46, 51, 53, 61, 90. *Self-culture*: 40, 77, 109–10, 328. *Freedom* is used interchangeably with *independence* and is one of Thoreau's most frequently mentioned goods (7–8, 12, 15, 33, 37, 45, 56, 60, 63, 70, 84, etc.). *Friendship* receives its fullest discussion in Thoreau's earlier work, *A Week on the Concord and Merrimack Rivers* (Princeton: Princeton University Press, 1980), 259–89. In *Walden* in the chapter entitled "Solitude" Thoreau asserts a certain independence from the need for human friendship, while in "Winter Visitors" he obliquely discusses his friendships with fellow transcendentalists Channing, Alcott, and Emerson (*Walden*, 129–39, 267–70). *Knowledge*: 18, 20, 90, 95–97, 100, 321–22, 327, 330–31. *Achievement* in his chosen calling—writing—is referred to obliquely yet stirringly on 16–21, 162.

10. Thoreau, *Walden*, 76.

11. Thoreau, *Walden*, 91.

12. Thoreau, *Walden*, 15, 63.

13. Shaw, "A Virtue Ethics Approach to Aldo Leopold's Land Ethic."

14. Aldo Leopold, *A Sand County Almanac with Essays on Conservation from Round River* (New York: Ballantine Books, 1970), xviii–xix, emphasis added.

15. Leopold, *A Sand County Almanac with Essays on Conservation from Round River*, 102.

16. Leopold, *A Sand County Almanac with Essays on Conservation from Round River*, 291.

17. Leopold, *A Sand County Almanac with Essays on Conservation from Round River*, 244.

18. Leopold, *A Sand County Almanac with Essays on Conservation from Round River*, xvii, 50, 291.

19. For a detailed argument that aesthetic value can ground the preservation of nature, see Eugene Hargrove, *Foundations of Environmental Ethics* (Englewood Cliffs, NJ: Prentice Hall, 1989).

20. Although superficially more modest than Thoreau's *Walden*, Leopold's *Almanac* also suggests that its author is a better person than most, due to his knowledge and finer appreciation of the world around him. Leopold whizzing across the former tall-grass prairie on the "Illinois Bus Ride" is the only passenger who knows its natural history or recognizes its remnants. This knowledge makes him better than them. The nice way to put such a point is to say "you can improve your life through these activities" or, even more nicely, to simply suggest by example that such

possibilities are open to the reader. Leopold does the latter. Thoreau takes the more direct route, saying that "a person is a better person if they do x, y, or z, rather than pile up useless possessions" or, even more obnoxiously, "I am better than you, because I know x or do y." Nevertheless the authors imply the same ethical contrast by writing books in which they talk about themselves and their experiences to such a great extent. An environmental virtue ethics, like any virtue ethics, is essentially inegalitarian.

21. Leopold, *A Sand County Almanac with Essays on Conservation from Round River*, 37, 94, 92, 158–59.

22. Leopold, *A Sand County Almanac with Essays on Conservation from Round River*, 42.

23. Thoreau, *A Week on the Concord and Merrimack Rivers*, 37 (emphasis in the original). Note the fish puns.

24. Aristotle, *Nicomachean Ethics*, bk. 1, chap. 9. Similarly, perhaps, an environmental virtue ethics counters twenty-five centuries of privileging the mental by rephysicalizing the virtues. "If you have come quietly and humbly, as you should to any spot that can be beautiful only once," Leopold writes, if you "watch closely," "you may surprise a fox-red deer, standing knee-high in the garden of his delight" (*A Sand County Almanac with Essays on Conservation from Round River*, 55–56). Quietness and close watching are part of the virtue of humility here, not merely contingent aspects of the experience.

25. Leopold, *A Sand County Almanac with Essays on Conservation from Round River*, 262. Just as *nobility* is a key ethical term for Thoreau, so *beauty* is a key ethical term for Leopold. Here they clearly take us back to an ancient conception of ethics.

26. Responding to an earlier presentation of this chapter, Thomas Hill Jr. commented: "The term *naturalizing of virtue* suggests that what traits are virtues for a natural kind of being simply follows from an adequate account of its natural properties. If so, nonhuman animals and pine trees are capable of having, quite literally, some of the same virtues as we are because we have in common some of the same relevant natural characteristics. These are at best controversial philosophical claims. One does not have to suppose that the word *virtue* applies only to human character traits in order to doubt that normative terms, like *virtue* and *excellence*, and the names of specific virtues, do not reduce to any set of natural properties. . . . Would we not do better simply to admit that moral virtue terms, like *valor*, *prudence*, and the like, are extended to birds and trees metaphorically, to express a recommended attitude rather than to make a literal claim capable of 'naturalistic justification'?" The question of what makes a virtue a virtue, for people, birds, or pine trees, is not easy to answer. Aristotle, whom I follow, defines the virtues as qualities that allow a person to fulfill his or her proper or characteristic functions and to flourish as a good of his or her kind. This definition seems readily transferable to nonhuman beings, *provided* we see some important or foundational good in their being goods of their own kinds and we bother to learn their characteristic functions. The question of what virtues we share with nonhuman beings, then, will largely depend on how we characterize the lives that we and they lead. We might fall into anthropocentric error in two ways here: praising other beings for qualities that they do not have but which we value in humans; failing to praise other beings for their characteristic virtues, because these are not virtues in humans. As Hill correctly notes, the phrase "naturalizing virtue" has metaethical implications. I provide no general theory of virtue in this chapter. But regarding both human and nonhuman virtue, I believe a correct theory will drop the notion of "proper" functions, as it is found in Aristotle and the natural law tradition, and instead consider "characteristic" functions, the things we typically do. Virtues, on this view, will be those qualities that help us succeed in our typical activities: to do whatever we do, well. What traits are virtues for a natural kind of being will follow from an account of its life, along with a belief that such a life is worth living. This is "naturalizing virtue" in the right way. I can see no better foundation for our virtue judgments, for humans or nonhumans. (For the full text of

Hill's comments, see *Philosophy in the Contemporary World* 8, no. 2 [2001], which is devoted to environmental virtue ethics.)

27. Rachel Carson, *Silent Spring* (New York: Fawcett World Library, 1962), 169.

28. Quoted in Linda Lear, *Rachel Carson: Witness for Nature* (New York: Henry Holt, 1997), 424.

29. Carson, *Silent Spring*, 95, 73, emphasis added.

30. Carson, *Silent Spring*, 84, 97, 107, 118–19. Paul Shepard and William O. Douglas, quoted in Carson, *Silent Spring*, 22, 72.

31. Rachel Carson, *The Edge of the Sea* (Boston: Houghton Mifflin, 1955), 39.

32. Carson, *The Edge of the Sea*, 41, 15.

33. Carson, *Silent Spring*, 118.

34. Carson, *Silent Spring*, 261.

35. Rachel Carson, on *CBS Reports* (1962), quoted in Lear, *Rachel Carson*, 450. Thomas Hill has also suggested that "a proper humility" is an important environmental virtue. Hill likewise broaches the possibility that "aesthetic sensibility" is a virtue, a position that Carson and our other naturalists would certainly endorse. See Hill, "Ideals of Human Excellence and Preserving Natural Environments," 216, 219, 223.

36. "A conservationist is one who is humbly aware that with each stroke he is writing his signature on the face of his land. Signatures of course differ, whether written with axe or pen, and this is as it should be" (Leopold, *A Sand County Almanac with Essays on Conservation from Round River*, 73). "This is the only way, we say; but there are as many ways as there can be drawn radii from one center" (Thoreau, *Walden*, 11).

37. Thoreau, *Walden*, 20. On Thoreau's economic philosophy, see Philip Cafaro, "Thoreau and the Place of Economy," *Center: Architecture and Design in America* 11 (1999): 39–47.

38. Lear, *Rachel Carson*, 428–56.

39. Leopold, *A Sand County Almanac with Essays on Conservation from Round River*, 240.

40. But what should we do when there is a conflict of important interests between human and nonhuman beings? Perhaps my failure to ask or answer this question here fed the skepticism of one anonymous reviewer, who doubted that virtue ethics could help "solve real ethical quandaries." It is not clear that deontological, Utilitarian, or contractarian moral theories fare better in the face of such quandaries; still, that hardly absolves virtue ethics from its alleged failure to speak to such hard questions. What should we do when human and nonhuman interests conflict? Neither Leopold nor Carson asks this question directly, insofar as I know. Thoreau answers it at length in the chapter of *Walden* entitled "The Bean-Field." There he notes that woodchucks "have nibbled for me a quarter of an acre clean" out of two and a half acres planted, and he immediately goes on to ask: "But what right had I to oust johnswort and the rest, and break up their ancient herb garden?" (*Walden*, 155). His answer—the only answer, he suggests, that could justify such vandalism—is that, like his neighbor the woodchuck, he had to eat or starve. Thoreau's more general answer to "the question" seems to be as follows: take only what you truly need from the earth, appreciate what nature does with the remainder, and be grateful for both. This, I believe, is the best answer we can give to this question.

41. See Yuriko Saito, "Appreciating Nature on Its Own Terms," *Environmental Ethics* 20 (1998): 135–49.

42. Baird Callicott has tried to divorce Leopold's land ethic from a commitment to wilderness preservation, unconvincingly, in my opinion. Whatever the merits of Callicott's views on the misguidedness of wilderness preservation efforts, they are clearly a long way from Leopold's views. After all, Leopold was the prime mover behind creation of the first Forest Service "primitive area" and a founder of the Wilderness Society. For Leopold on the value of wildness and wilderness, see Leopold, *A Sand County Almanac with Essays on Conservation from Round River*,

104–8, 120, 137–41, 150–58, 258–60, 264–79, 281–90. For Callicott on the relative unimportance of wilderness to Leopold, see J. Baird Callicott, "The Wilderness Idea Revisited: The Sustainable Development Alternative," in *The Great New Wilderness Debate*, ed. J. Baird Callicott and Michael Nelson (Athens: University of Georgia Press, 1998), 337–39; and J. Baird Callicott and Eric Freyfogle's introduction to Aldo Leopold, *For the Health of the Land: Previously Unpublished Essays and Other Writings* (Washington, DC: Island Press, 1999), 3–7.

43. Rachel Carson, *The Sea around Us*, rev. ed. (New York: Signet, 1961), 106, 45.

44. Carson, *The Sea around Us*, 29–30. Carson first published these words in 1951. By the time a revised edition was published ten years later, she and the rest of the scientific community were much more aware of anthropogenic changes and threats to the ocean. See Carson, *The Sea around Us*, x–xii.

45. Thoreau, of course, is the premier poet and defender of wilderness. See Thoreau, *Walden*, 207–8, 317–18; and Henry David Thoreau, "Walking," in *The Natural History Essays* (Salt Lake City: Peregrine Smith, 1980), 93–136.

46. Carson, *The Sea around Us*, 47.

47. Thoreau, *Walden*, 127.

48. Strong arguments for this conclusion include Lester Milbrath, "Redefining the Good Life in a Sustainable Society," *Environmental Values* 2 (1993): 261–69; and Jan Boersema, "Environmental Quality and the Quality of Our Way of Life," *Environmental Values* 4 (1995): 97–108.

PART 2

ENVIRONMENTAL VIRTUE ETHICS THEORY

Ideals of Human Excellence and Preserving Natural Environments

Thomas Hill Jr.

I

A wealthy eccentric bought a house in a neighborhood I know. The house was surrounded by a beautiful display of grass, plants, and flowers, and it was shaded by a huge old avocado tree. But the grass required cutting, the flowers needed tending, and the man wanted more sun. So he cut the whole lot down and covered the yard with asphalt. After all it was his property, and he was not fond of plants.

It was a small operation, but it reminded me of the strip-mining of large sections of the Appalachians. In both cases, of course, there were reasons for the destruction, and property rights could be cited as justification. But I could not help but wonder, "What sort of person would do a thing like that?" Many Californians had a similar reaction when a recent governor defended the leveling of ancient redwood groves, reportedly saying, "If you have seen one redwood, you have seen them all."

Incidents like these arouse the indignation of ardent environmentalists and leave even apolitical observers with some degree of moral discomfort. The reasons for these reactions are mostly obvious. Uprooting the natural environment robs both present and future generations of much potential use and enjoyment. Animals too depend on the environment; and even if one does not value animals for their own sakes, their potential utility for us is incalculable. Plants are needed, of course, to replenish the atmosphere quite aside from their aesthetic value. These reasons for hesitating to destroy forests and gardens are not only the most obvious ones but also the most persuasive for practical purposes. But, one wonders, is there nothing more behind our discomfort? Are we concerned solely about the potential use and enjoyment of the forests, etc., for ourselves, later generations, and perhaps animals? Is there not something else that disturbs us when we witness the destruction or even listen to those who would defend it in terms of cost/benefit analysis?

Imagine that in each of our examples those who would destroy the environment argue elaborately that, even considering future generations of human beings and animals, there are benefits in "replacing" the natural environment that outweigh the negative utilities that environmentalists cite.[1] No doubt we could press the argument on the facts, trying to show that the destruction is shortsighted and that its defenders have underestimated its potential harm or ignored some pertinent rights or interests. But is this all we could say? Suppose we grant, for a moment, that the utility of destroying the redwoods, forests, and gardens is equal to their potential for use and enjoyment by nature lovers and animals. Suppose, further, that we even grant that the pertinent human rights and animal rights, if any, are evenly divided for and against destruction. Imagine that we also concede, for argument's sake, that the forests contain no potentially useful endangered species of animals and plants. Must we then conclude that there is no further cause for moral concern? Should we then feel morally indifferent when we see the natural environment uprooted?

II

Suppose we feel that the answer to these questions should be negative. Suppose, in other words, we feel that our moral discomfort when we confront the destroyers of nature is not fully explained by our belief that they have miscalculated the best use of natural resources or violated rights in exploiting them. Suppose, in particular, we sense that part of the problem is that the natural environment is being viewed exclusively as a natural *resource*. What could be the ground of such a feeling? That is, what is there in our system of normative principles and values that could account for our remaining moral dissatisfaction?[2]

Some may be tempted to seek an explanation by appeal to the interests, or even the rights, of plants. After all, they may argue, we only gradually came to acknowledge the moral importance of all human beings, and it is even more recently that consciences have been aroused to give full weight to the welfare (and rights?) of animals. The next logical step, it may be argued, is to acknowledge a moral requirement to take into account the interests (and rights?) of plants. The problem with the strip miners, redwood cutters, and the like, on this view, is not just that they ignore the welfare and rights of people and animals; they also fail to give due weight to the survival and health of the plants themselves.

The temptation to make such a reply is understandable if one assumes that all moral questions are exclusively concerned with whether *acts* are right or wrong and that this, in turn, is determined entirely by how the acts impinge on the rights and interests of those directly affected. On this assumption, if there is cause for moral concern, some right or interest has been neglected; and if the rights and interests of human beings and animals have already been taken into account, then there must be some other pertinent interests, for example, those of plants. A little reflection will show that the assumption is mistaken; but, in any case, the conclusion that plants have rights or morally relevant interests is surely untenable. We do speak of what is "good for" plants, and they can "thrive" and also be "killed." But this does not imply that they have "interests" in any morally relevant sense. Some people apparently believe that plants grow better if we talk to them, but the idea that the plants suffer and enjoy, desire and dislike, etc. is clearly outside the range of both common sense and scientific belief. The notion that the forests should be preserved to avoid *hurting* the trees or because they have a *right* to life is not part of a widely shared moral consciousness, and for good reason.[3]

Another way of trying to explain our moral discomfort is to appeal to certain religious beliefs. If one believes that all living things were created by a God who cares for them and entrusted us with the use of plants and animals only for limited purposes, then one has a reason to avoid careless destruction of the forests, etc., quite aside from their future utility. Again, if one believes that a divine force is immanent in all nature, then too one might have reason to care for more than sentient things. But such arguments require strong and controversial premises, and, I suspect, they will always have a restricted audience.

Early in this century, due largely to the influence of G. E. Moore, another point of view developed that some may find promising.[4] Moore introduced, or at least made popular, the idea that certain states of affairs are intrinsically valuable—not just valued but valuable, and not necessarily because of their effects on sentient beings. Admittedly Moore came to believe that in fact the only intrinsically valuable things were conscious experiences of various sorts, but this restriction was not inherent in the idea of intrinsic value.[5] The intrinsic goodness of something, he thought, was an objective, nonrelational property of the thing, like its texture or color, but not a property perceivable by sense perception or detectable by scientific instruments. In theory at least, a single tree thriving alone in a universe without sentient beings, and even without God, could be intrinsically valuable. Since, according to Moore, our duty is to maximize intrinsic value, his theory could obviously be used to argue that we have reason not to destroy natural environments independently of how they affect human beings and animals. The survival of a forest might have worth beyond its worth *to* sentient beings.

This approach, like the religious one, may appeal to some but is infested with problems. There are, first, the familiar objections to intuitionism, on which the theory depends. Metaphysical and epistemological doubts about nonnatural, intuited properties are hard to suppress, and many have argued that the theory rests on a misunderstanding of the words *good, valuable*, and the like.[6] Second, even if we try to set aside these objections and think in Moore's terms, it is far from obvious that everyone would agree that the existence of forests, etc., is intrinsically valuable. The test, says Moore, is what we would say when we imagine a universe with just the thing in question, without any effects or accompaniments, and then we ask, "Would its existence be better than its nonexistence?" Be careful, Moore would remind us, not to construe this question as, "Would you *prefer* the existence of that universe to its nonexistence?" The question is, "Would its existence have the objective, nonrelational property, intrinsic goodness?"

Now even among those who have no worries about whether this really makes sense, we might well get a diversity of answers. Those prone to destroy natural environments will doubtless give one answer, and nature lovers will likely give another. When an issue is as controversial as the one at hand, intuition is a poor arbiter.

The problem, then, is this. We want to understand what underlies our moral uneasiness at the destruction of the redwoods, forests, etc., even apart from the loss of these as resources for human beings and animals. But I find no adequate answer by pursuing the questions, "Are rights or interests of plants neglected?" "What is God's will on the matter?" and "What is the intrinsic value of the existence of a tree or for-est?" My suggestion, which is in fact the main point of this chapter, is that we look at the problem from a different perspective. That is, let us turn for a while from the ef-fort to find reasons why certain acts destructive of natural environments are morally wrong to the ancient task of articulating our ideals of human excellence. Rather than argue directly with destroyers of the environment who say, "Show me why what I am doing is *immoral*," I want to ask, "What sort of person would want to do what they propose?" The point is not to skirt the issue with an ad hominem but, rather, to raise a different moral question, for even if there is no convincing way to show that the de-structive acts are wrong (independently of human and animal use and enjoyment), we may find that the willingness to indulge in them reflects the absence of human traits that we admire and regard morally important.

This strategy of shifting questions may seem more promising if one reflects on cer-tain analogous situations. Consider, for example, the Nazi who asks, in all seriousness, "Why is it wrong for me to make lampshades out of human skin—provided, of course, I did not myself kill the victims to get the skins?" We would react more with shock and disgust than with indignation, I suspect, because it is even more evident that the ques-tion reveals a defect in the questioner than that the proposed act is itself immoral. Sometimes we may not regard an act wrong at all though we see it as reflecting some-thing objectionable about the person who does it. Imagine, for example, one who laughs spontaneously to himself when he reads a newspaper account of a plane crash that kills hundreds. Or, again, consider an obsequious grandson who, having waited for his grandmother's inheritance with mock devotion, then secretly spits on her grave when at last she dies. Spitting on the grave may have no adverse consequences, and per-haps it violates no rights. The moral uneasiness that it arouses is explained more by our view of the agent than by any conviction that what he did was immoral. Had he hes-itated and asked, "Why shouldn't I spit on her grave?" it seems more fitting to ask him to reflect on the sort of person he is than to try to offer reasons why he should refrain from spitting.

III

What sort of person, then, would cover his garden with asphalt, strip-mine a wooded mountain, or level an irreplaceable redwood grove? Two sorts of answers, though ini-tially appealing, must be ruled out. The first is that persons who would destroy the environment in these ways either are shortsighted, underestimating the harm they do, or else are too little concerned for the well-being of other people. Perhaps too they have insufficient regard for animal life. But these considerations have been set aside in order to refine the controversy. Another tempting response might be that we count it a moral virtue, or at least a human ideal, to love nature. Those who value the environment only for its utility must not really love nature and so in this way fall short of an ideal. But such an answer is hardly satisfying in the present context, for what is at issue is *why* we feel moral discomfort at the activities of those who admit-tedly value nature only for its utility. That it is ideal to care for nonsentient nature beyond its possible use is really just another way of expressing the general point that is under controversy.

What is needed is some way of showing that this ideal is connected with other virtues, or human excellences, not in question. To do so is difficult, and my suggestions, accordingly, will be tentative and subject to qualification. The main idea is that, though indifference to nonsentient nature does not *necessarily* reflect the absence of virtues, it often signals the absence of certain traits that we want to encourage because they are, in most cases, a natural basis for the development of certain virtues. It is often thought, for example, that those who would destroy the natural environment must lack a proper appreciation of their place in the natural order and so must either be ignorant or have too little humility. Though I would argue that this is not necessarily so, I suggest that, given certain plausible empirical assumptions, their attitude may well be rooted in ignorance, a narrow perspective, inability to see things as important apart from themselves and the limited groups they associate with, or reluctance to accept themselves as natural beings. Overcoming these deficiencies will not guarantee a proper moral humility, but for most of us it is probably an important psychological preliminary. Later I suggest, more briefly, that indifference to nonsentient nature typically reveals absence of either aesthetic sensibility or a disposition to cherish what has enriched one's life and that these, though not themselves moral virtues, are a natural basis for appreciation of the good in others and gratitude.[7]

Consider first the suggestion that destroyers of the environment lack an appreciation of their place in the universe.[8] Their attention, it seems, must be focused on parochial matters, on what is, relatively speaking, close in space and time. They seem not to understand that we are a speck on the cosmic scene, a brief stage in the evolutionary process, only one among millions of species on Earth, and an episode in the course of human history. Of course, they know that there are stars, fossils, insects, and ancient ruins; but do they have any idea of the complexity of the processes that led to the natural world as we find it? Are they aware how much the forces at work within their own bodies are like those that govern all living things and even how much they have in common with inanimate bodies? Admittedly scientific knowledge is limited, and no one can master it all; but could one who had a broad and deep understanding of his place in nature really be indifferent to the destruction of the natural environment?

This first suggestion, however, may well provoke a protest from a sophisticated antienvironmentalist.[9] "Perhaps *some* may be indifferent to nature from ignorance," the critic may object, "but *I* have studied astronomy, geology, biology, and biochemistry, and I still unashamedly regard the nonsentient environment as simply a resource for our use. It should not be wasted, of course, but what should be preserved is decidable by weighing long-term costs and benefits." "Besides," our critic may continue, "as philosophers you should know the old Humean formula, 'You cannot derive an *ought* from an *is*.' All the facts of biology, biochemistry, etc. do not entail that I ought to love nature or want to preserve it. What one understands is one thing; what one values is something else. Just as nature lovers are not necessarily scientists, those indifferent to nature are not necessarily ignorant."

Although the environmentalist may concede the critic's logical point, he may well argue that, as a matter of fact, increased understanding of nature tends to heighten people's concern for its preservation. If so, despite the objection, the suspicion that the destroyers of the environment lack deep understanding of nature is not, in most cases, unwarranted, but the argument need not rest here. The environmentalist might amplify this original idea as follows:

> When I said that the destroyers of nature do not appreciate their place in the universe, I was not speaking of intellectual understanding alone, for, after all, a person can *know* a catalog of facts without ever putting them together and seeing vividly the whole picture that they form. To see oneself as just one part of nature is to look at oneself and the world from a certain perspective that is quite different from being able to recite detailed information from the natural sciences. What the destroyers of nature lack is this perspective, not particular information.

Again our critic may object, though only after making some concessions: "All right," he may say,

> *some* who are indifferent to nature may lack the cosmic perspective of which you speak, but again there is no *necessary* connection between this failing, if it is one, and any particular evaluative attitude toward nature. In fact, different people respond quite differently when they move to a wider perspective. When *I* try to picture myself vividly as a brief, transitory episode in the course of nature, I simply get depressed. Far from inspiring me with a love of nature, the exercise makes me sad and hostile. You romantics think only of poets like Wordsworth and artists like Turner, but you should consider how differently Omar Khayyam responded when he took your wider perspective. His reaction, when looking at his life from a cosmic viewpoint, was "Drink up, for tomorrow we die." Others respond in an almost opposite manner with a joyless Stoic resignation, exemplified by the poet who pictures the wise man, at the height of personal triumph, being served a magnificent banquet and then consummating his marriage to his beloved, all the while reminding himself, "Even this shall pass away."[10]

In sum, the critic may object, "Even if one should try to see oneself as one small transitory part of nature, doing so does not dictate any particular normative attitude. Some may come to love nature, but others are moved to live for the moment; some sink into sad resignation; others get depressed or angry. So indifference to nature is not necessarily a sign that a person fails to look at himself from the larger perspective."

The environmentalist might respond to this objection in several ways. He might, for example, argue that even though some people who see themselves as part of the natural order remain indifferent to nonsentient nature, this is not a common reaction. Typically, it may be argued, as we become more and more aware that we are parts of the larger whole we come to value the whole independently of its effect on ourselves. Thus, despite the possibilities the critic raises, indifference to nonsentient nature is still in most cases a sign that a person fails to see himself as part of the natural order.

If someone challenges the empirical assumption here, the environmentalist might develop the argument along a quite different line. The initial idea, he may remind us, was that those who would destroy the natural environment fail to *appreciate* their place in the natural order. "Appreciating one's place" is not simply an intellectual appreciation. It is also an attitude, reflecting what one values as well as what one knows. When we say, for example, that both the servile and the arrogant person fail to *appreciate* their place in a society of equals, we do not mean simply that they are ignorant of certain empirical facts but, rather, that they have certain objectionable attitudes about their importance relative to other people. Similarly, to fail to appreciate one's place in nature is not merely to lack knowledge or breadth of perspective but to take a certain attitude about what matters. A person who *understands* his place in nature but still views non-sentient nature merely as a resource takes the attitude that nothing is *important* but human beings and animals. Despite first appearances, he is not so much like the pre-Copernican astronomers who made the intellectual error of treating the Earth as the "center of the universe" when they made their calculations. He is more like the racist who, though well aware of other races, treats all races but his own as insignificant.

So construed, the argument appeals to the common idea that awareness of nature typically has, and should have, a humbling effect. The Alps, a storm at sea, the Grand Canyon, towering redwoods, and "the starry heavens above" move many a person to remark on the comparative insignificance of our daily concerns and even of our species, and this is generally taken to be a quite fitting response.[11] What seems to be missing, then, in those who understand nature but remain unmoved is a proper humility.[12] Absence of proper humility is not the same as selfishness or egoism, for one can be devoted to self-interest while still viewing one's own pleasures and projects as trivial and unimportant.[13] And one can have an exaggerated view of one's own importance while grandly sacrificing for those one views as inferior. Nor is the lack of humility identical with belief that one has power and influence, for a person can be quite puffed up about himself while believing that the foolish world will never acknowledge him. The humility we miss seems not so much a belief about one's relative effectiveness and recognition as an attitude that measures the importance of things independently of their relation to oneself or to some narrow group with which one identifies. A paradigm of a person who lacks humility is the self-important emperor who grants status to his family because it is *his*, to his subordinates because *he* appointed them, and to his country because *he* chooses to glorify it. Less extreme but still lacking proper humility is the elitist who counts events significant solely in proportion to how they affect his class. The suspicion about those who would destroy the environment, then, is that what they count important is too narrowly confined insofar as it encompasses only what affects beings who, like us, are capable of feeling.

This idea that proper humility requires recognition of the importance of nonsentient nature is similar to the thought of those who charge meat eaters with "speciesism." In both cases it is felt that people too narrowly confine their concerns to the sorts of beings that are most like them. But, however intuitively appealing, the idea will surely arouse objections from our nonenvironmentalist critic. "Why," he will ask,

> do you suppose that the sort of humility I *should* have requires me to acknowledge the importance of nonsentient nature aside from its utility? You cannot, by your own admission, argue that nonsentient nature is important,

appealing to religious or intuitionist grounds. And simply to assert, without further argument, that an ideal humility requires us to view nonsentient nature as important for its own sake begs the question at issue. If proper humility is acknowledging the relative importance of things as one should, then to show that I must lack this you must first establish that one *should* acknowledge the importance of nonsentient nature.

Though some may wish to accept this challenge, there are other ways to pursue the connection between humility and response to nonsentient nature. For example, suppose we grant that proper humility requires only acknowledging a due status to sentient beings. We must admit, then, that it is logically possible for a person to be properly humble even though he viewed all nonsentient nature simply as a resource. But this logical possibility may be a psychological rarity. It may be that, given the sort of beings we are, we would never learn humility before persons without developing the general capacity to cherish, and regard important, many things for their own sakes. The major obstacle to humility before persons is self-importance, a tendency to measure the significance of everything by its relation to oneself and those with whom one identifies. The processes by which we overcome self-importance are doubtless many and complex, but it seems unlikely that they are exclusively concerned with how we relate to other people and animals. Learning humility requires learning to feel that something matters besides what will affect oneself and one's circle of associates. What leads a child to care about what happens to a lost hamster or a stray dog he will not see again is likely also to generate concern for a lost toy or a favorite tree where he used to live.[14] Learning to value things for their own sake, and to count what affects them important aside from their utility, is not the same as judging them to have some intuited objective property, but it is necessary to the development of humility and seems likely to take place in experiences with nonsentient nature as well as with people and animals. If a person views all nonsentient nature merely as a resource, then it seems unlikely that he has developed the capacity needed to overcome self-importance.

IV

This last argument, unfortunately, has its limits. It presupposes an empirical connection between experiencing nature and overcoming self-importance, and this may be challenged. Even if experiencing nature promotes humility before others, there may be other ways people can develop such humility in a world of concrete, glass, and plastic. If not, perhaps all that is needed is limited experience of nature in one's early, developing years; mature adults, having overcome youthful self-importance, may live well enough in artificial surroundings. More importantly, the argument does not fully capture the spirit of the intuition that an ideal person stands humbly before nature. That idea is not simply that experiencing nature tends to foster proper humility before other people; it is, in part, that natural surroundings encourage and are appropriate to an ideal sense of oneself as part of the natural world. Standing alone in the forest, after months in the city, is not merely good as a means of curbing one's arrogance before others; it reinforces and fittingly expresses one's acceptance of oneself as a natural being.

Previously we considered only one aspect of proper humility, namely, a sense of one's relative importance with respect to other human beings. Another aspect, I think, is a kind of *self-acceptance*. This involves acknowledging, in more than a merely intellectual way, that we are the sort of creatures that we are. Whether one is self-accepting is not so much a matter of how one attributes *importance* comparatively to oneself, other people, animals, plants, and other things as it is a matter of understanding, facing squarely, and responding appropriately to who and what one is, e.g., one's powers and limits, one's affinities with other beings and differences from them, one's unalterable nature, and one's freedom to change. Self-acceptance is not merely intellectual awareness, for one can be intellectually aware that one is growing old and will eventually die while nevertheless behaving in a thousand foolish ways that reflect a refusal to acknowledge these facts. On the other hand, self-acceptance is not passive resignation, for refusal to pursue what one truly wants within one's limits is a failure to accept the freedom and power one has. Particular behaviors, like dying one's gray hair and dressing like those twenty years younger, do not *necessarily* imply lack of self-acceptance, for there could be reasons for acting in these ways other than the wish to hide from oneself what one really is. One fails to accept oneself when the patterns of behavior and emotion are rooted in a desire to disown and deny features of oneself, to pretend to oneself that they are not there. This is not to say that a self-accepting person makes no value judgments about himself, that he likes all facts about himself, wants equally to develop and display them; he can and should feel remorse for his past misdeeds and strive to change his current vices. The point is that he does not disown them, pretend that they do not exist or are facts about something other than himself. Such pretense is incompatible with proper humility because it is seeing oneself as better than one is.

Self-acceptance of this sort has long been considered a human excellence, under various names, but what has it to do with preserving nature? There is, I think, the following connection. As human beings we are part of nature, living, growing, declining, and dying by natural laws similar to those governing other living beings; despite our awesomely distinctive human powers, we share many of the needs, limits, and liabilities of animals and plants. These facts are neither good nor bad in themselves, aside from personal preference and varying conventional values. To say this is to utter a truism that few will deny, but to accept these facts, as facts about oneself, is not so easy— or so common. Much of what naturalists deplore about our increasingly artificial world reflects, and encourages, a denial of these facts, an unwillingness to avow them with equanimity.

Like the Victorian lady who refuses to look at her own nude body, some would like to create a world of less transitory stuff, reminding us only of our intellectual and social nature, never calling to mind our affinities with "lower" living creatures. The "denial of death," to which psychiatrists call attention, reveals an attitude incompatible with the sort of self-acceptance that philosophers, from the ancients to Spinoza and on, have admired as a human excellence.[15] My suggestion is not merely that experiencing nature causally promotes such self-acceptance but also that those who fully accept themselves as part of the natural world lack the common drive to disassociate themselves from nature by replacing natural environments with artificial ones. A storm in the wilds helps us to appreciate our animal vulnerability, but, equally important, the reluctance to experience it may *reflect* an unwillingness to accept this aspect of ourselves. The person who is too ready to destroy the ancient redwoods may lack humility, not so much in the sense that he exaggerates his importance relative to others but, rather, in the sense that he tries to avoid seeing himself as one among many natural creatures.

V

My suggestion so far has been that, though indifference to nonsentient nature is not itself a moral vice, it is likely to reflect either ignorance, a self-importance, or a lack of self-acceptance that we must overcome to have proper humility. A similar idea might be developed connecting attitudes toward nonsentient nature with other human excellences. For example, one might argue that indifference to nature reveals a lack of either an aesthetic sense or some of the natural roots of gratitude.

When we see a hillside that has been gutted by strip miners or the garden replaced by asphalt, our first reaction is probably, "How ugly!" The scenes assault our aesthetic sensibilities. We suspect that no one with a keen sense of beauty could have left such a sight. Admittedly not everything in nature strikes us as beautiful or even aesthetically interesting, and sometimes a natural scene is replaced with a more impressive architectural masterpiece. But this is not usually the situation in the problem cases that environmentalists are most concerned about. More often beauty is replaced with ugliness.

At this point our critic may well object that, even if he does lack a sense of beauty, this is no moral vice. His cost/benefit calculations take into account the pleasure others may derive from seeing the forests, etc., and so why should he be faulted?

Some might reply that, despite contrary philosophical traditions, aesthetics and morality are not so distinct as commonly supposed. Appreciation of beauty, they may argue, is a human excellence that morally ideal persons should try to develop. But, setting aside this controversial position, there still may be cause for moral concern about those who have no aesthetic response to nature. Even if aesthetic sensibility is not itself a moral virtue, many of the capacities of mind and heart that it presupposes may be ones that are also needed for an appreciation of other people. Consider, for example, curiosity; a mind open to novelty; the ability to look at things from unfamiliar perspectives; empathetic imagination; interest in details, variety, and order; and emotional freedom from the immediate and the practical. All these, and more, seem necessary to aesthetic sensibility, but they are also traits that a person needs to be fully sensitive to people of all sorts. The point is not that a moral person must be able to distinguish beautiful from ugly people; the point is, rather, that unresponsiveness to what is beautiful, awesome, dainty, dumpy, and otherwise aesthetically interesting in nature probably reflects a lack of the openness of mind and spirit necessary to appreciate the best in human beings.

The antienvironmentalist, however, may refuse to accept the charge that he lacks aesthetic sensibility. If he claims to appreciate seventeenth-century miniature portraits but to abhor natural wildernesses, he will hardly be convincing. Tastes vary, but aesthetic sense is not *that* selective. He may, instead, insist that he *does* appreciate natural beauty. He spends his vacations, let us suppose, hiking in the Sierras, photographing wildflowers, and so on. He might press his argument as follows:

> I enjoy natural beauty as much as anyone, but I fail to see what this has to do with preserving the environment independently of human enjoyment and use. Nonsentient nature is a resource, but one of its best uses is to give us pleasure. I take this into account when I calculate the costs and benefits of preserving a park, planting a garden, and so on. But the problem you raised explicitly set aside the desire to preserve nature as a means to enjoyment. I say, let us enjoy nature fully while we can, but if all sentient beings were to die tomorrow, we might as well blow up all plant life as well. A redwood grove that no one can use or enjoy is utterly worthless.

The attitude expressed here, I suspect, is not a common one, but it represents a philosophical challenge. The beginnings of a reply may be found in the following. When a person takes joy in something, it is a common (and perhaps natural) response to come to cherish it. To cherish something is not simply to be happy with it at the moment but to care for it for its own sake. This is not to say that one necessarily sees it as having feelings and so wants it to feel good; nor does it imply that one judges the thing to have Moore's intrinsic value. One simply wants the thing to survive and (when appropriate) to thrive, and not simply for its utility. We see this attitude repeatedly regarding mementos. They are not simply valued as a means to remind us of happy occasions; they come to be valued for their own sake. Thus, if someone really took joy in the natural environment but was prepared to blow it up as soon as sentient life ended, he would lack this common human tendency to cherish what enriches our lives. While this response is not itself a moral virtue, it may be a natural basis of the virtue we call "gratitude." People who have no tendency to cherish things that give them pleasure may be poorly disposed to respond gratefully to persons who are good to them. Again the connection is not one of logical necessity, but it may nevertheless be important. A nonreligious person unable to "thank" anyone for the beauties of nature may nevertheless feel "grateful" in a sense; and I suspect that the person who feels no such "gratitude" toward nature is unlikely to show proper gratitude toward people.

Suppose these conjectures prove to be true. One may wonder what is the point of considering them. Is it to disparage all those who view nature merely as a resource? To do so, it seems, would be unfair, for, even if this attitude typically stems from deficiencies that affect one's attitudes toward sentient beings, there may be exceptions, and we have not shown that their view of nonsentient nature is itself blameworthy. But when we set aside questions of blame and inquire what sorts of human traits we want to encourage, our reflections become relevant in a more positive way. The point is not to insinuate that all antienvironmentalists are defective but to see that those who value such traits as humility, gratitude, and sensitivity to others have reason to promote the love of nature.

Notes

1. When I use the expression "the natural environment," I have in mind the sort of examples with which I began. For some purposes it is important to distinguish cultivated gardens from forests, virgin forests from replenished ones, irreplaceable natural phenomena from the

replaceable, and so on; but these distinctions, I think, do not affect my main points here. There is also a broad sense, as Hume and Mill noted, in which all that occurs, miracles aside, is "natural." In this sense, of course, strip-mining is as natural as a beaver cutting trees for his dam, and as parts of nature, we cannot destroy the "natural" environment but only alter it. As will be evident, I shall use *natural* in a narrower, more familiar sense.

2. This chapter is intended as a preliminary discussion in *normative* ethical theory (as opposed to *metaethics*). The task, accordingly, is the limited, though still difficult, one of articulating the possible basis in our beliefs and values for certain particular moral judgments. Questions of ultimate justification are set aside. What makes the task difficult and challenging is not that conclusive proofs from the foundation of morality are attempted; it is rather that the particular judgments to be explained seem at first not to fall under the most familiar moral principles (e.g., utilitarianism, respect for rights).

3. I assume here that having a right presupposes having interests in a sense that in turn presupposes a capacity to desire, suffer, etc. Since my main concern lies in another direction, I do not argue the point but merely note that some regard it as debatable. See, for example, W. Murray Hunt, "Are Mere Things Morally Considerable?" *Environmental Ethics* 2 (1980): 59–65; Kenneth E. Goodpaster, "On Stopping at Everything," *Environmental Ethics* 2 (1980): 288–94; Joel Feinberg, "The Rights of Animals and Unborn Generations," in *Philosophy and Environmental Crisis*, ed. William Blackstone (Athens: University of Georgia Press, 1974), 43–68; Tom Regan, "Feinberg on What Sorts of Beings Can Have Rights," *Southern Journal of Philosophy* (1976): 485–98; Robert Elliot, "Regan on the Sort of Beings That Can Have Rights," *Southern Journal of Philosophy* (1978): 701–5; Scott Lehmann, "Do Wildernesses Have Rights?" *Environmental Ethics* 2 (1981): 129–46.

4. G. E. Moore, *Principia Ethica* (Cambridge: Cambridge University Press, 1903); *Ethics* (London: H. Holt, 1912).

5. G. E. Moore, "Is Goodness a Quality?" in *Philosophical Papers* (London: George Allen and Unwin, 1959), 95–97.

6. See, for example, P. H. Nowell-Smith, *Ethics* (New York: Penguin Books, 1954).

7. The issues I raise here, though perhaps not the details of my remarks, are in line with Aristotle's view of moral philosophy, a view revitalized recently by Philippa Foot's *Virtue and Vice* (Berkeley: University of California Press, 1979), Alasdair McIntyre's, *After Virtue* (Notre Dame: Notre Dame Press, 1981), and James Wallace's *Virtues and Vices* (Ithaca: Cornell University Press, 1978) and other works. For other reflections on relationships between character and natural environments, see John Rodman, "The Liberation of Nature," *Inquiry* (1976): 83–131; and L. Reinhardt, "Some Gaps in Moral Space: Reflections on Forests and Feelings," in *Environmental Philosophy*, ed. Mannison, McRobbie, and Routley (Canberra: Australian National University Research School of Social Sciences, 1980).

8. Though for simplicity I focus upon those who do strip-mining, etc., the argument is also applicable to those whose utilitarian calculations lead them to preserve the redwoods, mountains, etc., but who care for only sentient nature for its own sake. Similarly the phrase "indifferent to nature" is meant to encompass those who are indifferent *except* when considering its benefits to people and animals.

9. For convenience I use the labels *environmentalist* and *antienvironmentalist* (or critic) for the opposing sides in the rather special controversy I have raised. Thus, for example, my "environmentalist" not only favors conserving the forests, etc., but finds something objectionable in wanting to destroy them even aside from the costs to human beings and animals. My "antienvironmentalist" is not simply one who wants to destroy the environment; he is a person who has no qualms about doing so independent of the adverse effects on human beings and animals.

10. "Even This Shall Pass Away," by Theodore Tildon, in *The Best Loved Poems of the American People*, ed. Hazel Felleman (Garden City, NY: Doubleday and Co., 1936).

11. An exception, apparently, was Kant, who thought "the starry heavens" sublime and compared them with "the moral law within" but did not for all that see our species as comparatively insignificant.

12. By "*proper* humility" I mean that sort and degree of humility that is a morally admirable character trait. How precisely to define this is, of course, a controversial matter; but the point for present purposes is just to set aside obsequiousness, false modesty, underestimation of one's abilities, and the like.

13. I take this point from some of Philippa Foot's remarks.

14. The causal history of this concern may well depend upon the object (tree, toy) having given the child pleasure, but this does not mean that the object is then valued only for further pleasure it may bring.

15. See, for example, Ernest Becker, *The Denial of Death* (New York: Free Press, 1973).

CHAPTER 4

Environmental Virtue Ethics: Half the Truth but Dangerous as a Whole

Holmes Rolston III

Nature and Character

"Know thyself." "The unexamined life is not worth living."[1] Socrates' classic wisdom invites us to figure out who we are. But there is complexity beguiled by these seemingly simple maxims. On an elemental level, we often gain lessons in encounters with nature, with nonself. Confronting our surroundings and sources integrates us, protects us from pride, gives a sense of proportion and place, and teaches us what to expect and what to be content with. Living well involves catching certain natural rhythms. We learn humility, simplicity, frugality, serenity, freedom, and self-confidence. These virtues are neither modern nor postmodern; they are perennial and universally available.

Folk wisdom is routinely cast in this natural idiom. The farmer urges, "Work, for the night comes when man's work is done." "Make hay while the sun shines." "What you sow, you reap." "Into each life some rain must fall." "All sunshine makes a desert." "By their fruits shall you know them." "The early bird gets the worm." "The loveliest rose has yet its thorns." "The tree stands that bends with the wind." "Every mile is two in winter." "If winter comes, can spring be far behind?" The mariner says: "Time and tide wait for no man." "The north wind made the Vikings."

The sage in Proverbs admonishes the sluggard to consider the ways of the ant and be wise. The psalmist notices how we are like grass that flourishes but is soon gone, and those who understand the "seasonal" character of life are better able to rejoice in the turning of the seasons and to do everything well in its time. Jesus asks us, in our search for the goods of life, to consider the natural beauty of the lilies of the field, which the affected glory of Solomon could not surpass; and he points out birds, who, although hardly lazy, are not anxious or worried about tomorrow. Often, major religious seasons are naturally scheduled: Christmas comes at the winter solstice; Easter, with the bursting forth of spring; and Thanksgiving, with the harvest.

An inclusive moral virtue, well-rounded excellence of character, comes in significant part, although by no means in the whole, from this natural attunement. Here living well requires that we be properly sensitive to the flow of nature through us and its bearing on our habits of life. Otherwise, life lacks propriety; we do not know our place under the sun.

We need caution. Human virtues are multileveled. That nature builds character is but half the truth and absurd if taken for the whole. That would omit all the civic virtues, without which we could not be human. Character is developed in a dialectic of nature and culture. "Man is by nature a political animal."[2] Humans are animals who build themselves a polis, a city, and love to socialize within it. "Man is the animal for whom it is natural to be artificial."[3] *Homo sapiens* is "the natural alien."[4] What humans "naturally" do when they encounter nature is build a culture differentiating (alienating) ourselves from nature. Agriculture, business, and industry are our real vocation. Virtue has to be "cultivated," "cultured." Living with wild nature in nostalgic simplicity and frugality, these "humanists" will say, is romantic nonsense that forgets how much the human genius lies in exodus from and resourceful transformation of nature. The modern word for this is "Develop!"

In this human genius, humanizing our lives on Earth, nature is not to be praised. Nature only serves as an occasion for the construction of human virtues; the natural wisdom I was alleging earlier only reveals the virtues that develop in humans when we confront nature. We resourcefully take advantage of nature when it serves; we rebuild nature when it opposes us, an opportunist surmounting of nature in which successful humans exhibit remarkable powers. If we are to be human, then we have to distinguish ourselves from nature. Development and culture just *are* the human relationship with nature. We inhabit culture within nature, bracketing ourselves off from wild nature with an insulating culture. In doing this we demonstrate our excellences.

But this anthropocentric account of the nature–culture encounter is too one-sided. Evolution and ecology have taught us that every kind of life is what it is environmentally, in its surroundings, not autonomously. Humans too are environmental reciprocals, indebted to our environment for what we have become in ways that are as complementary as they are oppositional. Dialectically, the character is achieved within us, but the context is relational. Nature is not sufficient to produce these virtues, but it is necessary for them. With our evolved hands and brains, humans are realizing in the strong and good life something of the strength and goodness that nature has disciplined into its creatures and is bequeathing to us. In our cultural genius, nature remains in, with, and under us, a womb that we never really leave.

Further, in these cultures that we develop, the humanists will say (and correctly so), nature gives no ethical guidance for interhuman affairs. The virtues of culture are not present there. Nowhere in wild nature does one learn to keep promises, or to tell the truth, or to respect property and not steal, or to seek the greatest good for the greatest number, or to be just and charitable, or to forgive sins. So there does seem to be force in the claim that human virtues must transcend any elemental harmony with wild nature.

Nevertheless, human conduct must also be an appropriate form of life toward our environment, toward what the world offers us. Build cultures and cultivate our moral lives though we may, none of us is wise who does not ultimately make peace with the natural order. Wallace Stegner epitomizes this memorably:

Something will have gone out of us as a people if we ever let the remaining wilderness be destroyed; if we permit the last virgin forest to be turned into comic books and plastic cigarette cases; if we drive the few remaining members of the wild species into zoos or to extinction; if we pollute the last clear air and dirty the last clean streams and push our paved roads through the last of the silence, so that never again will Americans be free in their own country from the noise, the exhausts, the stinks of human and automotive waste. And so that never again can we have the chance to see ourselves single, separate, vertical and individual in the world, part of the environment of trees and rocks and soil, brother to the other animals, part of the natural world and competent to belong in it. . . .

We simply need that wild country available to us, even if we never do more than drive to its edge and look in, for it can be a means of reassuring ourselves of our sanity as creatures, a part of the geography of hope.[5]

So, for the sake of our own identities, of being who we are where we are, of being at home in the world, we need to maintain the integrities of the fauna and flora on our landscapes. Else we will become strangers to our places; we will be misfits, upsetting residents. We reach the truth that we are embodied persons. But this embodiment in place is entwining the character of the inner self with the character of the outer, natural world, that is, relocating, dislocating the virtues of the self, putting the self in its place.

Virtuous Persons Embodied in Their Places

"Life in an unexamined world is not worth living either." With this more inclusive maxim, I claim to be wiser than Socrates. Yes, the unexamined life is not worth living, but I disagree with Socrates' avoidance of nature, thinking it profitless: "You see, I am fond of learning. Now the country places and trees won't teach me anything, and the people in the city do."[6] Walt Whitman has quite the opposite conviction:

Now I see the secret of the making of the best persons,
It is to grow in the open air, and to eat and sleep with the earth.[7]

A rural New Yorker reflected over his environment, in late November, with a strong sense of satisfactory residence:

The wind sweeps out of the west, with the faint breath of blizzard far away; but the skies are clear, without even the shredded, high-flying clouds of storm. And so November leans toward December, and late autumn creeps past, silent as the stars. The hush of winter approaches, and short days lie upon the land. Now is the time that the countryman has the country to himself. The visitors are gone, vacations over. Even the migrant birds are gone. The squirrels go quietly about their business. And a man has time to survey his world and understand his own place in it, if he is ever to understand.

> Now it becomes clear that it isn't the little pleasures of the country that
> make life worth living there. It is rather the big assurances. The little plea-
> sures are for the casual visitor; but one must live with the wind and the
> weather and know the land and the seasons to find the certainties. The flash
> of a goldfinch or the song of an oriole can delight the senses; but the knowl-
> edge that no matter how sharp or long the winter, they will be back again
> for another spring provides an inner surety. To see a hillside white with dog-
> wood bloom is to know a particular ecstasy of beauty; but to walk the gray
> winter woods and find the buds which will resurrect that beauty in another
> May is to partake of continuity. To feel the frost underfoot and know that
> there is both fire and ice in the earth, even as in the patterned stars over-
> head, is to sense the big assurances.
>
> Man needs to know these things, and they are best learned when the si-
> lence lies upon the land. No one can shout them. They need to be whis-
> pered, that they may reach the questing soul.[8]

Now we are recognizing how persons cannot be human if displaced but, rather, must
be resident in their local environments. Here they sense the recurrent universals particularly displayed in that place—the seasons, the regenerative powers of life, life per-
sisting in the midst of its perpetual perishing: the "big assurances." A person in his or
her biography—as much as an ecologist with a field grid, a geneticist with a breeding
experiment, a taxonomist with a type species, or a mathematician with a set of algebraic equations—is a detection device for catching something of the richness and integrity of what is taking place on the landscape.

This results in human virtues but simultaneously takes the focus off the self.
Virtue cannot be self-contained but must be in place, and now the integrity of place—
as much as the integrity of persons resonating with their places—is what is really impressive. Nature is a vast scene of birth and death, springtime and harvest, permanence
and change; of budding, flowering, fruiting, and withering away; of processive unfolding; of pain and pleasure; of success and failure; of ugliness giving way to beauty
and beauty to ugliness. From the contemplation of it we get a feeling for life's transient
beauty sustained over chaos. There is a music to it all—and not the least when in a minor key. Though we are required to spend our lives in struggle, yet we are able to cherish the good Earth and accept the kind of world in which we find ourselves. We are
finding out who we are by finding out where we are and how we are emplaced there.

The dialectic between environmental resistance and conductance continues. Certainly, there is struggle in nature. But there is also, and even more, adaptedness. There
is resistance to life, but there is support of life. The account that the examined life
reaches when examining the world contains both elements—and not merely as a nonsensical mixture of goods and evils. One discovers a nature where the evils are tributary
to the goods, "a table prepared in the midst of my enemies."[9] It is not death but, rather,
life, including human life fitted to this planetary environment, that is the principal mystery that has come out of nature. For several billion years, the ongoing development and
persistence of that life, reaching the most complex achievements yet known in human
life, have been the persistent features of nature behind which the element of struggle is
contained as a subtheme. Our conduct ought to fit this natural life story.

We must anxiously preserve a discontinuity between the organism and physical nature, between the self and its resident world. The centripetal self maintains its integrity against a centrifugal wildness. Each species, each individual, sets a boundary between itself and the rest of nature, and in humans that discontinuity is enormously greater than elsewhere. This spirited agency is the distinctly human genius, the human virtue, wrested from nature; and, except as we insist otherwise, the accidents of external nature will destroy it. We maintain our being by being over against nature. We delight in personal narrative as we learn to travel through the world. This is the elation of auto/biography.

The pilgrim, the settler, the explorer—all were admired for their prowess against their environment. The wild continent was tamed; forests, cleared; roads, built; rivers, bridged—and often in the name of religion, for the Judeo-Christian faith urged conquering nature and redeeming the fallen world. Scientists and engineers, physicians and farmers, as they have conquered famines, sickness, and natural disasters, remain heir to this hope of gaining security by overcoming a threatening nature. The primary virtue here is a resolute courage. The sagas of the pioneers are spine-tingling, and in scouting or Outward Bound our youth still seek the outdoor experience as bracing and even challenging. An early and provident fear of nature is felt by all roused to work for shelter or to prevent hunger, by all wary of natural hazards, by all who button up before winter. The ego boundary must also be maintained in competition and cooperation with other human selves in the social world. But this is always within the fundamental tension of the human self against the natural world. Humans too live in Darwin's world, with a struggle for survival, for adapted fit. But the human genius is an exodus from natural selection into cultural prowess.

Still, our homes are cultural places in their construction, but there is always a natural foundation, a sense of belongingness to the landscape. For all those boundaries that we defend against the external world, our virtues are not confined to those of maintaining our separateness. The American settlers found that they had no sooner conquered a wilderness than they had come to love a land. Theirs was a promised land, even though they fought for it—nor are these biblical allusions incidental. After the conquest, there was time to rejoice in the sunshine and the rain, in seedtime and harvest, in peaks and prairies, in the orchard in bloom, in the smell of the newly mown hay.

We flourish with our landscapes, with trees and grass, flowers and gardens, lakes and sky. We cherish our hills of home, our rivers, our bays, and our country drives. Most of us identify so with some countryside that we get a lump in the throat when we must leave it or when we return after an absence. We have deep affections toward persons and communities, but our affections toward the city, per se, are often exceeded by those that we have toward the landscape. The notion of evolved fittedness includes congeniality, as well as opposition, but Darwin never quite said this. Nature is not a home ready at hand, and we must live in our built environments, urban and rural. Our virtues defend the organic self, but they also stretch it out to integrate it into its place.

In an analysis of the autobiographies of 300 geniuses, Edith Cobb concludes that they characteristically recall from their middle childhood a period "when the natural world is experienced in some highly evocative way, producing in the child a sense of some profound continuity with natural processes." It is to this encounter that, in the creativity of their adult years,

> these writers say they return in memory in order to renew the power and impulse to create at its very source, a source which they describe as the experience of emerging not only into the light of consciousness but into a living sense of dynamic relationship with the outer world. In these memories the child appears to experience both a sense of discontinuity, an awareness of his own unique separateness and identity, and also a continuity, a renewal of relationship with nature as process.[10]

The child is exalted by a rediscovery of those powers of autonomous agency in which the race has evolved, but the dominant impulse is a sense of immanence in the natural process, more relational than oppositional. To finger a stick, to throw rocks into the creek, to build a fire, to run with a dog across a field, to watch the sparrows— all awaken a sense of wonder at both the natural drama and the part the person is permitted to play in it. Nature is a foil for the self, yet so diversely so across the many cultures and centuries of these geniuses that human virtues are forged in environmental reciprocity. In Hegelian terms, the person is an evolutionary thesis of nature, set in antithesis to it and yet drawn toward synthesis with it.

In his autobiography, Carl Jung recalls being gripped in early childhood by the large stones in his family garden and returning there to regain those emotions in his adult years. With advancing age, he developed an intricate symbolic relationship with the stone "Tower," a rustic house that he himself built by stages on the scenic upper lake of Zurich. In this rural place, he writes,

> I am in the midst of my true life, I am most deeply myself. . . . At times I feel as if I am spread out over the landscape and inside things, and am myself living in every tree, in the splashing of the waves, in the clouds and the animals that come and go, in the procession of the seasons. There is nothing in the Tower that has not grown into its own form over the decades, nothing with which I am not linked. . . . Silence surrounds me almost audibly, and I live "in modest harmony with nature." . . .
>
> There is so much that fills me: plants, animals, clouds, day and night, and the eternal in man. The more uncertain I have felt about, myself, the more there has grown up in me a feeling of kinship with all things.[11]

The myth of Antaeus is true: man is an invincible wrestler but loses his strength if he takes both feet from his mother earth. Adam lost his Eden when he spurned it and fell into labor and pain. Human virtues lie in defending the self, aloft and transcendent over nature, but they also lie in fitting ourselves into the natural environment that transcends us. If we wish to call this an *environmental* virtue ethics, then we have to recognize that any such virtues, lodged in humans, require for these humans to be well placed in their worlds. The better name for such an ethic might be an *ecological* virtue ethics, for human virtues of this kind always require an ecology. Inevitably, we both defend our lives and find our places. In that sense, insofar as we flourish, these are virtues that we all live by. But they are virtues that some of us live for—they give significance to life.

Selves Caring for Others

"Know thyself." To Socrates again, I have a reply: "Know others." Virtues must be extended not only to caring for integrity of place but further, to caring for others in those places. On the positive side, an admirable trait in many persons is their capacity to appreciate things outside themselves, things that have no economic, medical, or industrial uses, perhaps even no recreational, aesthetic, or scientific value. An interest in natural history ennobles persons. It stretches them out into bigger persons. Humans must inevitably be consumers of nature; but they can and ought sometimes be more: admirers of nature. That redounds to their excellence. One condition of human flourishing is that humans enjoy natural things in as much diversity as possible—and enjoy them at times because such creatures flourish in themselves.

On the negative side, there is something small-spirited about the inveterate exploiter of nature. There is always something wrong with callous destruction. Vandals destroying art objects also ruin their own character. Americans are ashamed at having destroyed the passenger pigeon and the vast buffalo herds. Greatly imperiled today are the American native fish; about 70 percent of endangered and threatened fish species worldwide are in North America.[12] This is especially true of fish in the U.S. West, which are much jeopardized by dams, irrigation, water development, and pollution. The Endangered Species Committee of the Desert Fishes Council has identified 164 fish species in North American deserts that are endangered, vulnerable, or rare; eighteen have already become extinct.[13]

Americans should be ashamed if they destroy these desert fish; they are more excellent persons if they conserve them. Destruction of these desert fish is "uncalled for." Short of overriding justifications, humans really ought to save these native fish—including those species from which we can gain no conceivable economic, ecological, aesthetic, recreational, scientific, educational, historical, or other benefits. Humans of decent character will refrain from needless destruction of all kinds, including the destruction of even "unimportant" species. We can always gain excellence of character from acts of conservation. We have a duty to our higher selves to save these fish.

A human virtue is generated, actualizing a uniquely human capacity and possibility for excellence, when a person respects a wild animal's life for what that life is in itself, a different and yet related form of life. This triggers awareness of otherness and feeds back into our own sense of identity and integrity. So we are figuring out who we are as a consequence of figuring out who they are. We do realize something special about our own capacities. We can reflect on the manifest destiny of humans on Earth, on our human overtaking of the North American continent, and on the (perhaps inevitable) tragedy of the displaced wildlife and fish, if also now the open possibility of preserving some space on our landscape for the greatly displaced native fauna. We can be altruistic toward the fish and take care to conserve runs on our rivers where these fish can swim free there again, as they did for millennia before Europeans came. The fish, of course, have no analogous possibilities of being altruistic toward humans or of appropriately respecting the otherness of the human form of life, with its cultural developments.

Humans are unique and superior in their cognitive, critical, and ethical capacities; they are Earth's "overseers"—they see over the whole as no other species does. But their superiority is linked in a feedback loop with the whole; they realize their oversight only with care and concern for the Earth, for the fauna and flora on the planet on which they reside, and for the whole biotic community. We can care for the fish; they cannot care for us. And we realize our excellence in caring for these species that we have put into jeopardy.

But why is callous destruction of desert fish "uncalled for," if not because there is something in the fish that calls for a more appropriate attitude? Excellence of human character does indeed result from a concern for these fish, but if this excellence of character really comes from appreciating otherness, then why not value that otherness in wild nature first? Let the human virtue come tributary to that. It is hard to gain much excellence of character from appreciating an otherwise worthless thing. One does not gain much nobility just from respecting curios. To prohibit the needless destruction of fish species seems to depend on some value in the species as such, for there need be no prohibition against destroying a valueless thing. The excellence of human character depends on a sensitivity to excellence in these marvelous fish flourishing in the desert.

The human mind grows toward the realization of its possibilities (excellences) by appropriate respect for nature (fish), but that respect is the end and the growth is the by-product. It is even true that realizing this excellent humanity in *Homo sapiens* is a greater value than the flourishing of fish life in *Cyprinodon diabolis*, but the realizing of excellent humanity here is exactly the *expansion* of human life into a concern for fish life for what it is in itself, beyond concern for utility, resource conservation, or self-development. Here humans are higher than fish only as and because humans, moving outside their own immediate sector of interest, can and ought to be morally concerned for fish, whereas fish have no moral capacities at all. Fish can neither cognitively entertain a concept of humans nor evaluate the worth of humans. What *higher* means here is having the capacity to be concerned for the "lower." Humans are subjectively enriched in their experience as and because they love the other, nonhuman species for what they objectively are.

This caring needs to be elicited by the properties of what is cared for. Will anything do as an object of my caring, just so long as my caring for it builds my character? No, the virtue appearing in the caregiver must have some appropriate connection with value in what is cared for. There needs to be something worthwhile out there that excites my admiration. On some occasions, I might be even more virtuous for loving worthless things—as is claimed when saints love sinners despite what they are, not because of what they are. But even here the sinner is made in the image of God, destroyed though that image now is, and the saint believes that the sinner can be regenerated.

We may say, before callous destruction of passenger pigeons, bison, or desert fish: "No *self-respecting* person would do that." Yes, but the reason is that my *respect for the other*, which ought to be realized and respected within myself, is diminished, not that my self-respect per se has tarnished. It is virtuous to recognize the rights of other persons, but the motivating force is their rights that I appreciate, not my self-respect. With the fish in jeopardy, we should care for a form of life that has an intrinsic value; this places some claim on the humans inhabiting the U.S. West. The motivation for acting with concern for the other cannot be based simply on the consequences for me of caring for the other.

Now we worry that the person embodied in his or her resident environment is but half the truth. I care about the fish in the West where I reside, but many areas that I wish to preserve have nothing to do with my sense of place. I want to save mountain gorillas but have only seen wild gorillas in Uganda two days in my life. I want to save Antarctica and have only been there once; nobody lives there. I wish to save the vestimentiferans living at the deep ocean hydrothermal vents, but these are no part of my experienced nature. The world is a plural place. I am no doubt a resident of Earth, but I am not a resident of most environments on Earth. Most of these others, both other persons and other animals and plants, I do not encounter at all, although I have some knowledge that they are there and often in jeopardy. So I contribute to an African mission hospital and join the Worldwide Fund for Nature. Is this because of my search for personal virtue?

Human Virtue and Intrinsic Natural Value

A human virtue, in the current meaning of the term, is an admirable human characteristic acquired by reason and will. Gaining virtue will be assisted of course by upbringing and community encouragements; nor is it possible without genetic endowments. But virtues are achievements, not endowments. In this sense, perfect pitch, though an admirable trait, is not a virtue. Virtues are acquired excellences.[14] This is one reason why any concept of animal virtue is difficult. Animal excellences are largely genetic endowments; we are uncertain how much (if at all) the dominant wolf has his position by praiseworthy effort. A preferable term is animal (and plant) *values*, evolutionary and genetic achievements that are embodied in these organisms. The individual organism inherits such skills, coded in the genotype and displayed in the phenotype. We admire and respect such lives, among the marvels on Earth.

To a limited extent, especially with the higher animals, we can also wonder about the acquired achievements of an individual within its own lifetime, although, lacking access to their psychology and restricted by quite limited encounters with wild lives, we are often uncertain how much of this achievement is related to an individual's resolution, endurance, courage, or animal "virtue." We are likely to be more persuaded about such "virtues" with our pet dogs, possibly also with wolves, but rather skeptical about their existence in fish and rather sure that they are not present in butterflies.

Environmental virtues, as achieved by humans, will initially involve concern for human quality of life. But our deeper ethical achievement needs to focus on values as intrinsic achievements in wild nature. These virtues within us need to attend to values without us. Perhaps one starts with a love of nature that is tributary to self-love. Later one discovers that this self-love is quite inclusive, for the health of myriad nonhumans is implicated, entwined with ours. One is called to an active concern and positive engagement with the object of encounter. The other cannot be seen simply as a source of personal transformation. We must make the model at least an ellipse with two foci: human virtue and natural value.

Environmental virtue ethicists may reply that they quite agree. An environmental virtue ethic that has as its primary focus human self-development is immature. A more mature ethic takes value in nature as an essential focus: "In an environmental virtue ethics, human excellence and nature's excellence are necessarily entwined"; "an environmental virtue ethics may start from a concern for human interests, but it cannot remain there."[15] To be truly virtuous one must respect values in nature for their own sake and not as tributary to human flourishing. But if indeed intrinsic value in nature has become primary to the ethic, to call such an ethic a (human) environmental virtue ethics is no longer an adequately descriptive title. The virtue ethic is only a "start-up ethic," which can only get us halfway there. The better name would be an environmental value/virtue ethic, keeping both foci of the ellipse prominent.

My worry is that if an environmental virtue ethics is unable to disentwine human virtues from intrinsic values in nature, whether in practice or in principle, the glass remains half full and never fills up. The reason may be that there is a leak in the bottom as well. The full ethic affirms these intrinsic values in nature out there quite independent of their human entwinement. Maybe the cart is hooked up to the horse, but the horse has to go before the cart, not the cart before the horse. No, that is a misleading analogy, the virtuous may reply. Half a loaf is better than none. Virtue ethics can get you half the loaf, even if not the full loaf. But if we are appealing to proverbs, recall also the reply: half a horse is worse than no horse at all. Half this ethic might be less vital than we realize.

A more promising vocabulary is that of "integrity," for *integrity* can suggest being integrated within as well as integrated without. Humans, animals, and plants can all be said to have their "integrity," although the single term hides radical differences in their kinds of integrity. "Welfare" is also an inclusive category, for well-being is both within the self and without in wild lives. Recalling etymological roots, this focus on what is one's own (*proprium*) is improper if it does not equally keep in sight the goods proper to, owned by, others. These species have been around for millions of years. And why save them? It makes *me* a better person. My quality of life is entwined with theirs. But that confuses the by-product with the located focus of value. The wild other does not become valuable if and when it results in something valuable for me. It is valuable for what it is, whether I am around or not, and recognizing that value does valuable things to me. Such an ethic is best called a value-based ethic, not a virtue-based ethic.

Excellence is intrinsically a good state for the self, but there are various intrinsic goods that the self desires and pursues in its relation to others that are not "self states" of the person who is desiring and pursuing: the welfare of other humans or of desert fish. The preservation of the fish is not covertly the cultivation of human excellences; the lives of these fish in the desert is the overt value defended. An enriched humanity results, with values in the fish and values in persons compounded—but only if the loci of value are not confounded. Environmental virtue ethics, taken for the whole, is a misplaced ethic, a displaced ethic. It seems unexcellent—cheap and philistine—to say that excellence of human character is what we are after when we preserve these endangered species. We want virtue in the human beholder that recognizes value in the endangered species. Excellence of human character does indeed result, but let the human virtue cherish the value found in nature.

In another version of this argument, humans ought to preserve an environment adequate to match their capacity to wonder. Human life is often routine and boring, especially in town and on the job, and the great outdoors stimulates wonder that enriches human life. The desert evokes the sense of the sublime, and these curious desert fish can certainly serve as objects of wonder. We have a duty to our higher selves to keep life wonderful. But if the excellence of character really comes from appreciating something wonderful, then why not directly attach value to this other? If a person were to make a large donation to the Desert Fishes Council and, being asked what motivated his charity, replied that he enjoyed now and again an experience of wonder when he (rather rarely) actually saw rare fish, we should rightly react that, using the fish to enrich his experience, he does not yet genuinely care for them.

Virtue ethicists will caution that some seeming virtues can be appearances. For example, what if I give to a charity calculating how much I must donate to purchase a desired increase in my public reputation? My sought-for status does not match my inner intent. But what if I give to a charity knowing within myself that it is the right thing to do? I want to be that kind of person; and, what if, after the gift, I feel good about myself and I think of myself as a better person for what I have done? We do not expect one to feel bad about oneself if one also believes that one has done the right thing. Am I doing good in order to feel good about it?

This ancient Socratic puzzle, "No evil can come to a good man," is still a puzzle in contemporary psychology, where it is difficult to isolate disinterested helping of others (altruism) from the personal rewards of so doing, or to isolate which explanatory level is most significant in human moral behavior, both ideal and real.[16] Socrates seems to have argued that the personal benefits from doing the right always left the good person better off, more virtuous. But if that becomes the good person's motive, is one acting in self-interest or in the interests of others? If when we do the right, the two are always inseparable, then we cannot act selflessly. But surely we often can and ought to be concerned for others in independence of our own gain?

One does indeed want to keep life wonderful, but the logic is topsy-turvy if we only value the *experience* of wonder and not the *objects* of that wonder. Merely valuing the experience commits a fallacy of misplaced wonder; it puts the virtue in the beholder, not in the species beheld. Earth's five to ten million species are among the marvels of the Universe, and fish tenaciously speciating in the desert are exceptional even on Earth. Valuing species and speciation directly, however, seems to attach value to the long-standing evolutionary products and process (the wonders, the wonderland), not merely to subjective experiences that arise when late-coming humans reflect over events (the felt wonder).

Evolutionary development in these fish runs to quantitative extremes, and human awareness of this can enrich our quality of life. But what is objectively there, before human subjective experiences, is already quality in life, something remarkable because it is exceptional. If you like, humans *need* to admire and respect these fish more than they need bluegrass lawns, or an overpopulated Arizona, or a few more beef cattle, or introduced game fish. That is a moral need. Humans need development sensitizing them to values intrinsic in nature more than they need water development; they need a moral development constraining any water development that endangers species.

Authorities are to be commended because, on the Virgin River drainage in Utah in 1980, they abandoned the Warner Valley project lest it jeopardize the woundfin, *Plagopterus argentissimus*, and built the Quail Creek project instead.[17] Humans needed to do that. But the focus of this *need* cannot be simply a matter of human excellences. The alternate dam was not built in order to generate noble human character or to preserve experiences of wonder (although both of these things happened). The alternative was chosen to preserve notable fish and their natural excellences.

It is safe to say that, in the decades ahead, the quality of life in the American West will decline in proportion to the loss of biotic diversity, though it is usually thought that we are sacrificing biotic diversity to improve human life. So there is a sense in which humans will not be losers if we save endangered fish, cactuses, snakes, toads, and butterflies. There is a sense in which those who do the right thing never lose, even when they respect values other than their own. Slave owners do not really lose when they free their slaves because the slave owners become better persons by freeing their slaves, to whom they can thereafter relate person to person. Subsequent human relationships will be richer. After we get the deepest values clear in morality, only the immoral lose—that is Socrates' argument. Similarly, humans who protect endangered fish will, if and when they change their value priorities, be better persons for their admiring respect for other forms of life.

But this should not obscure the fact that humans can and sometimes should be short-term losers. Sometimes we ought to make sacrifices, at least in terms of what we presently value, to preserve species. On such occasions humans might be duty-bound to be losers in the sense that they have sacrificed values and adopted an altered set of values, although they would still be winners for doing the right thing. Ethics is not merely about what humans love, enjoy, and find rewarding or about what they find wonderful, find ennobling, or want as souvenirs. It is sometimes a matter of what humans *ought* to do, like it or not, and these *oughts* may not always rest on the likes of other humans or on what ennobles character.

Sometimes we ought to consider worth beyond that within our selves. It would be better, in addition to our preferences, our self-development, our self-interest, our concern, to be virtuous, to know the full truth of the human obligation—to have the best reasons, as well as the good ones. If one insists on putting it this way—emphasizing a paradox in responsibility—concern for nonhumans can ennoble humans (although this concern short circuits if the concern is explicitly or tacitly just for noble humans). Noblesse oblige. But those who act responsibly with concern for their nobility miss the mark. The real concern is for the other benefited. Genuine concern for nonhumans could humanize our race all the more.

That is what the argument about environmental virtue ethics seems to be trying to say, but if taken as the whole truth, it confuses a desirable result with the primary locus of value. A naturalistic account values species and speciation intrinsically, not as resources or as a means to human virtues. The value at stake precedes, overleaps, and (if we act rightly) succeeds our human presence. I need something bigger on my horizon than my virtues.

Any seeking of excellences, worrying about personal achievements, trying to act nobly, checking my contributions to my community flourishing but double checking against my own flourishing, finds that the sought-after excellence leaks away because there is a hole in the bucket. If we ever get the slightest suspicion that one is cultivating virtues by using (even reverencing) another, that person's entire moral stance is undermined by the smell of hypocrisy. The positive is inverted to a negative, rather like putting a minus sign before a positive value in an algebraic parenthesis. In the end the quest for human virtues is not just misplaced; it backfires.

Environmental virtue ethics here confronts a version of the ancient paradox of hedonism, that aiming for pleasure is a sure way not to get it. The self curves in on itself and becomes ingrown. The logic moves too close to the classic self-defeating character of self-interest, including my enlightened self-interest. There is a parallel paradox classically found by the theologians: one must lose one's life to find it. One cannot care for others in order to gain reward, looking for stars in one's crown, but neither can one care for others selflessly without being rewarded. The virtuous have to crack a paradox. C. S. Lewis warns: "You can't get second things by putting them first; you can get second things only by putting first things first."[18]

You cannot become virtuous by putting this human concern first; you get such virtue only by putting first a respect for life's intrinsic value, which preceded, envelops, and surrounds us and of which we are a subsequent and marvelously endowed participant. "Reverence for life," Jason Kawall tell us, is in humans "an environmental virtue."[19] But put first things first: life in nonhuman (and human) others, and second things second, one's virtues. Life will be inadequately reverenced if I respect the lives of others with the increase of my virtue in mind. The foundation here is a life ethics, not a virtue ethics.

"Genuine virtue" promotes "ecosystem sustainability," claims Louke van Wensveen. There is a feedback loop: "Ecosystem sustainability is a necessary condition for the cultivation of a virtue"; "a genuine virtue includes the goal of ensuring necessary conditions for its cultivation." But what are we really sustaining here: human virtue and its underlying ecosystemic grounds or ecosystems with values more comprehensive than human virtues? Lest "ecosystem sustainability is only brought in as a means for human moral agency," Wensveen has to caution, "to say that ecosystem sustainability is a necessary condition for the cultivation of a virtue is not to say that it is *only* that. . . . We know that ecosystem sustainability is *also* a necessary condition for the existence and functioning of many nonhuman beings, including nonhuman animal and plant species and individual organisms within ecosystems."[20] But then, as I am arguing, a virtue ethics is only halfway there without this additional component. If so, this sustainable-virtue-entwined-with-sustainable-ecosystems loop is not the final concern of the ethic at all. This is really an ethic about a sustainable biosphere. Again, first things first.

"Virtue ethics is more concerned with cultivating an excellent, praiseworthy character," concludes Bill Shaw. And he continues: "Beyond that, there is nothing in virtue ethics that precludes the position that the 'good' consists in part of something like 'integrity, stability, and beauty' of the natural world 'for its own sake.'"[21] Virtue ethicists, it seems, are continually having to notice this "beyond" that their ethic is tending not to address. My argument here is that going "beyond" is no permitted option but, rather, is essential to any authentic environmental ethic. Those who remain more concerned with cultivating their character miss the point of the ethic.

Henry David Thoreau is often taken as a role model environmentalist. But Thoreau, retreated to Walden, out by himself and cultivating his experiences, seems rather too concerned with what he can get out of life: "I went to the woods because I wished to live deliberately, to front only the essential facts of life, and see if I could not learn what it had to teach, and not, when I came to die, discover that I had not lived. . . . I wanted to live deep and suck out all the marrow of life."[22] A straightforward paraphrase is: "I went to the woods to find myself, to get the most out of life." Each person ought indeed to "find himself" (Socrates' "examined life"); but what one finds in the woods is others' "not self" (as one ought to also find in town). This leaves us wondering: Where is the concern for others, people or plants, except as they serve his autobiographical and educational interests?

Thoreau writes: "In Wildness is the preservation of the World. . . . From the forest and wilderness come the tonics and barks which brace mankind"; "our village life would stagnate if it were not for the unexplored forests and meadows which surround it. We need the tonic of wildness."[23] Amen; human life is incomplete without encounter with wildness. But looked at again, there is a worry: Is wildness to be conserved *only* as a bracing tonic, as medication to insure our health? Only for the marrow we can suck and sweeten our lives? Is not wildness here being preserved not so much for itself as in order that *our* human world be preserved? What Thoreau gets out of it keeps returning as the bottom line.

Daniel Botkin reports: "Thoreau's rationales were human oriented. I found little if any discussion in his writings of an intrinsic value of nature independent of the ability of human beings to benefit from it. Thus, of the [several] reasons to conserve nature, Thoreau would seem to have supported all but what is today called the moral."[24] John Broderick agrees: "To Thoreau the final importance of nature is in its effect on man."[25] Maybe Thoreau, overly concerned about his self-development, did not learn what those woods really had to teach: respect for the integrity of wild lives.

Philip Cafaro concludes: "Thoreau was a leading exponent of 'virtue ethics': that half of ethics which talks less about our duties and responsibilities to others, and more about our opportunities for personal development and flourishing. . . . These arguments need to be made along with intrinsic value arguments if we are to convince people to take the steps necessary to protect the natural world." He notes: "Thoreau is a virtue ethicist: particularly in *Walden* he focuses less on our duties toward others and more on questions of [personal] excellence and flourishing."[26] But Cafaro insists that Thoreau knew as well the other half of ethics, concern for intrinsic value in nature. For example, Thoreau admires the fish, such as shad, imperiled by dams in the eastern rivers: "Away with the superficial and selfish phil-*anthropy* of men,—who knows what admirable virtue of fishes may be below low-water mark."[27] Thoreau is using the word *virtue* in the archaic sense of an "excellence," survival skills in the migratory fish (with no reference to praiseworthy character achievement, thus analogous to perfect pitch in humans). Thoreau's concern for fish here is a predecessor to the contemporary concerns for endangered fish that we were considering earlier. Such achievements in the fish are, as Cafaro notices, now better termed "intrinsic values." If so, then the other half of Thoreau's ethic is better termed a value-based ethic and not a virtue-based ethic.

Meanwhile, we still worry that this more ultimate half of the ethics lies more often in the background than the foreground. True, Thoreau is in the woods rejoicing in these animals and plants he encounters; but his more evident concern is for bracing tonics and sucking the marrow out of life. Examining "Thoreau's project of self-fashioning," Jane Bennett finds that even his cultivation of his naturalist skills were "techniques of the self."[28] For Thoreau, "in the end those who seek to protect wild nature do so as much for their own sakes as for Nature's."[29]

If we compare Thoreau with other icons of environmentalism, we can see that this search for self-fulfillment does not dominate the concerns of Aldo Leopold, or Rachel Carson, or Jane Goodall, or E. O. Wilson, because all these persons are overwhelmed by self-transcending commitments that are orders of magnitude greater than themselves. Leopold seeks a land ethic, the integrity of the biotic community; Carson laments the vanished warblers, the silent spring, the vanished fish in the dying ocean; Goodall respects the chimpanzees; Wilson (*pace* his "selfish genes") cares deeply for the ants. No doubt each could say that we care for the other lest we lose something of our character. Wilson can appeal to our human "biophilia," "the human bond with other species," genetically based and cultivated for our flourishing.[30] But what each most fears is the loss of these wild others, for their own sakes, not some loss of our experiences that we would have been the better for. Of course, each will say, "I win when they win." Second things follow first things. But none will say: "I save them as bracing tonic; with them I suck the most marrow from life." That puts second things first, and would-be winners become losers.

We can worry about such displacement in Robert L. Chapman's account of environmental virtue ethics:

> Virtue ethics is more interested in character development, and while we can attribute intrinsic value to the "integrity, stability and beauty" (harmony) of the biotic community, it remains a human activity that will be evaluated from a human-in-nature perspective. . . . We are not only valuing human excellence but also the *place* from which it arises. It is not as if we locate intrinsic value in the world of nature and human value is an adjunct to it. . . . Human value is recorded within the incunabula [cradle] of nature; you cannot properly value one without the other. Living well and the activities that promote the good life result from environmental sensitivity (a complex concatenation of values). . . . Cooperation exemplified by virtuous actions preserves a place for human participation and ultimately a place-based identity befitting human development.[31]

A charitable bending of this passage might find an ethic with two foci: human virtues and natural values. But the more straightforward account is that human value here is not an adjunct; it is, rather, the sine qua non. Humans must win often enough to have their vital needs met, but they can and ought to behave with caring concern for fauna and flora because the result of this is that they become quite excellent humans. Human virtue is not the only good in the world, but still it comes across as the ultimate good, for that is the way this "virtue ethics" is titled and identified. If you want to promote your physical and psychological health, then you ought to encounter nature. If we want a healthy society, then we need to preserve nature so that we still have something natural with which to have such encounters.

That, happily, solves the is/ought problem, for it is rather easy to move from what is healthy to what one ought to do. That, however, also brings this worry: We seem to make love of nature tributary to self-love. But when we frame nature up in terms of what it can contribute to our virtue, this puts nature in the wrong reference frame.

Ethics is about optimizing and conserving moral and other values. This is a more comprehensive question than whether the self has optimized its own excellences. The focus on human virtue leads us to make the fallacy of misplaced location. Some critics complain that to locate value in nature commits the naturalistic fallacy. But for those who take seriously the richness of biodiversity on Earth, to locate value solely in humans commits the humanistic fallacy. Virtue ethics, if this half-truth is mistaken for the whole, becomes a light-in-the-refrigerator theory of value. Perhaps value is there in the dark but is unseen until humans open the door; the light comes on, and what was once in the dark lights up human virtues. The fallacy is that such humans are really "in the dark" about the depth of values in nature beyond their own lighting up.

The virtuous naturalist, if we must say it, is ennobled, but the person is not ennobled alone and isolated but, rather, only as reconnected into a larger value web. The self knows its ecology. It is not that what we choose is satisfying and that brings our good. Rather, what is satisfying is our good; and the environmental component is that we find the ecology we inhabit satisfying. This ecology can be satisfying to us if and only if it is both resource and residence, only if we use it but also live in meaningful community. We are not choosing it for our virtue, but our virtue is bound up with it.

Would we choose conservation without our resulting virtue? That is a difficult question, not because we think we ought to answer yes or are reluctant to say no. Rather, we do not know how to answer either yes or no. We are constituted in these relationship with these natural others, and we find such a constitution to be enriching; and we also find these natural things, the fauna and flora, adapted fits in their places, a wealth of biodiversity, whether or not we are there to become virtuous by our experiences of encounter. We do want to say: Yes, we want the animals and plants to flourish whether or not we are around to be virtuous.

If we answer, No, we would not choose these things without our accompanying virtues, then just that choice—not choosing them—makes us less virtuous, as well as dissatisfied. Constituted by our ecological communities (as also by our cultural communities), there is no other happiness to be chosen elsewhere. There are other ingredients to becoming virtuous, but they now are conjoined with this ecological one. Repudiating the natural world in which we reside, repudiating our ecology, is itself unsatisfying. Not choosing these ecological goods in order to gain virtues elsewise is a logical and empirical impossibility. All the other, nonnatural goods, whatever they are and whatever their importance, are undermined with the loss of these natural values.

These fauna and flora have a good of their own, they are located in a good place, they are desired for their own sake: and appreciating them is my flourishing; that is a win–win situation. Oppositely, losing them is losing the quality of life that comes based on them, as well as them being lost in their own right; that is a lose–lose situation. One thing we want to do, in addition to promoting our personal self-interests, is to be responsible members of a community with integrity. That sense of belonging to a healthy society—and, in environmental ethics, of belonging to a healthy ecosystem—that too is part of our self-interest, but now the self is entwined with the community destinies. We win when we assume responsibility for heritages that are greater than we are. Some things have to be won together. Our sense of what our interest is includes the welfare of the community we inhabit. The human excellence view, if the half-truth is taken for the whole, falls into concern with what a virtue-enhancing view of self is. But we fully flourish not with the excellence of an "own self" but in celebrating the display of excellences in the surrounding world, both there with us and there without us. Humans are the only species capable of enjoying the promise of culture; humans are also the only species capable of enjoying the splendid panorama of life that vitalizes this planet. Humans can and ought to inherit the Earth; we become rich with this inheritance, as and only as we oversee a richness of planetary biodiversity that embraces and transcends us.

Notes

1. Socrates, *Apology*, trans. H. N. Fowler, in *Plato I*, vol. 1 (Cambridge: Loeb Classical Library, Harvard University Press, 1977), 38. "Know thyself" was inscribed upon the Delphic oracle.

2. Aristotle, *Politics*, I, 2, 1253a.

3. Lucius Garvin, *A Modern Introduction to Ethics* (Cambridge, MA: Houghton Mifflin, 1953), 378.

4. Neil Evernden, *The Natural Alien: Humankind and Environment* (Toronto: University of Toronto Press, 1993).

5. Wallace Stegner, "The Wilderness Idea," in *Wilderness: America's Living Heritage*, ed. David Brower (San Francisco: Sierra Club Books, 1961), 97–102.

6. Plato, *Phaedrus*, trans. H. N. Fowler, in *Plato I*, vol. 1 (Cambridge: Loeb Classical Library, Harvard University Press, [1914] 1977), 230d.

7. Walt Whitman, *Leaves of Grass* (Ithaca: Cornell University Press, [1860] 1961), 319.

8. "The Certainties," *New York Times*, 28 November 1948: 8b.

9 This is in the words of Psalm 23.

10. Edith Cobb, "The Ecology of Imagination in Childhood," *Daedalus* 88 (1959): 538–39. See also Edith Cobb, *The Ecology of Imagination in Childhood* (New York: Columbia University Press, 1977).

11. Carl G. Jung, *Memories, Dreams, Reflections*, trans. Richard Winston and Clara Winston (New York: Vintage Books, 1963), 225–26, 358–59.

12. Dana R. Ono, James D. Williams, and Anne Wagner, *Vanishing Fishes of North America* (Washington, DC: Stone Wall Press, 1983); W. L. Minckley and James E. Deacon, *Battle against Extinction: Native Fish Management in the American West* (Tucson: University of Arizona Press, 1991).

13. Jack E. Williams et al., "Endangered Aquatic Ecosystems in North American Deserts with a List of Vanishing Fishes of the Region," *Journal of the Arizona–Nevada Academy of Science* 20 (1985): 1–62.

14. There is a now archaic sense of *virtue* that refers to any efficacy or power. In this sense even inanimate things, such as minerals, have virtues. The etymological root is the Latin *vir*, "man," hence *virile*, "having manly strength."

15. Philip Cafaro, "Thoreau's Environmental Ethics in *Walden*," *The Concord Saunterer* (N.S.) 10 (2002): 43; Philip Cafaro, "Thoreau, Leopold, and Carson: Toward an Environmental Virtue Ethics," *Environmental Ethics* 22 (2001): 14.

16. Socrates, *Apology*, 41d. Psychologists interested in altruistic motivation have often claimed that persons, aroused by the plight of others, may act to aid them but that the real goal is to reduce unpleasant arousal, not directly to help others. One acts so as to incur the least costs and most benefits in terms of feeling good about oneself and having others think well of oneself. Because helping others is obviously often accompanied by feeling good about one's success in so doing, it is difficult to isolate selfish and unselfish motives.

In the years between 1962 and 1982, there were over 1,000 empirical studies of altruism, and a review of them leaves the matter unsettled (John F. Dovidio, "Helping Behavior and Altruism: An Empirical and Conceptual Overview," in *Advances in Experimental Social Psychology*, ed. L. Berkowitz [New York: Academic Press, 1984]) but does not eliminate the possibility that on occasion moral altruism is the primary determinant. One hardly wants or expects to find many occasions on which the altruist feels bad about his or her altruism, or feels indifferent, or is censured by others, and the debate almost becomes moot.

However, in studies over the last decade designed to isolate these motives, the egoistic hypothesis that seeming altruism is in fact done to reduce negative arousal has met serious empirical challenge. There is "impressive support for the empathy-altruism hypothesis," which specifies "that empathic emotion evokes truly altruistic motivation, motivation with an ultimate goal of benefiting not the self but the person for whom empathy is felt," and this is important "for our understanding of human nature" (C. Daniel Batson and Laura L. Shaw, "Evidence for Altruism: Toward a Pluralism of Prosocial Motives," *Psychological Inquiry* 2 [1991]: 107–22; and Kristen R. Monroe, *The Heart of Altruism* [Princeton: Princeton University Press, 1996]).

17. James E. Deacon, "The Endangered Woundfin and Water Management in the Virgin River, Utah, Arizona, Nevada," *Fisheries* 13, no. 1 (1988): 18–24.

18. C. S. Lewis, *First and Second Things*, ed. Walter Hooper (London: HarperCollins, 1985), 22.

19. Jason Kawall, "Reverence for Life as a Viable Environmental Virtue," *Environmental Ethics* 25 (2003): 339–58.

20. Louke van Wensveen, "Ecosystem Sustainability as a Criterion for Genuine Virtue," *Environmental Ethics* 23 (2001): 232–34.

21. Bill Shaw, "A Virtue Ethics Approach to Aldo Leopold's Land Ethic," *Environmental Ethics* 19 (1997): 64.

22. Henry David Thoreau, *Walden and Other Writings of Henry David Thoreau* (New York: Modern Library, 1950), 81–82.

23. Henry David Thoreau, "Walking," in *The Natural History Essays*, Henry David Thoreau (Salt Lake City: Peregrine Smith, 1980), 613; Thoreau, *Walden*, 283.

24. Daniel Botkin, *No Man's Garden: Thoreau and a New Vision for Civilization and Nature* (Washington, DC: Island Press, 2000), 54.

25. John Broderick, "Thoreau's Proposals for Legislation," *American Quarterly* 7 (1955): 289.

26. Cafaro, "Thoreau's Environmental Ethics in *Walden*," 18, 35, cf. 24.

27. Henry David Thoreau, *A Week on the Concord and Merrimack Rivers* (Princeton: Princeton University Press, 1983), 37; Cafaro, "Thoreau's Environmental Ethics in *Walden*," 20.

28. Jane Bennett, *Thoreau's Nature* (Thousand Oaks, CA: Sage Publications, 1994), 16, 25–29.

29. Cafaro, "Thoreau's Environmental Ethics in *Walden*," 47.

30. Edward O. Wilson, *Biophilia* (Cambridge: Harvard University Press, 1984).

31. Robert L. Chapman, "The Goat-Stag and the Sphinx: The *Place* of the Virtues in Environmental Ethics," *Environmental Values* 11 (2002): 136.

CHAPTER 5

Virtue Ethics as Foundational for a Global Ethic

Laura Westra

Virtue Ethics and the Environment?

When we consider virtue ethics in relation to the environment, we start with two major obstacles: (1) the strongest representatives of virtue ethics flourished either in the distant past or, if more recently, in the era when environmental degradation was hardly a moral issue; and (2) most virtue ethics formulations depend on an essentialist understanding of human nature, an approach that is often deemed to be unacceptable today. In this chapter I will focus on just two major exponents of the virtue ethics tradition, Aristotle and Kant.[1] For both it is necessary to accept their view of what a human being is and should be, and if their essentialism is not accepted, then whatever can be learned from their doctrines will be lost or misrepresented.[2] What should be learned from them, without misunderstanding, is that a proper conception of human excellence is foundational for any ethical inquiry. Indeed, I shall argue that proper conceptions of both human excellence and the health and integrity of natural systems are central to a global ethic of human rights, environmental rights, and ecological rights. I begin with discussion of the essentialisms of Aristotle and Kant, respectively.

The Aristotelian Good

Amartya Sen discusses Aristotle in support of his "capabilities" approach to the "well-being" or the "welfare" of people, a seemingly fruitful approach to a global ethic. After acknowledging that Aristotle would reject "opulence as a criterion of achievement" with which to judge the goodness of human activities, he says that Aristotle analyzes *eudaimonia*, or human happiness, "in terms of valued activities."[3] However, this misrepresents Aristotle's conception of the highest telos of a human being. Various "valued activities" may be used as means to reach *eudaimonia*, but *eudaimonia* is not a bundle or an aggregate of activities as such. It is unitary as a goal, as it emerges as the component of the full development of man's proper function: "The human good turns out to be the activity of soul in accordance with virtue and, if there is more than one virtue, in accordance with the best and the most perfect."[4] Thus, it is one, the best, not a bundle of valued activities. Richard Kraut explains: "When Aristotle says that activity in accordance with the best virtue is the good he is saying that it should be our ultimate end. He is not merely saying that it is *a* good; it is *the* good."[5]

If this is the case, then Sen cannot be right. "Capabilities," including the "freedom" to make choices, have a lot to do with the means to happiness or *eudaimonia* but nothing to do with what is constitutive of it, as that is not the result of choices, no matter how free, but, rather, represents the full actualization of our potential as humans. We can no more "choose" to be properly actualized in a different way than an embryo can "choose" to become a horse if it is originally human. Of course, this claim and the extreme essentialism it represents are precisely one of the major difficulties I note above. But if we truly wish to establish an Aristotelian foundation for a global ethic, we cannot discard the main goal of his own doctrine.

We find a much better link between virtue ethics and a global ethic if we consider the *conditions* under which the human function and human flourishing can be fulfilled. This insight provides the basis of the arguments to follow. It is more than saying with Holmes Rolston that "even for humans one cannot have a sound economy/culture in a sick environment."[6] Rather, it lays down the foundations for the main conclusion of this work: that an environment fully capable of supporting life is a human right, not simply an option desired by certain groups, such as affluent Westerners. I have argued elsewhere that Aristotle's conception of *ergon* applies equally to natural systems and to humans.[7] The telos of humans is the full flowering of their capacity to be virtuous and intellectual beings. The telos of natural systems is to continually unfold to their full "mature state" (*akme*), for the fully actualized form (*eidos*) is normative in biology.[8] Here is John Cooper on this last point: "Living things are better than non-living things and existence than non-existence, so the continuous existence of living things is an important good; but since individual animals and plants are all perishable it is only by constant replacement that this good can be achieved."[9] Furthermore, "everything seems to fit together and the environment is such as is needed to support the kinds of plants and animals there actually are."[10]

John Rist captures the crucial Aristotelian point at work here as follows: "Nature always strives for the better . . . and Aristotle goes on to tell us what that means: being is better than non-being."[11] The implication of Aristotle's position is supported by modern science, especially epidemiology, a science that clearly links human survival, health, and normal function to the life-sustaining functions and processes of normally healthy ecosystems.[12] Thus, rather than finding biocentric holism (the position I have defended) "misanthropic" or "inimical to human rights," the opposite is clearly true: respect for the intrinsic value of natural entities and processes is necessary and basic to the respect for human rights, and this truth is both global and universal.[13] We need to consider what constitutes the basic requirement for the presence of all life, so that human life can develop and fulfill its potential for virtue and thus for happiness.

Thus, we look to the preconditions of virtuous activity, such as enough fortune to enhance our activity, the presence of limited external goods (that is, such goods as may be had without excess), and both friendship and amusements.[14] Although *eudaimonia* is indeed "complete and self-sufficient," as Aristotle has it, and we can only declare a life to have been happy when it is indeed "complete," these practical pre-conditions to the actualization of our proper function are instrumental to *eudaimo-nia* and our good.[15]

How, then, does this feature of virtue ethics help clarify how we can properly ap-ply it to better understand and support a global ethic? For Aristotle, as for Kant as we will see below, the main concern was the human life, not the human habitat. So em-ploying virtue ethics as part of the conceptual foundations for a global ethic requires establishing that environmental rights, or (better yet) "ecological rights," are a re-quirement for human life and flourishing.[16] I have elsewhere argued that the "princi-ple of integrity"—nothing can be moral that is in conflict with the physical realities of our existence or cannot be seen to fit within the natural laws of our environment—is a principle of ethics, rather than of environmental ethics, as any specious separation of humans from their natural habitat is inappropriate both conceptually and scientif-ically and therefore practically invalid.[17] There is, therefore, a constant interface be-tween environment and human life and flourishing that renders environmental rights as foundational to basic human rights.[18] Aristotle's virtue ethic thus makes a contri-bution to the human rights argument, in relation to a global ethic, even though his thought predates any explicit discussion of human rights. As we shall see, these con-nections among human flourishing, human rights, and a global ethic are also present in Kant's virtue ethic.

The Kantian Basis for Human Rights (and Beyond): The Background of a Kantian Global Ethic

The argument above for recognizing the connections among Aristotelian virtue ethics, human rights, and global ethics is not based on some casual remarks that may be found in Aristotle's writings regarding the environment but, rather, on his central argument in the support of life and the respect for the unfolding of all things, which includes re-spect for the required preconditions of the life of a truly human agent. The connection between environmental degradation and human life, health, and normal function thus rests on the inviolability of human rights. Human rights extend beyond the rights of the human person, to the generic right to life, including our habitat. This position is, I have argued above, Aristotelian and philosophically and historically defensible. How-ever, its defense can also be found in international law. Because in contemporary in-ternational law concerning human rights a Kantian approach is more in evidence, I will here be taking that approach in explicating the relationships among human flour-ishing, the preconditions of human flourishing, ecological rights, and human rights as they are, or should be, embodied in international law.

The foundational arguments proposed by Alan Gewirth help to shed light on that basic connection between humans and their habitats. Gewirth argues that it is only par-tially correct that human rights are based primarily on human dignity. He prefers to base "human rights on the necessary conditions of human action," as morality is intended to give rise to moral action.[19] Gewirth adds that "human rights are the equivalent to 'natural' rights, in that they pertain to all humans by virtue of their nature as actual or prospective agents."[20] He cites five reasons in support of his claim:

1. "the supreme importance, of the conditions of human actions"
2. action is "the common subject matter of all moralities"
3. "action" is more specific and less vague than "dignity" or "flourishing"
4. "action" ultimately secures "fundamental moral status" for persons
5. "action's necessary conditions provide justification for human rights—as every agent must hold that he has a right to freedom and well-being as the necessary conditions of his actions."[21]

Beyleveld and Brownsword argue that the "basic" or "generic needs" that represent the preconditions of all action including moral action are "freedom or voluntariness" and "well-being or purposiveness," where the former are procedural and the latter are "substantive"; and they view freedom as instrumental to well-being.[22] I propose inverting this order. Life, health, and the mental ability to comprehend and choose precede the exercise of voluntariness and are not only necessary for it but sufficient, when all these conditions are in fact present.

In essence, this has been the argument of the previous section: "basic rights" represent the minimum all humans are entitled to, and they are prior to all other rights, both conceptually and temporally.[23] For Gewirth as well, life and the capacities named above can be "threatened or interfered with."[24] Thus, to say that we have rights is to say equally that the preconditions of these rights represent something we are entitled to have not only in morality but also in the law. In other words, any legal instrument that supports the existence of human rights ipso facto ought to proclaim the requirement that their preconditions be equally supported and respected. Importantly, the introduction of "preconditions" means the introduction of conditions that are not only conceptually but temporally prior to agency; hence the protection of these preconditions entails the acceptance of potential consequences in the protection of agency, and I have defended the acceptability of potentiality arguments (in general) elsewhere.[25]

Kant defends the infinite value of life, as someone whose generic capacities to be human, with all that it might entail, is not eliminated by present adverse conditions, such as regular drunkenness, for instance. However, nonhuman animals have also been recognized to have purposiveness, as well as nociception at early stages of their development.[26] If, at the least, duties are owed to all beings capable of sentience and agency in various proportions, then the duty is not specific but, rather, can be owed to all life and to its preconditions. That is to say, by extending the meaning of *dignity* from its modern sense of *dignitas*, to its classical Greek sense of "within the natural laws of the universe," one may be able to place Kant's imperatives within the more far-reaching imperatives of the "principle of integrity."[27] In this case, anything that conflicts with the "dignity" of natural universal laws is prima facie suspect; hence, at the minimum, it requires serious justification, beyond "preferences" or economic advantages.[28] Therefore, it is clear that the absolute respect for life that Kant supports must also be extended to the basic ecological requirements of life.

So far the argument has shown that no hard and fast line can be drawn between animals (human and nonhuman alike) and their habitat, if we take human rights seriously. Hence, support and respect for ecosystems constitute at the same time support for all creatures that depend on ecosystem services for their survival, their health, and their optimum function. This ultimate connection is perhaps clearer in the case of people from developing countries, especially those who live outside city centers, because they depend immediately and directly on the land, the water, and the climate and are not therefore protected from natural disasters or extreme biotic impoverishment. However, the preceding shows that it is true for all humans, whose "ecofootprint" necessarily extends well beyond their urban habitat.[29]

So although neither Aristotle nor Kant expressed concern for the environment, we have seen that Aristotle recognized the necessity for certain conditions to be present to enable a human being to live the moral life and to achieve happiness. Kant, however, viewed all prudential imperatives as hypothetical, not categorical, so a two-step argument is required to establish the right to the preconditions of life.[30] As Nancy Sherman argues, for Kant, "a noble character will be freed from both the turbulence of affect and the desperate edge of passion. For Kant, more than the Stoics, *apatheia* really does become *eupatheia*, a state of good or wholesome emotions that support duty."[31] Therefore, even for Kant some "preconditions" may be required at least to support our commitment to duty.

Moreover, we can find an environmental component at the start of the character formation of the willing, moral agent, as the precondition of the agent's ability to will; but also we can find it at the end stage, near the achievement of the goal of morality. This is true for Aristotle but even more clearly so for Kant. For Aristotle, his emphasis on friendship and on the possibility of having a community of other reasoning agents, as well as a well-governed polis, indicates that a social/political goal was compatible with his doctrine, although the emphasis for Aristotle was always on the character of the agent.[32] A much more global reach can be found in Kant's cosmopolitanism, which I consider in the next section.

Kantian Cosmopolitanism as a Global Ethic

Kant explicitly extends his virtue ethics beyond one's own character. We find this in the formulation of the categorical imperative, as he prescribes "how we must treat ourselves and others in virtue of our legislative status," and in his vision of the Kingdom of Ends that makes us part of a social community "in which each person is regarded as an equal and autonomous agent."[33] No global ethic can be designed that does not include both respect for all humanity and a social community governed by the same principles that direct our interpersonal relations. Both principles are basic to the perpetual peace that is foundational to Kant's cosmopolitanism.

To establish the "cosmopolitan scope" of Kantian doctrine, Onora O'Neill uses environmental examples as the most apt to illustrate the reach of Kant's thought for both spatially and temporally distant persons: "In the contemporary world, people act on quite strong assumptions even about the most distant stranger. . . . [A] background assumption of most affluent lives is that state power will effectively keep most distant strangers more or less in their place in their poverty."[34] We may not accept O'Neill's argument about the element of "intent" present in the awareness of the relative safety of our economic well-being from desperately poor but distant people. But her point is basic to Kant: Universalism translates into cosmopolitanism in practice. What she terms the "hard cases" are examples of the temporally distant, that is, future generations, who are not able to be specified or counted and, especially, are not capable of present interaction. Yet the "immense influence" of our current activities, especially our irresponsible use of fossil fuels and natural resources in general, is undeniable. Hence, it is wrong to think that we need to have a clear and specific individual in mind before any individual can be included in our moral consideration.[35] Thus, the cosmopolitan aspect of Kantianism forms an excellent basis for a global ethic, as justice demands "the rejection of injury," whether direct or indirect, "through damage to the social fabric of the natural world."[36] In the previous section I argue that the vulnerability imposed by environmental disintegrity is especially evident in the populations of developing countries. By attacking the preconditions of their ability to act and to will, that is, "the material bases of their lives and action," we run counter to both the language and the spirit of the categorical imperative.[37]

For the most part, today's talk about human rights, outside the realm of armed conflicts, centers on religious or sexual rights or the right to secede on the part of groups in order to acquire national status. It seems that the most fundamental right, the basis of all others, has been quietly forgotten. The right to life has become, if not obsolete, at least politically incorrect because of its possible conflict with other rights. Yet unless one returns to the defense of the most basic rights of all, it will not be possible to protect humankind globally and to indict those who breach those rights and punish them with the severity appropriate to those crimes.

It is not my intention to view other rights violations as unimportant but simply to emphasize that our right to make any and all choices, be they political, religious, or personal, starts with being not only alive but in a condition that renders us capable of thinking, acting, and pursuing various goals: "And part of what it means to be able to enjoy any other right is not to be prevented from exercising it by lack of security or subsistence. To claim to guarantee people a right that they are in fact unable to exercise is fraudulent, like furnishing people with meal tickets but providing no food."[38] "Basic rights are the morality of the depths," and they represent "everyone's minimum reasonable demands upon the rest of humanity."[39] Subsistence rights include the bare necessities we all need—our habitat's conditions of "unpolluted air, unpolluted water, adequate food, adequate clothing, adequate shelter."[40] We may note that although some of these subsistence rights are at least present in the language of the *Universal Declaration of Human Rights*, neither the *International Covenant on Economic, Social and Cultural Rights* (1966) nor the *International Covenant on Civil and Political Rights* (1966) specifies that, beyond the right to life, the triad of air/water/food that is safe, hence supportive of life, is an actual right.[41]

In addition, although we may think of the two 1966 covenants as needed to improve the life of developing countries' citizens, the "triad" is emphatically not present as a right of citizens of affluent, technologically advanced democracies any more than it is a clear right in the impoverished South. The role of poverty in depriving people of their rights and thus of basic justice worldwide is amply documented: "Severe poverty has consequences: 790 million persons are not adequately nourished, while one billion are without safe water and 2.4 billion without basic sanitation . . . ; more than 880 million lack access to basic health services . . . ; about one billion are without adequate shelter and two billion without electricity."[42] Epidemiological data also exist about the lack of less than healthy air/water/food in the North/West, where particulates in the air, ozone layer depletion, unsanitary water, and food laced with hormones, chemicals, and other additives promote a wide range of disease including a "cancer epidemic" among citizens far removed from poverty.[43]

In order to strengthen the principles that would sustain laws to protect basic rights, the first step is to leave behind any form of reasoning that is purely consequential, in favor of a deontological approach. We need the adoption of universal principles that impose the obligation to ensure respect for life's infinite value, in the Kantian sense. Respect for life, O'Neill contends, means rejecting not only the infliction of direct harms but also that of "indirect injury" to the "natural world."[44] She argues that such injury may be "gratuitous," that is, simply undertaken because it is "convenient for the powerful," or it can be "systematic," that is, taken for granted as a normal way of conducting business or governing society.[45] In either case, there is a deep injustice in the destruction of natural environments.

In the first place, their destruction is unjust because it is a further way by which others can be injured: systematic or gratuitous destruction of the means of life creates vulnerabilities, which facilitate direct injuries to individuals. Destroying (parts of) natural and man-made environments injures those whose lives depend on them. Second, the principle of destroying their reproductive and regenerative powers is not universalizable.[46]

Thus, it is not an abstract cosmopolitanism that is advocated; we must ensure that justice should prevail globally in a practical sense, by "identifying compatible institutions and practices."[47] Note that although O'Neill does not clearly state this, *we all* depend on natural systems in various ways, and to be deprived of them is a severe attack on our life, health, and natural function.[48] This attack extends to a plurality of others everywhere now, as well as to future generations, whose ability to survive, thrive, and have their rights protected must also be respected.[49] Our interconnectedness, to all living things and processes, not only today but also in the future, ensures that this dimension of our obligations cannot be avoided, and it represents the basis of ecological concern.[50]

Whoever the humans of the future might be, they will share our finiteness and vulnerability; hence, in Kantian terms, "inclusive principles of indifference to and neglect of others also cannot be universalized."[51] Shue adds: "The infant and the aged do not need to be assaulted in order to be deprived of health, life or the capacity to enjoy active rights. The classical liberal main prescription for the good life, do not interfere with thy neighbor, is the only poison they need."[52] We can add to this all debilitated persons, malnourished or weakened adults, infants and the aged, and all of us who are exposed continually to unsafe living conditions.

Human Rights, Environmental Rights, Ecological Rights: The Road to Kant's Cosmopolitanism

The argument of the previous sections traced the connections between human and ecological rights in a way that includes both humans and nonhuman nature, both parts and processes. In it I assumed, without proposing a separate argument at this time, their unity through human health considerations. (I have argued elsewhere about the human health impacts of disintegrity.)[53] The intimate connection between human health and ecological integrity is and remains not only a rights argument but an environmental argument at the same time.

Environmental ethicists may prefer to argue directly for respect or for the rights of the natural environment. A large, rich literature already exists on those topics; thus, it is not necessary to revisit those arguments at this time. But there is a vast difference between the force of moral argument, strong though it is, and the potential force of the law. In my recent work I have chosen to focus primarily on the latter, without, however, abandoning the results of years of research that supports my philosophical position.[54]

It is best, I believe, to stress the human rights component of the argument while, at the same time, not denying its intimate connection to the habitat of the humans in question. The proverbial canary in the mine example is only persuasive because the demise of the canary is inescapably related to that of the miner. But the law and, for the most part, moral theorists as well, right or wrong, give much greater weight to the death of the miner than to that of the bird. Thus, in the interest of protecting the latter as well as the former, it is appropriate to turn to the major human rights doctrines, especially that of Kant, without forgetting the intrinsic value of nonhuman nature. The universalism that is foundational to Kant's moral thought translates into cosmopolitanism in his political thought, especially in *Perpetual Peace*.[55] The "republic" to which Kant aspires in that work is quite different from the present instantiation of liberal democracy in individual states. It is also different from governance based on legal instruments of international law, all of which are based on negotiations, are influenced by the economic motive, and embody the injustice present in the vast differences in status and power that are present within states and among them.[56]

From the standpoint of environmental rights, although the traditional view is that international law is only concerned with the rights and obligations of states, there have been significant changes recently. The global reach of most environmental problems, as I have argued, demands an international reach in the law and serious considerations of those who are physically harmed, hence not only of states. In recent decades the language of environmental rights and even of environmental crimes has entered the discourse of global governance.[57] Human rights are central to environmental concern, but the Rio Declaration only asserts that "human beings are at the center of concerns for sustainable development. They are entitled to a healthy and productive life in harmony with nature." But a clearer presence of human rights in international environmental law is undisputed as references to "a healthy, or decent, or viable environment are present in any number of treaties, declarations and resolutions."[58] These are typically referred to as "third-generation" or "solidarity rights," coming as they do after civil and political rights and economic, social, and cultural rights.[59] Nevertheless, these rights, some argue, straddle all other kinds.[60] I, however, have argued even further that environmental rights are primary, as they are basic, necessary before all other rights can be sought or enjoyed, because they represent the very preconditions of human agency.[61]

In 1994 the United Nations produced a "Final Report" on human rights and the environment by the Economic and Social Council Sub-commission on the Prevention of Discrimination and Protection of Minorities. The rights proposed in this report include the following:

1. freedom from pollution, environmental degradation, and activities that adversely affect the environment or threaten life, health, livelihood, well-being, or sustainable development;
2. protection and preservation of the air, soil, water, sea-ice, flora and fauna, and the essential processes and area necessary to maintain biological diversity and ecosystems;
3. the highest attainable standard of health;
4. safe and healthy food, water, and working environment;
5. adequate housing, land tenure, and living conditions in a secure, healthy, and ecologically sound environment;
6. ecologically sound access to nature and the conservation and sustainable use of nature and natural resources;
7. preservation of unique sites;
8. enjoyment of traditional life and subsistence for indigenous people.[62]

The anthropocentric bias present in this document is offset by the additional power and higher profile that environmental instruments gain by being clearly coupled with human rights. However, an even better approach is the one proposed by Prudence Taylor, with her concept of "ecological rights."[63] These rights are based on ecological reasons (touched on by 2 and 6 above), and hence they go specifically beyond the anthropocentric reach of environmental rights. Taylor suggests that ecological rights ought to be considered automatically as limits to any transaction involving property rights.

Another sign for hope can be found in the case law of a supranational institution such as the European Court of Justice.[64] That court has successfully used Article 8 of the European Convention of Human Rights in cases such as *Guerra v. Italy* and *Lopez-Ostra v. Spain* not only to defend the "biological integrity" of those who protested the noxious effects of the pollutants and effluents of nearby industrial operations on their lives and those of their children but also to force the closure of those plants. Protection was thus extended to the life and health of these citizens and also to their "family life and home." These concerns were judged to supersede the economic concerns that had led their respective national courts (in Italy and Spain) to reject their claims, before the case was brought to the E.U. court.[65]

In these cases, the local ecology and the impact of inappropriate and hazardous industrial practices on the lives and health of the affected families were viewed as intimately connected, so that the defense of one would imply that of the other. Nor is this approach limited to developed states or the European Union: "India, Pakistan, Bangladesh, the Philippines, Malaysia and several Latin American jurisdictions have also embraced public interest litigation on environmental issues."[66] Finally, an additional right was recently brought into focus: the right to access to information and participation of all citizens in environmental decision making, implying the full flow of information even across borders.[67]

Conclusion

Virtue ethics is foundational for a global ethic in that it articulates—in its Aristotelian and Kantian forms—conceptions of both human excellence and the health and integrity of natural systems. It also emphasizes the importance, indeed, the primacy, of meeting the preconditions for achieving that health and excellence, which for humans includes meeting the preconditions for moral agency. These preconditions in turn imply the need to support and maintain ecological integrity. However, the international discourse is the discourse of human rights. So we must emphasize the human rights dimension of this ethic and its implication for international law. Human rights approaches are, I have argued, supported by virtue ethics, the ethic of integrity, and are indispensably valuable for the advancement of an environmental agenda, for they are the most likely to elicit universal support and, perhaps, to give rise to possible means to enforce compliance. In addition, human rights violations are not treated exclusively as torts but, rather, are viewed for the most part as crimes and thus are considered far more serious than regulatory breaches.[68] Therefore, the moral arguments of Aristotle and Kant, the nature of international discourse, and recent legal developments together favor a cosmopolitan rights approach as the most likely to offer the promise of a sounder ecological form of global governance.

Notes

1. I will not argue that Kant is a virtue ethicist. I will simply point to the Kantian scholars who have accepted that proposition and stipulate now that I have found their arguments entirely persuasive. See, for instance, Onora O'Neill, *Towards Justice and Virtue* (Cambridge: Cambridge University Press, 1996); Marcia Baron, *Kantian Ethics Almost without Apology* (Ithaca: Cornell University Press, 1995); Nancy Sherman, *Making a Necessity of Virtue* (Cambridge: Cambridge University Press, 1997); and Stephen Engstrom and Jennifer Whiting, eds., *Aristotle, Kant and the Stoics* (Cambridge: Cambridge University Press, 1996), particularly J. B. Schneewind's "Kant and Stoic Ethics" and Julia Annas's "Aristotle and Kant on Morality and Practical Reasoning."

2. An example of this is Robert Solomon's misuse of Aristotelian virtue ethics in his version of business ethics ("Corporate Roles, Personal Virtues: An Aristotelian Approach to Business Ethics," in *Applied Ethics: A Reader*, ed. E. Winkler and J. Coombs [Oxford: Blackwell Publishing, 1993], 201–21). For example, *pace* Solomon, Aristotle's moral theory does not recommend "learning" morality from the community but simply starting with a community-based

rough understanding of right and wrong, before discourse may ensue and philosophical moral progress can be made. The journey of moral understanding is based on the "function" of human being, and only builds on the initial unthinking acceptance of community-based standards, to reach eventually the goal of full, rational understanding not only of what is good but also, even more important, of why it is so.

3. Amartya Sen, "The Living Standard," in *The Ethics of Consumption* (Lanham, MD: Rowman and Littlefield, 1997), 305.

4. Aristotle, *Nicomachean Ethics* 1098a16–18.

5. Richard Kraut, *Aristotle on the Human Good* (Princeton: Princeton University Press, 1989), 238.

6. Laura Westra, *An Environmental Proposal for Ethics: The Principle of Integrity* (Lanham, MD: Rowman and Littlefield, 1994), 133.

7. Westra, *An Environmental Proposal for Ethics*, 134–42.

8. Anthony Preus, "*Eidos* as Norm in Aristotle's Biology," in *Aristotle: Essays in Ancient Greek Philosophy*, ed. John P. Anton and Anthony Preus (Albany: State University of New York Press, 1983), 340–63.

9. John Cooper, "Hypothetical Necessity and Natural Teleology," in *Philosophical Issues in Aristotle's Biology*, ed. A. Gotthelf and James G. Lennox (Cambridge: Cambridge University Press, 1987), 247.

10. Cooper, "Hypothetical Necessity and Natural Teleology," 248.

11. John Rist, *The Mind of Aristotle* (Toronto: University of Toronto Press, 1989), 122.

12. Colin L. Soskolne and Roberto Bertollini, "Global Ecological Integrity and 'Sustainable Development': Cornerstones of Public Health" (Rome: World Health Organization, European Centre for Environment and Health, Rome Division, July 1999), available at www.euro.who .int/document/gch/ecorep5.pdf.

13. Westra, *An Environmental Proposal for Ethics*, 134–42.

14. Kraut, *Aristotle on the Human Good*, 159–65.

15. Aristotle, *Nicomachean Ethics* 1097a15–b21; T. H. Irwin, "Kant's Criticism of *Eudaimonia*," in *Aristotle, Kant and the Stoics*, ed. Stephen Engstrom and Whiting Jennifer (Cambridge: Cambridge University Press, 1996), 72–73.

16. Prudence Taylor, "Ecological Rights," *Georgetown International Environmental Law Review* 10 (1998): 309.

17. The principle of integrity is explicated and defended in Westra, *An Environmental Proposal for Ethics*. See also Laura Westra, *Living in Integrity: A Global Ethic to Restore a Fragmented Earth* (Lanham, MD: Rowman and Littlefield, 1998).

18. P. W. Birnie and Adam Boyle, *International Law and the Environment* (Oxford: Oxford University Press, 2002), chap. 5.

19. Alan Gewirth, *Human Rights: Essays on Justification and Applications* (Chicago: University of Chicago Press, 1982), 5.

20. Gewirth, *Human Rights*, 7.

21. Gewirth, *Human Rights*, 5.

22. Deryck Beyleveld and Roger Brownsword, *Human Dignity in Bioethics and Biolaw* (Oxford: Oxford University Press, 2001), 71.

23. Henry Shue, *Basic Rights: Subsistence, Affluence and U.S. Foreign Policy* (Princeton: Princeton University Press, 1996), n. 4.

24. Beyleveld and Brownsword, *Human Dignity in Bioethics and Biolaw*, nn. 27, 70; Gewirth, *Human Rights*, nn. 23, 54.

25. Laura Westra, "Environmental Rights and Human Rights: The Final Enclosure Movement," in *Human Rights*, ed. R. Brownsword (Oxford: Hart Publishing, 2004).

26. Thomas Regan, *The Case for Animal Rights* (Berkeley: University of California Press, 1983); David De Grazia, *Taking Animals Seriously* (New York: Cambridge University Press, 1996), n. 35.

27. Westra, *An Environmental Proposal for Ethics*, 96–97.

28. Laura Westra, "The Disvalue of Contingent Valuation and the Accounting Expectation Gap," *Environmental Values* 9 (2000): 153–71.

29. W. E. Rees and M. Wackernagel, *Our Ecological Footprint* (Gabriola Island, BC: New Society Publishers, 1996); William E. Rees and Laura Westra, "When Consumption Does Violence: Can There Be Sustainability and Environmental Justice in a Resource-Limited World?" in *Just Sustainabilities*, ed. Julyan Agyeman, Robert D. Bullard, and Bob Evans (London: Earthscan Publications, 2003), 99–124.

30. Irwin, "Kant's Criticism of *Eudaimonia*," 78–91.

31. Sherman, *Making a Necessity of Virtue*, 167.

32. Sherman, *Making a Necessity of Virtue*, 285.

33. Sherman, *Making a Necessity of Virtue*, 286.

34. O'Neill, *Towards Justice and Virtue*, 114–15.

35. O'Neill, *Towards Justice and Virtue*. See also Derek Parfit, *Reasons and Persons* (Oxford: Oxford University Press, 1984); Laura Westra, *Ecoviolence and the Law: Supranational Normative Foundations of Ecocrime* (Ardsley, NY: Transnational Publishers, 2004).

36. O'Neill, *Towards Justice and Virtue*, 174.

37. O'Neill, *Towards Justice and Virtue*, 174.

38. Shue, *Basic Rights*, 27 n. 4.

39. Shue, *Basic Rights*, 18 n. 4, 19.

40. Shue, *Basic Rights*, 23.

41. United Nations, *Universal Declaration of Human Rights* (UNGA Res. 217[LII], UN GAOR, 3d Sess., Supp. NO.13 @71, U.N. Doc. A/810 [1948]), A.25; United Nations, *International Covenant on Economic, Social and Cultural Rights* (993 U.N.T.S. 3, 1976 Can. T.S. No. 46 [1966]); United Nations, *International Covenant on Civil and Political Rights* (999 U.N.T.S. 171, 1976 Can. T.S. No. 47 [1966]).

42. Thomas Pogge, "Priorities of Global Justice," in *Global Justice*, ed. T. H. Pogge (Oxford: Blackwell Publishers, 2001), 6–23, citing the U.N. Development Programme.

43. David Fidler, *International Law and Public Health* (Ardsley, NY: Transnational Publishers, 2001); Westra, "The Disvalue of Contingent Valuation and the Accounting Expectation Gap"; A. J. McMichael, "Global Environmental Change in the Coming Century: How Sustainable Are Recent Health Gains?" in *Ecological Integrity: Integrating Environment, Conservation and Health*, ed. D. Pimentel, L. Westra, and R. Noss (Washington, DC: Island Press, 2000); Samuel Epstein, *The Politics of Cancer* (San Francisco: Sierra Club Books, 1978).

44. O'Neill, *Towards Justice and Virtue*, 174–75.

45. O'Neill, *Towards Justice and Virtue*, 175.

46. O'Neill, *Towards Justice and Virtue*, 176.

47. O'Neill, *Towards Justice and Virtue*, 179.

48. Soskolne and Bertollini, "Global Ecological Integrity and 'Sustainable Development.'"

49. Edith Brown-Weiss, "Intergenerational Equity," in *Environmental Change and International Law*, ed. Edith Brown-Weiss (Tokyo: United Nations Press, 1992), 385–412.

50. Laura Westra, Peter Miller, James R. Karr, William E. Rees, and Robert Ulanowicz, "Ecological Integrity and the Aims of the Global Ecological INTEGRITY Project," in *Ecological Integrity: Integrating Environment, Conservation and Health*, ed. David Pimentel, Laura Westra, and Reed Noss (Washington, DC: Island Press, 2000), 19–41.

51. O'Neill, *Towards Justice and Virtue*, 193 n. 14.

52. Shue, *Basic Rights*, n. 19.

53. Westra, *Living in Integrity*; Westra, *Ecological Integrity*.

54. D. Pimentel, L. Westra, and R. Noss, *Ecological Integrity in the World's Environment and Health* (Washington, DC: Island Press, 2000); Westra et al., "Ecological Integrity and the Aims of the Global Ecological INTEGRITY Project."

55. H. Reiss, ed., *Kant: Political Writings*, 2d ed. (Cambridge: Cambridge University Press, [1795] 1991), 93–130.

56. Edward S. Herman and Noam Chomsky, *Manufacturing Consent* (Amherst, NY: Prometheus Books, 2002).

57. Birnie and Boyle, *International Law and the Environment*, chap. 5; Westra, "Environmental Rights and Human Rights."

58. Birnie and Boyle, *International Law and the Environment*, 252.

59. See United Nations, *International Covenant on Economic, Social and Cultural Rights*; United Nations, *International Covenant on Civil and Political Rights*.

60. Birnie and Boyle, *International Law and the Environment*, 253.

61. Gewirth, *Human Rights*; Westra, "Environmental Rights and Human Rights."

62. U.N. Sub-commission on the Prevention of Discrimination and Protection of Minorities, Economic and Social Council, "Final Report" (UN Doc. E/CN.4/Sub.2/1994/9 [1994]).

63. Taylor, "Ecological Rights."

64. J. H. H. Weiler, *The Constitution of Europe* (Cambridge: Cambridge University Press, 1999).

65. Westra, "Environmental Rights and Human Rights."

66. Birnie and Boyle, *International Law and the Environment*, 264.

67. U.N. Economic Commission for Europe, *Convention on Access to Information, Public Participation in Decision-Making and Access to Justice in Environmental Matters*, adopted 25 June 1998, Arhus.

68. Westra, "Environmental Rights and Human Rights."

CHAPTER 6

A Virtue Ethics Approach to Aldo Leopold's Land Ethic

Bill Shaw

Introduction

Moral philosophers tend to approach the subject of environmental ethics from the same two perspectives that they approach every other subject within their domain. The perspectives center on issues of "the good," that is, good for the human community, and "the right," that is, the rules of right conduct. Their mission, so to speak, is to "search for knowledge of the good life and right conduct."[1] That certainly includes the common understanding of the word *ethics*, but it is not at all clear that these perspectives are sufficient for environmental ethics.

In a broad sense, an ethic is a way of life or an attitude toward life. It distinguishes social from antisocial behavior on the basis of a commitment to certain values of the human community—values that underlie any attempt to understand and articulate the right and the good. The ethical life as we live it day to day is guided by a sense of meaning and purpose that has to do in part with feeling and emotion and in part with rational processes.

If we conceive of ethics as a system of values or a set of attitudes that differentiates between the good for the community and the bad, we might conceive of the project of environmental ethics as an attempt to extend the notion of the good to embrace a community beyond that of human beings. Such a project engages both our emotional and our rational resources as we reflect upon, and develop, a moral concern toward the natural world as a whole. This concern, and the ethics it engenders, leads us to explore our relationships with the world around us.

Relationships, specifically ecological relationships, are clearly the centerpiece of environmental ethics. After all, ecology is the study of the relationships of organisms with one another and with the environment. A good place to begin this study is with the work of a person who was an ecologist rather than a moral philosopher. I am referring to Aldo Leopold and to his famous work, "The Land Ethic."[2] Leopold has long been recognized as one of the most significant figures in the development of the environmental ethics—especially the more controversial, nonhuman-centered strain of this movement identified with preservationist theories, ecocentrism, deep ecology, and the like.[3] In this chapter, I would like to use some of the basic principles at work in "The Land Ethic" to launch a discussion of two things.

First, I examine the possibility of a paradigm shift in everyday ethical attitudes. This examination will focus on the interests that are at stake in such a shift and the difficulties inherent in a modification of our ethical perception. Second, I consider the possibility of "land virtues" that may provide us with an avenue for circumventing some of the difficulties inherent in a paradigm shift.

One way to understand "the land ethic" is to look upon it as a set of attitudes and practices toward the unfolding or blossoming of natural systems (ecosystems) in accordance with their purpose or telos. This naturalistic trajectory is, of course, highly controversial as a general approach to ethical theory.[4] With regard to environmental ethics in particular, the observation that the environment evolves continuously (rather than crystallizing at a particular stage) has served to challenge this idea.[5] It should be noted, however, that human communities evolve as well, and no one has thought to jettison virtue ethics for that reason alone. Further, it appears that an Aristotelian conception of the "good" of natural systems, in reference to their nature and telos, is operating in Leopold's notion of the "integrity" of natural systems. I will have more to say about this later.

Because ecosystems include nonhuman as well as human subjects among their "citizens," Leopold's ethic does indeed demand a reevaluation and a reorientation in our thinking. The object of this process is to bring into harmony these nonhuman and human subjects by bestowing a special status upon those systems exhibiting a telos (in Aristotle's terms, a "nature," a "way of being"). A forest, no less than a human, exhibits the capacity for internal self-direction—for growth, for blossoming, for achieving its telos—and for that reason forests and other natural systems are respected as citizens in this new paradigm. Of great significance is the corollary of this proposition: human beings are reduced from masters of the land to "plain member and fellow citizens." How might something like this be rendered plausible and desirable, that is, in the interests of human and nonhuman subjects alike?

The attitudes and practices that serve the ultimate good in this new paradigm—the land virtues—tend to preserve the integrity, stability, and beauty of natural systems.[6] Vices tend to destabilize and to destroy these characteristics of natural systems. They send shock waves through the environment—the greenhouse effect, ozone depletion, eutrophication, loss of species, and desertification—that jeopardize all living systems. The significance of adopting virtue language and its relation to these problems will be discussed momentarily.

The Land Ethic

Clearly, an environmental ethic is an intangible thing. In an effort to explore it further, it is necessary to consider what is "good" from a different perspective—an environmental perspective. The next step, then, will be to ask what might count as the "good" in an ethic based upon a fundamental moral regard for the environment.

A. THE GOOD

Aldo Leopold envisions "the ultimate good" not as happiness but as *harmony* within the biotic, or living, community. The biotic community is one that is composed of natural, living systems including nonhuman and human members. In Leopold's scheme of things, the word *land* stands proxy for life and for the source of life, for example, the soil, water, plants, and animals. Harmony within this community—specifically, the integrity, stability, beauty of the community—is the ultimate good. Everything aims at harmony, but, given its scope and complexity, it is not one of those subjects that can be specified with precision.[7]

Because humans are included in this community, Leopold evidently views "the good for humanity" as compatible with, or a subset of, "the good for the biotic community." This is obviously a crucial issue, and the connection between the entirety of the biotic community and the subcommunities within it (including the human community) will have to be addressed, as will the question of the status of individual members of the biotic community vis-à-vis the whole. The fear, if well grounded, that neither the human community, nor any of its members, nor any individual member of any other biotic community has any value apart from the whole, would certainly constitute a radical departure from the standard course of ethical theory.

Bentham, however, would admit into the moral community any being capable of feeling pain, so animals with a nervous system less developed than ours could get in. Albert Schweitzer extended this community by advocating a "reverence for life," but these views have been largely ignored by mainstream philosophy. Bentham, Schweitzer, and more recently Peter Singer and Tom Regan all appear to be arguing for an extentionist approach, but one that maintains a human center. What *seems* to be implied in Leopold, however, is much more holistic. With the biotic community as a whole occupying the center, human rights, interests, and preferences can no longer dominate the stage as a privileged and unqualified "trump."

Clearly then, we need to address two major issues before we can continue. The first concerns the question of extending the boundary of the moral universe to biotic communities, to beings with a telos. Why is this morally just? The second issue revolves around the question of the status of the human component within an expanded moral community. Is there any room for a hierarchical conception of moral worth within the "land ethic," or is such a vision to be dismissed as unjustifiably anthropocentric? If human beings are obliged to abandon the center of the moral universe, then Leopold's vision is surely to be seen at odds with the interests of the most articulate citizens of this universe. First, however, let us approach the issue of the extension of the boundaries of moral standing.

We might ask, Why let "them" in?[8] Why admit something as intangible as "the land" into the moral community? One would not have to go far to hear arguments that there is not enough harmony within moral community now. How is that going to change for the better by granting something like citizenship to "land"? And, finally, what does it mean as a practical matter to admit land into full citizenship? Would that mean the "land" gets a voice, a vote, a veto? Would it hold the ultimate "trump"?

1. Why Let "Them" In?

Leopold views the admission of land into the moral community as a natural extension of ethics. In the evolutionary or historical sense, as we understand it, family groups of humans and certain nonhuman animals survive and prosper by developing modes of cooperation within the group. It has been the natural or evolutionary development for groups with the greatest internal harmony and cooperation to flourish and to be successful in extending their boundaries.

Group bonds, group loyalty, or group identification—the internal harmony or cohesion that forestalls splintering or deterioration within the group—also fosters or enhances the group's success in competition with other groups (the gentlest and most cooperative member of the group may be its fiercest defender).[9] Through the process of natural selection, cohesive groups (and group members with the most highly developed sense of cooperation) are the "fittest." Consequently they "survive" in competition with others.

These "modes of cooperation," observable in other and lower life-forms (i.e., in natural systems or biotic communities), can be articulated as an "ethic" only with the imaginative and intellectual powers of human beings, but they are nevertheless real and valid processes. These instinctive or genetic forces at work in nonhuman systems find their near-counterpart, though not their exact mirror image, in the human "affective domain" (i.e., the "emotional" side). Human feeling, sentiment, and emotion, then, account for the origin of ethics in the Darwinian sense.[10]

While this sort of account begs the charge of having committed the "naturalistic fallacy," it appears, nonetheless, to have a certain intuitive appeal. This is especially true with regard to the process of giving an account of why, both intellectually and emotionally, a paradigm shift in our ethical regard both appears to be, and "ought" to be, taking place. I will return to the issue of the naturalistic fallacy a little later.

Leopold seems to be absorbing some key elements of the Darwinian account. He sees the extension of ethics to the land as "an evolutionary possibility and an ecological necessity." So, in answer to the question, "Why let 'them' in?" Leopold responds that "all ethics so far evolved rest upon a single premise: that the individual is a member of a community of interdependent parts. His instincts prompt him to compete for his place in that community, but his ethics prompt him also to cooperate (perhaps in order that there may be a place to compete for)."[11]

Ecosystems come to this cooperative/interdependent stage naturally, and they do so in order to survive and prosper. It seems, then, to make a lot of intuitive sense to recognize the accumulated evolutionary wisdom of natural systems and adopt that paradigm, perhaps somewhat modified, or borrow its most important lessons. This accumulated wisdom, and the good sense of being guided by it, urges the expansion of our ethical universe beyond the bounds of the human community. After all, our existence and our culture are intricately bound to the land, and our continued well-being clearly depends upon a recognition and strengthening of our ties to it. Still unresolved, however, is the status of the human community within Leopold's expanded moral sphere, and we turn now to that issue.

2. What Does It Mean to Admit "Land" as a Full Citizen?

Suppose this is a correct, or at least a plausible, interpretation of Leopold. Are we all truly equal now—a fish and a tree and you and me? This way of regarding the shift in our moral concern is clearly not in keeping with the radical individualism that characterizes Western democracies. And while the intuitive appeal of a society built in harmony with the land is great, it seems to break down when plants and animals are placed on the same level as the human community.

Leopold, however, does not insist on that degree of equal citizenship, for he accepts that "a land ethic of course cannot prevent the alteration, management, and use of these 'resources,' but it does affirm their right to continued existence, and, at least in spots, their continued existence in a natural state."[12] As we move from conqueror to plain member and citizen of the land community, we must show "respect" for biotic communities and community members, but, at the same time, we can alter, manage, and use the land (natural systems, ecosystems) as a resource. Many times we have little other choice, and, of course, it will not come as a shock to observe that each biotic community uses other communities as resources as well.

In those times of little choice, and perhaps even because of the very narrowness of those choices, we see other ethical systems operating in ways that reinforce a virtue ethics analysis. In Kantian terms, it may be argued that we can treat the land instrumentally (that is, as a means to an end) but not merely as a means.[13] We can eat the fish and use the forest to build our houses, as long as we maintain a fundamental moral regard for the integrity of the biotic system. Likewise, Locke's development of social contract theory and private property is not inconsistent with an environmental mandate to leave "enough, and as good . . . in common for others."[14] If that phrase can plausibly be read into a contemporary setting, "others" might well be taken to mean other members of an expanded moral universe.

One must then acknowledge that our need to use the land does not license a radical freedom to abuse it. We are not entitled to pillage or waste, to ruin or destroy natural systems. This means that land use and forestry practices, indeed, the economics of the forestry industry, would have to be revamped to accommodate the owl community as well as other endangered species. Why? Because the owl, like her human fellow creatures, has intrinsic value.[15] Intrinsic value is attributed to things that participate in the dynamic relationships characteristic of a biotic community. This applies as well not only to the owl but to the owl habitat (old forests). To respect one is to respect the other and so on for the myriad interdependencies of other living systems.

What then of the owl when the owl habitat has economic value for the human community—when old forests are needed to build warm houses and to keep our loggers employed? How would a person inspired by the land ethic deal with that problem? Is there some priority built into the ethic that would justify the sacrifice of a species (first the habitat, then the owl) to the development of another housing tract in New York, California, or Texas? And what of the issue concerning the sacrifice of individuals, human or otherwise, in the interest of the biotic community as a whole?

Leopold does not make it easy for us to resolve these problems. In speaking of land as a resource, he says that the land ethic cannot prevent the "alteration, management, or use." That implies that the land (including products of the land and members of the biotic community) can be consumed or used instrumentally, as a means to an end. But, as has been already noted, the ethic "does affirm [the land's] right to continued existence, and, at least in spots, [its] continued existence in a natural state."[16] In the closing section of this piece, he concludes as follows: "It is inconceivable to me that an ethical relation to land can exist without love, respect, and admiration for land, and a high regard for its value. By value, I of course mean something far broader than mere economic value; I mean value in the philosophical sense."[17]

This clarification, however, does not resolve all our problems. Even in the "philosophical" sense, the word *value* means different things (e.g., instrumental and intrinsic to name just two). Giving Leopold a probable and plausible reading, however, he is most likely to be saying, "Preserve the biotic community!" with emphasis on *community*. And if the existence of a biotic community hangs in the balance, make certain that the sacrifice is amply justified by the preservation of another biotic community of greater "integrity, stability, and beauty."[18] These values, which seem to be at the core of "The Land Ethic," distinctly prefer the living to the nonliving and, among the living, the "community" that is the most clearly defined by these criteria.

Is the human community, then, at the top of this "pecking order"? That suspicion has limited deniability, and it brings to the forefront a prominent and problematic bias. If we really mean to give owl citizens a legitimate vote, make them full citizens, and give them the kind of respect that we accord ourselves, the pecking order will have to be revamped. Otherwise, a wise old "philosopher" owl will hoot, "There is nothing new here—just the 'same ole, same ole,' with a slightly different spin."

So we are left with some serious tensions at work in Leopold's conception of the "land ethic." On the one hand, he clearly seems to suggest that the integrity of biotic communities is the fundamental concern of the land ethic. He acknowledges, however, that different components of the biotic community are in competition with one another—the human community and the owl community have competing interests in certain areas. The question is: Can Leopold successfully make sense of, and adjudicate between, competing sets of interests within a world of biotic communities while holding fast to the holistic paradigm governing the land ethic?

B. THE LAND VIRTUES

Why introduce virtue language at this point? I believe it can be helpful for a number of reasons. Clearly, this examination of the land ethic has opened up a myriad of difficulties. On what grounds are we attributing intrinsic value to participants in the biotic community? What could possibly be the basis for the claim that the land has a "right" to continued existence, as Leopold suggests? Is this a moral right, a legal right, or perhaps both? And even if we grant such rights, on the basis of value or interests, for example, how do we begin to develop a theory to guide us through the process of adjudicating between competing sets of interests and rights? Do we really want to frame the notion of an environmental ethic in terms of a litany of who has claims against whom and who has a right to what?

Virtue language, I believe, allows us to circumvent, or at least to place on the back burner, some of these divisive issues. In order to begin addressing these concerns, we need the mediation of virtue ethics analysis to explore the sorts of attitudes and habits we are in fact cultivating toward the environment or, perhaps more importantly, to explore the sorts of attitudes and habits we should be cultivating.

In virtue ethics we are able to stop fretting about what claims the environment has against us, what rights we may be impinging upon, and concentrate on the more important question of how we as moral agents ought to relate to other environmental communities. From this perspective, the fundamental moral question is not "Who has what against me?" but, rather, "What kind of person should I be?" and, given the enormous complexities and uncertainties of ecological relationships, "How should a person act to foster the well-being of all living communities?" Leopold, prophetically I believe, underscores the necessity of changing attitudes before changing laws: "Obligations have no meaning without conscience," he relates, "and the problem we face is the extension of the social conscience from people to land."[19]

1. Virtues and Rules

To begin with, virtues are stable propensities to excel or character habits that are instilled into us from our early years and for as long as we are capable of moral growth. Second, virtues are "means" or midpoints between excess and deficit. A person who exhibited the virtue of honesty would be discrete enough not to "spill his guts" at every opportunity to be heard but forthcoming enough to volunteer information that was relevant to a discussion and not privileged. Finally, virtues are not the same as rules, and the person of virtue is not a mere rule follower living in blind obedience to a fixed position. A virtuous person is a person of character and judgment. Virtues cannot be formulated with the precision of a rule because they require decisions to be made under unique and challenging circumstances. In making these decisions, a virtuous person harnesses the emotional (affective) and the cognitive (rational) aspects of one's psyche.[20]

It is wrong, however, to suggest that virtue ethics is hostile to rules, even if, at bottom, virtues are contextual. Good rules for children to learn would be "Never tell a lie," "Be kind to animals," and "Don't play with matches." A virtuous person would have been conditioned for so long and so well by parents and friends that such a rule would be internalized—it would become a "natural" habit, that is, second nature. In educating children, rules have their place. However, in the life of an adult, rules either are too rigid or narrow for the kinds of judgments that have to be made or are too abstract to give any valuable guidance.

2. Land Virtues and Social or Interpersonal Virtues

Honesty, thoughtfulness, and prudence, the examples utilized in the paragraph above, are very important social or interpersonal virtues. Honesty and thoughtfulness are frequently characterized as moral virtues (character habits that are good in themselves), and prudence, a nonmoral virtue (generally equated with enlightened self-interest). These and other such internalized virtues are constituents of the good, but the good consists of external elements as well (good laws, good fortune, good health, good climate).[21] All of these goods relate in some way to Leopold's vision of a land ethic—an ethic in which the good of the biotic community is "integrity, stability, and beauty." The role of the land virtues should be to foster or advance that good. We would then instill in our children such great respect for those values that it would become natural, or second nature, for them to act in ways that supported the well-being of biotic communities.

The land virtues would not repeal or replace the social or interpersonal virtues. Instead, the land virtues would exist in phase with them.[22] The virtues of courage, temperance, truthfulness, and justice as we have come to know them, or the Christian virtues of faith, hope, and charity, have little to say to us about how to treat Citizen Owl. But a new concept of the good (a new order or new paradigm) at least gives us a clue—members of the biotic community are to be treated with respect; they must be treated as citizens who have intrinsic value or value in themselves and as citizens who are not to be put in jeopardy for any but the most compelling reasons.

3. Land Virtues

Beginning with the notion that it is the community rather than the individual community member that takes precedence in "The Land Ethic," and that the "good" of the community consists of its harmony of elements—integrity, stability, and beauty—then the "land virtues" will be those character habits that foster the "good." This kind of regard for the land, sometimes even approaching a spiritual regard, is commonplace in other, supposedly less advanced cultures and, to borrow a familiar example, is classically illustrated by the attitudes of the North American native peoples. Those were "simpler times," to be sure, but this window into the past gives exposure to a heritage that seems worthy of recapture and of adapting to a contemporary setting.

What are the virtues, then, that we could call "land virtues"? I will advance no more than three, though others can be advanced.[23] Each of the three I want to consider is an adaptation of a traditional virtue: respect (ecological sensitivity), prudence, and practical judgment.

(a) The first of these, respect for biotic communities (hence, ecosystems and ultimately the biosphere), equates with a respect for things with a telos.[24] The human community is not isolated from the environment but a part of it—part of a greater whole that functions in very complex and dynamic, if not fully understood, ways. This is something we must bear in mind when we try to cultivate an appropriate attitude toward the environment and deliberate about ethical choices. After all, things with a telos are, literally, things with a purpose, things with intrinsic value. Respect for this intrinsic value cautions us that they are not merely for our play but are placed here by nature for purposes we may not even fully understand.

Thus, although the well-being of the community comes first, this does not mean that individual members of the community can be sacrificed for mere trivial ends. While the deer and quail and trout communities can survive with fewer members, they are not purely "game," that is, they are not candidates for waste, depletion, or extinction by hunters and fishers. On the supposition, however, that hunting and fishing is a significant need (physical needs such as food or shelter or even a psychic need), that justification will hold only so long as it does not undermine the "good," which incorporates the "integrity, stability, and beauty" of the species or biotic community.[25]

(b) The virtue of prudence embodies the age-old wisdom that enlightened, long-term well-being, rather than immediate preference gratification, is more likely to advance the good. There is always the risk, however, that the perceived long-term good may never materialize and that the short-term gain, in retrospect, would have been the better choice. This serves to remind us of the deficiency of our science and of our lack of understanding of human and ecological affairs. Setbacks of this nature do not undermine the virtue of prudence. It is heir to many such setbacks. But our experience teaches that on the whole we should cultivate the habit of "not rushing to judgment." On the contrary, we should be thoughtful, considerate, and sometimes even plodding on how best to advance the good. Prudence, being the midpoint between "a mad rush into oblivion" and an "intransigent do-nothingness," has particular relevance to the good of ecosystems. "Ecosystems that are stable relative to characteristic fluctuations or stresses in which they have evolved may not be stable relative to human-induced stress no matter how diverse they are, simply because shifts in the characteristic diversity induced by high technology or large population influxes are not the kinds of stress to which even the most diverse ecosystems have evolved a resistance."[26]

The prudent course of action for the human species, or the course of action exhibiting a high degree of "enlightened self-interest," would surely link the well-being of the ecosystem with our own. But we must make this realization a part of our general moral outlook before we can begin to sort out issues of genuinely competing interests. Otherwise, it would appear that the short-term, bottom-line, cost-benefit approach will win out again and again.

Finally, in regard to the virtue of prudence, there is no apology for the pursuit of self-interest. Self-interest, identified closely with the interest of the community (and most of the time even identical with community interest) has its place and is not to be confused with selfishness and the radical pursuit of freedom that is certain to be destructive of community bonds.

(c) Practical wisdom or judgment is the third of the "land virtues," and it should be understood as permeating the other two. Judgment is involved in showing "sensitivity" to ecological communities and their members and sorting out the rival claims and interests within and among communities. The same is true of acting with "prudence." In face of the uncertain environmental consequences of clearing the Brazilian rain forests, or of logging "old forests" in Washington and Oregon, what weight would an enlightened decision maker place on real human needs for food, clothing, and employment and what weight on the preservation of those ecosystems? Surely there are no rules here that will guarantee a single right answer.[27] It is, of course, important to proceed with sensitivity and with prudence, but when one has to make choices and the consequence of those choices cannot be known, what should guide that decision? For a person committed to "The Land Ethic," (i) the decision should advance a concept of the good that welcomes the "integrity, stability, and beauty" of biotic communities within its sphere, and it should exhibit the land virtues (respect, prudence, and practical judgment) in mediating the welfare of this expanded network of communities; and (ii) the decision should not rest on the uncritical assumption that in all of its aspects the human community is the most highly evolved and that it always exhibits the greatest degree of "integrity, stability, and beauty" (housing developments and golf courses piled upon aquifers are good evidence that certain preferences should be reexamined).[28]

Conclusion: Citizenship and the Land Ethic

Leopold's controversial work should not be taken as a political treatise or as an original work of ethical theory. He speaks of "citizenship," commonly understood as a political concept, and "respect," a term familiar to ethicists, but his overriding message pushes the language of these traditions to the limits—even beyond those limits. Central to his thought, however, is the compelling need to reconceptualize the "land," that is, to enter into a new relationship with the network of biotic communities that metaphorically compose the land.

In Leopold's view, land is community. More precisely, land is a web of interrelated and interdependent communities, and those relationships and dependencies are exposed to ever-increasing pressure, and sometimes even to extinction, by the human community. The human community is not the sole intruder on this web, however, it is only the most recent and the most dangerous.

Mankind's intrusions upon other biotic communities are led by the assumption that land is a resource. These forays are sometimes characterized by prudence (a virtue that includes a survival component) but also, and too frequently, by indifference, by ignorance, and by a materialistic, economic imperative. At some time or another, every biotic community treats one or more of its neighbors as a resource, but this is taken to be the "survival" mode, in a Darwinian sense that is beyond any moral condemnation. It is the human community alone (or a substantial segment of that community) that sees itself as virtually unrestrained in its pursuit of material well-being and looks upon all choices as economically driven.

Leopold arrives upon the scene as a modest but insightful professional, a forest and game manager. He does not invite us into a world of deep ecology. He does, however, urge upon us a different way of thinking, a different mind-set or paradigm. It may not be "new under the sun," but he makes no such claim. Leopold understands his ethic to be an extension of an anthropocentric vision. In a way that parallels the admission of "slave girls" into the human fold, he sees the protective cloak of the land ethic drawn warmly about the borders of neighboring communities. Communities that were once mere instruments, mere resources, mere property, are valued in a different light.

Leopold makes it clear enough that the new paradigm is not a new set of commandments or an ecological golden rule. Right and wrong, good and bad are assessed in terms of the tendency to produce or preserve "the integrity, beauty, and stability of the biotic community." This can be understood as a component of "the good," and "the good," since Aristotle's time, is the thing to be aimed for.

It would advance Leopold's case, and Aristotle's, if the components of the good were stationary targets and were profiled in stark clarity. Then we could correct our aim or even perfect it. But this degree of clarity is not one of the attributes of the good. It is, instead, an evolving target, and the elements that Leopold conjoins must take their place alongside other constituents of the good.

Beyond that, the land ethic and the virtues that advance it simply take time to do their work. This is no quick fix. The tradition of virtue ethics, so long absorbed with the good for humankind, is being asked to extend its territory and to enfold the good of biotic communities as well. As once it received into its realm the descendants of Odysseus's slave girls and elevated their status from chattel property to personhood, it now stands ready to welcome the "integrity, stability, and beauty" of biotic communities into its borders.

Notes

1. Susan J. Armstrong and Richard G. Botzler, *Environmental Ethics: Divergence and Convergence* (New York: McGraw-Hill, Inc., 1993), 52.

2. Aldo Leopold, "The Land Ethic," in *A Sand County Almanac and Sketches Here and There* (New York: Oxford University Press, 1949), 201–6.

3. See, e.g., Joseph Des Jardins, *Environmental Ethics* (Belmont, CA: Wadsworth Publishing Co., 1993), 189.

4. The "naturalistic fallacy" consists of a projection from an "is" to an "ought," i.e., from an empirical observation that things are a certain way to a moral judgment that things ought to be that way. A syllogism in the following form simply will not do: Objects of nature have a telos; man is an object of nature; therefore, man has a telos and ought to fulfill it. This conclusion will not do because the moral "ought" is nowhere entailed by either of the premises. If the conclusion went no further than "man has a telos," it would be a sound one because it followed logically from the premises. This article will not dispute the logic of syllogistic deduction. It will proceed, however, on the view that there is more to ethics than can be captured in this deductive format. Instead of empirical, or self-evident, premises from which certain conclusions follow, Leopold, as interpreted by this article, advances arguments to support the following claims: Objects of nature, including man, have a telos or purpose, and that purpose is to develop fully one's natural potential. This development (or fulfillment or flourishing) is best advanced in communities. These communities will exhibit a structure that fosters an overriding, collective purpose. The effort to achieve this purpose places the citizens of these communities in a dynamically cooperative/adversarial relationship with other communities. Things with a telos, therefore, share a common bond, a common striving. The conscious or unconscious sense of kinship or citizenship that emerges from a recognition of this bond is the basis, then, for the environmental ethic that is contended for in this article. For an interesting example of a teleological approach yielding a biocentric ethic, see Paul W. Taylor, "The Ethics of Respect for Nature," *Environmental Ethics* 3 (1981): 197–218.

5. Des Jardins, *Environmental Ethics*, 199.

6. In a few lines, one writer captures the basis for this paradigm shift (perception), speculates on its origin (rebirth of a sense of wonder), and supports it with a theory of virtue rather than one of rights and duties. "When perception is sufficiently changed, respectful types of conduct seem 'natural,' and one does not have to belabor them in the language of rights and duties.

Here, finally, we reach the point of 'paradigm change.' What brings it about is not exhortation, threat, or logic, but a rebirth of the sense of wonder that in ancient times gave rise to philosophers but is now more often found among field naturalists" (John Rodman, "Four Forms of Ecological Consciousness Reconsidered: Ecological Sensibility," in *Ethics and the Environment*, ed. D. Scherer and T. Attig [Englewood Cliffs, NJ: Prentice-Hall, Inc., 1983], 88–92).

7. Aristotle, *Nicomachean Ethics* 1094a1–3, 1094b13–14, 1098a26–30.

8. This phrasing of the issue already invites charges of an anthropocentric bias that either is ungrounded or at least must be argued for in the context of ethical theory in general.

9. Charles Darwin, *On the Origin of the Species* (New York: Modern Library, 1936).

10. An Aristotelian account bases ethics in a fusion of human reason and emotion. Unlike many classical approaches it does not dismiss or discount the importance of emotion in the rational process. On this account, an emotion captures both a belief and a judgment. If a belief is judged to have been violated, then it would be quite rational for that person to become emotional, e.g., angry that an injustice had been committed. Aristotle's concept of "the good," however, is the good for mankind. The faculty of reason, which distinguishes mankind from all other living species, is the criterion for entry into the Aristotelian moral community. In this account, nonhumans are valuable only instrumentally, i.e., they are valued only as resources for the well-being of the human community rather than intrinsically or in themselves. A revised Aristotelian account, however, an account roughly parallel to the Darwinian view but without basing ethics on human feeling or sentiment, might (1) expand the concept of "the good" to include all natural systems (and members of those system) with a telos or (2) sanction plural or parallel concepts of "the good" for nonrational natural systems and their members. See, e.g., Christopher D. Stone, *Earth and Other Ethics* (New York: Harper and Row, Inc., 1987). In either case, the survival interests of nonhuman natural systems would have to be "respected"; the "integrity, stability, and beauty" of these systems could not be eclipsed or extinguished except for more compelling, overriding interests.

11. Leopold, "The Land Ethic," 203–4.

12. Leopold, "The Land Ethic," 204.

13. Immanuel Kant, *Groundwork of the Metaphysic of Morals*, trans. Paton (New York: Harper and Row, Inc., 1956). A thoughtful rendering of Kant's imperfect duties, duties such as benevolence or (in an environmental setting) duties that go beyond minimum protections, is supportive of, though not identical with, the analysis above. In Kantian terms, such imperfect duties are duties of virtue, that is, duties that are meritorious but not required. Mark Sagoff, *The Economy of the Earth* (Cambridge: Cambridge University Press, 1988), 218–19.

14. John Locke, *Of Civil Government: Second Treatise* (Chicago: Regnery, 1955).

15. Owls have value in themselves, as do all things with a telos, including human beings. Beyond that, however, human beings have a self-consciousness or awareness of themselves and their surroundings. Presumably, neither owls nor other living things have this self-consciousness. This evolution in consciousness would support the claim of human beings to recognition within the biotic community as the member or citizen displaying the greatest degree of "integrity, stability, and beauty."

16. Leopold, "The Land Ethic," 233.

17. Leopold, "The Land Ethic," 224–25.

18. This interpretation of Leopold is attributed to Rodman, "Four Forms of Ecological Consciousness Reconsidered." In a reading that seems consistent with W. D. Ross's *The Right and the Good* (Oxford: Clarendon Press, 1950), it could be argued that there is a prima facie duty to foster the well-being of the biotic community unless that duty clashes with one toward a community of greater "integrity, stability, and beauty."

19. Leopold, "The Land Ethic," 209.

20. Eugene C. Hargrove, *Foundations of Environmental Ethics* (Englewood Cliffs, NJ: Prentice-Hall, Inc., 1989), 21–33.

21. Aristotle's notion of the "good" was modeled upon an idealized Athenian city-state—a materially prosperous, aristocratically governed city with just laws and with a subordinate role for women, disdain for non-Athenians, and slavery status for conquered peoples and for "natural" slaves. This is not likely to strike many people today as an appropriate model. While concepts of the "good" are various and tend toward abstractions, they commonly advance a world community characterized by peace and good order, material prosperity and brotherhood, respect for human dignity, and an equal opportunity for everyone to develop to the fullest of one's potential. In a way that is in keeping with this expanded notion of the good and with "The Land Ethic," this essay argues that Leopold would extend these components of the good to include respect for the "integrity, stability, and beauty" of the biotic community or respect for all things with a telos.

22. To render this view in the language of another writer, the compatibility of land and other virtues could be characterized as some version of moral pluralism rather than moral monism. Christopher Stone, "Moral Pluralism and the Course of Environmental Ethics," *Environmental Ethics* 10 (1988): 139–54. The "land virtues" (in a sense, "new kids on the block") would supplement the social or interpersonal virtues, not replace them. "The biosocial development of morality does not grow in extent like an expanding balloon, leaving no trace of its previous boundaries, so much as like the circumference of a tree. Each emergent, and larger, social unit is layered over the more primitive, and intimate, ones" (J. B. Callicott, "The Conceptual Foundations of the Land Ethic," in *Companion to a Sand County Almanac* [Madison: University of Wisconsin Press, 1987], 208, crediting Richard and Val Routley for the tree ring analogy). See also J. D. Heffernan, "The Land Ethic: A Critical Appraisal," *Environmental Ethics* 4 (1982): 235–47, for the notion that "the land ethic" supplements rather than displaces traditional social and interpersonal ethics.

23. A "proper humility" is one such virtue, by which the author means "that sort and degree of humility that is a morally desirable character trait. How precisely to define this is, of course, a controversial matter; but the point for present purposes is just to set aside obsequiousness, false modesty, underestimation of one's abilities, and the like" (Thomas E. Hill Jr., "Ideals of Human Excellence and Preserving Natural Environments," *Environmental Ethics* 5 [1983]: 219 n. 12). Another scholar proposes "openness" as an environmental virtue explicating "humility." "In a positive sense, openness is an environmental virtue that establishes an awareness of oneself as part of the natural environment, as one natural thing among many others" (Geoffrey B. Frasz, "Environmental Virtue Ethics: A New Direction for Environmental Ethics," *Environmental Ethics* 15 [1993]: 274).

24. Holmes Rolston III, no enthusiast of virtue ethics, may nevertheless be in phase with this source of value. "Excellence of human character does indeed result from a concern for [an endangered species in the desert Southwest that has no utility to humans], but if this excellence of character really comes from appreciating otherness, then why not value that otherness in wild nature first? Let the human virtue come tributary to that" (Holmes Rolston III, "Fishes in the Desert: Paradox and Responsibility," in *Battle against Extinction: Native Fish Management in the American West*, ed. W. L. Minckley and James E. Deacon [Tucson: University of Arizona Press, 1991], 99–100). Clarity regarding what is valued, and for what reason, is indispensable in the development of virtue, which, after all, must foster some sense of value or of the good. In a similar vein, Rolston writes, "If the excellence of character really comes from appreciating *otherness*, then why not attach *value* to this otherness? Why praise only the virtue of the beholder?" (*Environmental Ethics* [Philadelphia: Temple University Press, 1988], 118). One need not take issue with Rolston's point to observe (and he may agree) that virtue ethics

is only secondarily concerned with assigning praise or blame and that such judgments are a result of identifying the good to be promoted. Virtue ethics is more concerned with cultivating an excellent, prize-worthy character; it is about the attitudes and stable propensities of moral agents. Rather than to "tar" virtue ethics with the brush of Aristotle's humanist ontology, and to dismiss the insights it might provide, it might be well to call to mind that philosophers of contractarian, rights-, and duty-based traditions can be taken to be environmentalists only by inventive, even imaginative, interpretations. Beyond that, there is nothing in virtue ethics that precludes the position that the "good" consists in part of something like "integrity, stability, and beauty" of the natural world "for its own sake," as suggested above. If, in Rolston's view, an adequate environmental ethic must locate intrinsic value in the natural world, then virtue ethics is capable of meeting that concern, as discussed above. Finally, though, the issue of intrinsic value might even be seen as something of a "red herring," and this is particularly true if one adheres to a strict ontology of value. This is a notoriously difficult and divisive issue. After all, on what basis do we assign value? Is there a hierarchy of values? How do we adjudicate between competing values? Virtue ethics has the potential of avoiding some of these pitfalls, though perhaps not all of them, by refusing to draw a calculus of values, rights, and duties.

25. Of course, this same criterion can also be used to justify selective culling of wildlife populations through sport hunting. We must remember though that such actions would only be considered "virtuous" if they are proposed and carried out in such a way that is consistent with a fundamental and deep moral concern for the well-being of the whole of the biotic community. Many will undoubtedly be uncomfortable with the "conservationist" coloring of this result, however.

26. Heffernan, "The Land Ethic."

27. As Norman Myers, for example, has cogently pointed out, such considerations ought to remind us that problems of threatened species and disappearing forests can be realistically viewed only within a framework of relationships between the developed world and the developing world (*The Sinking Ark* [Oxford: Pergamon Press, 1979]). We can no longer afford to ignore global sociopolitical issues when dealing with issues in environmental ethics. This is not to claim, however, that rules are never appropriate or "affordable." It would be difficult to imagine an ethical system so complete in itself that it could not find strength in roughly parallel concepts of a contending system. Eugene C. Hargrove, "The Role of Rules in Ethical Decision Making," *Inquiry* 28 (1985): 3–42.

28. Among the many perplexing and unanswered questions are the following: (1) On these criteria, can it be persuasively maintained that nonhuman survival interests should take precedence (ever or under certain circumstances) over survival interests of humans? (2) Can important nonsurvival interests of humans displace the survival interests of other biotic communities?

CHAPTER 7

Virtue Ethics and Repugnant Conclusions

David Schmidtz and Matt Zwolinski

In a now-classic article, Thomas Hill showed how traditional deontological and teleo-logical theories can fail to track our moral intuitions regarding environmental issues. When Hill's neighbor cut down a beautiful avocado tree, Hill was indignant but paused to wonder whether he had any theoretical justification for his indignation. The problem was not that trees have rights or that Hill's neighbor had no right to cut down the tree. Hill's neighbor was depriving others of enjoyment of the tree, but although this was consistent with Hill's indignation, it did not really account for it.

Ultimately, Hill concluded, the core question was not what was wrong with the act but, rather, what was wrong with the person. "What sort of person," Hill asked, "would do a thing like that?" Hill's answer was that an admirable person would not do it. A person would have to be quite insensitive and lacking in humility. Interestingly, the humility about which Hill was talking is recognizably an ecological humility. It is what Aldo Leopold meant when he spoke of our need to acknowledge and ultimately cherish our proper status as citizens (not conquerors) of the biotic community.[1]

Like Hill, many of us who are disturbed by the callous treatment of our natural environment would feel uncomfortable arguing that trees, brooks, or sand dollars have a *right* to be left alone. Also like Hill, though, neither is our discomfort grounded in a calculation of aggregate utility.[2] The problem is that both deontological and teleolog-ical theories locate the source of our discomfort in the wrong sorts of considerations. As a result, they tend to give us false guidance in a variety of situations. One particu-larly notorious example is Derek Parfit's "Repugnant Conclusion." Our goal is to ex-plore a connection between the arguments of Parfit and Hill. Parfit conceived his re-pugnant conclusion as a problem for one version of a utilitarian value theory, but in this chapter, we generalize Parfit's argument. We suggest, first, that all utilitarian theo-ries of value face analogous problems and, second, that we cannot solve the problem (although we might be able to obscure it) by adopting a different kind of *act-centered* theory. Ultimately, repugnant conclusions suggest (we do not claim that they entail) problems for the whole idea that moral theorizing should culminate in a simple for-mula for right action. We need a different sort of theory. We need not merely a better formula but a better objective, as is hinted at in Hill's environmental virtue theory.

The Repugnant Conclusion

Standard versions of the principle of utility say something like this: An act is right if and only if it maximizes happiness. What does it mean to maximize happiness? First, the principle is referring to an aggregate: that is, the sum of everyone's happiness.[3] Second, the principle on its face is quantitative, referring to the kind of thing that can be maximized. Third, the quantity is most naturally thought of as a total sum, as opposed to an average. As Parfit notes, however, there is a problem with this seemingly innocuous third point.

Suppose we are deciding whether to have one or two children and have no reason to doubt that the two children would each be about as happy as the one. If the two children would each be as happy as the one, then we conclude that there is more total utility—indeed, about twice as much—in having two children than in having one.

On its face, we seem to have utilitarian grounds for having two children rather than one. However, as Parfit points out, when we endorse the principle that the right act maximizes *total* happiness, we commit ourselves to the repugnant conclusion that "for any population of at least ten billion people, all with a very high quality of life, there must be some much larger imaginable population whose existence, if other things are equal, would be better, even though its members have lives that are barely worth living."[4] Here is how Parfit reaches that conclusion. Figure 7.1 illustrates three possible populations. The width of the blocks represents the number of people living; the height represents their average quality of life. In population *A*, people's lives are, on average, well worth living. Population *B* differs from population *A* only in that, in addition to the population of *A*, it contains an added group. These people's lives are worth living too, though less so than the lives of the persons in population *A*. Let us stipulate that their existence does not affect the persons in population *A* at all—members of population *A* do not even know of this new group's existence. The question, then, is this: Do we make a situation *worse* by moving from *A* to *B*—that is, by the mere addition of persons whose lives are worth living?

It is hard to imagine condemning such an addition. By hypothesis, no one's rights are violated, total utility is higher, and each new person is happy to be there.[5] At very least, *B* seems *no worse* than *A*. How does *B* compare with *C*? In *C*, the better-off group from *B* has been made worse off. But their loss is smaller than the gain achieved by the worse-off group, so overall utility has risen. The resulting distribution is superior on egalitarian grounds as well. On various grounds, then, *C* is at least as good as *B*.[6]

The problem, of course, arises in the repetition of this sequence, as illustrated in Figure 7.2. For if the move from *A* to *C* is justified, then why not the move from *C* to *D* and so on, all the way to *Z*? In other words, if a state of affairs is made better (or at least, not worse) than another by doubling the population while decreasing average utility by less than 50 percent, why not continue until we are left with an *enormous* number of people whose lives are, on average, only *barely* worth living?[7]

This is the repugnant conclusion. To people seeing this puzzle for the first time, the conclusion that *Z* is morally desirable, or even that it is no worse than *A*, sounds absurd. How could a society be superior to another simply by virtue of being so much larger, when average members are so much worse off that *one more* traffic jam,

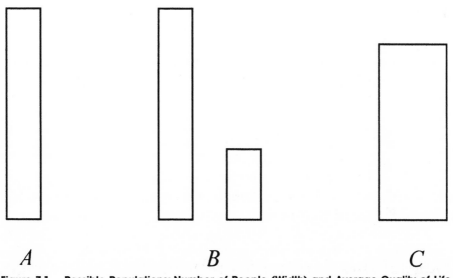

Figure 7.1.   Possible Populations: Number of People (Width) and Average Quality of Life (Height)

stubbed toe, or malfunctioning toilet will drive them to conclude that life is no longer worth living?

Generalizing: A Problem for Utilitarianism

Here is an easy response. Total utilitarianism works well enough in a world of fixed population, but in a world where population size is one of our choice variables, we need a more sophisticated metric. In this more complex world, the intuitive attraction of utilitarianism is better captured by *average* utilitarianism: the theory that an act is right if and only if it maximizes average utility. As Parfit was aware, though, average utilitarianism has its own version of the problem.

The "Other Repugnant Conclusion" is that for any population of people with a quality of life more or less like ours, say, we can imagine a smaller population (in the limit, a single, godlike Utility Monster) that is on average so much happier that it would

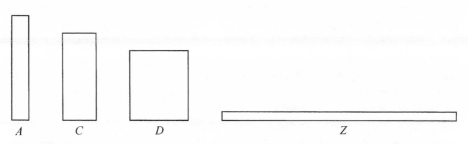

Figure 7.2.   The Repugnant Conclusion: Number of People (Width) and Average Quality of Life (Height)

be better if our population were replaced by that smaller one. Some environmentalists will not find this repugnant, but this is because they have other reasons to oppose over-population. To them, there are things in the world that matter more, maybe a lot more, than the happiness of persons. In other words, they are not utilitarians. To utilitarians, though, the *other* repugnant conclusion is almost as big a problem as the original.

To summarize, the problem in its general form is that we have two kinds of me-chanical measures of aggregate happiness: total and average. In practice it may be mas-sively difficult, indeed impossible, truly to arrive at any such measure. But the prob-lem suggested by our repugnant conclusions goes deeper: that is, we would not be able to trust a *number* even if it were easy to obtain and even if its accuracy were indu-bitable. The fact would remain that neither version of a utilitarian number—that is, neither total nor average happiness—reliably tracks intuitions that lead us to find util-itarianism plausible in the first place.

Generalizing Further: A Problem for All Act-Centered Theories

The problem, as we see it, is more than a problem for utilitarianism. It is a problem for all *act-centered* theories: that is, moral theories that take as their primary task the specification of action-guiding rules. From an act-centered perspective, it is difficult to explain *why* the repugnant conclusion is repugnant. We have already seen that utili-tarian theories, which base their evaluation of actions on their tendency to produce de-sirable states of affairs, are left with little means of stopping once they accept the de-sirability of the initial moves from A to B and B to C.

Deontological theories might appear to be in better shape. After all, they do not base their evaluations of an act's morality on its tendency to produce a certain state of affairs, so they can reject the move from A to B even if they judge B to be a better state of affairs. But it is an awkward response for a theory to bite the bullet and say (as the hardest forms of deontology say) that consequences should play *no* role in our evalua-tions of states of affairs. And this is all that is needed to get repugnant conclusions off the ground. For if C is superior to A on *some* morally relevant grounds, then the bur-den of proof is on the deontologist to show that there are countervailing moral con-siderations that override the moral case for moving from A to C. And this seems un-likely. Who is being treated as a mere means in the course of moving from A to C? Where in the chain is the step that cannot be universalized? For that matter, what is wrong with Z from a deontological perspective? Whose rights are being violated? More profoundly, whose rights are violated by the bare admission that Z is a better state of affairs? A theory might try to save face by insisting that the move from A to Z is for some reason impermissible, but quibbling about the propriety of the move would be too little too late. If a theory admits that Z is better, then it has already embarrassed it-self, regardless of whether it prohibits *moving* to Z.

Deontological theories are more apt for considering how to treat currently exist-ing people than for considering whether it would be good for an additional population to come into existence. Which is to say, deontological theories are less apt for a world where moral problems increasingly are taking on ecological dimensions.

Somehow, the initial utilitarian rationale for the move from *A* to *C* is spurious. Our conclusion ought to be that there is no reason at all for moving from *A* to *C*. In some way, a total utilitarian has the wrong idea, not about whether consequences are relevant but about the way in which consequences are relevant. An average utilitarian at best does only a little better. We may hope for some escape from the problem once we factor in environmental considerations, but it is built into the problem that life in the larger population is, after all, worth living. So whatever loss of environmental amenities people face, average people nevertheless are eking out lives worth living, even if only barely.

An anthropocentric deontology likewise would seem not to solve the problem, as there is no particular reason to suppose that members of this larger population are failing to treat each other as ends in themselves. A deontology expanded to embrace animal rights merely treats one symptom of a larger problem because the problem goes beyond our treatment of other sentient creatures to the wanton destruction of trees and such. The larger concern is not animal rights; it is more fundamentally an ecological concern, perhaps with aesthetic overtones.

Is There Another Way of Doing Moral Theory?

There would seem to be a more direct way of going to the heart of the problem, but it would involve giving up on standard act-centered moral theories. The heart of the task is at least in part a task of defining ideals of human excellence—defining a conception of the good life for a person that makes sense as an ideal, with no presumption that the ideal must be adopted as a goal to be promoted. We have other ways of responding to ideals; simply respecting them comes to mind, an attitude perhaps more in keeping with the intuitions that motivate deontology. Part of an ideal of human excellence could, in turn, incorporate forms of environmental sensitivity. Again, though, there is no assumption that environmental sensitivity must translate into an activist agenda—simply appreciating the beauty of nature is among the more admirable ways of being sensitive to it.[8]

Thomas Hill suggests that our discomfort with environmental exploitation is not wholly a product of our belief that environmental goods are being put to inefficient use or that those who exploit such goods are violating any rights in doing so. It is a mistake, he thinks, to suppose that "all moral questions are exclusively concerned with whether *acts* are right or wrong, and that this, in turn, is determined entirely by how the acts impinge on the rights and interests of those directly affected."[9] Instead, Hill suggests, we ought to ask, "What sort of *person* would destroy the natural environment?" Approaching the issue from this perspective allows us to see that "even if there is no convincing way to show that the destructive acts are wrong (independently of human and animal use and enjoyment), we may find that the willingness to indulge in them reflects the absence of human traits that we admire and regard as morally important."[10] People who carve their initials in 100-year-old saguaros might not be violating any rights, and the satisfaction they get might well outweigh the suffering caused to other sentient beings, but the fact remains that there is some defect in such people's characters. In Hill's language, they lack a kind of humility—an ability to appreciate their place in the natural order or to "see things as important apart from themselves and the limited groups they associate with."[11]

Hill's approach offers a natural, straight-to-the-point way of thinking about what Richard Routley called the "Last Man Argument."[12] Routley's thought experiment presents you with a situation something like this: You are the last human being. You shall soon die. When you are gone, the only life remaining will be plants, microbes, and invertebrates. For some reason, the following thought runs through your head: "Before I die, it sure would be nice to destroy the last remaining redwood. Just for fun." What, if anything, would be *wrong* with destroying that redwood? Destroying it will not hurt anyone, so what is the problem? The problem is, What kind of person would destroy that last redwood? What kind of person would enjoy such wanton destruction of such a beautiful, majestic, living thing? Hill's question seems like exactly the right question.[13]

Hill's approach also offers a way of dealing with repugnant conclusions. For even if we cannot provide a definitive account of the wrongness of preferring a society Z of the sort described in the repugnant conclusion, there remains *something* wrong with being the kind of person who would prefer Z. That something could be hard to articulate, but it is no less real for that. In any case, Hill does provide some pertinent articulation. The sort of person who would prefer Z is the sort of person who does not possess the humility that would lead a more virtuous person to see value in human society playing an appropriately limited role in the biotic community, for nonanthropocentric as well as anthropocentric reasons.

It is difficult to make accurate judgments of character without setting the context in some detail. And it is difficult to imagine a context in which a person's expressed preference for Z is worthy of being taken seriously enough to merit a moral evaluation. In the next section, we will attempt to describe a situation in which it makes sense to speak of a person "choosing" to move from A to Z. For now, though, suppose that someone you know were offered the option of snapping their fingers and thereby popping into existence a population either like A or like Z in some far-off and (otherwise) causally isolated universe. Presumably, as no other values are at stake, a disposition to choose population Z in such circumstances is simply part of what it *means* to believe that Z is a superior state of affairs to A.

Given this fact, then, what are we to say about the character of a person who prefers Z to A? Bear in mind that Z is, in the end, a fairly miserable place. People's lives are, it is true, still worth living—but only barely so. Think of how much misery a person can endure while still believing that life is worth living. Now think of a whole world—a very *crowded* world—filled with such people. What kind of person would bring *that* kind of universe into existence when one could just as easily have produced a universe with a smaller number of very happy people? What would be the point? Intuitively, there is *no* point, contra total utilitarianism.

The most natural explanation for such a disposition seems to be a sort of obsession. It is normal to think that the happiness of particular other people is important.

It is normal to generalize from this and think that happiness itself is important. It is *maniacal* to think that this abstraction translates into a reason to prefer, over *A*, the concrete misery of world *Z*. Like cases of obsession in general, what seems to have gone wrong here is an extreme inability to grasp the larger context. In this respect, it is not unlike a person who originally pursues cleanliness for the sake of health (and health for the sake of a long, enjoyable life) but ends up cleaning compulsively. Cleaning becomes the only thing that individual thinks about, preventing him or her from leading an enjoyable life and thus undermining the very value that led the person to pursue cleanliness to begin with. There is something wrong in being a person who would think of maximizing a happiness number, as if, from an *anthropocentric* perspective, what matters most were *happiness* rather than persons themselves (or something about persons other than their happiness, such as whether they achieve excellence).

Note on Contributing to Overpopulation

In the real world, of course, populations are never the product of any individual's choice. Individuals and families do not choose populations; they choose whether or not to have children. Populations emerge only as a (often unforeseen and unintended) consequence of the combination of many such decisions. The fact that we can raise questions about the character of one who holds a sincere preference for population *Z* might thus seem to have few implications for deciding what to say about people and policies that *actually move us* toward *Z*. Do character-centered ethics have anything to say about these more practical population-related questions?

Insofar as they are not the product of any single individual's choice, undesirable populations can be regarded as an externality along the lines of air pollution. No individual family's decision to limit the number of children it has significantly affects the size or well-being of the overall population, just as no commuter significantly affects the amount of smog in the air by choosing to ride a bicycle to work one day. In either case, however, the aggregate result of many individuals failing to make such decisions is tragic.

If the situation is such that adding large numbers to the existing population will contribute to an unsustainable (or undesirable) population growth, then to raise a large family is to fail to contribute to a sort of public good. In such a situation, achieving a desirable population requires a general policy of restraint on the part of most families, and to have a large family in such a situation is to ride free on the restraint of others. The irresponsibility here need not be calculated—many families simply will not know (and will not bother to find out) the consequences of having more children than they can afford. The point, however, is that where act-centered theories fall short of explaining the indignation we sometimes feel when confronted with free riding that does only minute harm, a character-centered theory provides a rich vocabulary for criticizing those who contribute to repugnant conclusions as shortsighted, irresponsible, weak-willed, selfish, and so on.

Does virtue ethics help to provide a specifically environmental perspective on what is wrong with people who contribute to overpopulation? First, a utilitarian can say that an act has bad environmental consequences, which counts for something. Second, a deontologist can say that an act that has sufficiently bad environmental consequences will as a result be nonuniversalizable and may also fail to treat other would-be users of the same environmental amenities as ends in themselves. Third, a virtue theorist can say that an actor is a bad person *qua* member of the biotic community, which is something else. A virtue theorist can acknowledge that the third conclusion is true partly because the first one is but can go on to say that there is more to being a good person than to act in a way that has good consequences. A good person is considerate and therefore *cares* about consequences. A good person is humble, in the sense of seeing oneself as a locus of value in a world where there are many loci of value, and it is not only humans who can be worthy of appreciation.

Intuition and Theory

One false ideal for moral theory is the idea that the right theory will be simple in the sense of being able to substitute for the wisdom of experience. Part of the point of the repugnant conclusion is that wise persons realize that the intuitions leading them to find utilitarianism plausible are not in fact captured by any simple formula.

It is not as if theory is a radical alternative to intuition. A theory is an attempt to capture our intuitions with a simple formula. How could we expect to do that without losing some of morality's intuitive nuance? Of course theories will have counterexamples! It is in our veins as philosophers to continue to test our theories against the intuitions we intend to articulate with our theories, and of course those articulations will be an imperfect match.

Theories try to systematize our intuitions, but that is like trying to launch a ballistic missile in a direction such that its simple trajectory will track the more complex trajectory of a guided missile. Counterexamples take the form of showing where the ballistic missile deviates from the guided missile's more convoluted path. This is not to express skepticism about the whole project of moral theorizing, so much as about the more particular assumption that act-centered moral theorizing is the way to go. Act-centered theories are one way of trying to articulate. There is no reason to assume that they are the best way. Nothing like that is guaranteed. What is more or less guaranteed—we see no counterexamples on the horizon!—is that act-centered theories will provide imperfect guidance.

We are not presenting this as a knockdown argument against act-centered theory. Our conclusion is that act-centered theory has a certain kind of value, not that it has no value. Virtue ethics reminds us that providing us with a decision procedure covering all possible situations is not the main purpose of moral theories (if it is even a purpose at all). The people for whom moral theories are intended are people already in the midst of living their lives. They come to philosophy hoping that it can help them reflect on their lives. A moral theory is successful if it provides that assistance and unsuccessful if it does not. Cases like the repugnant conclusion show us that an act-centered theory is not useful as a universal decision procedure. The proper lesson is not that act-centered theories are useless, though, but, rather, that we are better off treating act-centered theory as the sort of thing from which wise persons can gain insight that is useful, even if limited.

Summary

There are times, as Hill says, when the question is not what is wrong with the act but what kind of person would do it. The "Repugnant Conclusion" seems to show that there are cases where the moral problem, even from an act utilitarian perspective, is not straightforwardly a problem of how to maximize total utility. The "Other Repugnant Conclusion" seems to show that average utilitarianism does not solve the problem; therefore, even by its own lights, act utilitarianism, the simplest, most mechanical of all moral decision procedures, is not reliable as a mechanical procedure even in principle. Moral decisions require wisdom, not mere computational power, and there is no simple recipe for wisdom.

It is mere appearance, and misleading appearance, that act-centered theories are better than agent-centered ones at converting moral decision making from art into science. Prevailing act-centered theories incorporate theories of value that specify some of the considerations to which a wise moral agent will be sensitive. That is their contribution to moral wisdom. It is a significant contribution, but they have not done better than that and probably never will.

Human rights matter, as do animal rights, whenever they are at stake. Interests matter, when they are at stake. Treating persons as ends in themselves matters, when persons and their ends are at stake. Perhaps universalizability matters in some independent way, but if it matters in some independent way, it probably matters in virtue of what it says about an agent's character. The idea is that to act in a way that you could will to be universal law arguably is the essence of acting with integrity. That is, when we do that, we are acting from motives that we would not hesitate to make transparent, for all the world to see. If Kant was right, then acting in accordance with what one could will to be universal law is the essence of goodwill, which (although goodwill is a notoriously technical notion in Kantian scholarship) appears to be a state of character. A virtue theory might not agree with Kant that goodwill is the only thing good in itself but might readily agree that goodwill is basic and that unless one gets one's character in order, the other good things in life become ashes.

Finally, talk of rights, interests, and treating persons as ends seems especially apt when we are talking about how to treat persons, or perhaps other sentient beings, and that is what we were talking about in the previous paragraph. But what if the issue concerns a person's relation to an insentient creature such as a redwood or to the biotic community as such? Intuitively, Hill's question is *the* question.[14]

Notes

Acknowledgments. Dave Schmidtz (schmidtz@u.arizona.edu) thanks the Liberty Fund, all his colleagues and students at the University of Arizona, and our fellow campers at the 2003

Four-Corners Environmental Ethics Summit for their unwavering encouragement and support. Matt Zwolinski (mzwolinski@sandiego.edu) thanks the Earhart Foundation for research support and Julia Annas, Todd Stewart, and Jennifer Baker for wonderful discussions on these topics.

1. Aldo Leopold, *A Sand County Almanac* (Oxford: Oxford University Press, 1981).

2. For a wonderful presentation of this insight and its significance for contemporary environmental ethics, see Bryan G. Norton, *Toward Unity among Environmentalists* (New York: Oxford University Press, 1991).

3. It must seem obvious that we will have trouble contriving a number that reliably represents aggregate happiness, but utilitarians have little choice but to insist that it can be done. We accept the assumption for argument's sake.

4. Derek Parfit, *Reasons and Persons* (Oxford: Clarendon Press, 1984), 388.

5. The average utility of the entire population has, of course, decreased. But the average utility of the original group remains unchanged, and there are reasons to think that this should be the relevant consideration. If we judged the morality of an action based on the average utility of the population that exists *ex post*, rather than *ex ante*, then average utility would seem to condone (secretly) killing off anybody who was less happy than average. Surely this is not the way to make the world a happier place.

6. This is not to deny that there are impermissible ways of moving from *B* to *C* or even that a state of affairs that would otherwise be desirable can be rendered condemnable by being brought about in an impermissible way. So long as we assume that this is *not* the case, *C* looks preferable to *B*.

7. What does it mean to say that a life is only barely worth living? On its face, this description is compatible with a life being pretty miserable. This, at any rate, is the interpretation we operate with for the purposes of this chapter. On reflection, though, the judgment that a life is worth living might be one to which it is difficult to assign any concrete interpretation in the absence of a particular perspective. A person who is *already living that life* might be more disposed to sincerely believe that his or her life is worth living than a person who is observing the world from the outside, deciding whether or not it would be worth it to live that life (rather than remain in his or her current state of oblivion). Perhaps there are psychological forces that impel the persons living their lives to convince themselves that they are worthwhile. Or perhaps the fact that they are situated in a particular point in time is relevant (costs in the past are sunk, and there is always hope for the future). Are these reasons to discount the preference expressed by actual individuals? What is the alternative?

8. Freya Mathews, in "Letting the World Grow Old: An Ethos of Countermodernity" (in *Environmental Ethics: What Really Matters, What Really Works*, ed. David Schmidtz and Elizabeth Willott [New York: Oxford University Press, 2002]), argues that militant environmentalists make the same mistake as everyone else who seek to conquer the biotic community: failing to embrace a truly ecological ethos of "letting it be."

9. Thomas E. Hill Jr., "Ideals of Human Excellence and Preserving Natural Environments," *Environmental Ethics* 5 (1983): 190.

10. Hill, "Ideals of Human Excellence and Preserving Natural Environments," 192.

11. Hill, "Ideals of Human Excellence and Preserving Natural Environments," 216.

12. Richard Routley, "Is There a Need for a New, an Environmental, Ethic?" *Proceedings of the XVth World Congress of Philosophy* 1 (1973): 205–10.

13. This paragraph borrows from Elizabeth Willott and David Schmidtz, "Why Environmental Ethics?" in *Environmental Ethics: What Really Matters, What Really Works*, ed. David Schmidtz and Elizabeth Willott (New York: Oxford University Press, 2002).

14. David Schmidtz, in "Are All Species Equal?" (*Journal of Applied Philosophy* 15 [1998]: 57–67), argues that we can respect nature without being species egalitarians. Indeed, the view that potatoes and chimpanzees have equal moral standing is incompatible with genuine respect for nature. Genuine respect acknowledges what living things have in common but also acknowledges differences.

PART 3

ENVIRONMENTAL VIRTUES AND VICES

CHAPTER 8

Benevolence as an Environmental Virtue

Geoffrey Frasz

In 1988 the most prominent story in Alaska was not the attempt to open the Arctic National Wildlife Reserve to oil drilling, or the problems salmon fisheries faced, or the general economic downturn in Alaska but, rather, the attempts to rescue three gray whales trapped in the ice near Barrow, Alaska.[1] The episode demonstrated the way important traits of character can be extended from the world of interhuman relations to the nonhuman realm. That so many people with such seemingly diverse environmental views could be motivated to contribute time, money, and effort by a sense of benevolence, a concern for the suffering and possible death of three whales, indicates a need to explore the nature of benevolence as a central environmental virtue.

In this chapter I will present a general account of benevolence and then show how this virtue can be understood as an environmental virtue. After addressing some possible objections I develop an account of the environmental vices that hinder the development and expression of benevolence. I conclude with a discussion of why such a virtue should be cultivated by environmentally minded persons. I recognize that providing a full account of benevolence (a project that I reserve for a later time) will involve a detailed discussion of the specific environmental virtues (such as the environmental versions of compassion, friendship, kindness, and gratitude) that fall under the general category of environmental benevolence. Nonetheless, the discussion of environmental benevolence presented here will provide both an account of the common features such virtues will have and an account of why we ought to cultivate them.[2]

The Possibility of Benevolence as an Environmental Virtue

Writers on ecotheology have often acknowledged the role of benevolence in shaping environmentally desirable attitudes.[3] Donald Hughes, for instance, has argued that the influence of St. Francis plays an important, positive role in shaping Christian attitudes toward nature.[4] In addition to recognizing the goodness of all of God's creation, including the animals, St. Francis held that the fact of biodiversity in creation and the delight God takes in this diversity represent God's benevolent presence. From this Hughes argues that we have a duty not just to abstain from harming God's creations but also to adopt an attitude of respect for them.

Also writing on issues of Christianity and the environment, Holmes Rolston III points out that biblically based faith is founded on the belief that the covenanted Promised Land is sacred and good, separate from any instrumental value it might have for humans.[5] But the intrinsic goodness of the created world notwithstanding, Rolston worries that a Christian ethic that advocates virtuous treatment of humans may not easily be expanded into virtuous treatment of the nonhuman world and its inhabitants. He argues, however, that central tenets of Christian faith, including the promise of redemption, can be found in an ecological understanding of the land.

Although these accounts suggest that it is possible to cultivate a benevolent relationship with nature, they leave undeveloped the actual nature of benevolence as an environmental virtue, as well as the justification for why we would want to cultivate it. More helpful is Jennifer Welchman's account in which she argues that benevolence and loyalty are necessary features of good stewardship for the land.[6] One could, she argues, voluntarily act as a good steward for the land even if motivated by an enlightened anthropocentrism. Acts motivated by enlightened self-interest can include preservation of resources, biodiversity, and natural beauty. After all, benevolence toward our own descendents is a strong motivator for action. But what about motivation for the well-being of nonhuman others? Welchman argues that compassion alone is not enough to provide such a motivation. She concludes that benevolence, in the form of compassion for sentient beings, must be coupled with loyalty, in the sense of loyalty to one's moral integrity, in order to complete the necessary virtues of stewardship of nature. Unfortunately for the project at hand, she focuses all her attention on providing a well-developed case for this loyalty to one's moral integrity, leaving the notion of environmental benevolence underdeveloped.

Still more helpful to our project is the work of Frank Schalow, who takes the position that, from a Heideggerian perspective, the differences rather than the similarities between humans and animals provide an obligation for us to act in benevolent ways toward animals.[7] Schalow argues against those who take an egalitarian view based on recognized similarities between humans and animals and instead stresses two distinctive features of human life—freedom and language—to develop a notion of obligation to the welfare of animals. It is, he argues, these differences between humans and animals that make possible benevolent actions by humans toward animals. Providing support for Welchman's call for stewardship for the nonhuman world, Schalow argues for a nonanthropocentric perspective that emphasizes that "the abilities that distinguish us most from other creatures are precisely those with which we are endowed (rather than possess), and hence their exercise extends beyond the satisfaction of exclusively human interests."[8] Freedom is here viewed as a gift that allows for the possibility to simply let animals be instead of treating them as mere property for the satisfaction of human interests, and our capacity to use language makes it possible for humans to speak for animals, who cannot articulate directly what is in their own interests.

Schalow gives further support to Welchman's call for stewardship when he claims that "we are most fully human or 'authentic' when engaged in acts of stewardship rather than in exploitive pursuits. In becoming guardians, we display the 'care' (*Sorge*) that situates us within nature as a whole and fosters the possibility of a harmonious relation to those domestic animals dependent on us."[9] Such care is possible also regarding wild creatures because of our capacity to use language to disclose what is there, what is outside of us. Through my use of language to provide a word to a thing, I indicate it as something other than the "me" who does the naming. And through the process of acquiring, rather than simply using, language it is possible for us to "acquire it in harmony with an 'attunement' (*Stimmung*) that disposes [humans] to foster the manifestness of things, nature, and welfare of their animal counterparts."[10] By recognizing the significance of the difference between humans and animals it is possible to develop what I have elsewhere called a "proper humility" toward animals and the natural world. With such humility we can then truly speak for those who might suffer because of our actions.

Welchman and Schalow make the case for benevolent treatment of nonhuman entities as a necessary attitude for good stewards of the land. But they have not spelled out in detail what the characteristics of a benevolent steward are; nor have they shown why we should be such good stewards and cultivate this virtue. In what follows I first present an account of benevolence in interpersonal contexts and then expand the notion to include human–nature relationships, thereby showing how benevolence can be considered an *environmental* virtue. We will find that what is generally the case for interpersonal benevolence can be extended to the human–natural world relationship. An account of the vices associated with the absence of green benevolence is then presented. I finish by making the case that an environmental form of benevolence is needed for a person to be environmentally good and that the cultivation of benevolence makes it possible to live an environmentally good life.

The Virtue of Benevolence as Such

Benevolence as such is a genus or family of virtues that involve a direct concern for the happiness and well-being of others.[11] Virtues of benevolence include compassion, friendliness, kindness, and generosity. Feelings of affection need not be present for there to be benevolence, though the two traits are often found together.

The related vices of benevolence include jealousy, selfishness, greed, and profligacy, for these are traits that compete with the tendencies to promote the good of others. A lack of concern for the welfare of others can be expressed in hateful emotions or in grasping and self-centered behaviors that ignore or turn a blind eye to their welfare. What we find objectionable in such cases is that one's own good is sought without a concern or care for how one's actions may impact others. A greedy, selfish, or profligate person is one who is willing to expend irreplaceable resources to further one's own good without any real concern for how one's actions might impact the ability of others to further their own good. A jealous person may go so far as to hope for others to fail in their attempts to promote their own good because one believes that their success would frustrate one's own goals. Thus, the jealous person is not merely envious of the flourishing of others but, in fact, often actively seeks to harm the other or to keep the other from flourishing.[12]

Benevolence virtues are not forms of conscientiousness (which involves a commitment to social action), but the same action may be done out of sense of benevolence and conscientiousness. Someone who takes an active role in civic life, giving generously of her or his time and energy to help needy members of the community, may be motivated out of a sense of concern for the needy and out of a sense that such help makes for better communities.

The benevolent person does not merely seek to avoid wrong actions but, rather, seeks to promote the good of others. It is not enough to refrain from being jealous, or greedy, or self-indulgent, admirable as such restraint may be. What the virtuous person seeks is to be open to the concerns, interests, goals, and needs of others and to actively pursue plans that would help others in these respects. Benevolence therefore calls on us first to cultivate in our character an imaginative dwelling on the condition of the other. It involves discovering what the other, given his or her character, beliefs, and values, needs in order to flourish. Acting on this concern, in turn, improves the life of the benevolent person him- or herself directly, through the satisfaction of acting morally, and indirectly, through helping to create a better society for all.

In order to truly determine what is in the best interest of the other, one needs to gather information about the life and concerns of the other. This may involve something as simple as asking the other person what makes him or her happy or being open and sensitive to how persons' actions reveal what they seek in order to live flourishing lives. It also includes gathering insights provided by the human and social sciences regarding what is good for people and the communities of which they are a part. Because of a shared humanity, I can reason analogously from knowledge of my own self and what I need generally to be healthy, be productive, and flourish as a human being to what others may need (bearing in mind the dangers of confusing what is in my personal self-interest with what is in that of others).

Benevolence further involves a motivation to act on the knowledge of the other gained through this imaginative indwelling. This benevolent motivation to act may be expressed in different ways, reflecting the different virtues within the benevolent family of virtues, as well as the particular circumstances of the agent. A friendly person acts in ways that reflect the desire to do what will make the friend happy. Actions motivated by friendship can include gift giving, spending time with a friend (even if one would rather be elsewhere), or simply listening to what the friend wishes to say. Acts motivated by friendship may even involve not doing or not permitting something that the friend wants because we recognize that it would not truly promote the welfare of the other (friends don't let friends drive drunk, as the saying goes). A generous person is willing to give of her or his time, effort, money, and material goods to promote the welfare of others. A kind person is quick to see how one could help another and is prone to act in kind ways. A compassionate person is motivated by the suffering of others and acts in ways to relieve that suffering.

We judge the actions done from these different manifestations of benevolence as good actions. Their goodness comes from the attempt to move beyond acts of immediate self-interest to acts for the interests of others. This is why we consider benevolent persons to be praiseworthy and celebrate their actions. We hold that benevolent acts are good because they tend to foster good feelings based on mutual goodwill. This is a useful and satisfying result for a community. Such a concern is often recognized by other community members (though such a recognition is not necessary for benevolence to occur), and it gives rise to goodwill on their part. A community in which benevolence is a character trait in many of its members is more likely to be a place where the community itself and community members can flourish.

Benevolent virtues tend to support the self-esteem of those who are beneficiaries of the action, for they acknowledge that the other person is valuable and important, so much so that one is willing to expend resources promoting the other's flourishing. Such benevolent actions promote a sense of equality in the community by exemplifying that the flourishing of others and the community as a whole is just as important as one's own pursuits. The relationships based on virtues such as friendship and kindness are more satisfying relationships, ones that bring delight to one's own life as well as to one's friend's.

When others recognize that someone else is genuinely interested in their welfare and wishes to help promote it, sources of hostility and confrontation are less likely to provoke destructive or harmful reactions. Confrontations can be better avoided when community members are aware that others are not acting solely out of selfish or self-promoting concerns. When those shared concerns are recognized, it is more likely that community members can find common goals and solutions to community problems that are acceptable to all.

From these general reflections on benevolence we can indicate the central features of a benevolent act:

1. The agent engages in an imaginative reconstruction of the life of the other.
2. The agent attempts to determine what is in the best interest of the other.
3. The agent is motivated to act with the best interest of the other in mind.

The different species of benevolence—friendship, compassion, kindness, and so on—will reflect these characteristics in different ways and to different degrees and have as their focus different kinds of relations.

Actions that are fully characteristic of benevolence foster mutual goodwill, create satisfying relationships, forestall antagonism, and create an atmosphere where people can work out differences and achieve common personal and community goals. I will now show how considering benevolence as an *environmental virtue* enriches and expands our understanding of this family of virtues and provides insights into what characterizes an environmentally good person.

Benevolence as an Environmental Virtue and Its Corresponding Vices

If benevolence is an environmental virtue, then an environmentally good person has an active and consistent concern for the happiness, flourishing, health, interests, or well-being of both human and nonhuman others. An environmentally good person takes an active interest in promoting the flourishing of all the other members that make up the land. This expansion of the sphere of concern to nonhuman others makes up the first characteristic of environmental benevolence.

Through their actions many people already show a concern for individual living beings such as pets and household plants. Such a concern is praiseworthy, as are the efforts of people to rescue abandoned pets or feral cats and dogs and provide shelter to them. We recognize in the generous, compassionate actions of such people a genuine benevolent concern for the well-being of all such animals. But the expansion of the sphere of "others" must move beyond domesticated animals and cultivated plants: the fully environmentally benevolent person is concerned for nondomesticated life as well.

The expansion of the sphere of concern must include members of wild species—and not just individual members of those species that we find charismatic, fascinating, or enough like humans to evoke empathy. Benevolence of action must extend to all living creatures, even those we might find disturbing, distasteful, or uninteresting to us and our own concerns. It is one thing to act in benevolent ways to preserve those members of species that have high value to us, such as bald eagles or grizzly bears, but it is much harder to show concern for stinging flies, poisonous plants, and biting reptiles.

However, the expansion of concern should not be solely individualistic. What characterizes an environmentally benevolent person is also an active concern for whole species and particular places, biogeographic zones, ecosystems, and watersheds.[13] We are apt to praise sustained efforts on the part of individuals to preserve and protect an entire area. What makes their actions virtuous in part is a concern for the entire land, not just a concern for individual living things that make up that land. We see this concern reflected in support for wilderness areas and also for natural parks, forests, and grasslands.

As environmental benevolence has such an expanded sense of the other, the range of actions that may be done by the environmentally virtuous person will be varied and extensive. What can make the extension of concern to nonhuman others more likely is the realization that the flourishing of one's self and that of others occurs in, and is made possible by, an extended environmental community. This, in turn, requires the recognition that the notion of community must be expanded to include nonhuman entities, both living and nonliving. This expansion of community to include "the land" in Leopold's sense means that we must broaden our moral horizon to the point that we recognize that there are other citizens in our community besides present and future humans and that the interests of these citizens are also proper objects of our concern. Furthermore, this community requires an extensive abiotic structure to make the flourishing of all its citizens possible. Thus, an environmentally benevolent life involves "an excellence or relationships among the parts of the self and with the outside world."[14] In this way a flourishing land also provides the conditions for a flourishing human life.

I have argued elsewhere that the project of environmental virtue ethics in general has as its ontological basis human nature as flourishing in an expanded, mixed community of biotic and abiotic features.[15] The development of the environmental virtue of benevolence is a trait that makes such flourishing possible and provides for a bond of kinship with the land. An excellent human being is also an excellent environmental citizen, living an environmentally good life that maintains fidelity with the natural world and rejects human chauvinism and notions of human superiority.[16] The cultivation of environmental benevolence, along with the cultivation of what I have called a "proper humility," and the rejection of arrogance are part of the makeup of an environmentally good citizen of the land.[17] The flourishing as an ecological citizen that benevolence makes possible is good not only for the person but for the land as well.

The task facing an environmentally virtuous person is how to determine what is in the best interest of nonhuman others. This involves a further expansion of the capacity of imaginative dwelling on the condition of the other. We want to imaginatively enter into the life of the other, to see how the other lives, understand what the goals of this nonhuman other are. Because we cannot use spoken language to communicate with most animals and ask them what they need to live a good life, we must adopt other strategies for accumulating this knowledge. One way is to simply watch them over time as their life activities reveal to us goal-driven activities that reflect their needs. This can be done through sustained nature watching and observation of animals in their wild habitats. It can also be done indirectly through active study of accounts of animal behaviors. Thus, there is an important role for the biological and ecological sciences, for nature writing, and for personal accounts of encounters with wild creatures to help us better learn what is in their own best interests and what they need to live healthy, flourishing lives. In order to better learn this it will be necessary to cultivate those intellectual skills that improve our perceptive ability, as well as the moral traits to improve our willingness to expend the time and effort to let natural entities reveal themselves to us. We must cultivate what Linda Zagzebski calls "a sensitivity to detail" that involves refining our abilities to make fine distinctions among related kinds of natural entities and to develop and use a vocabulary that lets us express these distinctions.[18]

Coupled with this sensitivity are the hardy traits of character that are required for sustained involvement in the natural world on its own terms. Philip Cafaro points out that virtues such as persistence, patience, thoroughness, and continuous attentiveness (even when it involves personal discomfort on our part) make it more likely that a person will be able to learn what nature can teach.[19] Also needed are moral qualities such as openness to the other and humility in the face of limited or continually developing understanding of the diverse features of the natural world. We must cultivate an openness that heightens our sensitivity to the concerns, behaviors, subtle features, and goal-directed activities of nonhuman entities. Openness will prime us to what can be revealed. Humility will keep us open to novelty and new experiences as we recognize that we can continually learn from the wild, that we do not have all the answers, and that our skills for learning from nature may require further refinement or polishing.

Of course, as common members of a biotic community we all have basic needs that must be met in order that the goods of our own kind can be realized. All living things must have a healthy environment, free of pollutants, toxins, and other biohazards, in order to flourish. I recognize that what is necessary for me as a living thing may be what other living things need as well. What an environmentally benevolent person must strive to avoid is a confusion over what is specifically in one's interests as a human being and what is in one's interest as a living being, a member of the biotic community.

But whatever the mechanisms are, we look to an environmentally benevolent person as having enough concern for the well-being of others to use whatever means necessary to discover what it takes for that other to flourish—and act on this knowledge.

How do we identify an environmentally benevolent person? First, we look to see that there is a movement toward action. Does this person act consistently in ways that promote the well-being of other members of the biotic community as well as his or her own? We need to see actions of various kinds done over a period of time. It is not enough to act sporadically, spurred into action by a guilty conscience, moved periodically by magazine ads for help to save the whales or contribute to rain forest protection. Although such acts are good, virtue requires that these actions be done on a regular basis as a reflection of a key ingredient of a person's character. One swallow saved does not an environmentally benevolent person make, as Aristotle might have said!

The actual content of benevolent acts will vary from place to place and reflect the context of the action. What is required to promote the well-being of one group of living things may be different from what is needed to promote the health of a particular ecosystem. A compassionate person may work long hours as a volunteer at an animal rescue shelter, feeling the suffering of injured or needy stray animals. A generous person may give time and money to restore a wetlands habitat rather than to promote worthwhile self-interests. A friend of the land might simply spend time in nature, attuning oneself to what the land can teach about the processes and structures that contribute to the health of it and its members. A friend of the land might also tell stories to others, as Thoreau and Leopold did. In each case we judge the action as environmentally benevolent because it flows from a concern to identify what is in the best interest of the nonhuman others and then to consistently act on that knowledge.

Much of my argument for environmental benevolence is based on the movement from the traditional interpersonal notion of benevolence to an environmental version. I have argued that such an extension is possible, but a critic might ask: What is the range of this extension? For example, although compassion may appropriately be extended to any sentient creature, can it also be extended to nonsentient natural entities? If not, then benevolence might be limited to human–sentient creature relations. It might also be objected that because my account of traditional benevolence seems to involve a mutual recognition of what is in the well-being of each person, benevolence cannot be extended beyond those beings that could acknowledge our actions. Finally, it could be pointed out that I call for an imaginative entering into the life of the other, which would limit the scope of environmental benevolence to conscious beings for whom such an exercise might be plausible.[20] These are important and significant concerns that need to be addressed.

The first criticism has to do with whether one can be compassionate toward an entity that lacks sentience. Because compassion involves making a connection with the suffering of others, it is true that one can only be compassionate toward those natural entities that can suffer. But benevolence is not equivalent to compassion. Benevolence involves a family of related virtues, each of which involves a concern with the lives and condition of others. But this concern need not be limited to a condition of suffering. Concern for the well-being of another also includes elements of friendship, kindness, and respect, which can focus on the health, integrity, or overall well-being of an entity that is not sentient. So, for example, one can have a benevolent concern for the well-being of a forest and take action to restore or maintain forest health. Far from sentience being a prerequisite for genuine benevolence, the idea that it is betrays the lack of imagination mentioned earlier. Making sentience a necessary prerequisite for benevolence would be like making consciousness, or being human, or having white skin, or being a member of my local community a necessary prerequisite. What is lacking in such provincial, or racist, or speciesist views is the ability or willingness to take an active interest in the well-being of all others.

The second objection is that nonhuman others may not recognize our benevolent acts. Though it is true that in many interpersonal acts of benevolence there is a mutual recognition of the acts as such, this recognition is not necessary. One can act in a benevolent way to a child, a comatose patient, or even a fetus, none of which need be able to recognize that an action was done for his or her well-being. In the same way, one can act in friendly ways without the other even being aware of the performance of the action. I have argued elsewhere that acts of friendship can be done toward nonhuman natural entities such as the land, and in such cases acknowledgment is not even possible.[21]

The third objection deals with whether one can imaginatively enter into the life of the nonhuman other if that other is not conscious. The imaginative entering that is a part of benevolence involves attempting to find out what would benefit or harm that other. It is not trying just to think like that kind of thing. It is to ask oneself what actions would further or hinder the other's well-being. In the case of a conscious or sentient being, that entering is, perhaps, easier. But in any case benevolence requires me to move out of a self-referential mode (asking to what extent that other is like me, a conscious, sentient being with particular wants, desires, needs, etc.) and use my imaginative powers to see the world either from the perspective of another sentient being who is a center of a life or even as a natural entity that is made up of many biotic and abiotic parts, such as a swamp, forest, or ecosystem. I can meaningfully ask what actions would benefit or harm that kind of entity as well, even though it is not conscious or sentient. For example, I can harm a river or a bog by dumping a terrible poison into it, or damming it, or draining all its water for irrigation. Think of how the damming of the Colorado River harmed the riparian communities that required yearly flushing by the naturally occurring floods to replenish nutrients.

Environmental benevolence involves a concern for the well-being of another entity, and depending on the kind of natural entity it is, different aspects of benevolence will be appropriate to it. The environmentally benevolent person acts for the well-being or interests of individual living things, populations of living things, species, and the biotic community itself and avoids confusing self-interest alone with that of the land. I now turn to articulating the attendant vices that correspond to environmental benevolence. Previously, I presented some of the vices of general benevolence as traits that compete with our dispositions to act on behalf of the other. With an environmental focus, these vices reflect habits or traits of character that interfere with an active concern for nonhuman or natural entities. Such environmental vices can be seen as connected in a negative way to the three central features of environmental benevolence.

The first feature is the willingness to engage in an imaginative reconstruction of the lives and condition of nonhuman others. Traits such as human arrogance and chauvinism will cause us to view the condition of nonhuman others only in terms of our own satisfaction of human interests. They are seen only in instrumental terms and judged for their capacity to satisfy one's short-term personal preferences. This attitude is reflected in those who can see only the economic value of some members of a forest and dismiss as useless or worthless those other species that cannot be immediately harvested. It is reflected in the attempts to turn an old-growth forest rich in biodiversity into a monoculture crop field for trees that have high lumber value. Such a person, when considering an investment of time or money for a worthwhile cause, would ask, "What's in it for me?" A person who does not or cannot see intrinsic value in nature is closed to it and lacks the kind of openness to nature I have claimed is an important trait of an environmentally good person. Echoing the point made earlier by Schalow, such a person cannot hear what animals or the natural world are saying. Furthermore, it is not uncommon to find indifference to humans and nonhumans together in environmentally destructive acts. For example, mining operations in a fragile desert area not only despoil the land with toxic waste but also often cut and run when they close operations, leaving behind a human community that was dependent on the mine for jobs.

Jealousy and greed are thus environmental vices, for they are emotional attitudes that often lead to the harming of nature in an attempt to attain mastery over it. To greedily exploit a natural resource to the extent that other creatures suffer by one's actions, such as clear-cutting a forest to the point of destroying the habitats of the creatures living there, reflects a desire to only maximize one's own interests. Furthermore, these vices can be reflected in the willingness to turn a blind eye to environmentally destructive actions on the part of others. In southern Nevada, where drought conditions have gotten worse in the last few years, powerful gaming interests are able, through campaign contributions, to get local governments to provide them with exceptions to water use restrictions so that they may construct new hotels with extensive fountains and lagoons, while local residents face fines for washing cars in driveways.

Profligacy in the exploitation of natural resources is also a reflection of arrogance and lack of concern for the well-being of others. Overgrazing or overfishing of areas may produce short-term economic benefits for some, but they harm both the long-term interests of people and the heath of ecosystems. The extensive consumption of petroleum products, especially in automobiles, that puts places such as the Arctic Wildlife Refuge at risk through oil drilling is a reflection of such profligacy. It is difficult to imagine an environmentally benevolent person who drives an SUV around town and lives a high-consumption lifestyle.

The second feature of environmental benevolence involves finding some mechanism that reveals what is in the best interest of nonhuman others. Traits such as laziness and sloth are vices because they keep us from learning what is in the interest of other living things. A person who is unwilling to take the time and make the effort to travel into the nonhuman realm reflects this laziness. A somewhat comic example from recent Las Vegas events illustrates this. A brand new development of expensive homes had been built on the edge of town, not far from a large pig farm that had been in operation for many decades before development had spread toward it. Buyers of the new homes, which had not even been built yet, would travel to the developer's air-conditioned offices, look at photos and scale models of the new homes that were going to be built, and then buy a proposed home. When the new residents would move in later and catch a whiff of the hog farm, they would complain to the city government. But had they taken the time and made the effort to travel around the land, they would have been made aware of the farm. Instead, they were too lazy to examine their future surroundings and relied on salespeople to tell them about the land. Even today many of these same people have no interest in finding out where their clean water comes from and where their sewage goes. Such laziness is often a cause of neglecting to discover where runoff water from the floods (that come with regularity to desert areas) goes. Had they made an effort to investigate, they might have found out that the floodwaters go through their neighborhoods.

Slothfulness is reflected in a lack of interest in knowing or maintaining the well-being of other living things, even in cases as simple as keeping an aquarium clean of parasites or keeping a pet well groomed and healthy. A lack of interest in actively seeking out what information is needed to determine what it takes to keep a pet healthy reflects this vice. Intellectual laziness is also a vice in this context because there exists a tremendous amount of information gathered by naturalists, ecologists, animal lovers, and even pet fanciers on what is needed to promote the flourishing of living things and natural systems. Someone who is too lazy to take the time to learn about the natural world, either through personal experience or by relying on the information available from experts, is not going to be disposed to act in benevolent ways toward it.

Furthermore, because it is necessary to learn various intellectual skills and abilities, along with moral habits, from nature, the tendencies that work against such learning will be environmental vices as well. A lack of curiosity about the natural world, a lack of attentiveness, impatience, and the tendency to rush through encounters in the wild keep us from being able to learn what can be discovered. We see these habits in shallow tourist experiences, where the tour bus pulls up to a scenic area, the visitors step out quickly to take some photographs, they return just as quickly to the air-conditioned bus, and then it is off to the next photo opportunity. When people desire to encounter nature only through the frame of a bus or car window for momentary instances, they lack the necessary openness to experience readily available expert information that would make it possible for them to discover what nonhuman creatures need for their flourishing. Although such tourists may have a belief that they are open to natural beauty, the unwillingness to take the time needed for natural entities to reveal themselves makes them able to gain only a shallow understanding of the wild. Even if such tourists were armed with extensive, authoritative guidebooks and tape recordings that told them what they were seeing, it would be difficult for them to develop a greater sense of benevolence for nature without getting out and away from the bus, for deep encounters with the natural world require making real connections with nature, unmediated by glass, books, or well-intentioned bus guides. People who lack a sense of humility regarding their own ability to understand the natural world or who have an over-inflated sense of their abilities to comprehend what nature can teach us manifest the vices of arrogance and chauvinism that are expressed in phrases like "If you've seen one redwood, you've seen them all" or "This is nothing but an empty, barren desert with nothing of interest or value in it, so let's build a megaresort here."

The third feature of environmental benevolence is the motivation to act on the basis of what one has learned from nature. Thus, those traits and habits that keep us from acting on behalf of the good of nonhuman others are also environmental vices to be avoided. The traits of laziness and sloth mentioned earlier are relevant here, as is cynicism regarding the effectiveness of environmental action. An environmentally benevolent person recognizes that it is not possible to do everything necessary to promote the well-being of every creature. He or she recognizes that environmental protection efforts sometimes fail. Yet he or she is motivated to act nonetheless. The cynicism common in environmental critics leads them to fall into the "perfectionist fallacy." They will argue that attempts to act on behalf of the interest of nonhuman entities will not provide for a complete or total fulfillment of their needs, interests, or good; thus, such attempts should not be made in the first place. But a recognition that one cannot help all things at any given time to flourish does not mean that one should not do what one can reasonably do to help some creatures to flourish. We admire those who are able to bring about even a small improvement in the good of nonhuman entities.

In summary, the environmental vices that we want to avoid are traits or habits that keep us from being open to the nonhuman world and the lives of nonhuman others, unwilling or unable to determine what is in their interests, and unmotivated to promote the well-being of all the entities involved in our encounters with the natural world. In the next section I conclude with an account of why benevolence should be cultivated by anyone seeking to be an environmentally better person.

Why Cultivate Environmental Benevolence?

This question is a variation on the general question facing environmental virtue ethics: Why cultivate environmental virtue at all? It has echoes of one of the fundamental questions of ethics: Why should I be moral? My answer to this question is that a life that reflects this virtue produces a better life for the agent, a life that allows for the agent to flourish in ways that are appropriate to a rich, full, satisfying, environmentally good life.[22] This answer reflects the nature of a life fully characteristic of benevolent virtues as expanded into the biotic community.

A life informed by benevolence will be a life that fosters goodwill between humans and nonhuman creatures. Even when a natural entity cannot recognize the benevolence in environmental actions, the feeling of goodwill that can develop among the people doing the actions is a good. The various players in the Alaskan whale rescue came away from that action with a greater sense of goodwill on the part of others, even if those people had been adversaries on other environmental issues. This mutual goodwill can play an important role in forestalling further antagonisms when these same people square off in other environmental encounters. Each will be more aware that the other has been willing to avoid acting in solely self-interested ways, was willing to try to understand how things are for the others, and was motivated to act in ways that promote common interests.

The relationships that can develop when people display acts of environmental benevolence can be more satisfying ones. When people act in ways that promote the flourishing of both self and others, human and nonhuman alike, the relationships can be based on trust and a recognition of mutual interests. Such relationships are ones that we value already in our lives. Cultivating environmental benevolence makes it possible to have more such relationships, thereby enriching our own lives as well as those of others.

When people attempt to cultivate benevolence, they can resolve differences between their goals and those of the nonhuman world. Furthermore, because these are goals of the expanded biotic community of which both humans and nonhumans are a part, all can live better, richer, fuller, flourishing lives. Instead of seeing nonhuman entities as things to be fought, to be destroyed, or in opposition to our well-being, a sense of environmental benevolence makes it more likely that we can be open to and find common solutions to problems that promote the well-being of all concerned. Cultivation of benevolence makes it more likely that people can live a more harmonious life with the natural world that enriches ourselves and others.[23]

The value of benevolent practices comes from the fact that they allow us to feel the interconnectedness we have with other living things, other species, and ecosystems. These practices allow us to feel joy and happiness when all the members of a biotic community flourish and to feel distress when confronted with the suffering of living beings or with distressed, disturbed ecosystems. Beneficial practices allow us to experience the interrelatedness of all things, living and nonliving. They allow us to realize that we cannot act without affecting other living beings or other natural entities. Such recognition is empowering because we can set an ethical example for others to follow.

Benevolent practices are further desirable because they help define who we are. We can come to understand that in a fundamental sense we do not exist in the world as isolated, atomic individuals who simply act on objects outside of ourselves. Rather, we are relational beings, moral agents who act in specific social, historical, and ecological contexts. These interrelationships make up the core of who we are. To be human is to dwell in relations with the nonhuman environment. Benevolent practices reaffirm our human nature, celebrate it, and strengthen our ties with the other members of the biotic community. In cultivating the environmental virtue of benevolence we can discover who we really are and what it will take to live in a joyous way with the nonhuman world of which we are a part.

Notes

1. Patti H. Clayton, *Connection on the Ice: Environmental Ethics in Theory and Practice* (Philadelphia: Temple University Press, 1998).

2. In this discussion I follow the general characteristics of an environmental virtue as presented in Louke van Wensveen, "Ecosystem Sustainability as a Criterion for Genuine Virtue," *Environmental Ethics* (2001): 227–41.

3. For an example, see Carolyn M. King, "Ecotheology: A Marriage between Secular Ecological Science and Rational, Compassionate Faith," *Ecotheology* 10 (2001): 40–69.

4. Donald J. Hughes, "St. Francis of Assisi and the Diversity of Creation," *Environmental Ethics* 18 (1996): 311–20.

5. Holmes Rolston III, "Environmental Ethics: Some Challenges for Christians," *Annual of the Society of Christian Ethics* (1993): 163–86.

6. Jennifer Welchman, "The Virtues of Stewardship," *Environmental Ethics* 21 (1999): 411–23.

7. Frank Schalow, "Who Speaks for the Animals? Heidegger and the Question of Animal Welfare," *Environmental Ethics* 22 (2000): 259–71. For a consideration of the whale rescue and benevolence from a Heideggerian perspective, see also Clayton, *Connection on the Ice.*

8. Schalow, "Who Speaks for the Animals?" 265.

9. Schalow, "Who Speaks for the Animals?" 265–66.

10. Schalow, "Who Speaks for the Animals?" 268.

11. In this account of benevolence I have drawn extensively on the ideas found in James D. Wallace, *Virtues and Vices* (Ithaca: Cornell University Press, 1986).

12. Literature is full of examples of the hateful person who is envious of the good success or benevolent nature of another, believes him- or herself incapable of doing or being good in such a benevolent manner, and therefore actively seeks the destruction of the other. Herman Melville's story *Billy Budd* provides an excellent example of this pathology.

13. This account of environmental benevolence does not entail a position regarding the individualistic/holistic debate. It merely asserts that concern for nonhuman others, whether individual entities or otherwise, is a necessary part of environmental benevolence.

14. Lisa Newton, *Ethics and Sustainability: Sustainable Development and the Moral Life* (Englewood Cliffs, NJ: Prentice-Hall, 2003), 8.

15. Geoffrey Frasz, "What Is Environmental Virtue Ethics That We Should Be Mindful of It?" *Philosophy in the Contemporary World* 8 (2001): 8.

16. Newton, *Ethics and Sustainability*, 37.

17. Geoffrey Frasz, "Environmental Virtue Ethics: A New Direction for Environmental Ethics," *Environmental Ethics* 16 (1994): 259–74.

18. Linda Zagzebski, *Virtues of the Mind: An Inquiry into the Nature of Virtue and the Ethical Foundations of Knowledge* (Cambridge: Cambridge University Press, 1996), 95.

19. Philip Cafaro, "The Naturalist's Virtues," *Philosophy in the Contemporary World* 8, no. 2 (2001): 88.

20. I am grateful to Ronald Sandler for raising these critical questions in a reading of an earlier draft of this chapter. I am further grateful for all the helpful comments and editorial suggestions he and coeditor Philip Cafaro have made on this essay.

21. Geoffrey B. Frasz, "Can We Love the Land? (And Would We Want To?)," paper presented at the Northwest Conference of Philosophy, November 1997.

22. I recognize that another answer to this question is that we should act altruistically, even though this might not lead to a more satisfying result for the agent. Without developing my point further, I will say that I agree with Aristotle that a virtuous life will result in a more satisfying life, even if checkered with setbacks or defeats from time to time.

23. This point is made quite forcefully by Stephanie Kaza in her essay "Acting with Compassion: Buddhism, Feminism, and the Environmental Crisis," *Ecotheology* 1 (1996): 71–98.

CHAPTER 9

Gluttony, Arrogance, Greed, and Apathy: An Exploration of Environmental Vice

Philip Cafaro

Search on *vice* in the *Philosopher's Index* and not much comes up. Along with a lot of articles with "vice versa" in their abstracts there is one book, which is not about vice but about just political arrangements, and half a dozen articles, none well known, actually dealing with vice or particular vices.[1] Yet there are good reasons to explore vice. Dramatically speaking, vice is more interesting than virtue: think *Inferno* versus *Paradiso*; think Lucifer versus any other character, including God, in *Paradise Lost*. More important, the exploration of moral character has been one of the great steps forward in the "virtue ethics" revival of the past two decades, and considering vice in addition to virtue leads to a more complete treatment of moral character. How human beings fail can tell us much about ourselves. Perhaps nowhere are our failures more apparent than in our treatment of nature.

Public opinion polls repeatedly have shown that most Americans self-identify as "environmentalists" and support strong policies to protect the environment.[2] Yet these same people routinely behave in environmentally irresponsible ways. They plant thirsty bluegrass lawns and pour poisons on them to keep them free of dandelions. They buy gas-guzzling SUVs and drive them four blocks for a loaf of bread. We need to ask why, when it comes to the environment, our actions are so out of sync with our professed values, and we need to ask why in a way that leaves room for both political and personal answers.

To some degree our political, economic, and technological systems present us with environmentally unsustainable choices or strongly incline us in those directions. Our politicians fund highways, not bike paths or mass transit; corporate advertising stimulates environmentally costly desires, rather than encouraging contentment with what we have. Still, as consumers and citizens we usually have real choices, and we often choose the environmentally worse ones. No one forces us to buy big SUVs, build three-car garages, or let our bicycles rust. This chapter argues that we do these things because we are not the people we should be. Our poor environmental behavior stems, in part, from particular character defects or vices. Among the most important of these are gluttony, arrogance, greed, and apathy.[3]

To anticipate one criticism, exploring environmental vice at the individual level does not mean ignoring the larger, systemic causes of environmental degradation. Creating sustainable societies will demand fundamental political change. Citizens across the globe should work for the passage and enforcement of strong antipollution laws, more national parks and wilderness areas, funding for mass transit and taxes on personal cars, and measures to limit human population growth. Above all, we should work to end the power of large corporations to set environmental policy, directly or through their political tools. At the same time, those of us who care about nature have a responsibility to choose wisely in our everyday environmental decisions. The failures of our neighbors, or our leaders, do not absolve us from our personal environmental responsibilities. The world is an unjust place, but we should live justly within it.

Vice Defined

In common usage, a "vice" is a personal habit, a social practice, or an aspect of human character of which we disapprove.[4] We may speak of a person's habitual lying and nose picking as vices, of more or less widely practiced activities such as smoking and gambling as vices, and of character traits such as greed and gluttony as vices. From here on in, when I speak of a vice, I mean it in the sense of a character trait.

In many cases, when people call a character trait a vice, there is nothing more in their minds than a picture of certain behaviors and a swirl of negative emotions. Thinking human beings aspire to something more than this. We believe that our vice judgments can be right or wrong—or at least more or less plausible. We try to correct or improve them. How?

Traditionally, Western philosophers have invoked the concept of *harm* in order to clarify and justify their judgments about vice.[5] A vice harms the vicious person, those around him, or both. So, for example, gluttony may undermine the health of the glutton or predispose him to pay insufficient attention to what is really important in life. Avarice may tempt us to cheat our business partners or neglect the claims of justice and charity. Sloth undermines our ability to pursue valuable projects that give our lives meaning and which benefit society.

Judgments about the vices are thus derivative: they rest on particular conceptions of the "goods" that make up a good human life and on the general presupposition that the flourishing of the individual and society are important.[6] Lists of key vices and specific conceptions of particular vices have changed, as notions of flourishing have changed. Aristotle imagined human flourishing to consist largely in fulfilling the roles of friend, householder, and citizen in a fourth-century Greek polis. His "vices of character" hinder our performance of these roles and cut us off from the benefits they provide.[7] For Thomas Aquinas, human happiness finds completion in knowledge of and right relationship to God, in this world and the next. Hence, he defined the vices partly in terms of them separating human beings from God. Hence "worldliness" became a vice in the medieval tradition in a way that would not have made sense to the Greeks. For Montaigne and increasingly in the modern world, a sense of the preciousness and fragility of the individual self comes to the fore. Thus, cruelty emerges as a major vice (and diversity becomes a societal virtue).[8] Once again as in Greek times, a vice's evil is described not in terms of disobedience to God but in terms of how it undermines the happiness of individuals or their unlucky neighbors.

Throughout the evolution of the Western tradition and despite much variety, four commonalities tend to hold. First, selfishness and self-centeredness are condemned, whereas legitimate self-concern and self-development are praised. For Aristotle, "every virtue causes its possessors to be in a good state and to perform their functions well"; the vices undermine proper human functioning and well-being.[9] For Aquinas, too, the notion of virtue "implies the perfection of a power," whereas vice leads to weakness, failure, and, in extreme cases, a sort of disintegration of the self.[10] Even Kant, despite his caution that love of "the dear self" lies at the root of immorality, also argues that we have a duty to develop our talents and capabilities.[11] Vices hinder this legitimate self-development.

Second, and as a consequence, the tradition insists that vice is both bad for individuals and harmful to their communities. Indeed, individual writers have sometimes gone to extreme lengths here, arguing, for example, that we never benefit ourselves when we wrong others.[12] More sensibly, the tradition has argued that moral shortcuts to happiness in fact *tend* to place us on winding roads toward unhappiness. Sharp dealing in business leads people to distrust us, and hence we do not prosper; avarice helps us amass great wealth at the expense of our fellow citizens, who then hate us or plot our demise. In this way, the tradition often appealed to a broadened self-interest in order to convince people to act morally: our happiness is bound up with the happiness of others. This approach has largely been abandoned by modern moral philosophy, which has focused on direct appeals to altruism.

Third, the tradition sees vice as contradicting and eventually undermining reason, hence destroying our ability to understand our proper place in the world and act morally. Aristotle expresses this in his distinction between incontinence (the tendency to pursue pleasure even when we know it is wrong to do so) and the full-blown vice of intemperance (where the continued pursuit of illicit pleasure has so clouded our judgment that we no longer recognize right from wrong).[13] The vices are habits of thought and action. Left unchecked, they tend to cloud reason, the voice of both conscience and prudence.

Fourth, and partly as a consequence of this diminished rationality, the tradition sees vice as cutting us off from reality or at least from what is most important in life. This is most obvious in the late ancient and medieval periods; for Augustine and Aquinas, sin and vice cut us off from God, the highest reality.[14] But we also see this notion at work in Aristotle, where intemperance leads people to pursue gross physical pleasures at the expense of activities such as science and contemplation that connect us to higher things.[15] We see it in early modern times in Montaigne, where the vice of certainty blocks sustained inquiry into existence, and intolerance blinds us to our common humanity and a true understanding of the human condition.[16]

What holds these four aspects of vice together is that they all involve harm: to ourselves, to those around us, or to both. What constitutes harm, particularly beyond a core of obviousness, has varied widely in the tradition, along with the particular conceptions of human nature and the ultimate commitments held by philosophers. And until recently, philosophers have paid scant attention to human harms to the environment—or to the potential for those harms to rebound and harm us in turn.

Vice and Environmental Harm

Take a look at the arguments for environmental protection in op-ed pieces in the newspapers, in articles in *Sierra* or *Audubon* magazines, or in the classic works of Aldo Leopold or Rachel Carson.[17] Sometimes environmentalists appeal to human altruism. Air pollution from Midwestern power plants is killing trees and acidifying lakes in the Appalachian Mountains; a proposed dam out West will drown a river and perhaps extinguish a rare fish species. This harm to nature is, or would be, wrong, based on nature's intrinsic worth—a worth that may be expressed more in aesthetic or spiritual terms than directly in what philosophers recognize as ethical terms. As we are powerful, these arguments assert, so we should be just and merciful.

At least as often, environmentalists' arguments appeal to human self-interest. We should rein in water and air pollution because they harm human health. We should preserve an undeveloped tract of prairie, an unroaded forest, a wild and undammed river, because opportunities to know and appreciate nature will disappear if we do not do so. Scientists and artists will lose chances to study and appreciate wild nature; hunters, fishermen, and backpackers will lose recreational opportunities. We might be able to live without these activities, but at least some of us would not be able to live well or live the way we want to live.[18]

Both sorts of arguments are ubiquitous in the environmental literature. Both can be effective. One need not preclude the other. The first sort of argument finds direct (or intrinsic) value in nature's flourishing; the second sees human flourishing as dependent on nature's flourishing, which thus has derivative (or instrumental) value. In either case, harms to nature are ethically important. During the past thirty years, most environmental philosophers have focused on making the case for altruism, refining and developing the first sort of argument. Recently some philosophers have focused on refining and justifying the second sort of approach, arguing that we will be better and happier people if we appreciate and protect nature.[19]

The key idea behind such an *environmental virtue ethics* is that we cannot harm nature without harming ourselves. A basic human flourishing depends on a healthy environment (lead exposure can damage children's brains, leading to lower intelligence, mental retardation, and death, at progressively higher levels of exposure). Full human flourishing depends on a varied and stimulating environment, including accessible wild areas that preserve the native flora and fauna (children who grow up without chances to experience wild nature miss opportunities to appreciate beauty, understand human history and prehistory, and reflect on their place in the world). The complementary insight is that human flourishing does *not* depend on high levels of material consumption. In fact, when the acquisition of material possessions leads us to ignore higher pursuits, or when society's overconsumption undermines nature's health and integrity, our own lives suffer.

In her book *Dirty Virtues*, Louke van Wensveen shows that environmentalists often assert that certain vices are at the base of environmentally harmful behavior.[20] A *greedy* factory owner dumps untreated pollutants into a stream, even though she knows that it may harm fish in the stream or people who eat the fish. *Gluttonous* Americans consume too much food, energy, or raw materials; thus, we take more than we need from the Earth. To justify such vice judgments, environmental philosophers must provide convincing accounts of the motivations behind antienvironmental behavior. And they must show harm.

Consider how Aristotle discusses vice. In the *Ethics*, certain persistent and cohesive aspects of human personality are defined as character traits, and certain character traits are judged vices because they harm vicious individuals and those around them. Because for Aristotle a human being can only flourish in a polis and because one's happiness cannot be completely divorced from that of one's family, friends, and descendants, even the vices that seem primarily to harm others have a potentially self-destructive aspect. There are a number of well-worn paths by which other-directed harms may harm a selfish person, including poisoning his relationships with others and undermining the social cohesion on which a functioning polis depends. Ultimately, self-harms and other-directed harms cannot be completely separated.

The way to justify environmentalists' vice talk is similar. We need to show how environmental vices—which may be largely the same as the traditional vices or may include many new ones—harm the vicious person directly. We need to show how they harm those around him and future generations, people about whom he should care (for one thing, the selfish person's happiness is not so easily separated from theirs as he thinks). We must also show that there is another legitimate circle of moral concern, not recognized by Aristotle or the philosophical tradition, pleaded for in Leopold's *Sand County Almanac* and by legions of environmentalists since then: the wider circle of nonhuman nature. Harm within this circle is bad in itself, for it is real harm to entities that can flourish and are wonderful when they do flourish. And such harm rebounds, harming human communities and (sometimes) the individuals inflicting the environmental harms. Aristotle places us in a social environment and defines human flourishing accordingly. The fact that we also live in physical environments shows the need for this more encompassing view of human flourishing and moral concern.[21]

To anticipate another criticism, some philosophers will say that only when we show how vices harm vicious persons themselves have we given the strongest possible argument for their viciousness. Although I do think that showing the connection between vice and self-harm is one benefit of a virtue ethics approach, I see no reason to limit our conception of harm to self-harm. Self-concern and concern for others are both legitimate and necessary within ethics. There is something wrong with a person who brings all of her actions to the test of her own happiness, even when they obviously affect others. Similarly, there is something wrong with ethical philosophies that do so. An environmental virtue ethics may give us good self-interested reasons to rein in our environmental vices; it does not seek to reduce all vice to self-interest.

On the other hand, I see nothing wrong with curbing our vices because we believe that it is in our self-interest to do so. My colleague Holmes Rolston is worried that you will treat nature right for the wrong reasons.[22] I am more worried that you will not treat nature right at all, and I believe that any reason that convinces you to treat nature more gently is a good reason. Furthermore, a better understanding of our self-interest should lead to less materialistic lifestyles and more time exploring nature. Rolston's arguments for nature's intrinsic value deserve to prevail; they are more likely to prevail among people who have had experiences that help them understand and appreciate them.

In the end, as in interpersonal ethics, a complete environmental ethics will have to make a place for both altruism and enlightened self-interest. In truth we are all self-interested, although not exclusively so. In truth, our flourishing and nature's flourishing are intertwined. In what follows, I discuss four key environmental vices: gluttony, arrogance, greed, and apathy.[23] If I can show how these vices lead to harm, that will be all the justification you should need that they are worth reforming (certainly it is all the justification you will ever be able to get). The greater the harm—to oneself, to others, to nature, or to all three—the greater the incentive to reform.

Gluttony

"Gluttony: excess in eating and drinking" says my *American Heritage Dictionary*; the *Oxford English Dictionary* adds that the word may also refer to an excessive *desire* for food and drink and by a natural extension to many kinds of overindulgence (I may be a glutton for punishment, learning, or cheap romance novels). Despite the word's pejorative connotations, we tend to take a relatively benign view of this vice today. Few moralists treat overeating as a serious personal failing, on a par with such qualities as selfishness or cruelty. Earlier thinkers took gluttony more seriously. Aristotle devoted extensive attention to intemperance, defined as the vice regarding the pleasures of touch: primarily food, drink, and sex. Saint Paul inveighed against those "whose God is their belly." Not only was *gula* considered one of the seven deadly sins, but early church thinkers often put it at the head of the list.[24]

Perhaps the classic picture of the glutton is a man at table, stuffing in food with both hands, sauces dribbling down his chins, belly pushing back the table as he occasionally lurches into it. Unconcerned with quality, he is going for quantity. He does not talk to his dinner companions, even to comment on the food. He is all desire; there is something brutal and inhuman about him. Another picture of gluttony involves two women sitting in a fancy restaurant, simpering over the tomato bisque. One compares it with the soup she had at another restaurant three weeks ago; the other describes a version she made from a recipe taken from *Gourmet* magazine. We might call these women epicures rather than gluttons, and many would see nothing wrong with their behavior. Gregory the Great, who helped define the seven deadly sins for the medieval tradition, took a sterner and more encompassing view: "In another manner are distinguished the kinds of gluttony, according to Saint Gregory. The first is, eating before it is time to eat. The second is when a man gets himself too delicate food or drink. The third is when men eat too much, and beyond measure. The fourth is fastidiousness, with great attention paid to the preparation and dressing of food. The fifth is to eat too greedily. These are the five fingers of the Devil's hand wherewith he draws folk into sin."[25] Monkish quibbling? Or a recognition that beyond the health harms of gross gluttony, gourmandizing wastes our time and causes us to pay less attention to what is truly important? It depends on your view of human flourishing and the purpose of life.

Neither of these pictures is particularly appealing, yet our disapproval could be merely aesthetic. To show why gluttony is *morally* wrong, we must discuss the harms it generates. In the case of gluttonous eating, the most obvious harms fall on the glutton himself. Excessive eating leads to obesity, and the health dangers of obesity are well documented in the scientific literature. Of the ten leading causes of death in America, four show positive correlation to being overweight or the diet and activity patterns that lead to being overweight.[26] These include the three leading proximate causes of death—heart disease, cancer, and cerebrovascular disease (stroke)—as well as diabetes mellitus, the seventh leading cause. In addition to direct harms to health, obesity decreases happiness and well-being in less obvious ways that are harder to measure.[27] Overweight people tend to feel more lethargic. Obese individuals participate less often in many enjoyable physical activities, from sports to sex (this is a positive feedback problem: less physical activity leads to less energy, leading to less physical activity, etc.). The surgeon general has concluded that obesity is a major health problem in the United States.[28]

With fine gluttony, the argument that it harms the glutton is less clear. Gourmands may find a lot of pleasure savoring the sauces and comparing the wines. Gregory did not have to worry about whether his monks were enjoying themselves, but for most of us today pleasure is at least part of what we want out of life. Even from a hedonistic perspective, however, we may wonder whether developing a taste for finer things will lead to happiness in the long run. If we are no longer able to enjoy simple meals, or forget Seneca's words that "hunger is the best spice," or pay more attention to how our cooking turned out than to the friends around our table, or eat such rich foods that we get gout, the gourmet life may lead away from happiness. Too, our time is limited. Attention to trivia can lead us to neglect more important things.

So gluttony takes a direct toll on gluttons, but it also has environmental costs. In America, 1,265 species are listed as threatened or endangered under the Endangered Species Act: 519 animals and 746 plants.[29] The causes of extinction are complex, but scientists generally agree that habitat loss is primary. A comprehensive study has found habitat degradation/loss implicated as a cause for 85 percent of threatened and endangered species in the United States.[30] Crucially, in analyzing the causes of habitat loss, the study identifies agriculture (principally row cropping) as the leader, affecting fully 38 percent of all endangered species. Livestock grazing is also important, affecting 22 percent. In addition, agriculture is an important contributor to several other major causes of endangerment, including water developments such as reservoirs and dams (affecting 30 percent of species) and pollutants (20 percent).[31]

Now just as food consumption drives agricultural production, so food *over*consumption fuels a more environmentally harmful and intensive agriculture. A recent, comprehensive study by the U.S. Department of Agriculture's Economic Research Unit estimated that in 2000, Americans consumed an average of 2,800 calories per day, 25 percent more than the 2,200 calories needed to supply their nutritional and energy needs.[32] This translates directly into increased agricultural demand. All else being equal, Americans' habit of consuming approximately 25 percent more calories than necessary increases the amount of land needed to grow crops and graze animals by 25 percent. It increases the amount of pollutants dumped onto agricultural lands and running off into rivers and streams by 25 percent.[33] Excess food consumption harms Americans' health; if we take *ecosystem* health to include clean rivers and streams and robust populations of our native flora and fauna, we must conclude that excess food consumption also harms environmental health.

Because ecosystem health and human health are connected, a complete account of the harms of gluttony must extend further. Unhealthy ecosystems lead to direct human harms, for example, when people sicken from the air or water pollution generated by huge livestock confinement facilities. Ecosystem sickness also leads to intellectual and spiritual losses, as a dull and lifeless agricultural landscape becomes a bore to live and work in. Even if this landscape remains productive of agricultural products, it may no longer be productive of happy and healthy human beings.[34] In Illinois only one-ten thousandth of the original 37 million acres of tall-grass prairie remains: 3,500 acres occurring in small, isolated conservation areas.[35] Living in a monotonous sea of corn and soybeans has probably taken a toll on the minds of Illinois farmers.

Gluttony reminds us that the vices, although often selfish, harm both ourselves and others. Food overconsumption harms our health and lowers life expectancy, but it also harms nature. These harms to nature rebound, in turn, and cause new kinds of harm to human and nonhuman beings. So that in the end, it becomes difficult to separate harms to self and harms to others, harms to people and harms to nature. Our flourishing is tied up with the flourishing of others.

On the other hand, the example of gluttony reminds us that the calculus of harms does not always come out as neatly as moralists want it to. For the past thirty years, books like Frances Moore Lappé's *Diet for a Small Planet* have argued that overeating in the wealthy nations leads to Third World hunger.[36] The argument has developed momentum by virtue of endless repetition, but empirical studies show that the connection does not hold. Work by Amartya Sen and others suggests instead that political and economic factors within Third World countries are most important in causing famines and malnutrition: particularly civil war, indifferent governments, and terrible poverty.[37] This does not mean that rich, fat Americans should not do more to help the world's poor; it means that eating less food is unlikely to help feed them. However, eating less *will* lessen our agricultural footprint, helping all those other species that compete with us for habitat and resources. Gluttony's other-directed harms fall primarily on nonhuman others.

Again, the moralist may want to say that gluttony, like all vices, inevitably harms the glutton herself. But gluttony shows us that we may refine our vices, so as to direct more of their harm—perhaps *all* of their harm—toward others. I may dine out three times a week in spectacular restaurants, eating and drinking my way through my children's inheritance—without neglecting to hit the gym the next day, thus staying quite healthy. I may cook spectacular meals for myself and my friends, thoroughly enjoy both, and maximize my own pleasure—while greatly increasing my environmental harms. On average, it takes one cup of oil to grow, harvest, store, ship, and sell each cup of food (dry weight) consumed by Americans. Fine gluttony greatly increases this aspect of our agricultural footprint, as "the market" flies fish from New Zealand to Denver or strawberries from Chile to New York in January. This causes *us* no harm; furthermore, we may still get out and enjoy nature, perhaps even flying to New

Zealand or Chile to hike and ski. Still, a more comprehensive and accurate account of harm will teach us that we should limit our agricultural footprint and accommodate ourselves more to locally available foods. All important, unnecessary harm is wrong. Although it is possible to live a life in which we largely externalize the costs of our gluttony, we should not do so.

Virtue ethicists emphasize the childishness of gluttony. Aristotle believed that there is something crude and undeveloped in a person who seeks all happiness in the simplest ways.[38] "The gross feeder is a man in the larva state," wrote Henry Thoreau, "and there are whole nations in that condition, nations without fancy or imagination, whose vast abdomens betray them."[39] Similarly, virtue ethicists assert that self-development and lasting satisfaction come not through gluttony but through pursuing more adult pleasures and activities. "When someone lacks understanding," wrote Aristotle, "his desire for the pleasant is insatiable and seeks indiscriminate satisfaction."[40] In contrast, the pleasures of love and friendship, aesthetic appreciation and the pursuit of knowledge, will not pale or lead us to behave unjustly.

Traditionally, the virtue opposed to gluttony was *temperance* or moderate use. We may also speak of *gratitude* as a complementary virtue. Consider an American Thanksgiving. Originally it was a day set aside to thank the Lord for physical and spiritual sustenance, with roots in Indian green corn ceremonies with similar motivations. Now Thanksgiving is often just another excuse for Americans to pig out. The next day, we go shopping. I do not think that the answer to this is to fast on Thanksgiving but, rather, to give thanks, thoughtfully and sincerely. With gratitude will come understanding and acceptance of our environmental responsibilities.

Arrogance

With no other virtue/vice complex have Western attitudes varied so much as with pride, humility, and arrogance. The Sermon on the Mount exhorts us to live lives of meekness and humility. For Christians pride is a vice, because human beings are infinitely inferior to God and essentially equal to one another. We often go wrong in our social dealings precisely through a desire to assert our superiority over others. Contrarily, the ancient pagans tended to view pride as a necessary part of a good life. Because self-knowledge and striving to live well helped define the good life, if one lived well, one knew it and commended oneself for it. Humility was at best a just judgment of one's own mediocrity and at worst a failure to understand true human excellence and whether one had achieved it.[41]

We are heirs to this complex heritage. On the one hand, we condemn those who lord it over others. We dislike braggarts and prefer heroes who credit others for their successes or who downplay them. On the other hand, we scoff at obsequious people. We encourage our children to take pride in their schoolwork and other efforts and are proud of their achievements.

If we look to the harm criterion, I believe we will make a place for a proper pride as a virtue, with obsequiousness as one vice and arrogance as another. As Kant, our greatest exponent of egalitarian morality, puts it, we have no right to disrespect humanity in our own person; nor should we encourage others to do so through excessive meekness. Furthermore, part of our legitimate motivation for treating others morally is a sense that we exalt our own humanity in the process.[42] Still, arrogance—an overvaluation of ourselves and an undervaluation of others—remains a vice. The human harms that arrogance leads to are obvious, as we selfishly place our own interests far ahead of other people's.

Environmentalists and environmental philosophers see a similar arrogance in much of our treatment of nature. "Christian as well as non-Christian ecowriters warn against the prideful attitude that makes us humans think we are number one in the universe," Louke van Wensveen writes, "that we are . . . 'central and in control'." She notes that "the Latin term for pride, *superbia*, translates the Greek *huperbios*, which means 'above life'," and "the Latin term *humilitas* literally suggests closeness to 'humus', i.e., 'soil' or 'ground'."[43] An early attempt to articulate a better environmental ethics was titled "the arrogance of humanism."[44] Today philosophers speak of the arrogance of "anthropocentrism," the vain and selfish view that human beings alone are worthy of respect, whereas everything else in the world, including several million other species of life, only has value if it is useful to humans.

Arrogant indifference to nature and arrogant indifference to people often go together. For four decades, Chevron and Shell have been drilling for oil in the Niger Delta, making billions of dollars for their companies, their shareholders, and Nigeria's successive military and civilian dictators. Little of this wealth has made its way into the hands of the delta's inhabitants, who have had to bear the brunt of the environmental harms of oil drilling. These have included poisoned water and diminished fisheries, leading to sickness and hunger for many inhabitants. Efforts to protect the environment and other local interests have been brutally suppressed. Ken Saro-Wiwa and eight other leaders of the Ogoni people were executed following a show trial in 1995. Since then other activists have been jailed and tortured, as documented in a 200-page report from Human Rights Watch.[45]

In May 1998, more than 100 activists from the Ilaje people occupied a Chevron drilling platform and service barge in an effort to force the company's management to negotiate with them. Activists' demands included clean drinking water, electricity, environmental reparations for nearby villages, and rebuilding of eroding riverbanks. With work on the barge stopped, Chevron was losing money. After four days and while the activists believed they were still in negotiations, Chevron flew in members of the Nigerian military, who opened fire on the unarmed occupiers, shooting two of them dead. The rest were taken off to prison and tortured.[46]

The Nigerian armed forces were brought in on Chevron contractors' helicopters and given bonus pay by the contractor; the decision to bring them in was made by Chevron management. Nigeria's armed forces and police are notorious for human rights abuses. By bringing in the military and sending the activists off to jail, oil company managers knew what they were buying.

Bola Oyinbo, one of eleven protesters arrested, reported being handcuffed and hung from a ceiling hook for five hours, in an effort to extract a confession of piracy and destruction of property. The radio program *Democracy Now* asked Bill Spencer, a Chevron contractor in charge of servicing the barge, what he thought of the torture endured by Oyinbo and others:

Spencer: I don't think anybody here was under the impression that when you go to jail in Nigeria, it's pleasant.

Q: Was there concern about the young people who were held in detention. Was there any follow up?

A: By me? Not at all. No.

Q: Were you concerned about them in detention?

A: I was more concerned about 200 people who work for me. I could care less about the people from the village, quite frankly.

Q: Once your people were safe . . .

A: Did I personally have any concern for them, not one little bit. No.

The arrogance here is blatant. With this view of the Niger Delta's inhabitants, it is hard to imagine Spencer or the other oil men working there having much concern for the delta's fisheries or wildlife. Indeed, coming to Nigeria seems to provide them with a well-paid moral holiday. As Spencer puts it: "I'm not leading a moral campaign. We're just here to work. Strictly commercial venture. Not a political one."

But Chevron's and Shell's activities have enormous political consequences. Oil provides the government with 80 percent of its revenues. That money helped prop up military dictatorships for more than thirty years. The oil companies got what they wanted: zero accountability for the environmental and human harms caused by their activities, hence maximum profits. Only the Nigerian people suffered. Here is Bill Spencer again, on that subject:

> *Democracy Now:*   Do you have any reservation about working with those forces [Nigerian armed forces and police] knowing or acknowledging they can in fact be ruthless?
>
> *Spencer:*   No, I don't know. Life is tough here. And people, you often hear it said, that life is cheap here. I guess it is. It's looked at a little differently. I think that that's something that doesn't happen in our society. Life is a little more maybe precious or something. I think here or any of these developing countries it tends to be a little cheaper.

It is fascinating to see how arrogance can dim a man's sense of moral responsibility. This is how it *is* here, Spencer says, as if he and the oil companies are not helping to create the conditions in Nigeria from which they profit. But read the words of the activists describing what they hope to achieve: clean water, secure food, education for their children, and some say in how they are governed and how their environment is managed. *They* seem to think that their lives and the lives of their children are precious. Now we can begin to understand why Chevron managers prefer to send in the armed forces to kill these people and crush their spirit, rather than meet with them. If they heard them speak and looked them in the eyes, they would be forced to see them as human beings. That might get in the way of maximizing profits.

Examples of corporate arrogance are legion; arrogant environmental destruction by individuals is just as common. A good example in the United States is off-road vehicle

(ORV) use. Over the past three decades, ORVs have created major, well-documented harms to our public lands.[47] Four-wheelers have carved tens of thousands of miles of illegal roads onto our national forests, degrading wildlife habitat and causing erosion. Snowmobiles in Yellowstone National Park stampede wildlife and cause such serious air pollution that entrance guards have been forced to wear respirators. Jet skis dump up to one-quarter of their oil and gas directly into lakes and rivers, polluting them. While they trash nature, ORV users ruin the experience of other recreationists—who happen to be the vast majority of visitors to national parks and national forests.

The arrogance of many ORV users is palpable. Magazines such as *Petersen's 4-Wheel & Off-Road* or *4-Wheel Drive and Sport Utility Magazine* are filled with macho posturing. "Bud Vandermel chose to display some attitude coupled with Chevy prowess when building his '78 Scottsdale off-roader," begins a typical article: "Wanting to run with the big trucks, or wanting them to follow, Bud's off-road machine needed to be tall, and it needed to display dominance. To get the altitude, Bud installed 8-inch Skyjacker Softride leaf springs."[48] When Bud revs up his truck and heads into the backcountry, crashing through small trees and leaving tire tracks in the streams are part of the experience. At a minimum, ORVers do not care about their effects on the places they are tearing up. For some of them, harming nature is part of the fun.

These arrogant practices showcase important aspects of the vices. First, they tend to make us *selfish*. The ORV magazines rarely mention the obvious environmental harms ORVs cause or how annoying they are to other public lands users. In an extensive review, the few mentions I found of environmental harms all focused on the "environmental extremists" or "eco-wackos" complaining about them. Second, as Aristotle emphasizes, the vices *corrupt our reasoning abilities*.[49] In eight years teaching environmental ethics, I have read term papers on most major environmental issues, and some of the most illogical, rhetorically overblown, and willfully confused ones have been discussions of the ethics of ORV use by ORV enthusiasts. Third, vices come from and lead to *crude views of the good life* and make it hard to appreciate better ones. In discussing the experience of off-roading the emphasis is on fun, excitement, "the adrenaline rush." That is what people want—and it has nothing to do with understanding or appreciating nature. Indeed, it makes it harder for ORVers or anyone else to do so.

Vice cuts us off from reality, according to Thomas Aquinas. The arrogance of anthropocentrism cuts people off from the reality of nature. ORV users arrogantly destroy the wild nature that others want to appreciate and whiz through it so fast that they learn nothing about it themselves. In the Niger Delta, Chevron and Shell are arrogantly displacing traditional ways of life based on small-scale agriculture and sustainable fishing. Anthropocentrism as an intellectual outlook also cuts us off from reality, as we ignore nature's stories and tell truncated and false stories about ourselves.[50]

In the pursuit of virtue, *practices and laws* are crucial. ORV use is a good example of a practice that encourages anthropocentrism. If we want to live environmentally responsible lives, we will have to cultivate practices that lock in habits and ways of looking at the world that are nonanthropocentric. As Aristotle says, we learn to act morally by instilling proper habits, not by arguments. Activities such as bird-watching, trout fishing, wildlife photography, and backcountry camping instruct us in nature's diversity and beauty each time we engage in them. They teach us nature's stories, sharpening our senses and quieting our minds enough to appreciate them.[51] We should encourage our children in these practices—and we should keep them from engaging in what might seem like harmless fun on ORVs.[52]

For the irredeemably arrogant, of course, we need laws. Current efforts in the United States to replace strong environmental laws with voluntary environmental protection must be exposed and defeated. And as Peter Singer has recently argued, we must create an international legal order in which Chevron, Shell, and other corporations are held accountable for encouraging human rights abuses and propping up tyrannical regimes that abuse their own people.[53] Similarly, we must develop strong, binding international agreements to halt global warming, preserve endangered species and ecosystems, and reverse human population growth. Nothing less than this will succeed in preserving the flourishing natural world that an environmental virtue ethics insists is the prerequisite for human flourishing.

We cannot be good people without appreciating and developing those aspects of our humanity that distinguish us from the rest of nature: our abstract reason, our complex culture. Yet exalting our humanity does not mean focusing exclusively on these differences or setting ourselves up as tyrants over the rest of creation. Rather, the more we preserve and appreciate nature's beauty, the more we will flourish ourselves. The greater our moral restraint, the more a proper human pride will be justified.[54]

Greed

Greed is "an excessive desire to acquire or possess more than what one needs or deserves, especially with respect to material wealth."[55] It is natural to enjoy material possessions; it is necessary, in modern society, to deal with money. But the desire for wealth may prove excessive for several reasons. It may leave us perpetually unsatisfied; as one philosopher puts it, greed is "an insatiable longing" that actual possession cannot slake.[56] The greedy person is often portrayed as rich. He has more than most people, more, perhaps, than he knows what to do with. Still, it is not enough. Greed may also lead us to neglect other, more important aspects of life. Another picture of greed is the miser counting gold pieces, alone in a windowless room, without friends, without interest in the world outside. The clink, clink, clink of each coin as it hits the pile echoes hollowly down the empty halls.

These are just images, of course, proving nothing. To show greed's viciousness, we must explore how too great an emphasis on money or possessions leads to harm. We must show, too, that there are limits to what we need, deserve, or really can use here.

Greed is perhaps the most selfish-making vice; in its grip we become incapable of generosity and immune to the demands of justice. When Andrew Carnegie and Henry Clay Frick broke the Homestead steelworkers strike in 1892, they were among the wealthiest men in America, but they had no intention of sharing any more of that wealth with their workers than they could possibly avoid. No claims of justice, no consideration of the good uses their workers could put that money to or the sheer pointlessness of *them* amassing any more wealth, made any impression.

Cases such as Homestead or the oil companies' injustices in Nigeria show how greed can lead to great injustice. But even everyday, small-scale greed can lead to important harms, accentuating differences in wealth, fueling envy in the poor and vanity in the rich, and undermining the social bonds necessary for a happy society. Christians have criticized avarice above all for these social harms. "Now shall you understand that the relief for avarice is mercy and pity in large doses," Chaucer's Parson says: "Certainly, the avaricious man shows no pity nor any mercy to the needy man; for he delights in keeping his treasure and not in the rescuing or relieving of his fellow Christian."[57] Aquinas condemned the hoarding of unnecessary possessions in clear terms, stating that "whatever a man has in superabundance is owed, of natural right, to the poor for their sustenance."[58] To grasp possessions beyond this limit is unjust and idolatrous: the worship of Mammon.

To the traditionally recognized social harms of greed, environmentalists add harms to nature. Greed leads to environmental harms in three ways. First, when profit is placed over all other goals, greed leads businesspeople to break environmental laws or do the minimum necessary to comply with them. For example, a factory hog farm might be highly profitable; still, its owner wants more money. He doubles his hog sheds, increasing the stink breathed by the neighbors and his poorly paid workers. The resultant increase in manure overstresses his waste lagoons, causing overflows into a nearby river. This kills fish and other wildlife, drives anglers and canoers from the river, and decreases property values for dozens of his neighbors. Unfortunately, it is easy to find real examples where businesspeople break or bend environmental laws in pursuit of profit.[59]

Second, greed undermines the democratic political process. In his final year as CEO of Halliburton, an oilfield services and construction firm, Dick Cheney earned $26.4 million in compensation.[60] Upon taking office as U.S. vice president a year later, Cheney's main job was to chair a task force charged with setting U.S. energy policy. Its recommendations, developed in meetings closed to the public but open to friends and colleagues from the energy industries, read like a wish list from those same industries, including rollbacks of environmental regulations and tens of billions of dollars in unnecessary subsidies for new energy development. In the Bush administration, in one governmental department after another, industry lobbyists and managers are "regulating" their own industries, lining their friends' pockets just as their own pockets will be lined when they return to private life. In Cheney's case he does not even have to wait, for he continues to receive compensation from Halliburton while serving as vice president.[61] These are clear cases of greed trumping the public interest.

Third, greed leads to environmental harms by helping drive overconsumption among the general populace. Americans use vastly more oil, coal, water, metals, and other resources than our grandparents did, largely because we purchase lots of unnecessary things. Four and five year olds badger their parents for the latest plastic action figures and video games, which soon enough are dispatched to overflowing landfills. Middle-aged men with flagging libidos acquire mysterious desires for large, powerful cars—no matter that they already own cars or that the new Porsche or Hummer gets one-third the gas mileage and generates three times the CO_2 of the family's Taurus. All this overconsumption makes a pitiful enough spectacle, but the more important point is that it leads to great harms to nature. Human beings compete with millions of other species for the habitat and resources needed to survive. Like Carnegie and Frick 100 years ago we are willing to destroy other lives or monopolize the resources needed to preserve them for the most trivial reasons. At a minimum, justice would seem to demand that we avoid consumption that does *nothing* to further our happiness. But greed leads us on to ever more consumption.

In these ways, greed harms nature. But it also harms greedy people themselves. In the first place, there is no strong connection between increased wealth and happiness. Sages and philosophers have taught that "money can't buy happiness" for millennia— now science is starting to confirm it. Numerous studies in America have shown that beyond the poorest 10 to 15 percent of the population, there is no statistically significant correlation between wealth and subjective or objective measures of happiness.[62] You are no more likely to be happy earning $4,000,000 per year than $40,000. The factors that correlate most strongly with happiness are *security* of income—having some assurance that you and your family will have enough—and getting along well with your fellow workers and your spouse. But having some assurance that one has enough depends on being able to *recognize* that one has enough. Greedy people find this hard to do. Furthermore, studies have shown that people with more materialistic outlooks on life tend to have poor interpersonal relationships.[63] So the most proven, effective means to happiness tend to be beyond the reach of greedy people—no matter how wealthy they are.

Beyond the fact that material possessions are largely irrelevant to happiness, psychological studies show that a materialistic *outlook* on life tends to undermine happiness. One group of psychologists report:

> A growing body of research demonstrates that people who strongly orient toward values such as money, possessions, image, and status report lower subjective well-being. For example, [several studies] have shown that when people rate the relative importance of extrinsic, materialistic values as high in comparison to other pursuits (e.g., self-acceptance, affiliation, community feeling), lower quality of life is also reported. Late adolescents with a strong materialistic value orientation report lower self-actualization and vitality, as well as more depression and anxiety.[64]

Other studies have replicated these findings with college students and older adults.

Why are materialists less satisfied with life? One review article has considered various hypotheses and concluded that there is good evidence for three of them. First, materialists have poorer social lives, thus undermining their subjective well-being (but whether materialism is cause or effect remains unclear; unhappy people may grasp at materialistic values like straws). Second, it appears that "working toward material goals is less rewarding in the moment than working toward other goals." Anyone who has worked jobs that were enjoyable and challenging and jobs that were not knows this already. Third, the evidence suggests that the gap between what people have and what they want is more pronounced in the material realm than in other areas of life; hence focusing on material goals fosters dissatisfaction. It leads to a race to get and spend that leaves many people feeling hurried and harassed.[65]

Philosophers, following Thomas Aquinas, will add that materialism pales because it involves turning away from real goods to apparent goods.[66] When we are greedy, we neglect the real goods of activities for mere passive possession (the bird-watcher with top-of-the-line Zeiss binoculars who rarely gets up to hear the dawn chorus, the spoiled teenager with a fifteen-piece drum kit sitting unused in the basement). We reject the real goods of relationships for the apparent goods of triumphing over others (the CEO who cheats his employees out of their expected pension benefits and trades in his wife for a younger model). We neglect fulfilling, socially useful work for the trappings of status or success (the millionaire plastic surgeon specializing in boob jobs versus the humble pediatrician who volunteers at a free clinic twice a month).

In an excellent study of the seven deadly sins, Henry Fairlie notes that different societies predispose their members to different vices.[67] In America, we are raised to be greedy. Never before has a nation been so relentlessly bombarded by advertising; the average American child sees hundreds of thousands of television commercials by the time he or she reaches adulthood. Advertising emphasizes consumption as the primary means to happiness and works by increasing our dissatisfaction with life. As one marketer puts it: "Advertising at its best is making people feel that without their product, you're a loser. Kids are very sensitive to that. . . . You open up emotional vulnerabilities, and it's very easy to do with kids because they're the most emotionally vulnerable."[68]

This education in greed does not stop with childhood. Our colleges and universities teach applied avarice in their economics classes and business schools. At election time, candidates work to convince us that they can increase economic growth, without asking whether that growth will make us happier or better people. Institutions that once spoke out against materialism, above all the churches, have largely fallen silent about its dangers.[69]

We cannot eradicate the vices from human beings. However, there are practical steps we can take to limit greed and promote its contrasting virtues: thrift, modesty, generosity, and contentment. Individuals can focus on engaging in activities, rather than purchasing things. We can *share* things: buying a new lawnmower with several neighbors, for example, rather than buying one alone. We can stop watching television, eliminating much of the commercial incitement to greed from our lives. We can find alternatives to "recreational shopping" and other activities that cause wasteful consumption and leave us feeling unsatisfied.

At the political level, communities should ban billboards and commercial advertising in public schools. They should *require* recycling: current voluntary systems ensure that those who most need to learn restraint do not do so. More ambitiously, communities could pass sumptuary laws: limiting the size of houses, for example, to decrease human impacts on the landscape and standing incitements to envy. Beyond their direct environmental benefits, such measures would send a powerful, socially sanctioned message that greed is bad. Taking these personal and political steps would be good for us and good for nature.

Apathy

"Apathy" comes from the Greek *apatheia*, "without feeling"; one synonym in old English was *unlust*.[70] It is perhaps best understood as a lack: "lack of interest or concern, especially regarding matters of general importance or appeal . . . lack of emotion or feeling; impassiveness."[71] There is a close connection between apathy and laziness. Over the course of the Middle Ages, the two vices of *tristitia* (pessimism, despair) and *accidia* (apathy, "dryness of spirit") merged and morphed into the cardinal sin of sloth.[72] Calling apathy and sloth vices, or sins, emphasizes the active nature of a good human life.

Apathy is a key environmental vice, for several reasons. Our default procedures typically harm the environment, whereas doing better takes work, especially initially: bicycling to work rather than driving a car, setting up recycling bins rather than just tossing our garbage. One pop philosopher connects *all* our moral failures to laziness, and if this perhaps goes too far, it is true that doing right requires effort.[73] Often, we need to *think* our way toward better environmental solutions, and apathy shows itself in lazy thinking as well as in halfhearted action or inaction. Sluggish thinking tends to be selfish, short-term, and unimaginative. It reinforces passivity, as when my students' inability to imagine any way forward beyond American car culture, combined with their understanding of its environmental harms, leaves them feeling defeated and hopeless.

Thankfully, some of my students are not apathetic but, rather, are filled with passion and energy: to save Yellowstone's buffalo or Colorado's prairie dogs, to convince the university to purchase more recycled paper and wind power. Here, though, another problem can crop up, for too often their passions burn bright and flare out after a semester or two of activity, leaving them apathetic and disengaged. This is not just an issue for students learning about environmental issues for the first time; "burnout" among activists is a major problem for environmental groups, which depend on grassroots strength to combat the overwhelming monetary advantages of their opponents. When activists burn out, particular environmental efforts lose continuity and focus.[74]

The harms to nature from apathy are obvious: the old growth is cut, the refuge is drilled, the endangered species disappears. Polls might say that the great majority of the population supports preserving old growth, wilderness areas, or endangered species, but it is no matter if an active, eloquent few do not speak up on their behalf. "The broadest and most prevalent error requires the most disinterested virtue to sustain it," wrote Henry Thoreau, discussing his own society's apathetic acceptance of slavery.[75]

Apathy's harms to people are just as clear. Most simply, *apatheia* feels bad. A passive life is dull and boring. It lacks the engagement and interest in the world that are keys to happiness. It makes life seem meaningless, and meaning is as important as bread for living a fully human life.[76] Environmental apathy is especially pernicious for environmentalists; arguably, a person who has a strong sense of nature's beauty and worth, yet who cannot summon the energy to try to protect it, fails to live up to his or her full humanity.[77] Nothing makes us more fully human than the ability to articulate and live up to our ethical values. Environmentalists who do not act on their beliefs forfeit moral integrity.

With its focus on human flourishing, the virtue ethics tradition has generally praised the active life.[78] According to Aristotle, "Virtue is an ability [or power; *dynamis*] that is productive and preservative of goods, and an ability for doing good in many and great ways, actually in all ways in all things."[79] "By *virtue* and *power* I mean the same thing," wrote Spinoza: a power that allows us to become more fully ourselves.[80] Giving in to apathy means acquiescing in powerlessness. It means allowing others to circumscribe your life and your children's lives. Fighting for a special place or a beloved species, although it opens us up to disappointment, engages a basic human capability for political action. One of my students astutely suggests *vulnerability* and *ambition* as two virtues opposed to apathy.

A fear of vulnerability was partly behind the Stoic cultivation of *apatheia* as a virtue. Indifference toward "externals" beyond one's control allowed a person to take charge of his life and achieve happiness, the Stoics believed, while an unemotional rationality helped further just and successful action out in the world. The Stoic approach holds some appeal. It can further focus, hence effectiveness. Environmentalists do need to avoid fretting about events beyond our control, in a world with immense environmental problems and too much information about them. Nevertheless, cultivating environmental apathy seems misguided, for our happiness and flourishing depend, to an important degree, on flourishing natural and human communities. These must be defended. Environmentalists also *want* to explore and connect with these communities, which necessarily involves caring for them. There are many benefits to caring—but they cannot be divorced from the pain we feel when that which we care for is harmed.

Still, a person sometimes might be happier not caring about the environment and just living in it. From an individual point of view, being a free rider might make sense. In my home state of Colorado, many people take the attitude: "I'll float the rivers and ski the mountains, build my second home in prime elk habitat, enjoy it while I can, and not worry about tomorrow." These people may be happier than the people sitting through four-hour-long city council meetings, waiting nervously for a chance to speak for two minutes in favor of a new zoning ordinance. After all, you cannot sit in a meeting room and ski fresh powder at the same time. But with too many free riders, too much selfishness, the environment will be degraded, and soon enough the people living within it will suffer. I believe that those of us who enjoy nature's benefits have a duty to try to preserve it: for our communities and for future generations, for nature's sake and for our own.

In a recent article, Louke van Wensveen argues that genuine virtues must help ensure ecosystem sustainability.[81] As the virtues are virtues because they contribute to human flourishing and as flourishing is an ongoing project, the virtues must help secure the conditions necessary for their own cultivation. Traditionally, philosophers have emphasized the need to sustain the *social* conditions necessary for flourishing; today the evidence is clear that sustaining necessary *environmental* conditions is just as important. Wensveen's position seems unassailable.[82] It sets minimum standards for environmental concern that any plausible virtue ethics needs to uphold. Generalizing the point and shifting the focus from virtue to vice, I contend that any character trait, habit, institution, or way of life that cannot be sustained indefinitely is vicious. Furthermore, any character trait, habit, institution, or way of life whose current pursuit jeopardizes the well-being of others, now or in the future, is unjust. Apathy and indifference are socially and environmentally unsustainable. They cause, or allow, great harm. By these criteria, they are vices.

To fight apathy, we must find sustainable ways to engage in politics. Ideally, we will find political roles that we enjoy. Failing that, we will have to come up with tasks that we can tolerate for restricted amounts of time. Here we see particularly well the limits of general rules and prescriptions in ethics. People are different and suited to different social roles. The idea that you *should* engage in particular political activities will almost certainly fail to motivate sustained action. Instead, find out what you are good at and what you find enjoyable. Perhaps you like the excitement and combat of political campaigns; or the fleeting, minor celebrity of writing newspaper editorials; or the quiet, anonymous analysis of complex government policy proposals. Perhaps you would prefer teaching children the names of the flowers and birds in the local woods. All these activities are necessary in the ongoing struggle for nature.

To fight apathy and despair, we also need to find ways to *escape* from politics.[83] Aldo Leopold wrote that the price of an ecological education is to walk through a world of wounds. Leopold spent a good part of his life speaking out for wildlife and wilderness preservation, working politically to heal the wounds. But he also spent many hours planting trees and filling gullies on his sand county farm and many more hours hunting, fishing, bird-watching, snowshoeing, canoeing, and horse packing. No matter how dismal the environmental policies of the Soil Conservation Service or the State of Wisconsin were, Leopold could see the slow healing of land on his farm. No matter how often the Forest Service or Park Service punched roads into wilderness or exterminated predators, he found opportunities to explore and connect with wild nature. Leopold crafted a life that he found enjoyable and meaningful, that sustained him and made possible his lasting contributions to conservation. Our challenge is to do likewise. In the end, action is the only answer to apathy.[84]

Conclusion

Why do we harm nature? Because we are ignorant. Because we are selfish. Because we are gluttonous, arrogant, greedy, and apathetic. Because we do not understand our obligations to others or our own self-interest. We falsely assume that we can keep separate harms to nature and harms to humanity, harms to others and harms to ourselves. We do not see that environmental vices do not just harm nature; they harm us and the people around us. As I have shown in this essay, many of these harms are scientifically verifiable; the rest can be understood by anyone with open eyes and an open heart. The environmental vices are bad for us and bad for the Earth. For better and for worse, we really are all in this together.

Notes

1. Why is vice so little discussed in contemporary philosophy? Perhaps the failure comes from a discomfort with appearing too judgmental. When we assert that a particular action is wrong, we typically assume that people are free to act otherwise. Vice terms imply a deeper evil in people, harder to reform, certainly not to be shaken off by an argument or two. Similarly,

when we assert that particular social arrangements are unfair or unjust, we locate the primary evil in "the system." Vice terms, in contrast, locate evil squarely within people. It is fine to criticize particular acts or social arrangements; criticize people generally and you trespass on the sacred, humanity having replaced God as the divine object in modern secular philosophy. Locate a *persistent* evil in individuals, and you verge on a pessimism at odds with the Enlightenment optimism still at the heart of most moral philosophy.

2. See recent Gallup Earth Day polls, available at www.gallup.com (accessed 18 February 2004).

3. My sense is that these are our four most important, or cardinal, environmental vices because they are fundamental and lead to the greatest environmental harms. Justification of this claim lies beyond the scope of this essay, depending as it would on a fully developed moral psychology and a comprehensive account of environmental degradation.

4. See the *American Heritage Dictionary of the English Language* and the *Oxford English Dictionary* (3d ed.).

5. Louke van Wensveen, *Dirty Virtues: The Emergence of Ecological Virtue Ethics* (Amherst, NY: Humanity Books, 2000), 103–6.

6. In this way vice judgments are similar to virtue judgments. See Martha Nussbaum, "Non-relative Virtues: An Aristotelian Approach," in *The Quality of Life*, ed. Martha Nussbaum and Amartya Sen (Oxford: Oxford University Press, 1993), 242–69.

7. Aristotle also described human flourishing in terms of higher activities such as philosophical study and contemplation, leading to a different set of virtues and vices. These two different conceptions of happiness and virtue are incompletely integrated in his ethical philosophy.

8. See the essays "Of Cruelty" and "Cowardice, Mother of Cruelty" in Michel de Montaigne, *Essays*.

9. Aristotle, *Nicomachean Ethics* (Indianapolis: Hackett, 1999), 23 (bk. 2, chap. 6).

10. Thomas Aquinas, *Treatise on the Virtues* (Englewood Cliffs, NJ: Prentice-Hall, 1966), 57 (*Summa*, pt. 2, question 56).

11. Immanuel Kant, *Groundwork of the Metaphysic of Morals*, AK 397; Immanuel Kant, *The Doctrine of Virtue: Part II of The Metaphysic of Morals*, AK 384–91, 443–45.

12. If we take moral character to be the sole determinant of personal well-being, or infinitely more important than other aspects of personal well-being, then it becomes true that we cannot improve our own well-being by wronging others. However, these Socratic and Stoic views give morality more importance than it deserves. Morality is important, but it is not all-important. We can preserve the nobility behind the view that we can never benefit ourselves by harming others by saying instead that we never *should* benefit ourselves by harming others.

13. Aristotle, *Nicomachean Ethics*, 110–11 (bk. 7, chap. 8).

14. See, for example, Augustine's account of his theft of the pears in the *Confessions*, bk. 2.

15. Aristotle, *Nicomachean Ethics*, 48–49 (bk. 3, chap. 12), 160–61 (bk. 10, chap. 5).

16. Both these themes are treated in Montaigne's final essay, "Of Experience." On tolerance, see also "Of Cannibals."

17. See Bill Shaw, "A Virtue Ethics Approach to Aldo Leopold's Land Ethic," in this volume; and Philip Cafaro, "Rachel Carson's Environmental Ethics," *Worldviews: Environment, Culture, Religion* 6 (2002): 58–80.

18. This last point is important. We need not show that some aspect of environmental protection is a *necessary* condition for the happiness of *all* members of society; to show that it is an *important* condition for the happiness of *some* members of society may be all the justification we need for environmental protection. As Aldo Leopold wrote: "Mechanized recreation already has seized nine-tenths of the woods and mountains; a decent respect for minorities should ded-

icate the other tenth to wilderness" (*A Sand County Almanac with Essays on Conservation from Round River* [New York: Ballantine, 1970], 272).

19. The most comprehensive study so far, setting the agenda for future scholarship in this area, is Wensveen, *Dirty Virtues*.

20. Wensveen, *Dirty Virtues*, 97–103.

21. To be fair to Aristotle, he already had some sense of the importance of environmental protection to human flourishing. See Aristotle, *Politics*, bk. 7, chaps. 4–6, 11–12.

22. See Holmes Rolston III, "Environmental Virtue Ethics: Half the Truth but Dangerous as a Whole," in this volume.

23. Once again, though I believe that these are our cardinal environmental vices, sustaining that claim would require further elaboration and defense. Selfishness, injustice, and ignorance are also plausible candidates for cardinal environmental vices.

24. Morton Bloomfield, *The Seven Deadly Sins: An Introduction to the History of a Religious Concept, with Special Reference to Medieval English Literature* (East Lansing: Michigan State University Press, 1967), 59, 69. Bloomfield (*The Seven Deadly Sins*, 74–75) documents how, early in the medieval period, gluttony lost its place at the head of the list to pride; he speculates that as the list began to be used to guide moral life outside monasteries, sins of the flesh such as gluttony and lust came to seem less important than more socially damaging sins such as pride and avarice.

25. Geoffrey Chaucer, *Canterbury Tales* (New York: Covici and Friede, 1934), 603.

26. J. M. McGinnis and W. H. Foege, "Actual Causes of Death in the United States," *Journal of the American Medical Association* 270, no. 18 (1993): 2207–12.

27. One study notes that "aside from mortality rate . . . obesity substantially increases morbidity and impairs quality of life" (D. B. Allison, K. R. Fontaine, J. E. Manson, J. Steens, and T. B. Van Itallie, "Annual Deaths Attributable to Obesity in the United States," *Journal of the American Medical Association* 282, no. 16 [1999]: 1530).

28. U.S. Department of Health and Human Services, *The Surgeon General's Call to Action to Prevent and Decrease Overweight and Obesity* (Rockville, MD: Public Health Service, Office of the Surgeon General, 2001).

29. U.S. Fish and Wildlife Service, "Summary of Listed Species," available at http://ecos.fws .gov/tess_public/TESSBoxscore?format=display&type=archive&sysdate=5/01/2004 (accessed 14 May 2004).

30. D. S. Wilcove, D. Rothstein, J. Dubow, A. Phillips, and E. Losos, "Quantifying Threats to Imperiled Species in the United States: Assessing the Relative Importance of Habitat Destruction, Alien Species, Pollution, Overexploitation, and Disease," *BioScience* 48, no. 8 (1998): 607–15.

31. Wilcove et al., "Quantifying Threats to Imperiled Species in the United States." A more recent study has confirmed agriculture's leading role in species endangerment; see B. Czech, R. Krausman, and P. K. Devers, "Economic Associations among Causes of Species Endangerment in the United States," *BioScience* 50, no. 7 (2000): 593–601.

32. J. Putnam, J. Allshouse, and L. S. Kantor, "U.S. Per Capita Food Supply Trends: More Calories, Refined Carbohydrates, and Fats," *FoodReview* 25, no. 3 (2002): 2–15.

33. Of course, all else is not equal. For one thing, approximately 20 percent of the food produced in the United States is exported (see M. Reed, *International Trade in Agricultural Products* [Upper Saddle River, NJ: Prentice-Hall, 2001]). But this point cuts both ways: much of the food consumed today in America is imported, and its growing, harvesting, and shipping have environmental costs.

34. Robert Pyle, *The Thunder Tree: Lessons from an Urban Wildland* (New York: Lyons Press, 1993); Kent Meyers, *The Witness of Combines* (Minneapolis: University of Minnesota Press, 1998).

35. D. H. Chadwick, "American Prairie: Roots of the Sky," *National Geographic* 184 (October 1993): 116.

36. Frances Moore Lappé, *Diet for a Small Planet* (New York: Ballantine, 1991).

37. Amartya Sen, *Poverty and Famines: An Essay on Entitlement and Deprivation* (Oxford: Oxford University Press, 1981).

38. Aristotle, *Nicomachean Ethics*, 46, 48–49 (bk. 3, chaps. 10, 12), 157 (bk. 10, chap. 3).

39. Henry Thoreau, *Walden* (Princeton: Princeton University Press, 1971), 215.

40. Aristotle, *Nicomachean Ethics*, 49 (bk. 3, chap. 12).

41. Readers interested in the ancient pagan view should review Aristotle's discussion of magnanimity or "great-souledness" (*Nicomachean Ethics*, bk. 4, chap. 3). Aristotle there defines magnanimity (Greek *megalopsuchia*) as a virtue specifying the proper attitude toward honor, stating that the magnanimous man "thinks himself worthy of great honors, and is worthy of them." The associated vices are overvaluation of oneself, on the one hand, and pusillanimity, thinking oneself worthy of little, on the other. Interestingly, Aristotle thinks that the latter vice is more usual than the former.

42. For a good discussion of Kantian self-respect, see Thomas Hill Jr., "Servility and Self-Respect," *Monist* 57 (1973): 87–104.

43. Wensveen, *Dirty Virtues*, 98.

44. David Ehrenfeld, *The Arrogance of Humanism* (New York: Oxford University Press, 1978).

45. Bronwen Manby, *The Price of Oil: Corporate Responsibility and Human Rights Violations in Nigeria's Oil Producing Communities* (Washington, DC: Human Rights Watch, 1999).

46. This account of events in the Niger Delta, and the quotes from Chevron contractor Bill Spencer that follow, come from the *Democracy Now* radio program "Drilling and Killing: Chevron and Nigeria's Oil Dictatorship," produced by Amy Goodman and Jeremy Scahill, 30 September 1998, available at www.pacifica.org/programs/nigeria (accessed 13 February 2004).

47. For a comprehensive discussion and bibliography, see American Land Alliance, *Off-Road Vehicles: A Growing Threat to Public Lands and Waters*, available at www.americanlands.org/forestweb/offroad.htm.

48. Kevin McNulty, "Off-Road Attitude," available at www.off-roadweb.com/features/0202or_covertruck/index.html (accessed 12 February 2004).

49. Aristotle, *Nicomachean Ethics*, bk. 7, chaps. 7–8.

50. The arrogance of someone who holds to belief in a literal biblical creation, its combination of stubbornness and laziness, has a lot in common with the justifications for corporate crime and personal irresponsibility above. Anthropocentrism is not just a faulty value system but also a faulty way of understanding the world. In Aristotle's terms, it is an intellectual vice as well as a character vice.

51. It is no accident that most of our environmental heroes have been naturalists. See Philip Cafaro, "The Naturalist's Virtues," *Philosophy in the Contemporary World* 8, no. 2 (2001): 85–99.

52. For similar reasons, federal and state land management agencies should ban ORVs from our public lands. By allowing and often encouraging such use, they are creating a whole constituency of people who do not respect nature. They are training people *on* public lands to *trash* public lands.

53. Peter Singer, *One World: The Ethics of Globalization* (New Haven: Yale University Press, 2002), 104–5.

54. Ron Sandler makes the good point that arrogance is as much about what we think we can do as what we think we are worth. It is the former that is most in play in genetic engineering, damming and straightening rivers, industrial agriculture, and so on.

55. See the *American Heritage Dictionary*. Greed can also refer to an extreme desire for anything; as Chaucer says, "Avarice ne stont not oonly in lond ne in catel, but som tyme in science and in glorie" (quoted in the *Oxford English Dictionary* definition for *avarice*).

56. Wensveen, *Dirty Virtues*, 233.

57. Chaucer, *Canterbury Tales*, 601.

58. Thomas Aquinas quoted in Singer, *One World*, 185.

59. For examples of businessmen and businesswomen who are building profitable businesses that *enhance* environmental protection, see Steven Lerner, *Eco-pioneers: Practical Visionaries Solving Today's Environmental Problems* (Cambridge: MIT Press, 1998).

60. Gary Strauss, "Cheney as VP Faces a Serious Cut in Pay," *USA Today*, 26 June 2000. Available at www.usatoday.com/news/opinion/e2415.htm (accessed 15 June 2004).

61. John King, "Cheney Aide Rejects Halliburton Questions," *CNN.com/Inside Politics*, 16 September 2003. Available at www.cnn.com/2003/ALLPOLITICS/09/16/cheney.halliburton/index.html (accessed 15 June 2004).

62. These studies are summarized in Robert Lane, *The Market Experience* (Cambridge: Cambridge University Press, 1991), 524–47.

63. Tim Kasser, Richard Ryan, Charles Couchman, and Kennon Sheldon, "Materialistic Values: Their Causes and Consequences," in *Psychology and Consumer Culture: The Struggle for a Good Life in a Materialistic World*, ed. Tim Kasser and Allen Kanner (Washington, DC: American Psychological Association, 2004), 19.

64. Kasser et al., "Materialistic Values," 29 (in-text citations silently removed).

65. Emily Solberg, Edward Diener, and Michael Robinson, "Why Are Materialists Less Satisfied?" in *Psychology and Consumer Culture: The Struggle for a Good Life in a Materialistic World*, ed. Tim Kasser and Allen Kanner (Washington, DC: American Psychological Association, 2004), 45.

66. Bloomfield, *The Seven Deadly Sins*, 88.

67. Henry Fairlie, *The Seven Deadly Sins Today* (Washington, DC: New Republic Books, 1978), 25. Fairlie argues that American society instills avarice, gluttony, and lust in its members.

68. Nancy Shalek, quoted in Tim Kasser, *The High Price of Materialism* (Cambridge: MIT Press, 2002), 91.

69. Of course, one can take the view that our contemporary acceptance of greed is all to the good. Almost 300 years ago, Bernard Mandeville, in his *Fable of the Bees: Or, Private Vices, Public Virtues*, argued that the vices are in fact necessary to a happy and flourishing nation.

70. Bloomfield, *The Seven Deadly Sins*, 251.

71. See the *American Heritage Dictionary*.

72. Wensveen, *Dirty Virtues*, 100; Bloomfield, *The Seven Deadly Sins*, 96.

73. M. Scott Peck, *People of the Lie: The Hope for Healing Human Evil* (New York: Simon and Schuster, 1983).

74. Randy Larsen, "Tenacity as a Virtue," unpublished MS, 8. For a good discussion of issues surrounding apathy and activism, see Randy Larsen, "Environmental Virtue Ethics: Nature as Polis" (M.A. thesis, Colorado State University, Fort Collins, 1996), chap. 3.

75. Henry Thoreau, *Reform Papers* (Princeton: Princeton University Press, 1973), 72.

76. See Matthew 4:4.

77. David Schmidtz, "Are All Species Equal?" in *Environmental Ethics: What Really Matters, What Really Works*, ed. David Schmidtz and Elizabeth Willot (New York: Oxford University Press, 2002), 100.

78. Still, passivity remains a live option within virtue ethics, embraced in ancient times by Eastern Taoists and Western Cynics. Given how much environmental harm is caused by the human need to act, regardless of whether action is justified, an environmental focus may challenge

the traditional preference for activity within virtue ethics. Perhaps the most radical aspect of the U.S. National Environmental Protection Act is its requirement that federal managers consider a "no action" option before proceeding with projects.

79. Aristotle, *On Rhetoric* (New York: Oxford University Press, 1991), 79 (bk. 1, chap. 9).

80. Baruch Spinoza, *The Ethics and Selected Letters* (Indianapolis: Hackett, 1982), 156 (pt. 4, definitions). We see this equation of virtue, power, and activity in various archaic uses of the word *virtue*, when botanists or physicians write of the virtues of medicinal plants, for instance. Contrarily, many contemporary philosophers could agree with Ambrose Bierce's definition of virtue in his *Devil's Dictionary*: "virtues: certain abstentions."

81. Louke van Wensveen, "Ecosystem Sustainability as a Criterion for Genuine Virtue," *Environmental Ethics* 23 (2001): 232–34.

82. Wensveen's approach is challenged in Ronald Sandler, "The External Goods Approach to Environmental Virtue Ethics," *Environmental Ethics* 25 (2003): 279–93.

83. For a discussion of hope, despair, and political activism in environmental virtue ethics, see Philip Cafaro, *Thoreau's Living Ethics:* Walden *and the Pursuit of Virtue* (Athens: University of Georgia Press, 2004), 174–204.

84. Ed Abbey echoes Leopold and well sums up the claims of an environmental virtue ethics when he writes: "Do not burn yourselves out. Be as I am—a reluctant enthusiast . . . a part-time crusader, a half-hearted fanatic. Save the other half of yourselves and your lives for pleasure and adventure. It is not enough to fight for the land; it is even more important to enjoy it. . . . Enjoy yourselves, keep your brain in your head and your head firmly attached to the body, the body active and alive, and I promise you this much: I promise you this one sweet victory over our enemies, over those desk-bound people with their hearts in a safe deposit box and their eyes hypnotized by desk calculators. I promise you this: you will outlive the bastards" (quoted in Steve Van Matre and Bill Weiler, eds., *The Earth Speaks* [Greenville, WV: Institute for Earth Education, 1983], 57). Randy Larsen points out the appropriateness of this quote in his "Environmental Virtue Ethics."

CHAPTER 10

Vices and Virtues in Religious Environmental Ethics

Charles Taliaferro

Virtues and vices often depend on context. Some of the context involves the external circumstances; a person's active movement or stationary restraint may be courage or cowardice depending on which dangers and opportunities are in play. And some of the context involves more interior matters: a person's beliefs and desires, her or his physical and mental abilities. You and I may both walk across the same street in the same surrounding circumstances at the same time, and yet for me this is courageous (I am confronting and overcoming a physical or mental disability), whereas for you the event is of no particular importance.

The great religious traditions of the world have an important bearing on the philosophy of environmental virtues and vices because they portray competing, sometimes complementary, nonsecular accounts of our external circumstances as well as different interior philosophies of human beliefs and desires, our physical and mental abilities. The virtues and vices that are recognized in religious ethics often overlap those of secular ethics, but sometimes they differ in magnitude and kind. As I shall argue below, they differ in magnitude insofar as they treat some values with a higher intensity than one finds in a secular context, and they differ in kind insofar as they introduce virtues and vices not found in secular ethics. In this chapter I consider environmental virtues in a theistic context that is common to Judaism, Christianity, and Islam (the Abrahamic faiths). I then contrast it with a nontheistic Buddhist philosophy. The chapter concludes with reflections on religious virtues in a practical moral and political context.

Before considering religious virtues and vices at closer range, consider five general reasons for undertaking this study. First, one or more religious traditions may be true, for example, there is a God or the Buddhist view of the self is right.[1] If so, and if (as I shall argue) religious traditions present us with virtues and vices that expand secular ethics, then any comprehensive view of values must include religious ethics. The exclusion of religion from serious philosophical inquiry has become less fashionable in the last forty years. In the 1950s and 1960s, religious views of the cosmos were frequently cast as superstitious nonsense by anglophone philosophers in light of an empirical, scientifically grounded naturalism. For a range of reasons, such a rigorous naturalism (sometimes closely associated with logical positivism) was overturned or at least marginalized.[2] Naturalism is still a dominant intellectual force, but the idea that theories of the cosmos that challenge naturalism are incoherent (or even nonsensical or meaningless!) is no longer obvious or commonplace.[3] Recent decades have witnessed a renaissance of philosophy of religion, and there is now an impressive philosophical literature articulating and defending all the main world religions. Because philosophers today often take seriously the credibility of religious views of human nature and the cosmos, the inclusion of religious ethics in the study of environmental virtues is a natural development.[4]

Second, if a religious view of the cosmos proves to be adequate, it could provide an overarching grounding or justification for one's secular environmental ethics. Some applied environmental ethics simply assume a basic view of values—for example, pleasure is good, suffering is bad, biodiversity within sustainable limits is good, the avoidable involuntary infliction of cancer on the innocent is wrong, and so on. There is discussion of whether values are intrinsic, inherent, instrumental, or holistic, but this is often carried out without considering a comprehensive metaphysical framework that accounts for such values. There is a further task of offering an account of such values and disvalues: What is their origin? Are these values a reflection of largely human preferences and institutions, or are they instead derived from a transcendental source? Most theists, for example, understand the values of this cosmos to be grounded in the goodness of God.[5] My point is not that an acceptable environmental ethics must include an overarching, plausible metaphysics that bolsters and grounds secular ethics. As a subfield of philosophy, there is already more than enough for environmental ethicists to do besides debating comprehensive metaphysics. Still, this larger metaphysical task may be seen as a complementary project that (under ideal conditions) would provide a backing for environmental ethics.[6]

Third, even if we bracket questions about the truth of religious convictions, the majority of the world population is either identified as religious or is affected by religious traditions.[7] So long as you wish to carry out environmental ethics in a way that engages vast portions of the world population, some acquaintance with religious ethics is pivotal. An intelligent encounter with religious traditions may be especially important when environmental ethics addresses problems across cultures, when, for example, secular and religious values clash. An environmental ethic that ignores religious values is in danger of failing to engage and respond to the world population as it is today, substituting in its place an engagement with a limited academic community.[8]

Fourth, the study of religious ethics can provide lessons for secular environmental ethics. I cite just one example. In environmental ethics today there is some tension between those who emphasize the individual versus those who focus on species, collectives, or holistic values.[9] I suggest that the history of religious values—both in the West and in the East—provides some reason for questioning unbridled or extreme forms of both individualism and holism. Some middle ground is needed between a holist stress on universals and collectives, on the one hand, and individual, particular values, on the other. In Christianity, for instance, there is an important moral tradition that places enormous value on "agape" (a Greek term for love), which is theologically defined as selfless, unconditional love. In this tradition, the love of other persons must not include preferential friendships. The history of ethics in Christianity reveals, however, the unsustainability of an agape ethic and the need to allow for healthy, preferential friendships (sometimes referred to by theologians as "eros"). In theological terms, agape needs to make room for eros.[10] For a non-Western instance, consider the tension between Yang Zhu and Moism. Moism, named for the philosopher Mo Tzu (490–403), extols universal love of all persons over against Yang's ethic of self-interest. Yang was a kind of warring Ayn Rand who promoted a philosophy of *weiwo* (for myself). I believe that the history of Chinese ethics gives one reason to see the problem of Moist universal ethics (the movement did not win wide sustained following) being ungrounded in specific social contexts, as well as the problem of a narrow form of self-interested individualism.[11]

The unsatisfactory nature of these extremes was historically important in the search for a middle ground in Confucianism. Xingzhong Yao writes about the great Mencius's case for Confucianism, set forth in *The Book of Mencius* (300 B.C.E.):

> Mengzi [Mencius] believed that both [Mo Tzu and Yang Zhu], in one way or another, stripped morality from human relationships and made men no better than beasts. Opposing these doctrines Mengzi taught the Confucian understanding of individuals as members and participants in the wider society of family and the state. He called for all human relations to be based on family affections and believed that the world would be naturally at peace if only everyone respected the old people in their own family as they should be respected, and extending this respect to the old of other people's families; and cared for the young people in their own family as they should be cared for, and extending this care to the young people of other people's families.[12]

These sorts of lessons can, I think, provide a helpful perspective on secular environmental ethics.[13]

Finally, religious conceptions of human flourishing are important to consider, as they are, socially and philosophically, an important challenge to consumptive, economically defined values in popular culture, the marketplace, and politics. Although most of the world religions have had economic roles (witness Max Weber's study of religion in European culture), historically they have often delimited a sphere that is independent of economic values (e.g., the worth of a religious rite is not measurable solely in economic terms) and one that can serve as a base for critically assessing economic values. In *Spheres of Justice*, Michael Walzer discusses how religious concepts of divine grace can form an "autonomous sphere" set apart from the marketplace: "Here is perhaps the clearest example in our culture of an autonomous sphere. Grace cannot be purchased or inherited; nor can it be coerced. It cannot be had by passing an exam or by holding an office."[14] By taking seriously the sphere of religion, one may entertain values that are not narrowly restrained by the economy. Let us now turn to theistic values, virtues, and vices and then to nontheistic, religious ones.

Theistic Virtues and Vices

At the heart of Judaism, Christianity, and Islam is the thesis that the cosmos is itself the good creation of an all-good, -powerful, -knowing God. Theism is united in this core, value-centered philosophical position despite the divergent convictions in religious terms over the scope of divine providence (Has the messiah come? Was Jesus Christ God and man? Is Mohammed the great prophet of Allah?), God's nature (Is God triune? Is God eternal or temporal?), and how to understand religious scriptures.

In the field of environmental ethics, debate over religion in the 1960s until the early 1980s was often limited to theism and the question of whether Christianity in particular is responsible for the modern ecological crisis. The key essay that defined the parameters of this debate was Lynn White's "The Historical Roots of Our Ecological Crisis."[15] White castigates the Genesis account of creation on the grounds that it has historically been interpreted as identifying human beings as the central purpose of creation and licensing humanity in dominating (and thus exploiting) nature. He also laments that monotheism led to a desacralized view of the natural world. White's purpose was not altogether secular (he wished to revise or reform Christianity), though some subsequent philosophers have held that Christianity is thoroughly toxic from the standpoint of environmentalism.[16] Further work, however, has successfully challenged such a sweeping critique.[17] It is now widely recognized that although Christianity may be interpreted as fostering anthropocentric, exploitive policies, it may also be reasonably taken to foster an ethic of stewardship and respectful care for creation out of gratitude and worship of the God who "saw everything that [God] had made, and indeed, it was very good."[18]

A theistic environmental ethic may be seen through three, closely related tenets: creation, divine ownership, and the identification of natural goods with God's presence. I have already taken note of the centrality of God creating nature as good. It is interesting to note that the scriptural testimony to God as the supreme and sole creator is often couched in terms that praise or treasure natural goods. Consider this extensive passage from the Qur'an:

> And who other than He created the heavens and the earth and sent down for you water from the sky, whereby We cause to grow lush orchards—for it is not up to you to cause their tress to grow! Is there, then a god beside God? Yet these are the people who ascribe partners to Him! And who other than He made the earth a firm abode [for you], and set rivers traversing through it, and put firm mountains therein and sealed off one ocean from another? Is there, then a god beside God? . . . And who other than He responds to the distressed one when he calls Him and He relieves him of the distress and who had made you His vicegerent on earth? Is there, then a god beside God?—little do you reflect. And who other than He guides you in the darkness of the land and the sea? And who sends forth winds heralding His mercy [sc. rain]? Is there, then a god beside God? For exalted be He above what they associate with Him! And who other than He brings forth His creation and then re-creates it? And who gives you sustenance from the heaven and the earth?[19]

The common conviction among theistic Jews, Christians, and Muslims that nature is the creation of a good God has historically distinguished them from religious movements such as gnosticism, which denigrate the natural order.

The second tenet, divine ownership, comes in with the thesis that nature, as a creation of God, belongs to God: "The earth is the Lord's and the fullness thereof"; "to God belong all things in the heavens and the earth; And it is He that encompasseth all things."[20] Jews, Christians, and Muslims have differed over the meaning of this teaching, but there is consensus over the concept that creation itself is a bounteous gift. God owns the cosmos as Creator, and yet he gives it to his creatures for their good.[21] As such, gratitude is proper, as well as the respectful treatment of the gift.

The third tenet is God's affective identification with the values in the cosmos. That is, the cultivation of a good cosmos is seen in theism as participating in a God-given practice or, in more general terms, to participate in God's caring love of creation. There are abundant references in the Hebrew and Christian Bibles and the Qur'an to God's care of the cosmos. Consider this passage as representative: "Who hath cleft a channel for the waterflood, or a way for the lighting of the thunder; To rain on a land where no man is, On the wilderness where there is no man; To satisfy the desolate and waste ground; And to cause the bud of the tender herb to spring forth?"[22] Respectful, life-sustaining cultivation has been cast as the covenant between God and humanity.[23] By caring for creation one joins in a divine providence. Jonathan Helfand offers this succinct view of a religious ethic, which sees glad, respectful pleasure in creation as a part of life: "An evil person is considered dead, for he sees the sun shining but does not bless 'him who brings on the evening'; he eats and drinks and offers no blessings."[24]

Jews, Christians, and Muslims do not just provide a view of our cosmic context concerning the things around us; they also offer an engaging view of our beliefs and desires, our mental and physical abilities. Perhaps the simplest and most sweeping way to state this religious perception is that, according to Abrahamic faiths, the fulfillment of our beliefs and desires, our mental and physical life, is to be found (in part) by living in concord with God. God wills the consummate fulfillment of creation. Acting or living in solidarity with such a divine will is believed to answer (in part) our deepest human needs and longings. As Augustine put it, famously, "Our hearts are restless until they find their rest in Thee."[25] Theists have differed in their views about the extensiveness of the good of this "rest" or abiding in solidarity with God. Most, for example, believe in an afterlife for at least human beings, whereas some do not. Some hold that the natural world itself has been profoundly marred by human sin, whereas others do not.[26] Even so, there is a widespread common core conviction that (in the words of Thomas Aquinas) divine grace fulfills and perfects nature rather than destroys nature.[27]

The virtues that emerge from this theistic philosophy include the virtue of feeling gratitude in response to seeing nature as a gift, the virtue of caring for creation as a gift out of respect and gratitude, and the virtue of acting in solidarity with the good Creator. Religious vices take shape as the mirror opposite states of character and action: the vice of ingratitude out of vanity or malice, the exploitive destruction of a gift, and the repudiation and antagonism toward the good Creator of a gift. On this account, is anyone who has no knowledge of God or who thinks that there is no God—and thus anyone who does *not* see nature as a gift—guilty of vice? No. You can only deliberately repudiate a gift when you are aware that there is a gift to repudiate. Vice only comes into play when, say, you are aware that you have been given a gift (for example, you are given the gift of the kiss of life when you are rescued from death by a good person) and you destroy or repudiate the gift out of vanity (imagine that you belittle the gift of the rescue as unnecessary, and, out of pride, you lie, claiming that in reality it was you who did the rescuing).[28]

Consider an objection: The above portrait of virtues and vices is quite general. In practice, theistic religious traditions advance specific moral teachings that can be (from the standpoint of a secular ethic) deeply appalling. Theistic religious traditions have provided justifications for slavery, male domination, raising nonhuman animals for food and other ends, depriving native populations of land, aggressive wars, religious intolerance, the persecution of homosexuals, ecologically disastrous population policies, and so on. In this context, it is impossible to take up each of these issues, but it may be helpful to identify a general feature of theism that helps foster moral development and self-criticism within a religious tradition. Theism understands God to be impartial, all-knowing, and affectively apprised of the standpoint of all creatures.[29] Insofar as moral progress is achieved through impartiality, knowledge, and affective awareness of others, then the religious theist can hold that moral progress is made by the increasingly accurate, or a better understanding of, a God's-eye point of view. Let me illustrate how this works in light of a debate between theists on ethical vegetarianism.

Imagine that theists agree that in the Hebrew and Christian Bibles and the Qur'an there is a bona fide revelation of God and that in these scriptures the raising of nonhuman animals for food accords with what appear to be divinely revealed precepts. They nonetheless also believe God to be all good and that vegetarianism is ethically obligatory. Must the theist set to one side her or his ethical scruples and submit to a nonvegetarian authority?[30] No, it does not. Thinking ethically within a religious tradition should not be equated with the mandatory submission to a fixed moral teaching. There is a flexibility built in to most modern faiths that invites progressive, moral reflection. In this case that flexibility would be exercised and ex hypothesi progress would be made by one of the following two alternatives: first, denying that the scriptural precepts about eating animals are genuine; perhaps they are human in origin (the result of partiality, false beliefs, and a failure to appreciate animal consciousness) and not properly, divinely inspired. Our greater impartiality et ceteras allows us to see what is merely human and what transcends human self-interest. Contemporary theologians in each of the Abrahamic faiths distinguish the *inspiration* of scripture from its *inerrancy*, thus allowing that religious scripture and subsequent religious history can be progressive and (to some extent) revisionary. The second alternative is acknowledging that the relevant divine precepts are genuine but claiming that they were only an accommodation of human weakness (vegetarianism represents the ideal following of God) or that the conditions that countenanced nonvegetarian practices (and thus their divine permissibility) have changed. Many vegetarian Christians, for example, argue that the current meat industry is unjust because of the harm done to animals and because it is unnecessary for human flourishing. Perhaps the sacrifice of animals in the past was essential (in evolutionary history the consuming of animals was natural and not evil), but it is not now and so must be renounced. The structure of this reasoning is similar to what you find in the history of religion as ethicists critically reevaluate past judgments and seek greater clarity on moral concerns. So thinking ethically within a religious tradition does not amount to mandatory submission to fixed moral teaching. There is an appropriately critical attitude recognized by many religious ethicists as essential to moral and religious thinking.[31]

Theism, I suggest, elevates some virtues that are shared by secular ethics. In addition to the virtues of humility and self-respect, justice, and so on, there are the virtues—of the kind of impartiality, the desire for knowledge, and the affective appreciation of the points of view of others—that contribute to progress in religious and secular ethical reflection.[32] I have also, in this section, highlighted some alternative virtues and vices that come to the fore in a theistic cosmos. So, the virtues involving gratitude toward, and acting in solidarity with, God are virtues in Abrahamic faith, but in a nontheistic, secular context these would not be seen as virtues. Let us turn now to a nontheistic religion.

Buddhist Virtues

Buddhism is a rich tradition with many strands. The earliest versions are nontheistic in an interesting way. Though some early Buddhists were atheists, a common view is that God should be ignored even if there is a God.[33] This is largely because one goal of Buddhism is detachment from the concept of an enduring self (whether human or divine). Buddhism begins with a realization of the ill of suffering and its source. As Gautama Buddha teaches:

> Now this, O monks, is the noble truth of the cause of pain: that craving which leads to rebirth, combined with pleasure and lust, finding pleasure here and there, namely, the craving for passion, the craving for existence, the craving for non-existence.
>
> Now this, O monks, is the noble truth of the cessation of pain: the cessation without a remainder of that craving, abandonment, forsaking, release, non-attachment.[34]

The liberation from the cycle of rebirth (and thus redeath) is an emancipation from one's individual consciousness as an enduring thing. Gautama points to a transcendent consciousness, beyond all the distinctions that mark our ordinary ways of thinking and acting:

> All consciousness by which one could predicate the existence of the saint [someone meditating and engaging in a virtuous life], all that consciousness has been abandoned, uprooted, pulled out of the ground like a palmyra-tree and become non-existent, and not liable to spring up again in the future. The said, O Vaccha, who has been released from what is styled consciousness is deep, immeasurable, unfathomable, like the mighty ocean. To say that he is not reborn would not fit the case. To say that he is reborn would not fit the case. To say that he is neither reborn nor not reborn would not fit the case.[35]

The result is a state of being that goes beyond or displaces the God–cosmos distinction one finds in theism.

I highlight only two Buddhist virtues that emerge from this extraordinary tradition. One virtue may be seen as straightforwardly compatible with secular environmental ethics, whereas the second offers a distinct, alternative religious contribution. Buddhism is well known for its teaching that the natural world is in a state of impermanence and interconnection. Each thing exists in a state of relations with others. This is sometimes described as the doctrine of *Praitityasamutpada*, the "together-rising-up-of-things." The virtue called for here is to live in mindfulness of this interconnection of elements. This virtue may be seen as a quintessential ecological virtue. It is out of this wise understanding of interdependence that Buddhism goes on to see as vices what Buddha called the three fires of greed, delusion, and hatred. This wise realization of interconnection is, I think, at home in both Buddhist and secular ethics.

A more radical virtue rests in the life of compassion of a bodhisattva; this is one who attains but then postpones ultimate enlightenment in order to aid others. As Nan Huia-Chin writes, "The philosophy of Mahayana Bodhisattva opens up the Hinayana philosophy of detachment into a spirit of active entry into the world."[36] The bodhisattva helps others overcome their ignorance, craving, and grasping. I think the virtue of being a bodhisattva does not have a secular equivalent, for (in Buddhist tradition) this compassionate life is carried out in the midst of a religious conception of the cycle of life and rebirth (*samsara*) and the transcendental end of nirvana where a person realizes the transcendent consciousness (described above). A bodhisattva is not just a compassionate person; he or she lives in a world that has values and a structure that differ from a secular naturalism.[37] These Buddhist virtues— mindfulness and compassion—have commonly appealed to environmental contexts. They are employed, for example, in defense of nonexploitive treatments of land and animals.[38]

Religious Virtues in Context

The virtues and vices outlined above may come into environmental ethics on many levels. They can take explicit shape in outlining distinctive Buddhist or Christian views on animals, for example.[39] Or they may function below the surface, either enhancing or holding in check our secular environmental ethics. I close this chapter by highlighting a practical, moral, and political context in which religious virtues are sometimes explicit and sometimes implicit: agriculture.

Contemporary agrarians Wendell Berry, Marty Strange, and Wes Jackson have emerged over the last twenty-five years as leading advocates of alternative agriculture. Roughly, this means an agriculture that is practiced in light of ecology with the goal of long-term sustainability, the reduction or elimination of chemically intensive farming, and the promotion of more dispersed family- and community-oriented farming as opposed to industrially organized, capital-intensive, management-centered, corporate agriculture. Strange (who shares many of Berry's and Jackson's views on virtue) weaves together a case for such a virtue-oriented view of family farming.

Above all, family farming carries with it a commitment to certain values, entirely independent of the pettiness of economics. The agrarian tradition, of which family farming is a part, calls for people to be neighborly, to care for future generations, to work hard and to believe in the dignity of work, to be frugal, modest, honest, and responsible for and to the community. Family farming may be a business, but it is not just a business. It is a way of life as well. The farms in a family farming system operate in a social milieu that constrains the business behavior of farmers. Perhaps the best test of whether a farm is a family farm is this: Does the farmer feel more pain at the loss of a neighbor than joy at the opportunity to acquire that neighbor's land?[40]

The way of life that Strange advocates is, for Berry and Jackson, linked to a broader need for a culture of virtues that link persons and land. Berry writes:

A healthy culture is a communal order of memory, insight, value, work, conviviality, reverence, aspiration. It reveals the human necessities and the human limits. It clarifies our inescapable bonds to the earth and to each other. It assures that the necessary restraints are observed, that the necessary work is done, and that it is done well. A healthy farm culture can be based only upon familiarity and can grow only among a people soundly established upon the land; it nourishes and safeguards a human intelligence of the earth that no amount of technology can satisfactorily replace.[41]

If Berry is right, the resulting ideal may seem romantic or sentimental, but it may still (for all that) be an ideal to pursue.

When one undertakes to live fully on and from the land the prevailing values are inverted: one's home becomes an occupation, a center of interest, not just a place to stay when there is no other place to go; work becomes a pleasure; the most menial task is dignified by its relation to a plan and a desire; one is less dependent on artificial pleasures, less eager to participate in the sterile, nervous excitement of movement for its own sake; the elemental realities of seasons and weather affect one directly and become a source of interest in themselves; the relation of one's life to the life of the world is no longer taken for granted or ignored but, rather, becomes an immediate and complex concern. In other words, one begins to stay at home for the same reasons that most people now go away.[42]

So far the case for such an ideal alternative agriculture seems as open to the secularist as the religious believer, but Berry and Jackson go further. They draw on Christian views of land to bolster stewardship in light of God's goodness and contend further that this outlook supports what in Buddhism is called "right livelihood."

Berry develops his philosophy of land in light of the biblical narrative of God giving land ("the promised land") to the people of Israel. He uses this as a general outlook whereby all land should be seen as a gift:

It is a gift because the people who are to possess it did not create it. It is accompanied by careful warnings and demonstrations of the folly of saying that "My power and might of mine hand hath gotten me this wealth" (Deuteronomy 8:17). Thus, deeply implicated in the very definition of this

gift is a specific warning against *hubris*, which is the great ecological sin, just
as it is the great sin of politics. People are not gods. They must not act like
gods or assume godly authority. If they do, terrible retributions are in store.
In this warning we have the root of the idea of propriety, of *proper* human
purposes and ends. We must not use the world as though we created it ourselves.

The Promised Land is not a permanent gift. It is "given," but only for a
time, and only for so long as it is properly used. It is stated unequivocally,
and repeated again and again that "the heaven and the heaven of heavens is
the Lord's thy God, the earth also, with all that therein is" (Deuteronomy
10:14). What is given is not ownership, but a sort of tenancy, the right of
habitation and use: "The land shall not be sold forever: for the land is mine;
for ye are strangers and sojourners with me" (Leviticus 25:23).[43]

Berry depicts us as oriented to a giving, transcendent Creator whose calling to respectful land use is an opportunity to act in solidarity with God in a sacred order. In
Berry's work one can see each of the virtues I highlighted in the second section of the
chapter, and you may also see an ideal case of someone who promotes a religiously informed agrarianism that challenges our consumer-driven culture.[44]

This theology of land and land use has at least two consequences to consider in
practice and politics. First, formal agricultural education needs to be sufficiently open
so as to recognize agrarian values (religious and secular) as they function in social contexts. Berry and others stress how the virtues that function in good family farming
must be appreciated or inculcated in practice; they are not likely to be grasped in abstraction: "If family farming and good farming are as nearly synonymous as I suspect
they are, that is because of a law that is well understood, still, by most farmers but that
has been ignored in the colleges and offices and corporations of agriculture for thirty-
five or forty years. The law reads something like this: land that is in human use must
be lovingly used; it requites intimate knowledge, attention, and care."[45]

Gary Comstock points out the limitations of formal education versus the education and character formation that comes from participating in good family farming:

> Being a family farmer means caring for one's land. Such love cannot be
> taught in agricultural colleges; it is a practice that one learns at the feet of a
> master. It is knowledge of the heart, not the head, and it is best passed from
> generation to generation, not from agribusiness expert to agricultural stu-
> dent. This does not mean that newcomers cannot love the land; only that
> their doing so requires that they learn right emotions and intentions, not
> just right equations and ratios. This sort of care comes from lived experience
> and tradition—from memories, from the past. This provides a clear moral
> justification for giving preferential treatment to those farms that have long
> histories of having been family undertakings.[46]

This case for a practical encounter with family farming need not involve an explicit encounter with religious values, though in practice (given the current family farm population) it often will. Prominent contributors to environmental education have long
recognized the importance of taking agricultural practice and what might be called

"spirituality" seriously. Aldo Leopold, for example, claimed that there were "spiritual dangers in not owning a farm. One is the danger of supposing that breakfast comes from the grocery."[47]

Second, a closer look at the intermix of religious and secular virtues in agriculture can contribute to the debate on the political status of family farming. In the United States, there is debate over the extent to which current public policy gives an unfair advantage to corporate agribusiness. Debate also extends over the contribution of family farm culture to American culture at large. If Berry, Comstock, Strange, Jackson, and others are right, then family farming involves an interwoven set of goods such as the good of family or community, ecological health and sustainability, and neighborliness and civic virtues, which make an invaluable contribution to public life. Such claims need to be taken seriously in the debate over whether public funding should protect this virtuous way of life (or reduce the likelihood of it perishing). Of course, there are countless cases where family farms may fail to match the ideal of Berry and others. But we will not know this until we look closely for the virtues (and possible vices) that are at work. To do this calls for a comprehensive inquiry into secular and religious values.

In this chapter, I have sought to motivate the philosophical exploration of religious virtues in environmental contexts. I have proposed that theistic and nontheistic religions can provide philosophically interesting frameworks for identifying respectful environmental practices. As the case of agriculture shows, religious environmental virtues can function in a healthy environmental context in which the land is seen as a divine gift and caring for it is seen to be a divine vocation.

Notes

Acknowledgments. I thank Christina Herrmann, Ronald Sandler, and Brett Werner for helpful comments on an earlier version of this chapter.

1. I adopt what is often called a realist view of religion, according to which religions either make or assume assertions about the nature of reality that are either true or false. Some so-called nonrealists or antirealists, following Wittgenstein, see religions as "forms of life" without such commitments to what exists. For a discussion of realism and nonrealism, see my *Contemporary Philosophy of Religion* (Oxford: Blackwell, 1998).

2. For an overview of the outlook, see my *Contemporary Philosophy of Religion* and my *Evidence and Faith: Philosophy and Religion since the Seventeenth Century* (Cambridge: Cambridge University Press, forthcoming), chap. 8.

3. See, for example, W. Craig and J. P. Moreland, eds., *Naturalism: A Critical Appraisal* (London: Routledge, 2001).

4. The significance of the truth of one or more religions for environmental reflection may be brought to light in relation to Allen Carlson's views about the appreciation of nature. Carlson contends that although nature may be appreciated in terms of isolated individual objects (the appreciation of a rock, say, with no attention to geology) or of scenes (a picturesque landscape), it is better or deeper to see nature in its proper ecological framework (one grasps the relevant biota and abiota). Imagine that Christianity or Buddhism is true and credible. This would provide a fourth, deeper or wider, framework in which to appreciate

nature. See Allen Carlson, "Appreciation and the Natural Environment," *Journal of Aesthetics and Art Criticism* 37 (1979).

5. See, for example, R. M. Adams, *Finite and Infinite Goods* (Oxford: Oxford University Press, 1999).

6. To clarify my position, you might consider two views. In what may be called the "Hostage Model" environmental ethics is not adequate without an articulate, plausible metaphysics shedding light on the origin and nature of values. According to the "More Is Better Model" such a plausible metaphysic is valuable and thus desirable but not essential for an adequate environmental ethic. I am proposing the second, not the first, model.

7. For a good overview of the religious composition of the Western contemporary world, see R. Stark and R. Finke, *Acts of Faith: Explaining the Human Side of Religion* (Berkeley: University of California Press, 2000).

8. Reliable statistics are difficult to secure, but the *2003 Year Book of the Encyclopedia Britannica* includes figures such as the following: Christianity, 32.9 percent of the world population; Islam, 19.8 percent; Hinduism, 13.3 percent; Buddhism, 5.9 percent; and so on. In a pluralistic religious democracy like the United States explicit religious reasons may be shunned in policy making, but that does not mean that they are not operative socially and politically. See Michael Perry, *Under God? Religious Faith and Liberal Democracy* (Cambridge: Cambridge University Press, 2003).

9. So, for example, Tom Regan is more of an individualist than, say, J. Baird Callicott.

10. For a classic case of subordinating eros to agape, see Anders Nygren, *Agape and Eros*, trans. P. S. Watson (New York: Harper and Row, 1969). For an excellent critique and a case for a more balanced view, see R. M. Adams, "Pure Love," *Journal of Religious Ethics* (1980).

11. See Xingzhong Yao, *An Introduction to Confucianism* (Cambridge: Cambridge University Press, 2000).

12. From Yao, *An Introduction to Confucianism*, 74.

13. For further material on this, see my "Divine Agriculture: The Role of Philosophy and Theology in Agricultural Ethics," *Agriculture and Human Values* (fall 1992).

14. Michael Walzer, *Spheres of Justice* (New York: Basic Books, 1983), 244.

15. Lynn White, "The Historical Roots of Our Ecological Crisis," *Science* 155 (1967): 1203–7. This essay has been widely anthologized.

16. See, for example, the casual dismissal of Christianity in Paul Taylor's widely anthologized "The Ethics of Respect for Nature," in *Environmental Ethics*, ed. A. Light and H. Rolston (Oxford: Blackwell, 2003).

17. See, for example, Robin Attfield, "Christianity," in *A Companion to Environmental Philosophy*, ed. D. Jamieson (Oxford: Blackwell, 2003); and E. C. Hargrove, "Religion and Environmental Ethics: Beyond the Lynn White Debate," in *Religion and Environmental Crisis*, ed. E. C. Hargrove (Athens: University of Georgia Press, 1986).

18. Genesis 1:3 (NSRV).

19. Surah 27:60–64.

20. Psalm 24:1; Surah 4:26.

21. I defend the concept of divine ownership in "God's Estate," *Journal of Religious Ethics* 20, no. 1 (spring 1992).

22. Job 38:25–27.

23. See Genesis 8:8, 13.

24. Jonathan Helfand, "The Earth Is the Lord's: Judaism and Environmental Ethics," in *Religion and Environmental Crisis*, ed. E. C. Hargrove (Athens: University of Georgia Press, 1986).

25. Augustine, *Confessions*, first paragraph.

26. See Holmes Rolston III, "Does Nature Need to Be Redeemed?" *Zygon* 29 (1994).

27. See Thomas Aquinas, "De Veritate," Q.24, art. 8; and "Commentary on Boethius's 'De Trinitate.'" In the *Summa Theologiae*, Aquinas writes: "Gratia non tollat naturam sed perficiat" [Grace does not destroy/scrap nature but brings it to perfection].

28. The virtues cited here certainly have analogues in secular environmental ethics. One may even see them as cardinal virtues (e.g., respect, gratitude, and solidarity) or vices (e.g., vanity/arrogance, exploitiveness, ingratitude). But for the theist the respect, gratitude, and solidarity are with respect to the good Creator whom (ex hypothesi) the nontheist does not recognize. An atheist may be glad or reverential about nature (I have no doubt whatsoever over this), but "gratitude" is customarily something reserved for respectful, glad response to someone who has given one a gift. This is a position shared among many philosophers who otherwise hold very different views (e.g., Aquinas, Spinoza, Kant, and Hume).

29. For a further account of this thesis, see my *Contemporary Philosophy of Religion*.

30. For an overview of the issues, see R. A. Young, *Is God a Vegetarian?* (Chicago: Open Court, 1999).

31. See R. M. Adams's treatment of what he calls the "critical stance": "The [critical] stance amounts to at least this. For any natural, empirically identifiable property or type of action that we or others may regard as good or bad, right or wrong, we are committed to leave it always open in principle to raise evaluative or normative questions by asking whether that property or action-type is really good or to issue an evaluative or normative challenge by denying that it is really good or right" (*Finite and Infinite Goods*, 77–78). Adams argues that theism promoted a critical stance more thoroughly than nontheistic naturalism. See R. M. Adams, "Anticonsequentialism and the Transcendence of the Good," *Philosophy and Phenomenological Research* 67 (July 2003).

32. I am using the term *virtue* in an extended, broader use than in customary lists of virtues found in works by Aristotle and Aquinas. For a further, broader look at virtue, see my "The Virtues of Embodiment," *Philosophy* 76, no. 295 (January 2001). For a good account of the way arguments are conducted within religious traditions, see Basil Mitchell, *Faith and Criticism* (Oxford: Sarum Lectures, 1992).

33. See Paul Griffiths, "Buddhism," in *A Companion to Philosophy of Religion*, ed. P. Quinn and C. Taliaferro (Oxford: Clarendon, 1997).

34. Buddha, quoted in S. Randhakishnan and C. A. Moore, eds., *A Source Book in Indian Philosophy* (Princeton: Princeton University Press, 1957), 274.

35. Buddha, quoted in Randhakishnan and Moore, *A Source Book in Indian Philosophy*, 292.

36. Nan Huia-Chin, *The Story of Chinese Zen*, trans. T. Cleary (Boston: Charles E. Tutle, 1995), 52.

37. For an overview of the impact of Buddhism on environmental practices in Asia, see Christopher Chapple, "Jainism and Buddhism," in *A Companion to Environmental Philosophy*, ed. Dale Jamieson (Oxford: Blackwell, 2003). For further study of Buddhist and other religious environmental ethics, see M. E. Tucker and J. Grim, eds., *Worldviews and Ecology: Religion, Philosophy, and the Environment* (New York: Orbis Books, 1994).

38. For a fuller look at the nonsecular, doctrinal context of Buddhism, see Paul Griffiths, *On Being Buddha* (Albany: State University of New York Press, 1994).

39. See A. Linzey and T. Regan, eds., *Christianity and Animals* (New York: Crossroads, 1988); A. Linzey, *Animal Theology* (Urbana: University of Illinois Press, 1995); A. Linzey, *Christianity and the Rights of Animals* (New York: Crossroads, 1987); and M. E. Tucker and D. R. Williams, eds., *Buddhism and Ecology* (Cambridge: Harvard University Center for the Study of World Religions, 1997).

40. M. Strange, *Family Farming: A New Economic Vision* (San Francisco: Institute for Food and Development Policy, 1988), 35.

41. W. Berry, *The Unsettling of America* (New York: Avon Books, 1977), 43.

42. W. Berry, *The Long-Legged House* (New York: Harcourt, Brace, and Would, 1969), 88–89.

43. W. Berry, *The Gift of Good Land* (San Francisco: North Point Press, 1981), 270–71. Though I have given prominence to Berry's work, Wes Jackson is also an important reference point in mapping a theistic account of the virtues. See his *Altars of Unhewn Stone* (San Francisco: North Point Press, 1987).

44. Although Berry explicitly links his treatment of ecological stewardship with Buddhist right living, he does not develop this very extensively. I believe this is partly because of the fact that, historically, much of Buddhist ethics was fashioned in monastic, not familiar, contexts. Still, Buddhists have vied for the view that moral duties of compassion and care are sacred, and thus there is a serious kinship between Buddhism and Christianity.

45. W. Berry, *Human Encounters* (San Francisco: North Point Press, 1987).

46. G. Comstock, ed., *Is There a Moral Obligation to Save the Family Farm?* (Lincoln: University of Nebraska Press, 1987), 416.

47. Aldo Leopold, *A Sand County Almanac* (Oxford: Oxford University Press, 1949), 6.

CHAPTER 11

Cardinal Environmental Virtues: A Neurobiological Perspective

Louke van Wensveen

"We know that there are four cardinal virtues, viz. temperance, justice, prudence, and fortitude," wrote Ambrose, bishop of Milan, almost two millennia ago.[1] The label "cardinal" may well have been Ambrose's invention.[2] Derived from the Latin word *cardo*, which means "hinge," it expresses the idea that the moral life hinges on these four virtues. The idea itself is much older, however, having already been championed by ancient Greek philosophers, including Socrates, Plato, and Aristotle. They all agreed that we need to have the four cardinals or else our lives will turn to chaos. We will become failures in every personal and social respect. The cardinals bring our strongest passions in balance, these ancients would say. Only then can we begin to flourish, both internally and communally.[3]

The traditional list of four cardinals—practical wisdom, justice, temperance, and courage—has been stable for millennia.[4] In Western ethics, its contribution to human life remains practically unchallenged today. However, pedigree provides privilege but not proof. Recently, the world has been changing under severe environmental stresses, and human beings are consistently falling short in responding appropriately. Hence one may begin to wonder: Do the old cardinals still provide adequate guidance in this unfamiliar situation? Has the time perhaps come to supplement or even replace these rusty hinges with a smooth-turning, new set, with some cardinals that are explicitly *environmental* virtues?

To underscore the urgency of the question, consider how we spend our days. Much of the time, we are so busy pursuing our daily happiness that we do not even notice the decay around us (and, indeed, *inside* us). If we do, we may become so frightened that we swing into denial. Even if we find ourselves strong enough to look again, we risk being flooded by outrage, frustration, and eventually despair, which turns us into the sorts of sour pessimists nobody likes to follow. In short, our emotions keep us from responding swiftly and adequately to our growing environmental challenges.

Does this mean that we are less moral than previous generations? Possibly. In our modern predilection for spontaneity, perhaps we have become too eager to ignore the time-tested tradition of cardinal guidance of the passions. Perhaps all we need is a good sermon, urging us to cultivate the old virtues, pulling us back in line. However, rebellion against sensible advice is not exactly a modern invention, and if today we fail to come around, that may also be because under current circumstances we need *better* guidance than tradition now provides—and quickly too, because the stakes are so high.

Some readers will object at this point. Academic ethicists with solid grounding in Western virtue tradition may want to interpose that the cardinals express a truth for all times and that only the uninformed would undertake to doubt this. Meanwhile, environmental activists may want to suggest the opposite: that I just move on and not even frame the question in terms of a tradition that has so clearly proven obsolete (again, to all but the uninformed).

At the risk of alienating both sides, I intend to keep a middle course and *revisit* the tradition of the cardinal virtues from a biologically informed vantage point. Doing so, I contend, is neither so radical as to be unthinkable nor so backward as to be un-interesting.

Revisiting the tradition of the cardinals at this time is not unthinkable, if we consider that Western virtue ethics has traditionally taken its bearings from human biology.[5] Just as we are beginning to understand the unprecedented impact of our actions on the biological systems of the Earth, we are also for the first time in history beginning to understand the biology of the human emotions that undergird these actions. Thanks to recent advances in neuroscience, we are in a better position than the ancients ever were to judge how well the traditional cardinals shape our emotions, allowing us to pursue our goals in ways that are appropriate within our particular environments. Not to entertain this question at this time of unprecedented challenge as well as knowledge would be plain unreasonable.

In contrast, to consider the question already answered would be equally unreasonable, for aside from agreement among many environmentalists that this ancient virtue tradition is flawed, no clear alternative has yet emerged from their ranks. Meanwhile, just about everyone seems to favor some virtue or virtues for cardinal status. In other words, the *idea* that hinges are necessary for the moral life has not gone out of fashion but only a particular classical *model* of hinge. This begs the question: What makes the latest models better, apart from looks? And besides, how many hinges do we need to do the job? Apparently, not all is obvious. A philosophical inquiry therefore seems in order.

Back, then, to my question: *Do the four traditional cardinals provide adequate guidance in the face of current environmental challenges, or does the moral life now require explicitly ecological hinges?* Although I shall eventually develop my own systematic, philosophical approach to this question, I hope to do this in a way that broadly incorporates the intuitions and arguments of other environmental ethicists. Let me begin by outlining what they have been saying about the key attitudes belonging to an ecological way of life.

The State of the Art

First, there are some odd and misguided statistics. When I began to track the emergence of ecological virtue language more than a decade ago, it seemed like a good idea to count how many times, and in how many different sources, any particular virtue was mentioned in a representative sample of environmental literature. The combination of these figures, I thought, would show which virtues might be heading for cardinal status among the ecologically minded (who themselves seemed remarkably reluctant to use the label "cardinal" or even "virtue" plain and simple). Not that I saw cardinal status as a prize for the greatest number of sound bites. However, I had little else to work with, and it made sense to believe that if, for example, many environmentalists repeatedly urge, "Let's be humble!" this might be an indication of a key moral attitude for an ecological age.

Table 11.1 shows what I found.[6] That is an odd list. Although the top seems intuitive, the bottom does not. Try asking any ecologically minded person if those trailing virtues are indeed so negligible as to be effectively dispensable in an environmental ethic!

As the discrepancy indicates, we run the risk of missing some candidates if we approach the search for environmental cardinals as a popularity contest. This is actually not surprising (and I should have known better at the time). After all, quantity has never been a good measure of quality. Also, insofar as "hinge" habits are typically part of other praiseworthy character traits, they may be so obvious as not to require mentioning. Moreover, people are sometimes reluctant to put into words those basic attitudes that lie closest to their hearts, perhaps because they do not want to defame them, or make themselves vulnerable to judgment, or blunt their listeners' receptivity through overexposure. (At home, in order to prevent a reaction from my family, I usually do not advertise my love of simplicity. Recently, however, assuming myself alone, I did respond to a telemarketing survey from the auto industry in that spirit. When I put down the phone, my daughter emerged. "But Mom, we sound *Amish*!" she protested. So it goes.) Finally, like all of us, ecologically minded people may on occasion be unaware that they espouse certain core attitudes; they may even be self-deceived and deny it. By taking the approach of a popularity contest in search of cardinal environmental virtues, we may be blind to all these possibilities.

Table 11.1.   Frequency of Virtue Terms Found in a Review of the Post-1970 Environmental Literature

Rank	Virtue	Frequency	Sources
The Winner	Care	79	17
The Runner-up	Respect	65	12
Third Place	Love	54	12
Fourth Place	Compassion	34	12
	Reverence	29	12
	Humility	34	9
	Creativity	33	10
	Hope	29	9
	Sensitivity	29	6
Also Ran	Identification (with nature)	21	8
	Acceptance (of limitations)	20	9
	170 other virtues		
Barely in View	Diligence, Efficiency, Endurance, Forgiveness, Gentleness, Humor, Sincerity, Tolerance		

More than a decade has passed since I aborted my statistical efforts. In the meantime, some environmental ethicists have begun to identify one or more virtues as particularly important for inclusive, ecological flourishing. As a group, they give us quite a smorgasbord. At the risk of somewhat oversimplifying, I see their prime choices as falling into four irreducible groups (indeed, the number is no coincidence, and I shall come back to that), namely, virtues of position, care, attunement, and endurance. Let me provide a brief overview of these favorites and their supporters.

Virtues of position are constructive habits of seeing ourselves in a particular place in a relational structure and interacting accordingly. Environmental ethicists commonly argue that an ecological way of being and acting rests on seeing ourselves as responsive nodes in a complex network, rather than as overbearing top dogs in a linear hierarchy. In taking this view, they share the spirit of visionaries such as Francis of Assisi, Albert Schweitzer, and Aldo Leopold. Already in the 1940s, for example, Leopold suggested that each of us consider ourselves nothing but a "plain member and fellow citizen" in a larger ecological community.[7] Such a view implies a style of interaction that holds the middle between slavishness and bullying, namely, a dynamic process of listening, cautious trying, looking for feedback, and modifying when necessary.

Among modern environmental ethicists, Thomas Hill was the first to highlight virtues of position, recommending that we cultivate *humility, self-acceptance, gratitude,* and *appreciation of the good in others.*[8] That was back in 1983, when most environmentalists focused on a control-minded combination of voluntary simplicity and fixing problems through alternative technology. Hill's prophetic message has since found wide support among ecologically minded ethicists. For example, Bill Shaw enriches our understanding of virtues of position by exploring *respect, prudence,* and *practical judgment* (all also central attitudes in Aldo Leopold's land ethic).[9] Lisa Gerber, though not satisfied with a land ethic approach, nevertheless converges on the view that *humility* helps us overcome self-absorption; connect to a larger, more complex reality; and develop a sense of perspective on ourselves and the world.[10] A similar message is linked to the biblical *wisdom* tradition by Susan Power Bratton and Celia Deane-Drummond, both ecotheologians with backgrounds in biology.[11] The style of interaction that matches these habits of appropriate self-placement has typically been called *sensibility* or *sensitivity.* For example, John Rodman recommends "ecological sensibility," and Holmes Rolston speaks of "the sensitivity of the naturalist."[12]

Virtues of care are habits of constructive involvement within the relational structure where we have found our place. How widely do we cast our sensors in order to learn what is needed around us? How well do we understand various kinds of need? And at which setting have we chosen to begin receiving signals of need and become positively engaged? As Geoffrey Frasz points out, a mere attitude of humility is not enough as an ecological way of being. Only by cultivating a sense of *friendship* with the natural world do we begin to notice and address the needs around us.[13] Lisa Gerber similarly highlights *attentiveness* as a key environmental virtue.[14] According to Jennifer Welchman, the "stewardship virtue" of *benevolence* is an essential disposition for developing environmentally sensitive character.[15] Jim Nash advocates an attitude of *loving* nature.[16]

Virtues of attunement are habits of handling temptations by adjusting ("tuning") our positive, outgoing drives and emotions to match our chosen place and degree of constructive, ecosocial engagement.[17] This is key because without such personal adjustments, all our humility and respect, our wisdom and sensitivity, our attentiveness and friendship, may still amount to nothing. For example, what good does it do to the frog (or, indeed, myself) if I teach my children to love endangered amphibians only to turn around and satisfy my desire for a picture-perfect family home by moving into the new development that sits on what used to be prime frog habitat? For this reason, Jim Nash has become increasingly vocal as a defender of the central role of *frugality* in any environmental virtue ethic, that is, of "morally disciplined production and consumption for the sake of the social and ecological common good." Nash warns, however, that frugality must not be confused with sour self-denial. Although self-limiting, it is "an enriching norm that delights in the less consumptive joys of the mind and the flesh."[18] Phil Cafaro and Lisa Newton sound a similar tone by stressing the importance of *simplicity*.[19] Again, this is not a matter of bleak living but, rather, of rejoicing in the discovery that "less is more."

Finally, *virtues of endurance* are habits of facing dangers and difficulties by handling our negative, protective drives and emotions in such a way that we can sustain our chosen sense of place and degree of constructive ecosocial engagement. Again, this is crucially important if our commitment to a vision of ecological flourishing is going to be worth its salt. Life is full of obstacles, and if we do not have the character strength to face them, going instead with whichever wind blows the hardest, then we cannot be said to have an ethic at all. This is why Randy Larson argues that *tenacity*, a habit that holds the middle between apathy and obsession, must be added to Aristotle's list as a key virtue for environmentalists.[20] Similarly, Jennifer Welchman singles out the "stewardship virtue" of *loyalty*, which enables us to stand by our commitments in the face of challenges.[21]

Although some environmental ethicists emphasize one or more virtues in only a single group, others identify favorites in several categories. Few, however, stress key virtues across the entire range. In my book *Dirty Virtues* I argue that we can distinguish four cardinal virtues in the work of Thomas Berry, namely, reverence, attentiveness, creativity, and critical reflection.[22] These in fact correspond closely with the four categories I propose here. Stephen Bouma-Prediger, a Christian environmental ethicist, also covers all the bases in his discussion of fourteen ecological virtues, although he does not specify whether he considers all of them to be equally important.[23]

These virtues are the favorites among environmental virtue ethicists. Although no one has highlighted the entire batch, each virtue's essential goodness and importance are pretty uncontroversial. Together, they provide a rich picture of key ingredients for the moral life in an ecological age. We would likely do well to cultivate them all.

Does this mean that we may now identify these as *cardinal* virtues? Here I hesitate, for two reasons. First, rarely do environmental ethicists use the label "cardinal" themselves.[24] This may be an oversight, but it could also mean that something about the idea of cardinality does not sit well. Perhaps it has too strong an overtone of tradition, and tradition is a mixed blessing if you are looking to articulate new ways of being for an age marked by new challenges. Perhaps it sounds too hierarchical, as though the moral life consists of a ladder of virtues, with the elite on top.[25] Such an image might grate on your sensibilities if you espouse an egalitarian, inclusive worldview. Substantive reservations of this sort warrant careful reflection.

Second, even if we decide simply to attach the cardinal label to the environmental favorites, this would raise more questions than it appears to settle. For example, would it mean that some, or perhaps all, of the traditional four cardinals have been displaced? If so, then why? (Their dethronement, after more than two millennia of elite status, would deserve at least an explanation.) And if not, then what are the connections between the new, environmental cardinals and the traditional ones? Moreover, what exactly do we stand to gain by using the cardinal label? If it is just a fancy way of saying "crucial," then why not stick with the simpler term? If not, then what does the label add—and do all the environmental favorites indeed meet that criterion, whatever it may be?

A Proposal

These questions spur me to consider carefully, with an open mind as well as an eye to tradition, what might be the distinguishing mark of a cardinal virtue, the mark that sets it apart from other virtues. It cannot be the number of citations, as we saw. Nor can it be the production of the best end results in terms of our actions and their effects on the environment, for that is already one of the reasons why favorites tend to be favored, so it would not be a *distinct* mark of cardinality. Moreover, though the proof of the pudding is indeed in the eating, tastes differ, and what I might consider a culinary highlight a gourmand might rate as just slightly better than burnt porridge. And if the gourmand were to change my mind by claiming extensive experience and a seasoned attitude toward food, then we are back to square one, for in trying to distinguish cardinal virtues by their results, we would be judging those results by means of certain virtues.

Perhaps though, more subtly and with an eye to tradition, we might consider a virtue cardinal *if its cultivation provides a prerequisite for virtuous agency in general.*[26] Such a definition would in fact honor a central environmental concern, namely, that human agency be sustainable. Cardinal virtues would be those character traits without which our overall ability to act virtuously cannot be sustained. Elsewhere, I have used a synonymous definition to argue for the cardinality of temperance (renamed "attunement"): "The traditional idea that cardinal virtues function as hinges for the moral life suggests that they are necessary conditions for moral agency. . . . [E]cojustice is also a necessary condition for moral agency. . . . By contributing [in a necessary way] to ecojustice, namely through the adjustment of desires, attunement takes on a kind of cardinal significance that has been overlooked by the tradition."[27] This I would call *the broad definition of cardinality*. It does set cardinal virtues apart from just any intuitive favorites. However, many more virtues than the traditional four could meet the criterion. For example, humility, respect, cautiousness, cooperation, care, and benevolence would all be likely candidates for cardinality by this account. In the context of an ecojustice-based environmental ethic, one could think of such a broad group of cardinals as a safety net, "spun to help the Earth hold itself together."[28]

However, we may find the broad definition too broad to be useful. After all, it elevates any virtue that provides even the smallest prerequisite for general virtuous agency (or makes even the minutest, but essential, contribution to a prerequisite for virtuous agency, et cetera, ad infinitum) to the status of a cardinal virtue. Worse yet, *all* virtues would be cardinal by this criterion if we subscribe to the idea that the moral life represents a unity, which unravels as soon as we miss even a single virtue.[29]

Instead, I can see a more specific and interesting use for the idea of cardinality, one that I shall pursue here. It is based on *a narrow definition of cardinality*, which is consistent with (1) the broader, environmentally sensitive definition (that is, contained therein); (2) ancient Western virtue tradition; and (3) recently discovered constants of human neurobiology that are key to the moral life. To be specific, I propose that we understand cardinality in terms of those habitual (conditioned) neurobiological processes that are *always* part of an agent's virtue cultivation. We might then consider a particular virtue cardinal if its cultivation consists of *conditioning a particular type of neurobiological system that plays a pivotal role in processes of emotional fine-tuning by which agents are enabled to flourish and let flourish under changing circumstances*.[30]

This narrow definition of cardinality is consistent with the broader, environmentally sensitive definition insofar as "processes of emotional fine-tuning by which agents are enabled to flourish and let flourish under changing circumstances" belong to virtuous agency and insofar as playing a pivotal role in these processes fulfills a prerequisite for virtuous agency. Moreover, the narrow definition of cardinality avoids the objection of elitism because, from a process perspective, role fulfillment is not a hierarchical concept. Even a pivotal role only makes sense within a structure of embedded holism. Thus, this definition of cardinality would fit well with virtue theories developed in conjunction with ecological principles, including egalitarian theories.

The proposed narrow definition of cardinality is also in line with the tradition of understanding cardinal virtues to be *necessary constituents of all other virtues*.[31] In fact, the two definitions are substantially equivalent, the difference being only a matter of vocabulary. Why should this be an advantage? First, by honoring the history of a concept, we reduce the chance of confusion, which to my mind is a good thing. If we want to specify something else, we can always come up with a new name. (Perhaps we should start using the term *virtuous agency sustaining*, or something similar, for the broader definition outlined above.) Second, I believe that even today we can get a lot of benefit from the old idea of cardinality. After all, is it not extremely useful to search for, discuss, cultivate, and generally focus on those core character traits that belong to *any* virtuous pursuit? If we do not get *these* right, then we will never get anything right—except perhaps by luck. And the luxury of luck is decreasing proportionately to the rate of increase in environmental stresses. I propose, therefore, that we follow the ancients in asking what the necessary constituents of all other virtuous characteristics are—even if we translate the question and do not take their own answers a priori as given.

Finally, my proposed definition of cardinality is consistent with and draws attention to those recently discovered constants of human neurobiology that are key to the moral life. This is an advantage for three reasons. First, it too fits the traditional intuition that cardinal virtues are what they are because of basic structures of human biology.[32]

Although we might today reject the ancients' understanding of this biology, or focus more on the brain, it is easy to see the wisdom in the general idea that an ethical theory should pay heed to the biological givens of agents. How else can such a theory hope to provide realistic guidance? Second, by drawing our attention to the internal, biological systems of agents, the narrow definition of cardinality reminds us that humans too are *animals* and that their agency always involves a dynamic linkage between their internal biology and external social and ecological systems. Such a perspective on moral agency is a sine qua non for a consistent environmental—that is, systems-based—virtue ethic. Third, it also powerfully zooms in on previously unknown or neglected building blocks of human action. In fact, the neurobiological systems perspective on moral agency promises to do for the advancement of virtue cultivation what the microscope once did for the advancement of science.[33]

I propose, then, that we consider as the distinguishing mark of a cardinal virtue that its cultivation involves the conditioning of a particular type of neurobiological system that plays a pivotal role in any other process of virtue cultivation.[34] In taking this perspective, we honor modern ecological sensibilities as well historically acquired wisdom. We also position ourselves to make the most of recent work in neurobiology, which stands to revolutionize the human animal's potential to live a life of virtue.

The Blessed Brain: A Model

Which of the favorite environmental virtues deserve cardinal status? In order to answer this question, I must first show you what, in a nutshell, goes on at the level of neuro-biological systems when humans cultivate virtues. Let me do that by gradually leading you down from the level of ecological systems to the level of the human brain with the help of an extended illustration.

Imagine that we are visiting a rather funky exhibition of modern art. I am your tour guide. We stop at what looks like a triptych, the kind of three-panel, gilded painting you may have seen on a prior visit to a collection of medieval Western art.[35] This particular triptych is called *The Blessed Brain* because of the portrayal of a human brain—medial (internal, vertical) and axial (internal, horizontal) views, both with haloes—on the main panel. It is flanked by a lush and sunny landscape on the left panel and a picture of two tiny campers under an expansive evening sky on the right.

We first take a closer look at the painting on the left. The landscape scene is teeming with life. Among lush greenery and fanciful flowers in the forefront, we see birds of multicolored plumage, tree mammals large and small, reptiles with shiny scales, and, between molding leaves on the mossy ground, a frog on a mushroom. Rays of sunlight playfully invite us to peek through the foliage. At a slight distance we discover a clearing in the forest, where hoofed and clawed animals forage and hunt among the high grasses. One herd has adorned itself with garments, pigments, and ornaments. We catch its members staring and pointing in the direction of the sun—and then we see it too, as though simultaneously through a microscope and a telescope: the sky, full of gaseous atoms, swirling in four colored streams. And further behind these, much further, our moon, the familiar seven planets plus Pluto, the Milky Way, and then galaxy upon galaxy and clusters of galaxies, like shining soap bubbles in the unfathomable but finite darkness of an unlit stage.

This, you may have guessed already, is the artist's rendition of a just community. In a medieval triptych, the panel would have shown the New Jerusalem, shining on a distant hill. The vision before us looks more like a return to Paradise, also a biblical theme, yet with the realistic twist that hunting, death, and decay continue—presumably as long as planetary conditions remain favorable to carbon-based life.[36] Nor do the humans end up climbing to the top of the hill. They stay put as one species of earthlings among others. Given their particular mental capacities, however, they can from that humble vantage point appreciate the beauty of the whole arrangement, from microcosm to macrocosm.

As we shift our attention to the panel on the right, we realize from the fashion of their outfits that the two small campers under the broad evening sky belong to the adorned herd of animals. Relaxed in front of a shallow cave, a dwindling campfire and several chewed-off ears of corn between them, they are enjoying the last bites of their evening meal. Their bodies are slightly inclined toward each other, and their faces appear to be smiling. Perhaps they are a couple? We will never know; the artist does not care to give us any further clues.

In fact, the artist seems to have been more interested in painting the expansive sky above their tête-à-tête. Again unusual things are happening in the heavens. (We notice this only now, preoccupied as we were at first by the more recognizable dynamics between the two people.) Rather than hanging loose in the firmament, all the stars are placed on clusters of five thin, parallel lines. It looks at though we are witnessing what the ancients would have called the music of the spheres, portrayed as a grand orchestral score with a complex rhythmical arrangement. Far on the left, past the key signatures, small icons indicate the instrumentation. Surprisingly, the instruments only play as pairs, each couple having to share a single system of notes: oboe with flute, piccolo with French horn, cymbals with xylophone. Even more surprising, their notes are very measured: usually one shining star per system, often only in comfortable range for one of the two instruments. In this snapshot of cosmic harmony, apparently half the orchestra is keeping quiet or just barely whispering along!

I point out a sign on the wall, next to the triptych, on which the museum curators provide us with an interpretive key to the instrumentation. The cosmic score actually symbolizes the internal, affective state of the two happy campers. Each instrument represents a human emotion; its partner, an opposing emotion. Oboe and flute stand for sadness and joy; piccolo and French horn, for fear and daring; cymbals and xylophone, for scorn and wonder; and so on. Moreover, from the placement of the stars we can deduce that, in their peaceful after-dinner setting, the two people experience mostly positive, outgoing emotions. Just like the outer world in its peaceful evening manifestation, their inner worlds are molded constructively. They are in a state of virtue. Again, we are reminded of the common medieval practice to portray, on a side panel, the financial sponsor(s) of the triptych in a state of blessedness.

Finally, I draw your attention to the central panel, to the "Blessed Brain" itself. Though pictured as it might have been in an anatomy textbook, with medial and axial views, this is no ordinary brain—or so we are inclined to believe, for we find ourselves blinded by the thickly gilded rays of its double halo, rays that fan out all the way across the triptych's fold lines, onto the side panels. A bit overdone, perhaps? Indeed, a bit *anthropocentric*? Not so, the museum curators again inform us on their sign. Not today. It might have been in the Middle Ages, when the human footprint on the environment was still small enough for people to believe in a more mystical balancing force (for example, the "Blessed Heart") and consider trust in human powers idolatrous. However, in these days of human-induced environmental stresses, the human brain is *the hinge* on which the whole picture of harmony turns.[37] It connects inner biological dynamics with outer biological dynamics, emotions with ecology. If it does this well, then both dimensions can keep running harmoniously; if not, then both will falter and die.

I see you peer at the grayish cauliflower halves, unconvinced. Perhaps you are reminded of those shriveled-up body parts in gilded reliquaries that, belonging to an old tradition of saint worship, are believed to have magical powers. Let me quickly liberate you from that queasy association by drawing your attention to some down-to-earth details of anatomy and physiology, subtly highlighted by the artist in this rendering of the living brain.

In the medial view, our attention is drawn to a border region at the very bottom of the brain, just behind the brain stem. That is the *cerebellum*. It is the general coordinating center of a multicomponent system that fulfills a key role in the human ability to match external, situational features with internal, emotion-based responses.[38] The cerebellum contributes the capacity to ensure a *high-quality* integrated emotional response by applying quality standards learned from experience.[39] This involves the ability to pair external, situational features (communicated to the cerebellum by perceptual regions in the cerebral cortex) with remembered profiles of successful emotional responses in similar situations. Based on this pairing, the cerebellum then sends signals to the systems that are generating, at default levels, various components of the relevant emotions, affecting for example their trigger sensitivity or the intensity and duration with which they operate.[40] The entire process continues in the form of a feedback cycle as long as the situation (which will begin to include the effects of human action!) continues to trigger default emotional reactions that need to be modulated into a high-quality, integrated response.

In the Blessed Brain all of this works very well—hence the halo. We are, in fact, looking at a picture of excellence: at a *virtue* dedicated to ensuring the high quality of emotion-based human responses in specific situations. In fact, if we think about it, we are looking at not just any virtue but a *cardinal* virtue: at a conditioned biological process *that is a necessary ingredient of all other virtue cultivation*. After all, can you imagine doing anything well without the ability to judge how to strike the right tone in particular situations? Lacking that ability, you might have all sorts of lofty, cerebral goals, but you would never be able to implement them, for you could not select the circumstance-dependent means to get there. This is exactly what classical Greeks and Roman philosophers had in mind when they described *practical wisdom* and identified it as a cardinal virtue.[41] The artist of *The Blessed Brain* is thus suggesting that we associate the cerebellar feedback system with this ancient hinge of the moral life.

The artist goes further, however. As though it were a cartoon, the cerebellum of the Blessed Brain emits not only a golden halo but also a spray of tiny pearls, symbolizing the sweat of healthy effort. The artist wants to suggest that the cerebellum operates at a high level of sensitivity and activity, matching, and checking, and adjusting, and rechecking constantly—yet smoothly, without overexertion—to ensure the highest degree of attuned response. This is because the Blessed Brain belongs to a member of the adorned herd of animals, who see themselves as one species among others, which means that they typically have to keep close track of how they fit in. Had they thought of themselves as Kings of the Field (assuming they had the features to pull it off), they would have been much more likely just to go with their gut feelings, lording it over others as seemed convenient. They might have needed their cerebella to keep track of in-group competition, but otherwise this part of their brains would not have to be very highly sensitized. Thus, where one places oneself in terms of social relationships affects one's style of interacting. By seeing oneself as a responsive node embedded in a complex network, like the adorned herd, one becomes generally both more sensitive and more cautious—and thus more inclined to monitor and modify.[42]

Moving to the axial (horizontal cross section) view, we notice a central region at the very bottom of the frontal lobe. That is the *ventromedial prefrontal cortex*, a coordinating center in a multicomponent system that undergirds the human ability to respond *constructively* to complex social situations.[43] For example, the ventromedial prefrontal cortex plays a key role in enabling appropriate feelings of compassion, embarrassment, and mourning.[44] It ensures the fittingness of such responses by triggering the relevant emotional circuits precisely at those times and levels that match stored profiles of successful social reactions in similar situations.[45]

Again, in the Blessed Brain all of this works optimally. We are looking at a *virtue* dedicated to ensuring a *high quality* of social responsiveness, based on prior experiences and reflection on those experiences. Moreover, this too is a *cardinal* virtue, a conditioned biological process that is a necessary ingredient of all other virtue cultivation. After all, can you imagine functioning well as a social animal, a *zoon politikon*, without having the ability to empathize with your mates or to feel when you may have offended them and must make amends? The artist of *The Blessed Brain* wants us to associate the neurological underpinnings of this ability with the ancient cardinal virtue of *justice*. Justice's primary function has traditionally been understood as ensuring a balance of well-being in the world.[46] This necessarily involves the well functioning of an agent's ability to be triggered into reacting by perceptions of external imbalance.

Less traditionally, however, in the Blessed Brain the system has also been conditioned to respond to an *extended* range of triggers, predisposing its owner to care about the needs of organisms outside his or her own group. Again, this is because the Blessed Brain belongs to a member of the adorned herd of animals, who have developed a highly compassionate culture.[47] When we look again at the left panel, we notice how young children are affectionately held by their parents. By choosing this symbol of compassionate behavior, the artist hints at a reputed correlation between child-rearing practices and cultural levels of compassion.[48] Had the adorned herd of animals instead thought of themselves as Terminators, they would have exhibited the evolutionarily much more common pattern of limiting their compassion to group members while approaching strangers with default xenophobia and aggression. By seeing themselves from an early age as embedded in an extended network of nature, the adorned herd's members have become more socially sensitive to the larger community of life. Thus, they are more inclined to respond considerately to a wide circle of organisms.

Finally, back in the medial view, we notice what looks like a jumble of circular wires, some green and some red. They wind all over the place, from the brain stem through the midbrain (where it gets really tangled) into various areas of the cortex and back again, in greater and smaller loops. The curators tell us that the green wires, like green traffic lights, stand for neural circuits dedicated to goal-directed, positive emotions, popularly known as desires.[49] The red wires, like red traffic lights, stand for neural circuits dedicated to protective, negative emotions, such as fear, anger, and disgust. Together, these green and red wires fulfill a key role in the human ability to produce just the right sort of emotional mix to ensure personal flourishing in different situations.[50] Thus, they correspond with the pairs of instruments that play the music score representing the balanced inner state of the campers on the right panel. Each wire serves as a trained musician, primed to play his or her instrument masterfully and to respond individually to the needs of the moment—but always within the larger balance of the composition (cerebrally articulated, normative directions) and the conductor's integrating, situation-sensitive interpretation (cerebellar guidance).[51]

The green desire wires represent various brain systems dedicated to what neuroscientists call "pre-goal attainment positive affect." One wire is drawn more prominently than others: the artist of *The Blessed Brain* wants to focus our attention on a system characterized by the neurotransmitter *dopamine*. This system is symbolic for what goes on in the green zone because it gets us up and moving, instead of just daydreaming about what we would want to do.[52] (Other systems include those dedicated to testosterone, estrogen, and phenylethylamine, a key neurotransmitter in romantic love: all powerful movers as well!) The artist has highlighted two processing centers in the dopamine circuit: a region of the brain stem called the *ventral tegmental area* and a region of the left prefrontal cortex called the *nucleus accumbens*. Together they constitute a feedback system that indicates how close we are to reaching a predicted goal. When things go better than expected, the nucleus accumbens communicates this to the ventral tegmental area, which releases a lot of dopamine back to the nucleus accumbens. We experience strong feelings of pleasure (a "rush," "butterflies," etc.). If things simply go according to plan, or worse than expected, no such boost occurs.[53] Doesn't this explain why it often feels better to desire than to possess, and why we keep shifting our gaze to new shores?

In the Blessed Brain, this system functions excellently in the sense that its settings have been conditioned such that, no matter what happens, it tends neither to "overheat" nor to "freeze."[54] Within this comfortable range, it responds swiftly and effectively to signals from other parts of the brain (for example, the cerebellum), demanding upward or downward—usually downward!—adjustment of activity.[55] We are thus looking at a *virtue* dedicated to ensuring the *high-quality* responsiveness of pre-goal attainment affect. Moreover, this too is a *cardinal* virtue, for in order to do anything well, we clearly must have the ability to prevent our desires from undermining our plans and instead channel them into supporting paths. The ancients called this ability *temperance*, and the artist of *The Blessed Brain* suggests that the highlighted neurological system be associated with this ancient tradition.

Again, however, the artist does not exactly follow the traditional concept of temperance. The highlighted system of pre-goal attainment affect is based on dopamine, which facilitates desire in general. By contrast, temperance has traditionally been associated especially with the ability to moderate sexual desire (most vehement among the "desires of touch"), which would be facilitated more specifically by testosterone and estrogen.[56] The choice is a matter of where one believes the largest threat to rational action lies. In the judgment of the artist, the sustainability of human moral agency is most seriously endangered by general desire, which tends to be the driver behind unsustainable consumerist behaviors. The Blessed Brain, belonging to a member of the adorned herd, particularly excels in moderating general desire.

The red wires, dedicated to protective, "negative" emotions, also represent various systems. Again, one wire is drawn more prominently than others: the artist wants us to focus on a system in which *cortisol*, a steroid stress hormone, plays a key role. This system is symbolic for what goes on in the red zone because it gets us in gear for protective action, for fight or flight. And once more the artist has highlighted two processing centers in an intricate feedback loop: the *amygdala* and the *hippocampus*, both located in the temporal lobe. The amygdala receives visual and auditory triggers associated with danger and sets into motion a series of reactions that lead to the release of cortisol, which acts both in the body (e.g., by making your heart race, which also makes you *aware* that you are feeling afraid or angry) and on the hippocampus. The hippocampus in turn puts the breaks on the same system by signaling that the release of cortisol should be reduced. The ultimate degree of stress response thus depends on the relative strength of the messages from the amygdala and the hippocampus.[57]

In the Blessed Brain, the excellence of this system again resides in the conditioned settings, which prevent the extremes of overactivity as well as underactivity. Within the resulting range, the system is trained to a high degree of responsivity to incoming signals demanding upward or downward adjustment of activity. Again, the specifics of the situation usually require downward modulation: we normally have to calm our fears or reduce our anger.[58] All in all, we are looking at a *virtue* dedicated to ensuring the *high-quality* responsiveness of defensive human emotions. This too is a *cardinal* virtue, for in order to do anything well, we must have the ability to channel our fears and aggressive impulses into helpful, supporting paths. The ancients called this ability *courage*, and the artist of *The Blessed Brain* clearly suggests that the highlighted neurological system be associated with this ancient tradition.[59]

Once more, though, the artist modifies the ancient model by shifting the accent away from the traditional emphasis on personal death in battle as the trigger causing the most troublesome automated response that would call for moderation. Judging that people in modern times face an even more fear-inspiring prospect, namely, *species death through the death of nature*, the artist wants us to understand the courage that symbolizes excellence in all protective human responses, the courage portrayed in the Blessed Brain, as a constructive response to this ultimate possibility of environmental destruction.

We have come to the end of our tour. While you take a final look at the triptych, I sum up its basic message (like most medieval art, it contains a moral): Today, ecological flourishing, which includes human flourishing, depends on the fitting balance of a wide array of social, outgoing, and protective human emotions, which in turn depends on the well functioning of certain key parts of the human brain. These parts we might as well honor with a halo, for even though it is no mystery what they do, it is always miraculous when everything works well and is trimmed and trained to perfection.

Cardinal Environmental Virtues

With the help of the model of the Blessed Brain, I am now in a position to address the question before us: Which of the current environmental favorites are indeed *cardinal* virtues in the sense that their cultivation focuses on the conditioning of a particular type of neurological system with an essential role in all other virtue cultivation? Note that the model of the Blessed Brain does not exclude the possibility that there may be *more* cardinal virtues than the classical four! However, in the interest of intellectual hygiene, we should only explore this option if we can clearly establish that a certain environmental favorite conditions a distinctly different and equally essential neurological system.

By way of shortcut, I shall assume that any environmental favorites with core conceptual similarities to the classical four—despite perhaps somewhat different labels— are indeed cardinal virtues in the sense I have proposed. Other favorites may be related to a classical cardinal, either as *constituents* (conditioning a subpart of the essential system), or as *instantiations* (conditioning the system with respect to a particular type of trigger), or as *analogues* (conditioning a less representative system of the same essential type).[60] Alternatively, they may not be related to the classical four at all—in which case we still cannot exclude the possibility that they are cardinals too, for they may condition as yet unidentified neurological systems of cardinal importance. Then the search would be on for such systems.

When I discussed the environmental favorites above, I organized them in four categories: virtues of position, care, attunement, and endurance. I chose that format knowing that it would facilitate the task of examining how this as yet unorganized batch of virtues might line up with the neural processes I believe to be associated with the cultivation of the four classical cardinals. Although this task can only be completed with the help of additional neuroscientific studies, a philosophical categorization of experience can generate fruitful hypotheses for such studies. Personally, I expect *all* the current favorites to line up quite well with the neural processes underlying the cultivation of the traditional four cardinals. Let me briefly explain how I imagine, or predict, these connections.

VIRTUES OF POSITION

As we saw in the Blessed Brain, the cerebellar system associated with practical wisdom (or prudence, in Roman Catholic parlance) links information about external situations with learned profiles of successful integrated emotional responses, operating at a level of intensity that depends on an agent's sense of position in a particular relational structure. Also, the model of the Blessed Brain suggests that in an ecological age, a high degree of human "situation sensitivity" is indispensable for the integrated flourishing of external and internal biological systems. The exercise of practical wisdom thus takes on an intensified form, which environmentalists tend to refer to as *sensitivity*. This environmental favorite can therefore be considered a synonym of practical wisdom. Also, we saw in the Blessed Brain that the more modest one's sense of place, the more actively one will try to monitor and modify in order to respond fittingly to what is going on. Thus, the cultivation of practical wisdom has become integrally dependent on virtues such as *humility, respect,* and *gratitude,* all of which contribute to an agent's modest sense of place.[61] I am therefore inclined to characterize these environmental favorites as constituents of the cardinal virtue of practical wisdom.[62]

VIRTUES OF CARE

In the model of the Blessed Brain, the frontal lobe system associated with justice allows one to respond to social situations in constructive, compassionate ways. Thus, the cultivation of justice has become synonymous with caring. (The model therefore connects an ethic of justice with an ethic of care, often presented as philosophical rivals, insofar as they are associated with the same pivotal neural system.) Caring, however, is integrally dependent on the virtues of *benevolence* and *attentiveness,* by which one becomes well disposed and actively notices needs beyond one's own. These two environmental favorites I would therefore consider constituents of the cardinal virtue of justice.[63] Meanwhile, insofar as *friendship* and *love* represent different types of caring, each with a distinct intensity and accents that befit particular sorts of relationships, I would classify these favorites as specific instantiations of the general virtue of justice. This would also apply where the focus of friendship or love is nonhuman nature.

VIRTUES OF ATTUNEMENT

In the Blessed Brain, the dopaminergic system associated with temperance allows one to channel one's desires to support rather than undermine one's overarching plans. The model focuses on general desire, which drives ecologically harmful consumerist behaviors, rather than following Western virtue tradition in its preoccupation with "desires of touch." Thus, although the cultivation of temperance continues to include various instantiations of moderating behavior, the environmental favorites of *simplicity* and *frugality* have become symbolic for its core meaning. Meanwhile, chastity takes more of a backseat as an analogically related virtue, valued for its benefits in family planning and personal as well as social harmony but definitely not as a way to "chastise the flesh" in search of otherworldly pursuits.[64]

VIRTUES OF ENDURANCE

In the model of the Blessed Brain, the stress system associated with courage allows one to face dangers and difficulties such that one's protective emotions do not interfere with, and may even support, one's overall plans. As in classical Western virtue tradition, the model especially focuses our attention on the ability to channel the fear of death—yet with the twist that we must also learn to handle the fear (plausible or not) that our entire species may die through the death of nature. For those whose lives derive meaning from a sense of commitment, whether to future generations or to a divine creator, the environmental favorite of *loyalty* then becomes a key aspect—a constituent—of cultivating courage.[65] Meanwhile, the cultivation of courage proper has become synonymous with the environmental favorite of *tenacity*: maintaining a steady focus on what matters in an ecological age, rather than slipping into the unhelpful extremes of either apathy (freezing) or obsession (blindly fighting) in the face of widespread environmental deterioration.

It seems, then, that by the criterion of cardinality that I have proposed, all of the environmental favorites discussed above can be considered either cardinals themselves (sensitivity, tenacity), or related to a cardinal virtue as constituents (humility, respect, gratitude, benevolence, attentiveness, loyalty), or particular instantiations of a cardinal virtue (friendship, love, frugality, simplicity). One caveat is in order, however. My suggestion, though philosophically grounded, still only has the status of a hypothesis. By making the operation of certain biological systems part of the definition of cardinality, I have introduced the need for scientific testing in order to move from a hypothesis to a solid model of cardinal environmental virtues. Here I must hand on the gavel, for I am not qualified to carry out such research myself. I hope, therefore, that in the future neuroscientists will become as interested in studying the pathways of virtue as they are currently focused on studying the pathways of pathology.[66]

Pending such corroboration, I would argue that environmental virtue ethicists, as a group, have covered a wide spectrum of cardinal functions, subfunctions, and instantiations—at least as wide as the spectrum covered by the ancients of the West.[67] I do not think that this is just coincidence. Insofar as these cardinal aspects of virtue cultivation represent essential dimensions of human engagement with the world, based on our common biology as adaptable mammals, we may indeed *expect* them to turn up at the core of any virtue ethic, old or new.

Conclusion

With the emergence of environmental ethics, the classical list of cardinal virtues—practical wisdom, justice, temperance, and courage—has not been replaced; rather, it has been transformed for an ecological age. What was cardinal about the list more than two millennia ago, those core features necessitated by our biology, is cardinal now. Unless we radically evolve as a species (who knows how we will use genetic engineering?), we can expect this to remain the case for generations in the future. Nevertheless, accents and interpretations have shifted, and in their environmental articulation the cardinals have become explicitly responsive, not only to interhuman social relationships but also to broader ecological ones. Thus, along with genuine similarity, there is a real difference: not the sort of radical transformation that trashes what is old but, rather, the sort that rebuilds from the old root up, for that root contains the very systems by which we are able to respond to our ailing world—the biology of our brains.[68]

Notes

1. Cited in Thomas Aquinas, *Summa Theologica* II–I 61.1, trans. Fathers of the English Dominican Province (New York: Benziger Brothers, 1948). The citation is from Ambrose's commentary on the Gospel of Luke. Note that the term *prudence* (*prudentia* in Latin) here indicates the classical virtue of "practical wisdom" (*phronesis* in Greek). It should not be confused with the popular, modern meaning of *prudence* as self-regarding, shrewd judgment.

2. See "Cardinal Virtues," *Catholic Encyclopedia*, available at www.newadvent.org/cathen/03343a.htm (accessed 22 January 2004).

3. See Plato, "The Laws," in *The Laws of Plato*, trans. Thomas L. Pangle (New York: Basic Books, 1980), I.631; Aristotle, *Ethica Nicomachea*, trans. W. D. Ross, in *Introduction to Aristotle*, ed. Richard McKeon (New York: Random House, 1947), 308–543.

4. Other leading philosophers and theologians who used this list include the Roman orator Cicero, Pope Gregory the Great, the Muslim scholar al-Ghazali, the Jewish scholar Maimonides, and the Christian scholar Thomas Aquinas. Their interpretations are often quite liberal, reflecting their times and particular concerns. Ambrose, for example, used the four cardinals very cleverly to argue that what pagan tradition had identified as essential to the moral life was nothing but the eternal Christian truth of the gospel. See Ambrose, *De Officiis*, trans. H. de Romestin, in *The Nicene and Post-Nicene Fathers of the Church*, ed. H. Wace and P. Schaff (Grand Rapids: Baker Book House, 1980), 2d series, 10.

5. See Aristotle, *Ethica Nicomachea*, I.13.

6. The findings are based on eighteen environmental texts (monographs and anthologies) from the period 1970–92. The texts were selected to represent a cross section of authors from social ecology, land ethics, deep ecology, ecofeminism, creation spirituality, process philosophy/theology, mainstream Roman Catholic environmentalism, and mainstream Protestant environmentalism. The authors include Thomas Berry, Wendell Berry, Murray Bookchin, John Cobb, Bill Devall, Andrew Linzey, Jay McDaniel, Sean McDonagh, Joanna Macy, Arne Naess, James Nash, Rosemary Ruether, John Seed, George Sessions, and Charlene Spretnak. For the full list of virtues, see Appendix A in my book, *Dirty Virtues: The Emergence of Ecological Virtue Ethics* (Amherst, NY: Humanity Books, 2000), 163–65. I thank my research assistant, Kim Christiansen, for helping with the tabulation.

7. Aldo Leopold, *A Sand County Almanac and Sketches Here and There* (New York: Oxford University Press, 1949), 240.

8. Thomas E. Hill Jr., "Ideals of Human Excellence and Preserving Natural Environments," *Environmental Ethics* 5 (1983): 211–24. Here I shall treat "self-acceptance" as an aspect of humility and "appreciation of the good in others" as synonymous with respect, rather than as separate virtues.

9. Bill Shaw, "A Virtue Ethics Approach to Aldo Leopold's Land Ethic," *Environmental Ethics* 19 (1997): 53–67.

10. Lisa Gerber, "Standing Humbly before Nature," *Ethics and the Environment* 7, no. 1 (2002): 39–53.

11. Susan Power Bratton, "The Precautionary Principle and the Biblical Wisdom Literature: Toward an Ethic of Ecological Prudence in Ocean Management," paper presented at the Annual Meeting of the American Academy of Religion, Toronto, 2002; Celia Deane-Drummond, *Biology and Theology Today* (London: SCM Press, 2001), 89–90.

12. John Rodman, "Four Forms of Ecological Consciousness Reconsidered: Ecological Sensibility," in *Ethics and the Environment*, ed. Donald Scherer and Thomas Attig (Englewood Cliffs, NJ: Prentice-Hall, 1983), 88–92; Holmes Rolston III, *Conserving Natural Value* (New

York: Columbia University Press, 1994). I take John Rodman's notion of ecological sensibility to be substantially the same as Rolston's notion of the sensitivity of the naturalist.

13. Geoffrey B. Frasz, "What Is Environmental Virtue Ethics That We Should Be Mindful of It?" *Philosophy in the Contemporary World* 8, no. 2 (fall–winter 2001): 5–14.

14. Lisa Gerber, "Environmental Virtues and Vices," Ph.D. dissertation, Department of Philosophy, University of New Mexico, 1999.

15. Jennifer Welchman, "The Virtues of Stewardship," *Environmental Ethics* 21 (1999): 411–23.

16. James A. Nash, *Loving Nature: Ecological Integrity and Christian Responsibility* (Nashville: Abingdon Cokesbury, 1991).

17. Neuroscientists distinguish between positive and negative emotions. The terminology does not reflect a value judgment but, rather, describes the difference between leading the organism to reach out or to protect itself.

18. James A. Nash, "The Old Order Changeth: The Ecological Challenge to Christian Life and Thought," *Virginia Seminary Journal* (December 1997): 11.

19. Philip Cafaro, "Less Is More: Economic Consumption and the Good Life," *Philosophy Today* 42 (1998): 26–39; Lisa H. Newton, *Ethics and Sustainability: Sustainable Development and the Moral Life* (Upper Saddle River, NJ: Prentice-Hall, 2003).

20. Randy Larsen, "Environmental Virtue Ethics: Nature as Polis," M.A. thesis, Department of Philosophy, Colorado State University, 1996.

21. Welchman, "The Virtues of Stewardship."

22. Wensveen, *Dirty Virtues*, 66.

23. Steven Bouma-Prediger, *For the Beauty of the Earth: A Christian Vision for Creation Care* (Grand Rapids: Baker Academic, 2001), 137–60. The fourteen virtues are respect, receptivity, self-restraint, frugality, humility, honesty, wisdom, hope, patience, serenity, benevolence, love, justice, and courage. For a helpful table of these virtues and their corresponding vices, biblical texts, theological motifs, and ethical principles, see Steven Bouma-Prediger, "Response to Louke van Wensveen: A Constructive Proposal," in *Christianity and Ecology*, ed. Dieter T. Hessel and Rosemary Radford Ruether (Cambridge: Harvard University Press, 2000), 175.

24. In fact, Bouma-Prediger draws many parallels between Aristotle's catalog and his own list of key virtues for (Christian) ecological ethics but does not choose to label any of the latter as cardinals. Wisdom, justice, temperance, and courage all appear on Bouma-Prediger's list, with explicit nods to their classical status as cardinals. However, he does not lift these four above the other ten virtues on his list. See Bouma-Prediger, *For the Beauty of the Earth*, 137–60.

25. I have suggested this myself in "Attunement: An Ecological Spin on the Virtue of Temperance," *Philosophy in the Contemporary World* 8, no. 2 (2001): 74.

26. This would, by definition, also produce good because a (strong) concept of virtue implies that its results are what we call good—even if they may not be as planned, or desirable, by some external measurement. See Linda Zagzebski, *Virtues of the Mind: An Inquiry into the Nature of Virtue and the Ethical Foundations of Knowledge* (Cambridge: Cambridge University Press, 1996), 88–102.

27. Wensveen, "Attunement," 74.

28. Wensveen, "Attunement," 74.

29. On the so-called unity of the virtues thesis, see Aristotle, *Ethica Nicomachea*, VI.13.

30. This definition does not assume that moral agency belongs exclusively to human beings. In the remainder of my argument I shall, however, focus on human agency. Also, the definition does not deduce a normative category from biological processes but, rather, uses empirical knowledge about biological processes to arrive at the most precise and explanatory articulation

of cardinality, which I see as a descriptive (in the sense of empirically testable) qualifier of the normative concept of a virtue.

31. See, for example, Aquinas, *Summa Theologica* I–II 61.3–4.

32. Thomas Aquinas (see *Summa Theologica* I–II 61.2) associated prudence (practical wisdom) with the rational faculty, justice with the faculty of the will, temperance with the faculty of desire (the concupiscible), and fortitude with the faculty that resists evil (the irascible). He largely followed Aristotle in making these links to what they both understood as basic faculties of a biologically based human soul. Aristotle, in turn, had been influenced by the ideas of Plato and Socrates.

Today these links with human biology-based psychology are still widely acknowledged by neo-Thomist ethicists. Porter, for example, explains the historical staying power of the cardinals in terms of underlying psychological constants. See Jean Porter, "Perennial and Timely Virtues: Practical Wisdom, Courage and Temperance," in *Changing Values and Virtues*, ed. Dietmar Mieth and Jacques Pohier (Edinburgh: T&T Clark, 1987), 60.

33. Two well-known scholars working on this frontier are Paul Churchland and Antonio Damasio.

34. Yet a note of caution is in order, for brain systems are typically widely interconnected, dispersed over several areas, and multifunctional. See Antonio Damasio, *Looking for Spinoza: Joy, Sorrow, and the Feeling Brain* (Orlando: Harcourt, 2003), 165.

35. I focus on a Western art form because I want it to serve as a model for a concept of cardinality that stands in the Western tradition of Aristotelian ethics.

36. Planetary conditions will cease to be favorable to carbon-based life when the intensity of our sun increases to the point of evaporating the Earth's oceans. This is predicted to happen in roughly one billion years, well before the sun turns into a red giant, expanding to envelop the inner planets and then settling down as a white dwarf. See A'ndrea Elyse Messer and Vicki Fong, "Earth's Oceans Destined to Leave in Billion Years," press release, 21 February 2000, available at www.spaceref.com/news/viewpr.html?pid=908 (accessed 22 January 2004).

37. Many Christian theologians now also recognize this by stressing the theme of stewardship, which does not replace divine power but makes humans accountable agents on Earth. See, for example, Calvin DeWitt, *Caring for Creation: Responsible Stewardship of God's Handiwork* (Grand Rapids: Baker, 1998).

38. See Jeremy D. Schahmann and Deepak N. Pandya, "The Cerebrocerebellar System," *International Review of Neurobiology* 41 (1997): 31–60.

39. In humans, learning from experience can incorporate post-hoc reflection on experience, which may put the response in a more positive or negative light (i.e., by attaching positive or negative emotions to the memory), affecting the way it will be used as a guide in future situations. This process allows humans to marshal their "library" of experiences in the interest of more abstract, reason-based goals. See Damasio, *Looking for Spinoza*, 146.

40. Damasio, *Looking for Spinoza*, 78.

41. On practical wisdom, see, for example, Aristotle, *Ethica Nicomachea*, VI.5.

42. Increased triggerability and cautiousness may be associated with reduced levels of the neurotransmitter serotonin. Interestingly, serotonin levels are affected by social status, being generally higher in dominant individuals than in their subordinates. See M. J. Raleigh, M. T. McGuire, G. L. Brammer, D. B. Pollack, and A. Yuwiler, "Serotonergic Mechanisms Promote Dominance Acquisition in Adult Male Vervet Monkeys," *Brain Research* 559 (1991): 181–90. (The authors found consistent results in human males as well.)

43. See James K. Rilling, David A. Gutman, Thorsten R. Zeh, Giuseppe Pagnoni, Gregory S. Berns, and Clinton D. Kilts, "A Neural Basis for Social Cooperation," *Neuron* 35 (2002): 395–405.

44. On social emotions, see Jonathan Haidt, "The Moral Emotions," in *Handbook of Affective Sciences*, ed. R. J. Davidson, K. Scherer, and H. H. Goldsmith (Oxford: Oxford University Press, 2003), 852–70. Key neurotransmitters for mediating social emotions are the pituitary peptides oxytocin (in the presence of estrogen) and vasopressin. See Thomas Insel, "A Neurobiological Basis for Social Attachment," *American Journal of Psychiatry* 154 (1997): 726–36.

45. Damasio, *Looking for Spinoza*, 61–62. The left region seems to be instrumental in inducing pleasant social emotions, and the right region, in inducing unpleasant social emotions.

46. On justice, see Aristotle, *Ethica Nicomachea*, bk. 5.

47. Key aspects of such conditioning toward an extensively compassionate state of being include the ability to imagine how symptoms of need in others, including members of other species, would translate in terms of our own feelings, as well as personal memories of being treated compassionately while in need. Consequently, I think that we should not too easily dismiss "anthropomorphizing" as being opposed to environmental ethics. Insofar as we are enabled to care for others by projecting their perceived needs onto our own body maps, and their potential relief onto our own memories of relief, we actually *overcome* the anthropocentrism that makes us act as though the entire world turns around us. On the role of body maps in feelings, including empathetic feelings, see Damasio, *Looking for Spinoza*.

48. See, for example, Michel Odent, *The Scientification of Love* (London: Free Association Books, 1999). Others suggest a correlation between compassionate cultures and some forms of religious belief, such as animism and Mahayana Buddhism. See, for example, Richard J. Davidson and Anne Harrington, ed., *Visions of Compassion: Western Scientists and Tibetan Buddhists Examine Human Nature* (Oxford: Oxford University Press, 2002). See also the work of the Boston-based Institute for Research on Unlimited Love, available at www.unlimitedloveinstitute.org (accessed 22 January 2004).

49. R. J. Davidson and W. Irwin, "The Functional Neuroanatomy of Emotion and Affective Style," *Trends in Cognitive Sciences* 3 (1999): 11–21.

50. In this model, the ultimate mixing is done by the cerebellar system associated with practical wisdom.

51. Aristotle and Aquinas use the metaphor of free citizens, who are ruled by political (versus despotic) command. See Aquinas, *Summa Theologica* I–II 56.4 ad 3.

52. This is one reason why rational arguments cannot motivate us to act independently of emotions. See Damasio, *Looking for Spinoza*, 140–55.

53. See W. Schultz, P. Dayan, and P. R. Montague, "A Neural Substrate for Prediction and Reward," *Science* 275 (1997): 1593–99. See also R. A. Depue and P. F. Collins, "Neurobiology of the Structure of Personality: Dopamine, Facilitation of Incentive Motivation, and Extraversion," *Behavioral and Brain Sciences* 22, no. 3 (1999): 491–569.

54. Settings are determined by a host of factors, including the number and responsiveness of the receptors and reuptake pumps belonging to the neurons in the system. Neurons can grow or eliminate receptors over time.

55. Activity in this system can be decreased with a range of tricks, which over time can become second nature, including (1) removing external triggers that are firing up the system, i.e., the old advice to get out of tempting situations; (2) removing internal triggers that are firing up the system, such as memories or thoughts about desirables; (3) dividing the desirable into small and easily attainable subgoals, which will lower your excitability as you get used to meeting them (you may even lose interest in the desirable altogether); (4) raising your expectations so high that you set yourself up for disappointment whenever you get a glimpse of your desirable, which should also cool you down; (5) engaging in activities or thoughts that stimulate other neural systems with negative feedback links to the dopamine system. This is called reciprocal activation. See D. Watson, D. Wiese, J. Vaidya, and A. Tellegen, "The Two General Activation

Systems of Affect: Structural Findings, Evolutionary Considerations, and Psychological Evidence," *Journal of Personality and Social Psychology* 76 (1999): 820–38. For more specific, science-based advice on channeling desires, see Terry Burnham and Jay Phelan, *Mean Genes: From Sex to Money to Food, Taming Our Primal Instincts* (New York: Penguin 2000).

However, too little activity in the system is not helpful either, for that would leave us in a state of apathy and blunted alertness. Some individuals are predisposed to a low baseline activation level, suffering from characteristically low states of enthusiasm and energy. See R. J. Davidson, "Affective Style, Psychopathology and Resilience: Brain Mechanisms and Plasticity," *American Psychologist* 55 (2000): 1193–1214. They can condition themselves to increase activity by taking opposite actions to the ones listed above. According to Davidson, "Of particular importance here is the ability to inhibit negative affect that may have a deleterious effect on the promotion of anticipatory positive affect" ("Affective Style, Psychopathology and Resilience," 111).

56. Aquinas, *Summa Theologica* II–II 141.4, 151.3 ad 2. Ironically, a hunger for touching may be the less vehement aspect of sexual desire; it is especially facilitated by oxytocin.

57. Joseph LeDoux, *The Emotional Brain: The Mysterious Underpinnings of Emotional Life* (New York: Simon and Schuster, 1996), 241.

58. Different individuals have different baseline activation levels, affecting their characteristic states of anxiety and aggressiveness. As the successes of behavioral therapy show, however, many people can decrease activity in the stress system by using some of the following tricks, which over time can become second nature: (1) removing external triggers that are firing up the system; (2) removing internal triggers that are firing up the system, such as exaggerated fear-mongering scenarios that do nothing but paralyze us; (3) avoiding cortisone-conducive brain states, such as *prolonged* stress, which can damage the ability of the hippocampus to put on the breaks; and (4) engaging in activities or thoughts that stimulate other neural systems with negative feedback links to the stress system, such as exercising or confidence building. Crenshaw suggests that cortisol levels drop in response to pleasant music. See Theresa L. Crenshaw, *The Alchemy of Love and Lust: How Our Sex Hormones Influence Our Relationships* (New York: Simon and Schuster, 1996), 88.

Too little activity in the system is not helpful either, for then we will fail to react to real threats. We can try to avoid this other extreme by developing an opposite set of habits.

59. Insofar as the core of courage was traditionally believed to lie in providing resistance to fear (see Aquinas, *Summa Theologica* II–II 123.3), one might particularly associate this virtue with the tempering function of the hippocampus in the stress system.

60. These subcategories are comparable to Thomas Aquinas's (see *Summa Theologica* II–II 48.1) integral, subjective, and potential parts.

61. The trick is, of course, to be able to see oneself in a humble position without getting depressed as a result. Humility as a virtue thus requires learning to associate a modest view of oneself with positive feelings, such as satisfaction and joy. However, there is a potential for irony here (a problem that has haunted Christian monks over the centuries): by feeling good about one's humility, one risks becoming proud of it—which means that one has lost it! This also implies that the good effects of humility on practical wisdom, such as increased triggerability and cautiousness, have disappeared.

62. In neurological terms, constituent virtues can be associated with subcircuits in the main system. In the case of humility and respect, I suspect serotonin circuits to be involved. See Raleigh et al., "Serotonergic Mechanisms Promote Dominance Acquisition in Adult Male Vervet Monkeys."

63. I suspect that both involve oxytocin-related subsystems. Benevolence may be associated with the ability to maintain generally high levels of oxytocin in the brain, along with the ability

to moderate interfering influences, such as dropping levels of serotonin or rising levels of corti-sol and norepinephrine. Attentiveness may be associated with a trained ability to connect mem-ories of personal need with incoming information about other organisms. As a result, oxytocin-based behavior would be triggered.

64. For the traditional connection between chastity and chastising, see Aquinas, *Summa Theologica* II–II 151.1.

65. There may be a connection between loyalty as a character trait and the neural peptide vasopressin. See Insel, "A Neurobiological Basis of Social Attachment."

66. For an initial exploration in this direction, see Damasio, *Looking for Spinoza*, 170–75. Neu-robiological understanding of the pathways of virtue should also stimulate discussion about the potential role of therapy and medications in the cultivation of virtue and the overcoming of vice.

67. The question of whether there are additional cardinal functions, or different ways of characterizing the ones mentioned here, I leave open at this point. Certainly, the fact that the four main Confucian virtues of humaneness (*ren*), righteousness (*yi*), propriety (*li*), and wisdom (*zhi*) do not seem to line up in any simple way with this model suggests that there is more to be said.

68. For an excellent discussion on method in comparative virtue ethics, see Lee Yearley, *Men-cius and Aquinas: Theories of Virtue and Conceptions of Courage* (Albany: State University of New York Press, 1990), 182–96.

PART 4

APPLYING ENVIRONMENTAL VIRTUE ETHICS

Synergistic Environmental Virtues: Consumerism and Human Flourishing

Peter Wenz

There is no conflict at this time between anthropocentric and nonanthropocentric goals in the moral development of people in industrial countries. Exercising the traditional virtues of frugality, appreciation, temperance, self-development, dedication, benevolence, generosity, empathy, and justice fosters human flourishing around the world and protects nature. Traditional vices, on the other hand, including six of the seven deadly sins—greed, avarice, gluttony, envy, luxury, and pride—as well as intemperance, selfishness, and indifference, foster lifestyles among current industrial people that diminish human well-being and harm the environment. The linchpin is consumerism, as currently understood and practiced in industrial countries, because it relies on vices that harm both people and nature. Traditional virtues oppose such consumerism.

I begin by defining consumerism and illustrating its harmful environmental effects. I argue next that consumerism harms poor people in the Third World. I then contend that it harms industrial people. Finally, I argue that consumerism promotes and relies on the cultivation of traditional vices whereas traditional virtues foster human flourishing and environmental protection.

If I am correct about consumerism, then nonanthropocentric environmentalists have reasons to favor traditional virtues because their exercise tends to protect the nonhuman environment. Anthropocentrists have reason to support the same virtues because their exercise promotes human flourishing. Nonanthropocentric and anthropocentric considerations regarding human virtue and vice are thus mutually reinforcing. Each is stronger in combination with the other than alone, a relationship I define as synergistic.[1] In addition, if I am correct, defenders of traditional virtues have reason to embrace nonanthropocentric environmentalism because it supports many traditional virtues. I conclude by suggesting how synergistic environmental virtues should be manifest in practice.

Consumerism Harms the Environment

Current environmental problems stem largely from consumerism in industrial countries, such as the United States. Consuming goods and services is not the problem. Human beings, like all living systems, require material throughput. We need food, clothing, shelter, and, because we are culture-oriented primates, education. Many products of modern technology make life easier or more fun, such as washing machines, CD players, trains, and cars. Consumerism differs from the consumption of such items, however, in treating consumption as good in itself. Consumerism is the ideology that society should maximize consumption, pursue consumption without limit.

Consumerism dominates American politics. No candidate for national office ever suggests maintaining or reducing the American economy. Everyone supports economic growth. The economy is never large enough. Life would be better if more people had more jobs producing more goods and services and earning more money to spend on consumption. "Enough" is politically subversive in a consumerism-dominated culture.

Attempts at unlimited consumption, pursued as an end in itself, degrade the environment. Global warming, for example, threatens species with extinction because of rapid climate change.[2] The warming results primarily from increased emissions of greenhouse gases, such as carbon dioxide. The United States, with less than 5 percent of the world's population, emits 24 percent of carbon into the atmosphere, caused significantly by consumer preference for gas-guzzling light trucks and sport utility vehicles (SUVs).[3] Such vehicles promote economic growth more than efficient alternatives—fuel-efficient cars and public transportation—through increased gasoline sales and required expansion of parking facilities. Commitment to unlimited economic growth favors inefficient transportation that threatens biodiversity through global warming.

Consumerism harms nonhumans in other ways as well: "Aquatic songbirds, called dippers, for example, disappear from stream waters acidified by pine plantations and acid rain."[4] Pine plantations are monocultures created to serve a growing market for wood pulp and building materials. The size of the average American home increased more than 50 percent between the 1960s and the 1990s, adding to economic growth and to the demand for building materials from pine plantations.[5] Acid rain results primarily from burning fossil fuels rich in sulfur, most often to generate electricity to run increasing numbers of electric appliances and air conditioners. The economy grows when people build larger houses, buy and use more appliances, and use more air conditioning. But pine plantations and acid rain harm the environment and endanger many species.

Development economist David Korten explains why environmental decline tends to accompany the rise in production required by increasing consumption: "About 70 percent of this productivity growth has been in . . . economic activity accounted for by the petroleum, petrochemical, and metal industries; chemical-intensive agriculture; public utilities; road building; transportation; and mining—specifically, the industries that are most rapidly drawing down natural capital, generating the bulk of our most toxic waste, and consuming a substantial portion of our nonrenewable energy."[6] Environmental researcher Alan Durning agrees that consumer-oriented societies are most responsible for impairing environmental quality: "Industrial countries' factories generate most of the world's hazardous chemical wastes. . . . The fossil fuels that power the consumer society are its most ruinous input. Wresting coal, oil, and natural gas from the earth permanently disrupts countless habitats; burning them causes an overwhelming share of the world's air pollution; and refining them generates huge quantities of toxic wastes."[7]

Consumerism Harms Poor People in the Third World

Anthropocentrists would not care that environmental decline accompanies consumerism so long as people flourish. Advocates of global free market capitalism, such as Thomas Friedman, believe that growing economies will help all people in the long run, so consumerism, the engine of economic growth in capitalist societies, is good for people. He writes: "When it comes to the question of which system today is the most effective at generating rising standards of living, the historical debate is over. The answer is free-market capitalism. . . . In the end, if you want higher standards of living in a world without walls, the free market is the only ideological alternative left."[8] And all people can share in the cornucopia, according to Friedman:

> Countries . . . can now increasingly choose to be prosperous. They don't have to be prisoners of their natural resources, geography or history. In a world where a country can plug into the Internet and import knowledge, in a world where a country can find shareholders from any other country to invest in its infrastructure . . . , where a country can import the technology to be an auto producer or computer maker even if it has no raw materials, a country can more than ever before opt for prosperity or poverty, depending on the policies it pursues.[9]

Unfortunately, Friedman is wrong. The whole world cannot consume at the level of citizens of industrial nations. Friedman seems to have missed the difference between *anyone* being able to do something and *everyone* being able to do it. If I order twenty texts for a class of twenty-five students, anyone could have bought the book at the university store, but everyone could not. Similarly, even if Friedman were correct that any country may become rich like industrial countries (which is already problematic), environmental limits preclude most of the world's people living consumer lifestyles. David Korten writes: "If the earth's sustainable natural output were shared equally among the earth's present population, the needs of all could be met. But it is . . . clear that it is a physical impossibility, even with the most optimistic assumptions about the potential of new technologies, for the world to consume at levels even approximating those in North America, Europe, and Japan."[10] According to environmental researchers Mia MacDonald and Danielle Nierenberg, "If every person alive today consumed at the rate of an average person in the United States, three more planets would be required to fulfill these demands."[11]

Korten cites a study by William Rees, an urban planner at the University of British Columbia: "Rees estimates that four to six hectares of land are required to maintain the consumption of the average person living in a high-income country—including the land required to maintain current levels of energy consumption using renewable sources. Yet in 1990, the total available ecologically productive land area (land capable of generating consequential biomass) in the world was only an estimated 1.7 hectares per capita."[12] What is worse, the world's human population is expected to increase more than 50 percent over its 1990 level by 2050, whereas Earth remains stubbornly resistant to growth.[13]

This environmental analysis suggests what international economists actually observe: economic globalization, intended to increase world economic growth so that everyone can be prosperous consumers, impoverishes many people in the Third World. Some examples illustrate how this occurs. One goal of consumer society is to grow food efficiently so that more resources are available for optional consumer items. The United States often claims to have the world's most efficient agriculture because less than 2 percent of the population is engaged directly in farming.[14] Agricultural research to improve efficiency resulted in the high-yield varieties (HYVs) of wheat and rice behind the Green Revolution of the 1960s and 1970s.

Agriculture and food security are central to many Third World countries. HYVs were marketed to the Third World partly out of humanitarian concern for human nutrition and partly to make a profit from the sale of agricultural inputs. Such sales help the economy grow. The unintended result, however, was to impoverish many people in the Third World, explains Vandana Shiva, a physicist and the director of the Research Foundation for Science, Technology and Natural Resource Policy in India. HYVs yielded substantially more cash crops of wheat and rice per hectare than traditional varieties, which helped the economy to grow. But HYVs require much more water per bushel. Unfortunately, many poor countries, including India, suffer from water shortage. So HYVs required deeper wells, which only relatively wealthy farmers could afford. With more water being pumped, water tables lowered beyond the reach of poor farmers, who could no longer get enough water even for traditional varieties. Many farmers lost their farms and became landless peasants seeking work.

HYVs also need more artificial fertilizer than traditional varieties. This again helped the economy grow but limited access to poorer farmers who could not afford such fertilizer. Worse yet, the fertilizer made *bathau*, a wild plant freely harvested for its vitamin A, a weed that threatened cash crops. Herbicides, another bought input that spurs economic growth, became necessary. Not only could poor farmers ill afford herbicides, but the intended result of their application, killing *bathau*, deprived many poor people of a free source of vitamin A. As a result, tens of thousands of children in India go blind each year for lack of vitamin A.

Dependence on free sources of food and materials is common in the Third World. Equally common is their reduction by globalization efforts aimed at turning traditional societies into "emerging markets." Worldwatch researcher Aaron Sachs compares rural Thailand with areas in the Amazon rain forest:

> Many of the villagers, like the peoples of the Amazon rainforest, used to derive their income from forest products—charcoal, bamboo shoots, wild

mushrooms, squirrels, even edible toads. Small-scale subsistence farmers also depended on the forests to provide breaks against soil erosion and to regulate natural irrigation systems.

Because they get much of what they need free, traditional peasants add little to the GDP of Thailand. In addition, they are too poor to buy goods produced in industrial countries, so they add little to the economic growth that consumerism requires. Thailand is better integrated into a consumer-oriented world economy when its land is taken from peasants, its trees are sold to logging interests, and its agriculture produces goods for export.

But logging projects . . . have laid waste to the area's hillsides over the last three decades. Economists often point to Thailand as a clear success—and the country's lucrative exports, consisting mostly of agricultural products grown on previously forested land, have certainly helped boost the Thai economy. . . . However . . . , the poorest people . . . lost . . . their livelihoods.[15]

Shiva similarly criticizes monocultural commercial forestry in India for depriving poor people of free forest products:

An important biomass output of trees that is never assessed by foresters who look for timber and wood is the yield of seeds and fruits. Fruit trees such as jack, jaman, mango, tamarind etc. have been important components of indigenous forms of social forestry as practiced over the centuries in India. . . . Other trees, such as neem, pongamia and sal provide annual harvests of seeds which yield non-edible oils. . . . The coconut, . . . besides providing fruits and oil, provides leaves used in thatching huts and supports the large coir industry.[16]

David Korten gives examples of Third World industrialization that fosters economic growth as measured in purely monetary terms, ties poor countries ever closer to global consumerism, and is supposed to help the world's poor. In each case, however, such development harms poor people more than it helps them. Japan, for instance, wanting to avoid domestic pollution from smelting copper, financed the Philippine Associated Smelting and Refining Corporation:

The plant occupies 400 acres of land expropriated by the Philippine government from local residents at give-away prices. Gas and wastewater emissions from the plant contain high concentrations of boron, arsenic, heavy metals, and sulfur compounds that have contaminated local water supplies, reduced fishing and rice yields, damaged the forest, and increased the occurrence of upper-respiratory diseases among local residents. Local people . . . are now largely dependent on the occasional part-time or contractual employment they are offered to do the plant's most dangerous and dirtiest jobs.

The company has prospered. The local economy has grown. . . . The Philippine government is repaying the foreign aid loan from Japan that financed the construction of supporting infrastructure for the plant. And the Japanese are congratulating themselves for . . . their generous assistance to the poor of the Philippines.[17]

Korten claims that this case is typical of Third World industrialization:

> Rapid economic growth in low-income countries brings modern airports, television, express highways, and air-conditioned shopping malls . . . for the fortunate few. It rarely improves living conditions for the many. This kind of growth requires gearing the economy toward exports to earn the foreign exchange to buy the things that wealthy people desire. Thus, the lands of the poor are appropriated for export crops. The former tillers of these lands find themselves subsisting in urban slums on starvation wages paid by sweat-shops producing for export. Families are broken up, the social fabric is strained to the breaking point, and violence becomes endemic.[18]

And Aaron Sachs discusses one effect of desperate poverty and social disruption brought on by integrating traditional societies into the consumer-oriented global economy—child prostitution:

> Brazil alone has between 250,000 and 500,000 children involved in the sex trade, and a recent study conducted by the Bogota Chamber of Commerce concluded that the number of child prostitutes in the Colombian capital had nearly trebled over the past three years. . . . But the center of the child sex industry is Asia: children's advocacy groups assert that there are about 60,000 child prostitutes in the Philippines, about 400,000 in India, and about 800,000 in Thailand.[19]

Income and nutrition statistics also indicate that integrating Third World countries into the economic system that supports First World consumerism hurts the world's poor:

> In 1960, the per capita gross domestic product (GDP) in the 20 richest countries was 18 times that in the 20 poorest countries, according to the World Bank. By 1995 the gap between the richest and poorest nations had more than doubled—to 37 times.
>
> To a large extent, these vast income gaps drive global consumption patterns. Disproportionate consumption by the world's rich often creates pollution, waste, and environmental damage that harm the world's poor. For example, growing demand for fish for non-food uses, mainly animal feed and oils, is diminishing the source of low-cost, high-protean nutrition for a billion of the world's poor people.[20]

In the year 2000, at least 1.2 billion people were hungry, and roughly half the human population lacked sufficient vitamins and minerals.[21] The World Health Organization reports that six million people die each year as a result of hunger and malnutrition.[22]

Environmental change brought on by consumerism could exacerbate this problem. Although global warming is not yet responsible for hunger and malnutrition, a one-meter rise in sea level, which such warming may cause, would inundate much cropland used by poor people for subsistence.[23] Global warming is also expected to lower soil moisture during the growing season in the world's breadbaskets—the U.S.

Great Plains, Western Europe, northern Canada, and Siberia—reducing yields and increasing the price of grain in world markets beyond the means of many people in the Third World.[24]

In sum, First World consumerism tends to harm people in the Third World, except for local elites. The environment could never support industrial lifestyles for all humanity, so the promise of currently poor people living consumer lifestyles is chimerical. Second, the pattern of development in Third World countries that ties those lands to consumerism in industrial countries tends to benefit only local elites and leave the vast majority much worse off than before, both materially and socially. Finally, gross statistics show that on balance consumerism increases income gaps between the world's rich and poor and jeopardizes food supplies for the poor.

Consumerism Harms Industrial People

Industrial people suffer from consumerism because it fosters perpetual discontent, social isolation, and depression. Here is how. A consumer society must have a growing economy to provide jobs and incomes needed for more consumption. Advertising whets people's appetites for consumption. Radio talk show host Dave Ramsey writes in his 1999 book *More Than Enough* that these ads work largely by sowing discontent: "Professional marketers and advertisers understand that they have to point out a need to you so you will recognize a need you didn't know you had. When you recognize that need, [a] process . . . has started [that] will end in frustration and finally purchase. . . . If you are a good marketer or advertiser your job is to bring dissonance or a disturbance to the person receiving your message. . . . That is the essence of marketing, to create an emotional disturbance."[25] Alan Durning adds:

> Advertisers especially like to play on the personal insecurities and self-doubt of women. As B. Earl Puckett, then head of the Allied Stores Corporation put it 40 years ago, "It is our job to make women unhappy with what they have." Thus for those born with short, skinny eyelashes, the message mongers offer hope. For those whose hair is too straight, or too curly, or grows in the wrong places, for those whose skin is too dark or too light . . . advertising assures us that synthetic salvation is close at hand.[26]

Such discontent interferes with human flourishing.

Discontent also motivates consumers to work more hours to earn the money needed for desired purchases. One result is social isolation because people have less time for leisure, friends, and family. As a social species, people flourish only when they have close personal relationships, but the work time that consumerism demands interferes with such relationships. Ramsey writes:

> A workaholic gerbil in a wheel invented the stupid phrase "quality time." There is no question that quantity time is what is needed to develop strong fruitful relationships. We are failing miserably in this culture by not slowing down enough to enjoy each other. . . .

> When I was growing up in the sixties, my mom would often be at a neighbor's kitchen table having a cup of coffee at midmorning while the kids played. . . . The evenings would find half the neighborhood gathered on a deck or patio to enjoy a night of interaction. We camped together, the men fished together, and as a kid you could get your butt busted by any adult in the neighborhood. There was a real sense of community.
>
> What has stolen our ability to find those luxurious hours to invest in family and friends? Several things have stolen that time. We are so marketed to that we have started to believe that more stuff will make us happy. But in this country, more stuff has resulted in more debt. What debt means is that we end up spending our every waking hour working to pay off our bills.[27]

Vicki Robin and Joe Dominguez, authors of the best-seller *Your Money or Your Life* concur: "It would seem that the primary 'thing' many people have sacrificed in 'going for the gold' is their relationships with other people. Whether you think of that as a happy marriage, time with the children, neighborliness, a close circle of friends, shopkeepers who know you, civic involvement, community spirit, or just living in a place where you can walk to work and the beat cop is your friend, it's disappearing across the country."[28]

The fruits of working outside the home often further impoverish family life and imperil human flourishing. As noted earlier, the size of homes increased in the late twentieth century. More children have their own bedrooms with their own TVs, computers, video players, and electronic games, decreasing the need to interact with other family members. For example, Robert Putnam reports in *Bowling Alone*, "The fraction of sixth-graders with a TV set in their bedroom grew from 6 percent in 1970 to 77 percent in 1999."[29]

Consumer items can also impair the sense of community. Air conditioning is one example. Older homes had porches, which were the coolest spots on hot summer days. Neighbors talked or visited porch to porch while avoiding indoor heat. Now people remain in their houses, isolated from neighbors, to avoid the heat. Air conditioning is wonderful and a lifesaver for some, but it does detract from a sense of community.

The car is another example. Cars are here to stay, but that does not tell us how many we should have or how best to use them. Cars have enabled people to move to suburbs where they live farther from neighbors and where neighbors commute in different directions to their respective jobs. The economy grows because more production is needed per capita when each person has his and her own car. "By 1990," Putman notes, "America had more cars than drivers." What is more, "the fraction of us who travel to work in a private vehicle rose from 61 percent in 1960 to 91 percent in 1995, while all other forms of commuting . . . declined."[30] Unlike private vehicle commuting, public transportation and walking foster the kind of community involvement that people need to flourish. As Putnam found:

> The car and the commute . . . are demonstrably bad for community life. In round numbers the evidence suggests that *each additional ten minutes in daily commuting time cuts involvement in community affairs by 10 percent*— fewer public meetings attended, fewer committees chaired, fewer petitions signed, fewer church services attended, less volunteering, and so on. . . .

Strikingly, increased commuting time among the residents of a community lowers average levels of civic involvement even among noncommuters.[31]

Gary Gardner, the director of research for the Worldwatch Institute, cites research showing that consumerism does not foster human flourishing. He notes

the failure of advanced industrial societies to deliver widely their most hyped product: well-being, or happiness. Studies of societal happiness show that income growth and happiness, which once marched upward together, have been uncoupled. In the United States, for example, the share of people describing themselves as "very happy" declined from 35 percent in 1957 to 30 percent today [2001], despite a more than doubling of income per person. For many of us, it seems, the more we ask consumption to fill our lives, the emptier we feel.[32]

Increasing rates of depression also show that the social isolation that consumerism fosters interferes with human flourishing: "Today, a quarter of Americans live alone, up from 8 percent in 1940, and at least 20 percent of the population is estimated to have poor mental health. By contrast, the Old Order Amish people of . . . Pennsylvania, who have a strong community life made possible in part by their car-free, electricity-free lifestyles, suffer depression at less than one-fifth the rate of people in nearby Baltimore."[33] Gardner also refers to a British study by Tim Jackson and Nick Marks released in 1999:

Their research analyzed the doubling of individual spending by Britons between 1954 and 1994, and found that most of the increase was an effort to meet non-material needs—needs for affection, leisure, and creativity, etc.—through the consumption of material goods . . . , needs that, in an age of fewer options and more social contact, had been met in their families and communities. But the literature on psychology is clear: we fool ourselves if we believe that nonmaterial needs can be met through the consumption of goods. Instead, love, self-esteem, and self-actualization are best gained through personal, social, and cultural interaction.[34]

In a consumer society people look for love in all the wrong places and remain frustrated. This should come as no surprise. "Money can't buy happiness" is a common observation. The Beatles added "Can't Buy Me Love," and June Allyson and Mel Tormé sang "The Best Things in Life Are Free." So in sum, consumerism degrades the environment, further impoverishes poor people in the Third World, and impairs the ability of industrial people to lead fulfilling lives.

Consumerism Promotes Recognized Vices

In 1956 Lewis Mumford pointed out a transformation in accepted virtues and vices that accompanies industrial civilization: "Observe what happened to the seven deadly sins of Christian theology. All but one of these sins, sloth, was transformed into a positive virtue. Greed, avarice, envy, gluttony, luxury and pride were the driving forces of the new economy: if once they were mainly the vices of the rich, they now under the doctrine of expanding wants embrace every class in [industrial] society."[35] Consumer society cultivates *greed*, the unlimited desire for more. Without greed consumer demand would flag, the economy would slump, and people would lose their jobs. *Avarice*, an inordinate desire for wealth, is implied by greed. People who want more and more of what money can buy desire unlimited amounts of money.

Gluttony is excessive food consumption. It seems that immoderate consumerism spawns overeating. Worldwatch researchers Gary Gardner and Brian Halweil report:

> Today [2000] it is more common than not for American adults to be overweight: 55 percent. . . . Moreover, the share of American adults who are obese has climbed from 15 to 23 percent just since 1980. And one out of five American children are now overweight or obese, a 50 percent increase in the last two decades.
>
> Treating the effects of obesity in the United States . . . costs more than $100 billion annually—more than 10 percent of the nation's bill for healthcare.[36]

In England adult obesity doubled during the 1990s to 16 percent.[37]

Envy is essential in a consumer society. Advertisers portray people with a product as having a better life than those without it. Consumers must envy the life of those with the product, or they would not buy it. Envy must often be strong enough to motivate hard work or long working hours to afford the product.

Pride is a factor in such motivation. Advertisers invite consumers to take pride in their ability to afford expensive or attractive goods and services. Ads often show others admiring a new car, window treatment, or hair color. If the item is a true *luxury*, then pride is enhanced. Luxury is no vice in a consumer society because, after all, you are worth it.

In medieval times, the deadly sin of *luxuria* referred to sexual lust, not luxury in the contemporary sense. But sexual lust, too, is promoted in a consumer society because sex helps to sell products. Good-looking people appearing in ads are often posed and attired to suggest sexual interaction. It seems that the more clothing Abercrombie and Fitch sell, the less their catalog models wear. The woman posing by a new car is meant to suggest desirable sex for car buyers. Victoria's Secret ads are (nearly) soft porn.

Sloth is the only one of the seven deadly sins that is not considered a virtue in a consumer society, perhaps because people must work more and more hours to produce the increasing volume of goods and services that consumerism requires. In addition to making virtues of what medieval Christians considered vices, consumerism fosters character traits that most people consider vices today. These include intemperance, selfishness, and indifference.

Intemperance is a lack of moderation or restraint. Consumerism cultivates and relies on intemperate consumers when economic growth rests in part on rich people creating jobs for others by, for example, building $2 million houses with six bedrooms for only two people. Even more consumers buy SUVs that are far larger than they need, cars with "performance" designed for professional racing, and mountain-climbing all-terrain vehicles to use in the flat Midwest. (Whose corn or soybean field do they imagine driving through?)

Selfishness is insufficient regard for the welfare of others. Consumerism fosters selfishness along with envy and greed. Envious people want the jobs, income, luxuries, recognition, and so forth that others have. They habitually compare themselves with those who have more and lament or resent their inferior position. This catalyzes greed. Such people have little mental energy to compare themselves with those who have less, so they tend selfishly to ignore occasions for helping the poor: hence the continuing appeal of middle-class tax cuts that reduce government programs needed by poor people.

As the tax cut example suggests, *indifference* follows selfishness. As people become more preoccupied with themselves, they pay less attention to other people's needs. Dramatic evidence comes from First World consumer indifference to the plight of poor people in the Third World who increasingly produce what we wear. According to David Korten, the footwear company Nike, for example,

> leaves production [of its shoes] in the hands of some 75,000 workers hired by independent contractors. Most of the outsourced production takes place in Indonesia, where a pair of Nikes that sells in the United States or Europe for $73 to $135 is produced for about $5.60 by girls and young women paid as little as fifteen cents an hour. The workers are housed in company barracks, there are no unions, overtime is often mandatory, and if there is a strike, the military may be called to break it up. The $20 million that basketball star Michael Jordan reportedly received in 1992 for promoting Nike shoes exceeded the entire annual payroll of the Indonesian factories that made them.[38]

This is typical, yet American consumers are so preoccupied with "stuff" that they ignore information about the near slave conditions of production that keep prices low. At the same time, however, our culture condemns the indifference of Germans during World War II who failed to help Jews. This is perverse. Opposing Nazi policies could be harmful to your health; buying domestically manufactured clothing is perfectly safe.

Traditional Virtues Oppose Consumerism and Promote Human Flourishing

Traditional virtues inhibit the consumerism that impairs human flourishing and degrades the environment. Consider *frugality*, which is, write Robin and Dominguez, "getting good *value* for every minute of your life energy and from everything you *have the use of*. . . . Waste lies not in the number of possessions but in the failure to enjoy them. . . . To be frugal means to have a high joy-to-stuff ratio. If you get one unit of joy for each material possession, that's frugal. But if you need ten possessions to even begin registering on the joy meter, you're missing the point of being alive."[39] Such frugality is closely allied to *appreciation*, the ability to appreciate and enjoy what you have. People who joyfully appreciate what they have are less likely to envy people who have more. They avoid the frustration and anger characteristic of envy and live happily without the compulsive consumption inherent in consumerism. Without compulsive consumption, they have fewer worries about money and more time to spend in meaningful relationships with family and friends. It is a win–win–win–win thing.

Temperance is another traditional virtue that opposes consumerism. When people have a sense of what is enough, they are more rational consumers. They have houses that are big enough but not so big as to waste space, money, and natural resources. Temperate consumers know when to stop eating, when they have enough clothing, and when a fancy wine is just too expensive. Advertisers and neoclassical economists oppose temperance. According to the economic theory dominant in consumer societies, people's wants are infinite, and there is no distinction between wants and needs, so any want can be considered a need. Hence, people are continually frustrated because they cannot have all that they are induced to think they need.

Practicing frugality, appreciation, and temperance creates opportunities to exercise another traditional virtue, *self-development*. At least some of the time saved from working to afford items that give little joy can be used to develop hobbies and skills. People can learn to play tennis, play the guitar, speak a foreign language, or knit. The sense of accomplishment from personal improvement in such pursuits cannot be bought. Of course, these pursuits also require some consumption, but it is not compulsive consumption. Practicing most sports and hobbies is much less expensive than acquiring material goods without sense or limit, especially when self-development is combined with frugality, appreciation, and temperance.

Dedication is another traditional virtue that stands between self-development and overconsumption. People who go quickly from one activity to another without the dedication needed for a reasonable chance of improvement or success may become major consumers of equipment, books, materials, and training. Embarking on a new activity often requires many purchases. On the other hand, those who, after some trial and error, dedicate themselves for years to one or more projects of self-development find long-term joy in the same books, equipment, and instruction. Such people tend to avoid overconsumption, especially, again, when their dedication is combined with frugality, appreciation, and temperance so that they avoid dedication to inherently wasteful or environmentally destructive pursuits, such as off-road racing.

People who avoid compulsive consumption find it easier to practice the virtue of *generosity* because they are not living on the edge of bankruptcy and can more easily live without the money and possessions that compete with generosity for personal resources. The possibility of generosity, in turn, promotes *empathy* with the plight of less fortunate people. Overspent and overworked Americans find empathy difficult because, lacking the means to be helpful (money and time), their insight into other people's troubles, which can be painful for anyone, is unrelieved by the joy of participating in improvement. Frugal, appreciative, and temperate people, by contrast, have the resources to be helpful and therefore the incentive to empathize with and help those less fortunate than themselves. The virtue of dedication can be used in projects of *benevolence* motivated by empathy.

Dedicated, empathic people engaged in projects of benevolence avoid the twin vices of indifference and injustice. Empathy itself opposes indifference. Injustice often results from people taking advantage of others, directly or indirectly, knowingly or unknowingly, as when Americans buy inexpensive clothing produced by child or near-slave labor. People whose sense of self-worth is tied to the amount of "stuff" they own resist paying the higher prices needed if workers are to receive just wages. By contrast, frugal, appreciative, temperate consumers can make justice a condition of purchase. Working conditions will improve in the Third World if enough consumers exercise these virtues.

Traditional Virtues and Environmentalism Are Mutually Reinforcing

I have argued that traditional virtues oppose consumerism and that consumerism is a major impediment to human flourishing and a major cause of environmental degradation. This makes traditional virtues an ally of both anthropocentrism and nonanthropocentric environmentalism. It means that anthropocentrism and nonanthropocentrism are mutually supporting through their different but complementary support for many traditional virtues and their different but complementary opposition to many traditional vices.

Imagine an anthropocentrist who is most interested in human flourishing. If the arguments given above are correct, such a person should promote traditional virtues as a means to human flourishing. At the same time, the exercise of these virtues will reduce human consumption and associated environmental degradation, a result favored on other grounds by nonanthropocentrists (who consider nature valuable in itself).

Now imagine a nonanthropocentric environmentalist who values nature for itself. She can argue that nonanthropocentrism among industrial people at this time calls for reduced consumption and therefore opposition to consumerism. If the arguments given above are correct, then consumerism is effectively opposed by traditional virtues, so the environmentalist has a nonanthropocentrically based argument for traditional virtues. These arguments reinforce anthropocentrically based arguments for these virtues. There is synergy here because the two sets of arguments for environment-friendly traditional virtues are stronger together than either set is alone.

An illustration may help to clarify the point. Consider nonanthropocentrists opposed to people driving gas-guzzling SUVs because such vehicles contribute greatly to rapid climate change that threatens many species with extinction. Such nonanthropocentrists have reason to oppose the vices of envy, pride, luxury, indifference, and selfishness because these vices are implicated in decisions to own SUVs. Advertisements for SUVs induce envy. Drivers take pride in owning a vehicle larger and more expensive than most others on the road. SUV owners seek the luxury of extra room in the vehicle and are selfishly indifferent to the effects of its greenhouse gas emissions on nature. So nonanthropocentrists oppose the traditional vices of envy, pride, luxury, indifference, and selfishness and support the traditional virtues of appreciation, frugality, and temperance, which incline people to reject SUVs in favor of more modest vehicles.

Anthropocentrists also have reasons to oppose SUVs on the ground that they promote climate change, which is likely to harm many poor people around the world by increasing vector-born diseases and reducing food availability.[40] Domestically, SUVs endanger people in smaller cars. SUVs also exacerbate dependence on foreign sources of oil, which motivates attempts to control oil-rich areas of the world, resulting in conflicts that take human lives. Finally, people trying to find happiness and fulfillment in the kind of car they drive are doomed to frustration because human flourishing cannot rest on any such basis. So anthropocentrists have their own reasons to oppose vices that promote SUV ownership and to favor virtues that discourage the purchase of an SUV.

The two sets of reasons against SUV ownership are compatible, complementary, and additive, as they are mediated by opposition to the same vices and promotion of the same virtues. Together these two sets of reasons are stronger than either set is by itself. Thus, there is synergy between them.

Here is another example of synergy. Anthropocentrists have reason to oppose the typical American diet because it impairs human health. It is rich in saturated fats and calories that lead to heart disease and obesity. Anthropocentrists have good reason, therefore, to oppose gluttony and promote temperance.

Nonanthropocentric considerations, such as those concerning the welfare of animals on factory farms, support the same changes of behavior through appeal to different traditional virtues—empathy, benevolence, and generosity. Americans overeat partly because food is inexpensive. It is inexpensive in part because of cruel methods of food production on factory farms. Continuing to eat factory-farm-produced food once its associated cruelties are known displays the vices of indifference and selfishness. Nonanthropocentrists who avoid factory-farm-produced food out of concern for animal welfare display the virtues of empathy and benevolence. Because they knowingly pay more for food, their choice displays the virtue of generosity as well.

Here nonanthropocentric considerations support the same behavior as anthropocentric considerations—reduced consumption of factory-farm-produced food—but do so through appeal to different traditional virtues and opposition to different traditional vices. The two lines of argument are compatible, complementary, and additive. There is synergy between them.

Practical Implications

In light of the arguments above, the following questions must be addressed: How should we expect people with the traditional virtues discussed above to act differently from most other people in society? How thoroughly should we expect them to reject consumerism? Must a virtuous person abjure automobile ownership? Must a virtuous person be a vegetarian? What are the practical implications of synergistic environmental virtues?

If virtue is to promote human flourishing, it cannot often require lifestyles so out of harmony with mainstream social expectations that virtuous people lack the companionship and camaraderie that flourishing as a social animal requires. To promote human flourishing, virtue must also avoid prescribing behavior that is impractical in the human-built environment, such as life without a car in many American communities.

I suggest addressing such matters with what I call the Principle of Anticipatory Cooperation (PAC). The PAC calls for actions that deviate from the social norm in the direction of the ideal that virtuous people aspire to for themselves and others but which do not deviate so much that virtue impairs instead of fosters flourishing. Consider, for example, car ownership and use. If life without a car is nearly crippling, the PAC does not require that virtuous people abjure car ownership and use. It requires only that they try to arrange their lives so that their car use and its adverse impacts are substantially less than is common in that society at that time. If most cars get twenty miles to the gallon, but good cars are available at reasonable cost that get thirty miles to the gallon, the virtuous person will, other things being equal, choose the more fuel-efficient car. She will also use public transportation and carpool more than is common when she can do so without bending her life out of shape. Her behavior anticipates more widespread participation in such practices and therefore helps to move society in a desirable direction.

If behavior like this becomes more common in society—average fuel efficiency approaches thirty miles to the gallon, for example, and car makers come out with reasonably priced cars that are even more fuel efficient—the virtuous person should, when finances permit, choose a car that is again considerably more fuel efficient than average. Absent some special need or problem, the virtuous person buying a new car today would choose a gas/electric hybrid that gets at least forty-five miles to the gallon. Similarly, if the transportation infrastructure changes to make public transportation more convenient and popular, the virtuous person will increase her use of public transportation so that it still exceeds the norm for people with similar transportation needs. A virtuous couple would likely be among the first to get by with only one car.

Virtuous people will try also to reduce below the common level their consumption of meat and animal products. Considerations of cruelty to livestock reared on factory farms may not require complete vegetarianism because in some places humanely raised livestock is available. But meat and animal products are nevertheless inefficient means of acquiring nutrition because livestock use most of nature's food-producing capacity for their own bodily maintenance. Only one-third to one-tenth of the nutrition that Earth produces reaches human consumers of meat and animal products. As people eat lower on the food chain they generally reduce the impact of their food consumption on the Earth and other species. The PAC requires, then, that people avoid the products of factory farms and reduce their consumption of meat and animal products below what is common in society, staying ahead of common practice as it (if it) moves toward a vegan norm.

The spirit of compromise in the PAC stems from two considerations. One, already mentioned, is that virtue should promote human flourishing; it would not if it required heroic sacrifice. The second consideration is justice. There is no justice in virtuous people trying to be perfect in social circumstances that make such attempts nearly self-destructive. Of course, the virtues considered here may require some short-term sacrifice. If my arguments are correct, however, the long-term result will be a better life. People who reject consumerism (without becoming utterly at odds with society) will flourish better than people whose lives are dominated by envy, greed, work, money worries, and separation from family and friends. People who reject consumerism in favor of traditional virtues will also lead more environmentally friendly lives.

In conclusion, people in industrial, consumer-oriented societies should cultivate traditional virtues to benefit themselves, other human beings, and the nonhuman environment. Anthropocentric and nonanthropocentric arguments for cultivating and exercising these virtues are mutually reinforcing, and their combination is synergistic. However, because the arguments for this conclusion depend on the baleful effects of consumerism, I draw no conclusions about virtue in nonconsumer-oriented societies.

Notes

1. For a more complete exposition of environmental synergism, see Peter S. Wenz, "Environmental Synergism," *Environmental Ethics* 24 (2002): 389–408.

2. Linda Starke, ed., *Vital Signs 2003* (New York: W. W. Norton, 2003), 84.

3. Starke, *Vital Signs 2003*, 40.

4. Starke, *Vital Signs 2003*, 82.

5. Dave Ramsey, *More Than Enough* (New York: Viking Penguin, 1999), 24.

6. David C. Korten, *When Corporations Rule the World* (West Hartford, CT: Kumarian Press, 1995), 37–38.

7. Alan Thein Durning, *How Much Is Enough?* (New York: W. W. Norton, 1992), 51–52.

8. Thomas L. Friedman, *The Lexus and the Olive Tree* (New York: Farrar, Straus and Giroux, 1999), 85–86.

9. Friedman, *The Lexus and the Olive Tree*, 167.

10. Korten, *When Corporations Rule the World*, 35.

11. Mia MacDonald with Danielle Nierenberg, "Linking Population, Women, and Biodiversity," in *State of the World 2003*, ed. Linda Starke (New York: W. W. Norton, 2003), 43.

12. Korten, *When Corporations Rule the World*, 33.

13. MacDonald with Nierenberg, "Linking Population, Women, and Biodiversity," 40.

14. For a critique of this view, see Peter S. Wenz, "Pragmatism in Practice: The Efficiency of Sustainable Agriculture," *Environmental Ethics* 21 (1999): 391–410.

15. Aaron Sachs, "The Last Commodity: Child Prostitution in the Developing World," *WorldWatch* 7, no. 4 (July–August 1994): 26–27.

16. Vandana Shiva, *Monocultures of the Mind* (London: Zed Books, 1993), 36.

17. Korten, *When Corporations Rule the World*, 31–32.

18. Korten, *When Corporations Rule the World*, 42.

19. Sachs, "The Last Commodity," 26.

20. Starke, *Vital Signs 2003*, 88.

21. Gary Gardner and Brian Halweil, "Overfed and Underfed: The Global Epidemic of Malnutrition," in *Worldwatch Paper 150* (Washington, DC: Worldwatch Institute, 2000), 7.

22. World Health Organization, *World Health Report 1998*, in Lester R. Brown, "Challenges of the New Century," *State of the World 2000*, ed. Linda Starke (New York: W. W. Norton, 2000), 7.

23. Grover Foley, "The Threat of Rising Seas," *The Ecologist* 29, no. 2 (March–April 1999): 77.

24. Peter Bunyard, "A Hungrier World," *The Ecologist* 29, no. 2 (March–April 1999): 87.

25. Ramsey, *More Than Enough*, 234.

26. Durning, *How Much Is Enough?* 119–20.

27. Ramsey, *More Than Enough*, 22–23.

28. Vicki Robin and Joe Dominguez, *Your Money or Your Life* (New York: Penguin Books, 1992), 142.

29. Robert D. Putnam, *Bowling Alone* (New York: Simon and Schuster, 2000), 223.

30. Putnam, *Bowling Alone*, 212.

31. Putnam, *Bowling Alone*, 213.

32. Gary Gardner, "The Virtue of Restraint," *WorldWatch* 14, no. 2 (March–April 2001): 14.

33. Gardner, "The Virtue of Restraint," 15.

34. Gardner, "The Virtue of Restraint," 18.

35. Lewis Mumford, *The Transformation of Man* (New York: Harper and Row, 1956), 104–5.

36. Gardner and Halweil, "Overfed and Underfed," 14, 8.

37. Gardner and Halweil, "Overfed and Underfed," 14.

38. Korten, *When Corporations Rule the World*, 111.

39. Robin and Dominguez, *Your Money or Your Life*, 167–68.

40. See Paul Kingsnorth, "Human Health on the Line," *The Ecologist* 29, no. 2 (March–April 1999): 92–94; Bunyard, "A Hungrier World"; and Korten, *When Corporations Rule the World*, 31–32.

CHAPTER 13

A Virtue Ethics Perspective on Genetically Modified Crops

Ronald Sandler

Genetically modified crops are here. In 2000 they constituted over one-fifth of the corn acreage, over half of the soybean acreage, and nearly three-quarters of the cotton acreage planted in the United States.[1] In 2002 over 58 million hectares (or 140 million acres) of agricultural land were sown with genetically modified crops worldwide.[2] It is clearly too late to ask whether the technology to create genetically modified foods should be developed. It is not, however, too late to ask whether, to what extent, and under what circumstances the technology should be used. That a society has the technological capacity to do something does not imply that the society ought to do it. Nor does a society's having the technological capacity to do something imply that the society will inevitably do it.[3]

Genetically modified organisms are created by the intentional genetic manipulation of microbes, plants, and animals by means of the transfer of genetic material among organisms—including organisms of different species—using recombinant DNA techniques.[4] There is considerable disagreement among both scientists and ethicists regarding whether promoting genetic modification in this way is simply a more sophisticated form of the kind of agricultural innovation that humans have been practicing by means of selective breeding and hybridization since the beginning of agriculture or whether it involves something significantly or even radically different from that tradition.[5] However, this issue—whether the technology is new in degree or new in kind—has been overemphasized in the context of ethical assessment.[6] Changes in degree can be ethically significant—discipline can become abuse, for example—and changes in kind can be ethically insignificant—replacing one's evening run with yoga, for example. The acceptability of genetically modified organisms must therefore be determined by considering the technology itself and its social and environmental implications directly, not by reflecting on how or to what degree the technology is unlike what came before it.

In what follows I develop a virtue ethics approach for making those kinds of assessments. In the next section I distinguish virtue ethics from modern moral philosophies such as utilitarianism and Kantianism, with an emphasis on articulating what is distinctive about the virtue ethics approach to providing action guidance. In the following sections I discuss where environmental considerations fit within the virtue ethic approach I have described. Then I apply the virtue ethics approach to the issue of genetically modified crops in particular, arguing that there should be a general presumption against their use. However, I show in the final section that the presumption is defeasible and that under certain circumstances some genetically modified crops are acceptable. Genetically modified crops that are likely to promote compassionate and just ends, and for which there are strong reasons to believe that they will not compromise the capacity of ecosystems (natural or agricultural) to produce sufficient external goods, should be promoted.

Virtue Ethics

Virtue ethics, as conceived here, is a particular method of ethics, in the same sense that utilitarianism and Kantianism are methods of ethics. It aims to provide a method for determining how one ought to act and what policies and practices one ought to support or adopt. Whereas utilitarianism evaluates actions in terms of their likely consequences and Kantianism evaluates actions according to whether they conform to the moral law, virtue ethics evaluates potential courses of action in terms of whether they hit the target of virtue or are what a virtuous person would do under the circumstances.[7] Virtue ethics thus involves a distinctive evaluative approach and set of central evaluative concepts. It does not deny that consequences or universalizability are relevant to ethical evaluation. However, the ultimate evaluative concepts in a virtue ethic are the virtues and vices—honesty, compassion, modesty, courage, intemperance, cruelty, arrogance, and so on.

The following, admittedly simplistic, example illustrates the virtue ethics method for determining what one ought to do in concrete situations. Suppose that you are deliberating about whether to lie to your professor regarding why you are late passing in your paper. The first step in the virtue ethics method is to determine which virtues are relevant in the situation. For example, compassion—the proper character disposition for human beings to have regarding decisions or actions with implications for the pain and suffering of others—is probably not relevant when deciding whether to lie to your professor about your paper. However, honesty—the proper character disposition for human beings to have regarding the withholding and disclosing of truth—clearly is relevant. Supposing for simplicity's sake that it is the only relevant virtue, the question then becomes determining what the honest person would do or what the honest thing to do is in this case. If it would be dishonest to lie, then it would be wrong to lie.

This is obviously a straightforward and unproblematic case for applying the virtue ethics method. Complexity arises when it is less clear what a virtue would require or there are multiple virtues that are operative. In those cases considerable reflection may be necessary for determining the substance of the dispositions that constitute the relevant virtues, as well as for determining which virtue or set of virtues is properly subordinated in that particular case. It may even require looking to role models or mentors for guidance or the application of moral wisdom.[8] (Moral wisdom is just a sensitivity, developed through attentive experience, regarding the application of the virtues in particular contexts.)[9] But despite its simplicity, the example does demonstrates what is distinctive about the virtue ethics method for determining what one ought to do in particular situations—the centrality of virtue- and vice-based concepts in reason giving.

Virtue Ethics and the Environment: The Production of External Goods

Where do environmental considerations fit within the virtue ethic framework discussed above? They assert themselves in both the development and the application of virtue. The environment is relevant to the development of virtue insofar as it provides certain goods that are necessary for the cultivation and maintenance of virtue, and it is relevant to virtuous action insofar as there are virtues the pertain to human interactions with the environment. In this section I discuss the role of the environment in the production of external goods. In the next section I discuss how the virtues can be normative for human interactions with the environment.

There has been disagreement among virtue ethicists, at least since Aristotle and the Stoics, regarding the role of external goods in human flourishing. The Stoics maintained (and stoic philosophers among us continue to maintain) that virtue is both necessary and sufficient for human flourishing. The virtues, after all, are excellences in character. A truly virtuous person is disposed to respond properly and perform fine actions regardless of what fortunes befall her or him. If the fortunes are unkind, then the virtuous person may not live the most comfortable or pleasurable life. In fact, a virtuous person may live a life of toil and hardship. But just as it is possible to live a comfortable and privileged life poorly, it is possible to live a difficult life well. Excellence in character alone, not external circumstance, is therefore what determines whether one lives one's life well.[10]

Aristotle, however, maintained (and Aristotelians among us continue to maintain) that virtue is necessary but not sufficient for human flourishing.[11] When we reflect on the lives of virtuous persons who have suffered misfortune and hardship, we can meaningfully say of them that their lives could have been better. Yes, they have done the best they could given their circumstances, but if they had greater comfort, better friends and family, or better health, then their lives would have been considerably improved. So although virtue is necessary for doing the best with what circumstances befall a person, the circumstances of fortune themselves contribute to the quality of life a person—virtuous persons included—is able to achieve.

But although they disagree about the intrinsic value of external goods—that is, about whether external goods are constituents of human flourishing—both Aristotelians and Stoics must acknowledge an indispensable instrumental role for external goods in human flourishing. This is because one cannot very well be virtuous or exercise virtue unless one is able to live to an age of moral maturity and maintain the conditions of moral agency, and external goods are essential to both of these. Moreover, the source of the relevant external goods throughout human history has been natural ecosystems. Here is Louke van Wensveen on this point:

> The cultivation of a virtue involves a person's ability to feel, think, and act in certain ways. Any feeling, thought or action is made possible thanks to physical conditions that sustain the person as a living being. Many of these essential physical conditions—such as oxygen, water, food, and fiber—derive from ecosystems. (By contrast, many of the physical conditions that may impede virtuousness, such as pollution and lack of food, can be linked to ecosystem stress.)
>   . . . The cultivation of a virtue also requires that a person can *continue* to feel, think, and act in certain ways over an indefinite period of time. Therefore, it implies that the supporting ecosystem must also endure over time, which is exactly what the notion of ecosystem sustainability conveys.[12]

On the basis of these considerations Wensveen concludes that "a genuine virtue includes the goal of ensuring ecosystem sustainability," for "a genuine virtue includes the goal of ensuring the necessary conditions for its cultivation."[13]

I have argued elsewhere that Wensveen's conclusion is too strong given her arguments.[14] The fact that there are external goods that have typically been provided by ecosystems and are requisite for the development and maintenance of moral agency (and thereby virtue) does not imply that a sustainable ecosystem is requisite for production of those external goods. Slowly degrading ecosystems (arguably such as the ones we currently occupy) can provide the requisite goods at least for the time it takes an individual to reach moral maturity. Moreover, it may be possible for technology to provide artificial alternatives for at least some of the essential external goods that ecosystems currently supply.[15]

But although Wensveen's argument cannot establish that virtue requires an individual to promote ecosystem sustainability regardless of historical context or society's technological capability, it does establish that there are certain external goods that virtue requires and that a virtuous person ought to take action to ensure their availability at least for her lifetime. Moreover, insofar as one's flourishing now depends on a justified belief that the people one loves—children, grandchildren, and perhaps great-grandchildren—will have a chance to flourish, one ought to act to ensure the requisite external goods for the next few generations as well. Furthermore, as a matter of historical fact, the natural environment is currently indispensable to the production of most of these goods. So a virtuous person located in this world at this time would not act in ways that jeopardize the environmentally provided external goods requisite for the maintenance of moral agency, and she will oppose the actions, practices, and policies of others that would do so. Given the virtue ethics account of right action, this is not only what the virtuous person would do, it is what any person ought to do. Because both Aristotelian and Stoic virtue ethics recognize virtue as necessary for human flourishing, this conclusion holds equally for both of them.

So the importance of the natural environment for the production of external goods that make virtuous action possible establishes a minimum level of consideration for the environment. One ought to act to maintain the capacity of the environment to provide the basic goods and conditions for the development and maintenance of moral agency, so long as there are no reliable artificial alternatives for those goods.

Virtue Ethics and the Environment: Virtues Regarding Environmental Interactions

Most ethicists who have argued that there are environmental virtues—virtues applicable to human interactions with the natural environment—have done so by extending conventional interpersonal virtues. They begin with a character disposition considered to be a virtue in interpersonal interactions or relationships, argue that environmental interactions are analogous in all morally relevant respects to interpersonal interactions (where "morally relevant" in this context refers to those features of the interaction that render the virtue appropriate to it), and conclude that the virtue is properly operative in environmental interactions or relationships as well. In this way Geoffrey Frasz has argued that friendship and openness with the land are environmental virtues, Jennifer Welchman has argued that benevolence and loyalty are environmental virtues, Ron Erickson has argued that solidarity is an environmental virtue, and Bill Shaw has argued that respect is an environmental virtue.[16]

In each case, the appropriateness of the extension depends on whether the environmental and interpersonal interactions share the morally relevant properties. For example, friendship with the land does not seem to be an appropriate case of extension. Friendship requires a history of active reciprocal concern for the best interests of the other, and "the land" lacks the psychological capacity for such concern. Perhaps we can speak metaphorically of friendship with the land or univocally of friendship with certain individuals within ecosystems (supposing there are nonhuman individuals populating them that possess the requisite capacities), but we cannot talk literally about the virtue of friendship with the land. However, it does seem legitimate to talk about compassion as an environmental virtue. Compassion is applicable in cases where one's decisions or actions have likely implications for the pain and suffering of others. Compassion is therefore normative in the not uncommon cases when human actions have likely implications for the pain and suffering of sentient nonhumans in nature. Extensionism is thus one way in which the virtues are appropriately brought to bear on human interactions with the natural environment. Human beings are, for example, generous when they expend much of their resources to protect the natural environment, patient when they lie still all day hoping for a glimpse of an elusive bird, and compassionate when they oppose trapping wild animals for sport.[17]

But although most environmental thinkers have been extensionists about environmental virtue, not all have. Notable among nonextensionists is Paul Taylor, who advocates an attitude of respect for nature that is not reducible to any combination of the conventional interpersonal virtues extended to ecological contexts.[18] The attitude is justified by a distinctively biocentric outlook, and central to it is the denial of human superiority and the acceptance of species impartiality:

> Given the acceptance of the biocentric outlook, the attitude of respect will be adopted as the only suitable or morally fitting attitude to have toward the Earth's wild creatures. One who takes the attitude of respect toward the individual organisms, species populations, and biotic communities of the Earth's natural ecosystems regards those entities and groups of entities as possessing inherent worth, in the sense that *their value or worth does not depend on their being valued for their usefulness in furthering human ends* (or the ends of any other species). When such an attitude is adopted as one's ultimate moral attitude, I shall speak of that person as having *respect for nature*.[19]

The justification for a distinctively environmental virtue is that there are issues unique to the human–nature relationship. When one considers the appropriate attitudes to take toward other human beings, one need not reflect on the importance of species boundaries, the place of the human species in ecosystems and natural history, or the value of nonhuman entities. Or, at least, these issues are peripheral there, whereas they are central when one considers the proper disposition to have toward the natural environment and the individuals that constitute it. This does not imply that one need not be tolerant, compassionate, or benevolent when dealing with the natural environment or the individuals that populate it; but it does suggest that a strictly extensionist account of environmental virtue will not be exhaustive.

Providing a comprehensive specification of the character dispositions that constitute a distinctively environmental virtue is not feasible within the context of this discussion. Moreover, any concrete specification of the dispositions is likely to be controversial. Most environmental philosophers who deny anthropocentrism would likely accept some likeness of Taylor's attitude of respect for nature. However, those who accept a sufficiently robust form of anthropocentrism will surely reject it, perhaps instead advocating a strictly conservationist attitude to maintain or increase the instrumental value of the natural environment.[20] So rather than attempting to establish one of these conceptions as the correct one, I will consider both of them when reflecting on whether agricultural biotechnology is contrary to virtue.

Agricultural Biotechnology and External Goods

From the virtue ethics perspective, then, an environmental assessment of a particular agricultural biotechnology involves (1) determining whether the technology will compromise the capacity of the natural environment to produce the goods essential to the development and maintenance of virtue and (2) determining if the technology is contrary to any of the virtues applicable to human interactions with the natural environment. In this section I discuss the external goods issues. In the next section I consider whether promoting agricultural biotechnology is contrary to any virtues that are normative for environmental interactions.

Are the technologies produced by the manipulation of the genetic sequence of plants used in agriculture likely to imperil the goods—food, clothing, water, and so on—requisite for the development and maintenance of moral agency? On first appearances one would think not. An essential property of all these technologies—the property that distinguishes them as agricultural technologies—is that they are designed to produce agricultural goods. Moreover, their advocates tout them as productively superior to nonengineered alternatives. They are purported to produce a more nutritious or flavorful product, or greater quantities of a product, or a less expensive or labor-intensive product, or a product that can be produced under otherwise forbidding conditions and so on.[21] Opponents of the technology often deny these claims, arguing that the technologies actually provide an inferior product, less agricultural security, or less product in the long run.[22] But no one denies that they produce agricultural goods. If they did not, then they would not be as common as they already are.

There is, however, the potential for unintended consequences with the adoption of any innovation. In this case opponents of genetically modified crops have argued that they are likely to affect natural ecosystems or the ecosystems that support the agriculture itself in ways that will ultimately undermine the production of external goods. There are concerns, for example, that unintended gene flow between genetically modified crops and their natural relatives will result in either superweeds (which will require ever increasing volumes of more and more concentrated herbicides to control) or organisms that will aggressively expand beyond their current ecological niche (which will compromise ecosystem stability and biodiversity).[23] There are concerns that the genetically modified organisms will themselves escape into the environment and outcompete native species or interbreed with them (which will also compromise ecosystem stability and biodiversity).[24] There are concerns that pests resistant to insecticidal genes will increase, rendering insecticides ineffective and pest problems worse than before the modified crops were introduced (which will require more frequent and intensive applications of chemical pesticides).[25] There are even concerns that the crops will decrease soil nutrient quality, thereby requiring intensive use of chemical fertilizers, a decrease in production, and ultimately the destruction of wild habitat to replace spent agricultural lands.[26]

These are legitimate concerns within the virtue ethics framework. If it is the case that any particular technology would involve ecosystemic disruption in such a way that it would undermine the production of the goods necessary for the cultivation of moral agency, then that technology ought not be used. Moreover, the effects of a particular technology must be examined synergistically. What is crucial is not what ecological effects a particular technology would have in isolation but, rather, what cumulative effects it would have given the other technologies in use as well as any stresses—such as habitat loss, recreational use, or climate change—to ecosystem stability. But to recognize the legitimacy of these concerns is not to concede that they render all genetically modified crops unacceptable. What it implies, instead, is that each genetically modified crop must be tested against the external goods criterion and that adoption of a particular technology should only take place if there are strong reasons to believe that it will not disrupt the integrity of the natural and agricultural ecosystems that we depend on for basic goods.

Nearly all genetically modified crops currently in the field have been engineered for herbicide tolerance, insect resistance, or both.[27] These technologies are thus an extension of the same intensive chemical and monocultural approach to agriculture that has become increasingly dominant over the last fifty years. Given the significant toll that this agricultural approach has taken on the ecosystems that support the production of primary goods—for example, the unintended elimination of nonpest species (plant, animal, and insect), soil erosion, desertification, decreased soil nutrients, loss of nutritional value in food products, contamination of aquifers and waterways, and the emergence of resistance species of pests—as well as the detrimental effects that it has had on food security in southern nations, close scrutiny of these new technologies is certainly justified.[28] Indeed, many of the objections that people have to genetically modified crops are based on the expectation that they will further promote chemical and monocultural agriculture and the deleterious effects associated with that approach to food production.[29]

Most other significant concerns involve the potentially detrimental effects that the unintended dispersion of genetically modified crops, or the dispersion of their modified genes, will have on supporting ecosystems.[30] From the perspective of the external goods criterion, then, the acceptability of a particular genetically modified crop is largely determined by whether it is likely to encourage increased monoculture and agrochemical use, as well as whether it contains genes that would be ecologically problematic were they to disperse beyond their intended fields. Are there any genetically modified crops that do not pose these risks?

There is at least one: golden rice.[31] Golden rice was engineered by scientists at the Swiss Federal Institute of Technology by inserting two daffodil genes and one bacterium gene into the rice genome. The modification enables the production of beta-carotene, the precursor to vitamin A, which is not otherwise present in rice. Scientists plan to crossbreed the engineered rice with local varieties favored by farmers in developing countries. The result will be a variety of rice—which will be made freely available to poor farmers in developing countries—that is well adapted to local environments and will provide a reliable source of vitamin A. This is significant because between 100 and 140 million children, many of whom live in developing countries where rice is a staple food, suffer from vitamin A deficiency, which in severe cases causes symptoms ranging from vision impairment to increased susceptibility to diarrhea and respiratory diseases.[32] The World Health Organization (WHO) estimates that between 250,000 and 500,000 vitamin A–deficient children go blind each year, half of whom die within a year of losing their sight. The WHO also estimates that of the nearly 600,000 women who die each year from childbirth-related causes, the majority of them die from complications that could be reduced by remedying vitamin A deficiency.[33]

Moreover, by incorporating the technology into locally favored seeds—rather than in a single product that would be controlled by transnational corporations such as Monsanto and Pioneer—the technology is being distributed in a way that will not displace local seed varieties (though, admittedly, they will be genetically altered). It is also significant that golden rice is not being billed as a panacea for vitamin A deficiency in the developing world. Researchers project that it will provide 15 to 20 percent of the recommended daily allowance of vitamin A.[34] It is thus intended to be a complement to traditional vitamin A sources, not as an option in competition with traditional crop diversity approaches for addressing the problem.[35] So it will not encourage further intensification of the agrochemical monoculture favored by transnational seed corporations.

Furthermore, because the transplanted genes increase vitamin production rather than hardiness, aggressiveness, fertility, or toxicity, it is difficult to construct any scenario according to which the transplanted genes would be detrimental to biodiversity even were they to spread through gene flow, interbreeding with wild plants, or unintended dispersal of the seed. The genetic modification simply does not confer a fitness advantage under any plausible environmental conditions. There is of course the possibility that such characteristics will be accidental to the genetic modifications of golden rice. But that can be determined in controlled field tests, which given the promise of the technology and the considerable reasons to think that it will not damage the capacity of natural and agricultural ecosystems to produce basic goods, should go forward. The results of those tests will then provide additional evidence as to whether golden rice satisfies the external goods criterion.[36]

However, most of the considerations that collectively suggest that golden rice promises to meet the external goods criterion do not apply to the preponderance of agricultural biotechnologies currently being promoted (and currently in use). The genetically modified soybeans, corn, and cotton that at present make up nearly the entirety of genetically modified plants cultivated in the world are designed to help large monocultural and agrochemical farms improve their yield and thereby turn a profit for the transnational corporations that manufacture and sell them. Indeed, they are inextricable from (and their use promotes) the intensive monocultural and chemical approach to agriculture that has greatly contributed to our agricultural and environmental problems.

So although concerns about the unintended ecological consequences of agricultural biotechnology ought to be taken seriously and can render particular technologies unacceptable, they do not justify global opposition to agricultural biotechnology. Each technology must be assessed individually because the details of the cases are crucial to determining whether a technology meets the external goods criterion.

Is Promoting Genetically Modified Crops Contrary to Virtue?

Those technologies that satisfy the external goods criterion might, however, still be objectionable from an environmental perspective if employing them is contrary to the proper disposition for human beings to have regarding natural or agricultural environments. That is to say, the genetic modification of crops might offend some virtue (either extensionist or nonextensionist) that is normative for environmental interactions. Indeed, some opponents of agricultural biotechnology have argued that there are particular virtues—respect for nature and humility—that are offended by any agricultural biotechnology.

Earlier I discussed two distinctly environmental virtues (I called them nonextensionist virtues) that one might advocate. One is conservationist, a disposition to maintain or increase the instrumental value of the environment (natural or agricultural). The other is nonanthropocentric, a disposition to respect the value of natural entities themselves. The former will certainly not justify universal opposition to genetic modification in agriculture. If a particular biotechnology increases (or does not decrease) the instrumental value of the environment, then it will not offend the conservationist virtue. However, those who appeal to respect for nature as grounds for opposing agricultural biotechnology will surely have something akin to Taylor's attitude in mind.[37] Do genetically modified crops unjustifiably discount the worth of individual organisms, species, or ecosystems?

In answering this question we need only consider those genetically modified crops that meet the external goods criterion, for if they do not meet that criterion, they are already unacceptable. The external goods criterion is in part concerned with the effects the technology might have on natural entities. So if some technology meets the criterion, its effects on those entities must be at least comparable to the effects of acceptable nonmodified crops. Therefore, those genetically modified crops that meet the external goods criterion will not be any more disrespectful to natural entities than nonengineered crops.

But perhaps it is not natural entities that are disrespected by the technology but, rather, agricultural ones. Is there any way in which the genetic modification of crops is disrespectful to agricultural ecosystems or to the species and individuals that are themselves genetically modified? The same point applies here as applies to whether genetically modified crops disrespect natural entities. If a genetically modified crop meets the external goods criterion, then its effects on the ecosystems that support the agriculture are comparable to those of nongenetically modified crops. Again, there is nothing that distinguishes them in this regard.[38] Moreover, it will be difficult to maintain that the technology is disrespectful to the modified crops and species themselves without being led to a similar conclusion. If genetically modified crops are disrespectful of species and individuals, it must be so in virtue of what genetic modification involves doing to them. But when the candidates are examined—it combines species, is anthropogenic, alters species from how they appear in nature, creates new species, and so on—we find that each is something that is done in conventional agriculture or occurs naturally. Nor in the case of genetic engineering is there necessarily a greater degree of genetic combination (remember that golden rice contains only three inserted genes). So even given the considerable assumption that ecosystems, species, and individual plants can in principle be disrespected—something that anyone who considers sentience or consciousness a necessary condition for moral considerability might deny—it does not appear that genetic modification is disrespectful in any unique way or to any unique degree.

These considerations do not, however, establish that pursuit of this technology does not display any extensionist vice. Indeed, several ethicists have suggested that doing so displays a certain sort of arrogance or hubris. Here is Carolyn Raffensperger's formulation of this charge:

> Humility would stand us in good stead, because we do not know all the consequences of engineering species. . . .

> The restraint we must practice is restraint from the hubris that has got-
> ten us into such technological messes time after time. Respect, humility, re-
> straint, even humor—that we have to learn all these lessons time and
> again—are as important as scientific knowledge and investigation and our
> boundless technological creativity. We cannot afford to leave values such as
> these at the door when talking about biotechnology.[39]

The objection here is that agricultural biotechnology is wrong because to engage in it is to "exhibit arrogance, hubris, and disaffection."[40] The problematic attitude, as Eric Katz puts it when discussing environmental restoration, is "the human presumption that we are capable of this technological fix [that] demonstrates (once again) the arrogance with which humanity surveys the natural world. Whatever the problem may be, there will be a technological, mechanical, or scientific solution."[41] This is not the objection that agricultural biotechnology somehow "transgresses the profound," "deviates from nature's design," or is in some other way "unnatural" and therefore wrong.[42] This argument trades on a more subtle concern about how we ought to understand our relationship with natural and cultivated environments and what norms should govern those relationships. Assessing the argument therefore requires determining what disposition is being expressed in the promotion of genetically modified crops and whether that disposition is indeed improper.

Proponents of the argument claim that the promotion of genetically modified crops as a solution to our immediate and long-term agricultural challenges expresses a technological, scientific, and domineering attitude toward the natural environment. They believe that those who support and pursue genetic engineering are expressing a disposition that favors controlling and manipulating nature rather than working with nature and accommodating ourselves to it. To paraphrase Bill McKibben, their impulse is not to adapt themselves and their lifestyle to the Earth but, in fact, to adapt the Earth to themselves and their lifestyle.[43] The question, then, is, What is wrong with that?

What is wrong with it from a strictly anthropocentric perspective is that it has fostered many of the agricultural and environmental problems that we now face. Among the world's critical agricultural problems are a decrease in the quantity of accessible and usable freshwater, topsoil loss, desertification, salinization, soil contamination, biodiversity loss, diseases and pests that can destroy entire crops, and increased social and political unrest as a result of all of the above. There is of course no single cause that can be credited with creating all of these problems. Each is the product of complex social, political, economic, and cultural factors. Still, it would be difficult to deny that humanity's attempts to control, manipulate, and dominate the natural environment have played a significant and critical role in their development. Damning rivers, filling in wetlands, cultivating water-intensive crops in inappropriate locations, clearing forests, monocultural agriculture, chemical agriculture, and species introduction and eradication are among the practices that involve manipulating and controlling nature, and all have in their own way contributed to the agricultural and environmental problems that genetically modified crops are supposed to alleviate. Moreover, as bad as these policies and practices have been for us, they have been considerably worse for wild nature and the individuals that populate it. As we have come to a point where we are concerned about our future, vast quantities of natural ecosystems and nonhuman beings have already been eradicated.

Given the historical record, it does appear to be hubris or arrogance for us to believe that the best way to address our agricultural problems is by further manipulation and domination of nature, which is precisely what agricultural biotechnology attempts to do. So the argument is not without merit—a disposition toward dominating and manipulating nature is an environmental vice—and there is at least one respect in which supporting and advancing the use of genetically modified crops are contrary to virtue.

Implications of the Preceding Argument

That the promotion of genetically modified crops betrays a lack of humility provides only a prima facie reason to resist their use. This can be seen quite clearly when we image a scenario in which the only available solution to mass starvation is the engineering and cultivation of a genetically modified crop that poses only a trivial environmental risk. A person who opposed the use of the crop in such a case would be accurately described as callous toward the suffering and deaths of others. What this illustrates is that there can be more than one virtue–vice paradigm operative in a particular case and that sometimes the course of action recommended by one virtue is properly subordinated to the course of action recommended by another. In this case compassion for the suffering of others requires that one act in a way that would under alternative circumstances be considered hubris. So although a disposition toward the domination and manipulation of the natural environment is an environmental vice, there may still be scenarios in which the virtuous person would do just that.

The upshot of this for the promotion and advancement of genetically modified crops in agriculture is that although there is a presumption against their use, some crops might still be acceptable under certain circumstances if there are compelling virtue-based reasons to use them. There must also be no overriding virtue-based reasons against their use. For example, the promotion of the technology must not be contrary to justice, as it would be if those who would benefit from its development are not the ones who would bear the associated burdens.[44] This is the case, for example, when Midwestern family farmers' tax dollars are used to support research at public institutions to develop genetically modified crops that benefit large corporate farms to the detriment of the same family farmers who were compelled (by taxation) to support the research.[45]

The genetically modified soybeans, corn, and cotton promoted by transnational agricultural corporations fail to meet these conditions (just as they had earlier failed to meet the external goods criterion). These technologies do not work to alleviate the suffering of the impoverished, eliminate global inequalities, or reduce the negative ecological impacts of agriculture. There are no social or ecological problems that these particular genetically modified crops effectively address. So in regard to these particular technologies the presumption against the use of genetically modified crops is not overcome. Once again, they ought not be supported.

This is not the case with golden rice, however. Golden rice appears capable of making a significant contributing to alleviating the suffering of some of the world's economically worst off. It has, in fact, been designed specifically for this purpose. It will be freely distributed to the most needy and will be used as a supplement rather than as a replacement of traditional sources of vitamin A. It will not promote chemical monocultural agriculture, and it will not diminish biodiversity because it is being engineered into locally favored rice varieties. Moreover, there is no better alternative currently available, for the cost and infrastructure limitations on a vitamin distribution solution are prohibitive. So in the case of golden rice there is a compelling virtue-based reason—compassion—in favor of the technology that overcomes the general presumption against genetically modified crops. Because golden rice has also been found to be acceptable according to the external goods criterion, the virtue ethics assessment of golden rice is that it ought to be supported and field tests of the technology should be permitted to go forward.

There are many more genetically modified crops in development. We have seen that neither a position of global opposition nor a position of global endorsement toward these technologies is justified. Each technology must be examined individually. If a particular technology fails to meet the external goods criterion or there are no virtue-based considerations that overcome the general presumption against genetically modified crops, then the technology ought to be resisted. However, if a technology satisfies the external goods criterion and there are compelling virtue-based reasons in favor of the technology, then it ought to be supported.

Notes

1. J. E. Carpenter and L. P. Gianessi, *Agricultural Biotechnology: Updated Benefits Estimates* (Washington, DC: National Center for Food and Agricultural Policy, 2001), 1.

2. See the International Service for the Acquisition of Agri-biotech Applications website, www.isaaa.org (accessed 3 January 2004). The area of land cultivated with genetically modified crops worldwide from 1997 to 2001—categorized by year, nation, and type of crop—can also be found at the GeneWatch website, www.genewatch.org (accessed 3 January 2004).

3. Bill McKibben provides examples of societies that have opted not to employ certain technologies in *Enough: Staying Human in an Engineered Age* (New York: Times Books, 2003), chap. 5.

4. This technology has been used to genetically modify animals. For example, scientists have inserted spider genes into the goat genome to create goats that produce silk proteins in their milk. The concern of this chapter, however, is limited to the genetic engineering of food crops.

5. These arguments can be found in Mae-Wan Ho, "The Unholy Alliance," in *The Ethics of Food*, ed. Gregory Pences (Lanham, MD: Rowman and Littlefield, 2002); Ronald Bailey, "Dr. Strangelunch: Why We Should Learn to Love Genetically Modified Food," in *The Ethics of Food*, ed. Gregory Pences (Lanham, MD: Rowman and Littlefield, 2002); and Norman Borlaug, "Are We Going Mad?" in *The Ethics of Food*, ed. Gregory Pences (Lanham, MD: Rowman and Littlefield, 2002), 74–79.

6. There is, however, a related issue that has significant regulatory importance in the United States. According to the Food and Drug Administration's "substantial equivalence" policy, a new variety of food crop is permitted to enter the market without full bureaucratic

review provided that it is substantially equivalent to an existing food crop. Substantial equivalence has typically been judged on the basis of the intrinsic properties of the food crops, not
the processes by which the crop varieties are produced. Proponents of genetically modified
crops have therefore argued that whether a certain crop is genetically modified is irrelevant to
the issue of substantial equivalence. A discussion of the regulatory question of substantial
equivalence, as well as an argument that judgments of substantial equivalence should include
considerations of production process, can be found in Mark Lappe, "A Perspective on Anti-
biotechnology Convictions," in *Engineering the Farm: Ethical and Social Aspects of Agricultural Biotechnology*, ed. Britt Bailey and Marc Lappe (Washington, DC: Island Press, 2002),
135–56. See also Michael Ruse and David Castle, eds., *Genetically Modified Foods: Debating
Biotechnology* (Amherst, NY: Prometheus Books, 2002), part 6, "Food Safety and Substantial
Equivalence."

7. It is often claimed that virtue ethics are circular because they define right action in terms
of what the virtuous agent would do while defining the virtuous agent as an individual who does
the right thing. This criticism is misplaced. Virtue ethics need not define the virtuous agent as
an individual who does the right thing. A virtuous agent is one who possesses the virtues, and
the virtues are character traits that a person needs to flourish or live well. For a detailed discussion of this point, see Rosalind Hursthouse, *On Virtue Ethics* (Oxford: Oxford University Press,
1999).

Another criticism against virtue ethics is that virtue ethics cannot provide substantive action
guidance for those who need it most—those who are not already virtuous. After all, one must
understand what the dispositions are that constitute honesty and compassion before one can obtain guidance from such directives as "act compassionately" and "be honest." The error in this
criticism is that it supposes that one must be compassionate to know what the compassionate
thing to do is in a particular situation (or be honest to know what the honest thing to do is).
This is simply false. Those who act without compassion often do so despite knowledge of what
the compassionate thing to do would be (and those who act dishonestly often do so despite
knowledge of what the honest thing to do would be). Moreover, it is false that an individual
who lacks understanding of the particular virtues has no recourse for obtaining knowledge of
what the virtuous thing to do is in a particular situation. Such a person can reflect (i.e., engage
in ethical theorizing) on what compassion is and what it calls for in the particular case (this is,
in fact, something we often do) or seek guidance from mentors or models who are their moral
superiors in this area (again, something that we often do).

8. Philip Cafaro discusses the importance of role models in environmental virtue ethics
in "Thoreau, Leopold, and Carson: Toward an Environmental Virtue Ethics," in this volume.

9. For a discussion of the role of moral wisdom in contemporary virtue ethics, see Hursthouse, *On Virtue Ethics*; and Rosalind Hursthouse, "Normative Virtue Ethics," in *How Should
One Live?* ed. Roger Crisp (Oxford: Oxford University Press, 1996), 19–36.

10. A second stoic argument is as follows: Because the objects of fortune—wealth, power,
privilege, etc.—can be used for either good or ill, they are not of themselves good. Only virtue
is essentially good because only virtue is always beneficial. The good human life involves possessing what is essentially or inherently good; only the virtues are essentially good; therefore,
possession of the virtues is both necessary and sufficient for human flourishing. For discussion
of the disagreement between Aristotle and the Stoics regarding external goods, see Julia Annas,
The Morality of Happiness (Oxford: Oxford University Press, 1993), chaps. 18–21. A contemporary proponent of the Stoic position is Lawrence Becker in *A New Stoicism* (Princeton: Princeton University Press, 1998). A classic example is Seneca, *Ad Lucilium Epistulae Morales* (Oxford:
Oxford University Press, 1965).

11. Aristotle, *Nicomachean Ethics*, trans. Terence Irwin (Indianapolis: Hackett, 1999), in particular, 1153b14–24, 1099b2–7. For a contemporary example, see Martha Nussbaum, *The Fragility of Goodness* (Cambridge: Cambridge University Press, 1986).

12. Louke van Wensveen, "Ecosystem Sustainability as a Criterion for Genuine Virtue," *Environmental Ethics* 23, no. 3 (2001): 233.

13. Wensveen, "Ecosystem Sustainability as a Criterion for Genuine Virtue," 233.

14. Ronald Sandler, "The External Goods Approach to Environmental Virtue Ethics," *Environmental Ethics* 25, no. 3 (2003): 279–93.

15. Cafaro calls this the "'artificial alternatives' argument: that when we have specified the good human life, we will find that it can be lived just as well in a largely artificial world—that we do not need wild nature" (Thoreau, Leopold, Carson, this volume). Hill makes a similar point in "Ideals of Human Excellences and Preserving Natural Environments" in this volume.

16. Geoffrey Frasz, "What Is Environmental Virtue Ethics That We Should Be Mindful of It?" *Philosophy in the Contemporary World* 8, no. 2 (2001): 5–14; Geoffrey Frasz, "Environmental Virtue Ethics: A New Direction for Environmental Ethics," *Environmental Ethics* 15 (1993): 259–74; Jennifer Welchman, "The Virtues of Stewardship," *Environmental Ethics* 21 (1999): 411–23; Ron Erickson, "On Environmental Virtue Ethics," *Environmental Ethics* 16 (1994): 334–36; Bill Shaw, "A Virtue Ethics Approach to Aldo Leopold's Land Ethic," this volume.

17. To get a sense of the variety and quantity of traditional interpersonal virtues that have been claimed as environmental virtues, see Louke van Wensveen, *Dirty Virtues* (Amherst, NY: Humanity Books, 2000), appendix A. Extension of vices to environmental interactions is also commonplace, and Wensveen has also compiled an extensive list of vices that have been claimed as environmental vices. However, philosophical work on environmental vice has lagged behind that of environmental virtue. Philip Cafaro's contribution to this volume is a considerable step toward remedying that disparity.

18. Paul Taylor, *Respect for Nature: A Theory of Environmental Ethics* (Princeton: Princeton University Press, 1986). Taylor does advocate the extension of several conventional personal virtues into the environmental sphere when he codifies the attitude of respect for nature with an ethical system that "embodies the attitude." However, the disposition that constitutes the attitude of respect for nature is not itself extensionist. Not all environmental philosophers agree that there is a uniquely environmental virtue. Susanne Foster has recently argued against the need for such a virtue in "Aristotle and the Environment," *Environmental Ethics* 24, no. 4 (2002): 409–28.

19. Taylor, *Respect for Nature*, 46.

20. The classic formulation of the conservationist attitude toward nature is in Gifford Pinchot, *The Training of a Forester* (J. B. Lippincott Co., 1937).

21. See, for example, Bailey, "Dr. Strangelunch", Borlaug, "Are We Going Mad?"; and Florence Wambugu, "Why Africa Needs Agricultural Biotech," in *Genetically Modified Foods: Debating Biotechnology*, ed. Michael Ruse and David Castle (Amherst, NY: Prometheus Books, 2002), 304–8.

22. See, for example, Lappe, "A Perspective on Anti-biotechnology Convictions"; Britt Bailey and Marc Lappe, *Against the Grain: Biotechnology and the Corporate Takeover of Your Food* (Monroe, ME: Common Courage Press, 1998); Peter Rossett, "Taking Seriously the Claim That Genetic Engineering Could End Hunger: A Critical Analysis," in *Engineering the Farm: Ethical and Social Aspects of Agricultural Biotechnology*, ed. Britt Bailey and Marc Lappe (Washington, DC: Island Press, 2002), 81–94; Vandana Shiva, "Genetic Engineering and Food Security," in *The Ethics of Food*, ed. Gregory Pences (Lanham, MD: Rowman and Littlefield, 2002), 130–47; Marc Lappe and Britt Bailey, "Biotechnology's Negative Impact on World Agriculture," in *The Ethics of Food*, ed. Gregory Pences (Lanham, MD: Rowman and Littlefield, 2002),

156–67; and GeneWatch, "Genetic Engineering: Can It Feed the World?" briefing paper (1998), available at www.genewatch.org/CropsAndFood/briefs.htm#Brief3 (accessed 17 November 2003).

23. See, for example, Norman Ellstrand, "When Transgenes Wander, Should We Worry?" in *Genetically Modified Foods: Debating Biotechnology*, ed. Michael Ruse and David Castle (Amherst, NY: Prometheus Books, 2002), 325–30; and GeneWatch, "Genetically Engineered Oilseed Rape: Agricultural Saviour or New Form of Pollution?" briefing paper (1998), available at www.genewatch.org/publications/Briefs/brief2.pdf (accessed 17 November 2003).

24. Lappe, "A Perspective on Anti-biotechnology Convictions."

25. Rossett, "Taking Seriously the Claim That Genetic Engineering Could End Hunger."

26. There have so far been few independent field studies completed that test the environmental impacts of genetically modified crops, and those that have been completed have thus far provided mixed results. For example, a recent study by the British Department for Environment, Food, and Rural Affairs on the effects of genetically modified crops on biodiversity found that "growing conventional beet and spring rape was better for many groups of wildlife than growing GM herbicide-tolerant beet and spring rape," whereas "growing herbicide-tolerant maize was better for many groups of wildlife than conventional maize" (www.defra.gov.uk, accessed 16 October 2003). Another example is a 2002 study by the Australian Bureau of Rural Sciences on the issue of gene flow from genetically modified crops, which concludes: "The actual amount of gene flow from GM crops and its consequences will depend on the crop, the transgene, the trait encoded, the particular environment and the risk management practices adopted" (www.affa.gov.au/corporate_docs/publications/pdf/innovation/Gene_flow_report.pdf, accessed 3 January 2004).

27. "Roundup Ready" soybeans engineered to tolerate Monsanto's Roundup herbicide are the most common. Corn, cotton, and potatoes have been engineered with toxin genes from the bacterium *Bacillus thuringiensis* so that they produce their own *B.t.* spores, a common insecticide used against cotton bollworm and European corn borer. The types and distribution of genetically modified crops used in commercial fields is tracked by GeneWatch (www.genewatch.org, accessed 17 September 2003).

28. See Lappe and Bailey, "Biotechnology's Negative Impact on World Agriculture"; and Shiva, "Genetic Engineering and Food Security."

29. See Shiva, "Genetic Engineering and Food Security"; Ho, "The Unholy Alliance"; Brian Johnson and Anna Hope, "GM Crops and Equivocal Environmental Benefits," in *Genetically Modified Foods: Debating Biotechnology*, ed. Michael Ruse and David Castle (Amherst, NY: Prometheus Books, 2002), 331–34; and Gary Comstock, *Vexing Nature? On the Ethical Case against Agricultural Biotechnology* (Boston: Kluwer, 2000).

30. See Ellstrand, "When Transgenes Wander, Should We Worry?"; and GeneWatch, "Genetically Engineered Oilseed Rape."

31. Others candidates include cereals that are tolerant of poor climate conditions, crops (particularly rice) with the ability to fix nitrogen, and cassava (a staple food in much of Africa) with resistance to the cassava mosaic virus. One genetically engineered product already in the fields that arguably satisfies the external goods criterion is a genetically engineered variety of papaya with resistance to the papaya ring spot virus that had decimated yields in Hawaii.

32. See the World Health Organization, www.who.int/nut (accessed 3 December 2003); and UNICEF, www.unicef.org/vitamina (accessed 3 December 2003).

33. See the World Health Organization, www.who.int/nut/vad.htm (accessed 3 December 2003). It should be noted that addressing the problem by distributing oral vitamin supplements is impractical, primarily because of cost and difficulties associated with infrastructure limitations.

34. Xudong Ye, Salim Al-Babili, Andreas Kloti, Jing Zhang, Paola Lucca, Peter Beyer, and Ingo Potrykus, "Engineering the Provitamin A (Beta-Carotene) Biosynthetic Pathway into (Carotenoid-Free) Rice Endosperm," *Science* 287 (2000): 303–5.

35. Ingo Potrykus, "Golden Rice and the Greenpeace Dilemma," in *Genetically Modified Foods: Debating Biotechnology*, ed. Michael Ruse and David Castle (Amherst, NY: Prometheus Books, 2002), 55–57; Gordon Conway, "Open Letter to Greenpeace," in *Genetically Modified Foods: Debating Biotechnology*, ed. Michael Ruse and David Castle (Amherst, NY: Prometheus Books, 2002), 63–64.

36. Detractors of golden rice have argued (1) that it will not be able itself to deliver the recommended daily amount of vitamin A; (2) that it will promote agrochemical monoculture; (3) that it will provide a foothold from which transnational corporations will be able to take control of rice production in developing countries; and (4) that it does not address the root causes of vitamin A deficiency: poverty and displacement of traditional diverse diets. See, for example, Vandana Shiva, "Golden Rice Is a Hoax: When Public Relations Replace Science," in *Genetically Modified Foods: Debating Biotechnology*, ed. Michael Ruse and David Castle (Amherst, NY: Prometheus Books, 2002), 58–62; and Greenpeace, "Genetically Engineered 'Golden Rice' Is Fools Gold," in *Genetically Modified Foods: Debating Biotechnology*, ed. Michael Ruse and David Castle (Amherst, NY: Prometheus Books, 2002), 52–54. Each of these concerns has been addressed above.

37. Taylor, it should be noted, defends the attitude of respect for nature as part of an ethic that applies to uncultivated or wild entities and ecosystems. He distinguishes environmental ethics from the ethics of bioculture, and the attitude of respect for nature is part of the former.

38. Of course, one response to these arguments is to claim that all crop agriculture is disrespectful and contrary to virtue. But those who oppose genetically modified crops would not welcome the conclusion. They might, however, be inclined to argue that all industrial agriculture is disrespectful of nature and therefore unacceptable. But even if that were true, it does not imply that the use of genetically modified crops in nonindustrial agriculture is disrespectful. Nor does it imply that there is greater or special disrespect, beyond whatever disrespect is inherent to industrial agriculture, when genetically modified crops are used in industrial agriculture.

39. Carolyn Raffensperger, "Learning to Speak Ethics in Technological Debates," in *Engineering the Farm: Ethical and Social Aspects of Agricultural Biotechnology*, ed. Britt Bailey and Marc Lappe (Washington, DC: Island Press, 2002), 133.

40. Comstock, *Vexing Nature?* 183. This objection can also be found in Bill McKibben, *The End of Nature* (New York: Anchor, 1999), pt. 2. A prominent defense of humility as an environmental virtue is in Thomas Hill Jr., "Ideals of Human Excellence and Preserving Natural Environments," in this volume.

41. Eric Katz, "The Big Lie: The Human Restoration of Nature," in *Environmental Restoration*, ed. William Throop (Amherst, NY: Humanity Books, 2000), 85–86.

42. For what are, in my estimation, decisive criticisms of this position, see Steven Vogel, "Environmental Philosophy after the End of Nature," *Environmental Ethics* 24, no. 1 (2002): 23–39; and Comstock, *Vexing Nature?* chap. 5.

43. McKibben, *The End of Nature*, 150.

44. The *Principle of Commensurate Burdens and Benefits*—that, all other things being equal, those who derive benefits should sustain the burdens associated with those benefits—which I am appealing to here, has been defended in Peter Wenz, "Just Garbage," in *Faces of Environmental Racism: Confronting Issues of Global Justice*, ed. L. Westra and B. Lawson, 2d ed. (Lanham, MD: Rowman and Littlefield, 2001), 57–71.

45. Comstock, *Vexing Nature?* chap. 1. Considerations of justice are also the basis for the charge of biopiracy—when a Western government grants patent rights to an individual or corporation for the modification of a species that has traditionally been used or cultivated by an indigenous group, whereupon the patent owner attempts to enforce that patent against the indigenous community—against transnational seed corporations and Western governments. See Vandana Shiva, *Biopiracy: The Plunder of Nature and Knowledge* (Boston: South End, 1997).

Contributors

Philip Cafaro is associate professor of philosophy at Colorado State University, with research interests centered on ethical theory and environmental ethics. A former interpretive ranger with the National Park Service, he monitors management activity on the Arapaho/Roosevelt National Forests for the Poudre Canyon Group of the Sierra Club. Cafaro is author of *Thoreau's Living Ethics:* Walden *and the Pursuit of Virtue* (University of Georgia Press, 2004).

Geoffrey Frasz is professor of philosophy at the Community College of Southern Nevada. He received a graduate certificate in environmental ethics and M.A. and Ph.D. in philosophy at the University of Georgia. In 1993 he published his first article on environmental virtue ethics and continues to work in this field. Each year Frasz teaches a course in environmental ethics that focuses on environmental issues in the southwestern United States.

Thomas Hill Jr. is Kenan Professor of Philosophy at the University of North Carolina at Chapel Hill. He previously taught at Pomona College and the University of California at Los Angeles. He has written extensively in moral and political philosophy. His essays are collected in *Autonomy and Self-Respect* (1991), *Dignity and Practical Reason in Kant's Moral Theory* (1992), *Respect, Pluralism, and Justice: Kantian Perspectives* (2000), and *Human Welfare and Moral Worth: Kantian Perspectives* (2002). He is coeditor (with Arnulf Zweig) of a new teaching edition of Kant's *Groundwork for the Metaphysics of Morals* (2003).

Holmes Rolston III is University Distinguished Professor and professor of philosophy at Colorado State University. He was Templeton Prize Laureate in 2003. He is featured in Joy Palmer, ed., *Fifty Key Thinkers on the Environment,* and has lectured on environmental ethics on seven continents.

Ronald Sandler is a assistant professor of philosophy in the Department of Philosophy and Religion at Northeastern University. His research is in the areas of environmental ethics, virtue ethics, and ethical theory in the early modern period. His work on environmental virtue ethics has appeared or is forthcoming in the journals *Environmental Ethics*, *Environmental Values*, *Agricultural and Environmental Ethics*, *Business Ethics Quarterly*, and *Philosophy in the Contemporary World*.

David Schmidtz is professor of philosophy and joint professor of economics at the University of Arizona. He is author of *Rational Choice and Moral Agency* (Princeton, 1995). He coauthored *Social Welfare and Individual Responsibility* (Cambridge, 1998) with Robert Goodin. His current projects are a book entitled *The Elements of Justice* (forthcoming from Cambridge) and another entitled *The Purpose of Moral Theory*.

Bill Shaw is Woodson Professor of Law and Ethics in Business at the McCombs School of Business, the University of Texas at Austin. He is the former editor in chief of the *American Business Law Journal* and the former president of the Academy of Legal Studies in Business. He writes for law and ethics journals and is author of the forthcoming *Aperia: A White Myth*.

Charles Taliaferro is a member of the Department of Environmental Studies and the Department of Philosophy, St. Olaf College. He has contributed to the journals *Environmental Ethics*, *Agriculture and Human Values*, and *Ethics, Place, and Environment*. He has also published in the *Blackwell Companion to Environmental Philosophy* (2003), *The Agrarian Roots of Pragmatism* (Vanderbilt University Press, 2000), and *Life Science Ethics* (Iowa State University Press, 2003). His most recent book is *Contemporary Philosophy of Religion* (Blackwell, 1998).

Louke van Wensveen is an ethics consultant based in Los Angeles. A Dutch native, she studied comparative religion, social ethics, and business ethics at Leiden, Harvard, and Princeton Theological Seminary. Before becoming an independent scholar in 2002, she taught as associate professor of theological studies at Loyola Marymount University. She is the author of *Dirty Virtues: The Emergence of Ecological Virtue Ethics*.

Peter Wenz is professor of philosophy and legal studies at the University of Illinois at Springfield and an adjunct professor of medical humanities at the Southern Illinois University School of Medicine. His published books are *Environmental Justice* (State University of New York Press, 1988), *Abortion Rights as Religious Freedom* (Temple University Press, 1992), *Nature's Keeper* (Temple University Press, 1996), and *Environmental Ethics Today* (Oxford University Press, 2001). He is currently writing a text in political philosophy.

Laura Westra received her first Ph.D. (philosophy) from the University of Toronto in 1983. Her second Ph.D. (jurisprudence) in international human rights and international environmental law is from Osgoode Hall Law School. She has published primarily in environmental ethics (fourteen books and approximately eighty chapters and articles). Her fifteenth book, *Ecoviolence and the Law* (Transnational Publishers, 2004), is taken from her thesis. Westra has worked with the World Health Organization, the IUCN Commission on Environmental Law, and the Earth Charter Organization, as well as with environmental justice groups in Alabama and Georgia.

Matt Zwolinski is assistant professor of philosophy at the University of San Diego. He has written on the separateness of persons, and his current research lies at the intersection of metaethics and normative ethics.

Index

Abbey, Ed, 158n84
Adams, R. M., 171n31
advertising, 150, 203, 208
aesthetic appreciation of nature, 33–34, 35, 43n35, 56–57
agent benefit, appeal to, 4–5
agriculture, 166–69, 200–201, 215–16, 220–27; and overproduction, 141–42
altruism. *See* self-interest
Ambrose, 173
anthropocentrism: criticized, 37–38, 42–43n26, 130, 156n50; defended 181–82; and GMOs, 225–26; synergistic with nonanthropocentrism, 209–10
Anticipatory Cooperation, Principle of, 211–12
apatheia, 152
apathy, 150–53
appreciation of nature, 38, 51–53, 71, 207–8
Aquinas, Thomas, 136, 137, 148, 191n32
Aristotle, 34–35, 79–81, 83, 88, 94, 102–3, 104n10, 105n21, 136, 137, 139, 143, 146, 151–52, 156n41, 217, 218
arrogance, 130, 143–47. *See also* humility; pride
artificial alternatives, challenge of, 39, 54, 62–63
attunement, 24, 61–62

benevolence, 9–10, 121–34. *See also* compassion

Bennett, Jane, 75
Berry, Thomas, 177
Berry, Wendell, 22, 166–69, 172n44
biotechnology, agricultural. *See* GMOs
The Blessed Brain, 180–86
Botkin, Daniel, 74
Bouma-Prediger, Stephen, 177, 190n23, 190n24
Bratton, Susan Power, 176
Broderick, John, 74
Buddha, Gautama, 165
Buddhist environmental ethics, 10, 165–66

Cafaro, Philip, 7–8, 10, 74, 127, 177, 229n15
cardinality of virtues, 10–11, 22, 23, 173–80, 186–88, 189n4, 194n67
Carlson, Allen, 169–70n4
Carson, Rachel, 1, 3, 35–37, 38–39
Chapman, Robert, 75–76
character, 111–12, 154n12; and ethics, 2
Chaucer, 148
Cheney, Dick, 148
Chevron, 144–45
Christianity and environmental ethics, 19, 121–22
Cobb, Edith, 65–66
compassion, 128–29, 166, 219. *See also* benevolence
Comstock, Gary, 168
Confucianism, 161
consumerism, 11, 197–212; and harms to nature, 198; and harms to the poor,

199–203; and harms to the rich, 203–7. *See also* overconsumption
convergence hypothesis, 20–21
Cooper, John, 80
courage, 185
creation, divine, 162–63
creativity, 65–66
curiosity, 131
cynicism, 132

Deane-Drummond, Celia, 176
dedication, 208
Dominguez, Joe, 204, 207
Durning, Alan, 198–99, 203

ecofeminism, 22, 23, 30n37
ecological virtue language: commonest virtues mentioned in, 174–77; examples of, 16–17; logic of, 20–26; philosophers neglect of, 17–18; reasons for its flourishing, 18–19
economics, proper role of, 37
empathy, 208
environmental character, 2–3
environmental ethics, 1–2; life-affirming, 32, 38–39; theistic, 159–69
environmental heroes, 2–3, 5, 7–8, 32–39
environmental virtue ethics: defined, 1–2; and environmental ethics, 6–7, 69–77; need for, 2, 19, 27–28, 31–32, 39–40, 47–50, 61–63, 79–83, 88, 93–94, 98–99, 107, 138–40, 197, 217–20; neglect of, 17–18; writings in, 28n8, 40n3
envy, 206
Erickson, Ron, 219
ethical theory: act-centered vs. character-centered, 110–11; point of, 114–15
excellence, 5, 8. *See also* virtue
extensionism, moral, 4, 33, 34, 93, 95–98, 126, 139; objections to, 128–29, 219–20

Fairlie, Henry, 150
feminism, and environmental ethics, 17, 21
flourishing: consumerism undermines, 197–212; defined teleologically, 95–97, 103n4; dependant on nature, 32–37, 47, 62–66, 79–83, 138, 142, 153; and external goods, 217–19;

foundational for environmental ethics, 79–81, 88, 126–28; human, 8–9, 11, 67–68, 76–77, 79–81; nature's, 94; theistic conception of, 163
Francis, Saint, 19, 26, 121–22
Frasz, Geoffrey, 9–10, 176, 219
Friedman, Thomas, 199
friendliness, 124
friendship, 219
frugality, 207–8

Gardner, Gary, 205, 206
generosity, 208
Gerber, Lisa, 176
Gewirth, Alan, 81–82
gluttony, 140–43, 206
GMOs, 11–12, 200–201, 215–16, 220–27
good life, 32–33
goods, external, 217–19; and agricultural biotechnology, 220–23
gratitude, 163
Gray, Elizabeth, 22
greed, 130, 147–50, 206
Gregory the Great, 140
Gruen, Lori, 23

Halweil, Brian, 206
Helfand, Jonathan, 163
Heller, Chaia, 23
Hill, Julia Butterfly, 1
Hill, Thomas, Jr., 8, 42–43n26, 107, 176
Hogan, Linda, 22
holism, environmental, 126, 160–61
hubris. *See* pride
Hughes, Donald, 121
humility, 36–37, 41–42n20, 51, 53–56, 105n23, 144, 193n61; and GMOs, 224–26. *See also* arrogance; pride
Hursthouse, Rosalind, 228n7, 228n9

imagination, 127, 129
indifference, 207
integrity: ecological, 8–9, 82, 86, 88; human, 70
intemperance. *See* temperance
interests, human and nonhuman, 43n40, 97–98. *See also* self-interest, and altruism
intrinsic values in nature, 8, 49–50, 69–77

Jackson, Tim, 205
Jackson, Wes, 166, 167, 172n43
joy, 38, 133
Jung, Carl, 66
justice, 183–84, 211; global, 83–87

Kant, Immanuel, 81–86, 104n13, 137,
    143–44
Katz, Eric, 225
Kawall, Jason, 73
Kheel, Marti, 23
Korten, David, 198, 199–200, 201–2, 207
Kraut, Richard, 80

land ethic. *See* Leopold, Aldo
land virtues, 9, 94, 100–102, 105n22. *See
    also* virtue, environmental
Lappé, Francis Moore, 142
Larsen, Randy, 158n84, 177
last man argument, 57, 112
law and environmental protection, 84,
    86–88, 146–47
Leopold, Aldo, 1, 9, 33–35, 37–39,
    43–44n42, 93–106, 153, 154–55n18,
    176
Lewis, C. S., 73
Linzey, Andrew, 23
loyalty, 122
lust, 206

Macy, Joanna, 18
mammon worship, 148. *See also*
    Friedman, Thomas; greed
Marietta, Don, 21
Marsh, Nick, 205
materialism and happiness, 149–50
McDonagh, Sean, 22
Mencius, 161
mindfulness 166
Montaigne, Michel, 136–37
Moore, G. E., 49
Muir, John, 1, 3
Mumford, Lewis, 205–6

Nash, James, 23, 176, 177
naturalism, ethical, 5, 30n37, 174, 178–88
neurobiology and ethics, 179–88
Newton, Lisa, 177
Norton, Bryan, 20–21

obesity, 141
Oelschlaeger, Max, 30n43
O'Neill, Onora, 83–84, 85
ORVs (off-road vehicles), 145–47
overconsumption, 130, 140–41, 148–49.
    See also consumerism

Parfit, Derek, 9, 107–9
perfectionist fallacy, 132
philanthropy, 33
Philippine Associated Smelting and
    Refining Corporation, 201–2
place, 63–66
Plumwood, Val, 17
population, human, 9, 108–14
practical wisdom, 101–2, 182–83
practices and environmental protection,
    132–33, 146–47
pride, 23, 167–68, 206. *See also*
    arrogance; humility
prudence, 101, 186–87
Putnam, Robert, 204–5

Raffensperger, Carolyn, 224–25
Ramsey, David, 203–4
real and apparent goods, 149–50
Rees, William, 200
religious arguments for environmental
    ethics, 10, 19, 23, 26–27, 49, 61,
    159–61, 177
repugnant conclusions, 9, 107–11;
    problematic for deontology, 110–11;
    problematic for utilitarianism,
    108–10
respect for nature, 21, 24, 37–38,
    100–101, 219–20; and GMOs, 223–24,
    231n37, 231n38. *See also* intrinsic
    values in nature
rice, golden, 222–23, 227, 232n36
rights: abused in Nigeria, 144–45;
    environmental, 9, 81–88; nonhuman,
    48–49; not everything, 17, 115;
    subsistence, 84–85
Rist, John, 80
Robin, Vickie, 204, 207
Rodman, John, 103–4n6, 176
Rolston, Holmes, III, 8, 80, 105–6n24,
    122, 139–40, 176
Routley, Richard, 112

Sachs, Aaron, 200, 202
Sandler, Ron, 11–12, 156–57n54
Schalow, Frank, 122–23
Schmidtz, David, 9
science, proper role of, 37
self-acceptance, 54–56
self-development, 74–75, 208
self-interest: and altruism, 31–32,
    37–38, 40, 40–41n5, 41n6, 43n40,
    64–66, 67–77, 78n16, 134n22,
    137–40, 160–61; enlightened, 4–5,
    31–32, 34, 39–40, 101, 132–33,
    138–40
selfishness, 74–75, 207
self-knowledge, 55–56, 67
self-respect, 68–69
Sen, Amartya, 79–80
sensitivity, 127
Shaw, Bill, 9, 73, 176, 219
Shell, 144–45
Sherman, Nancy, 83
Shiva, Vandana, 200, 201
Shue, Henry, 84, 85
silence, 63–64
simplicity, 33
sins, seven deadly, 205–6
sloth, 130–32, 151, 206. See also apathy
Solomon, Robert, 88–89n2
Spencer, Bill, 144–45
Spinoza, 152
Stegner, Wallace, 62–63
stewardship, 22, 122–22
Stoics, 152, 217, 218, 228–29n10
Stone, Christopher, 30n39
Strange, Marty, 166–67
superiority, human, 68
sustainability, ecological: criterion for
    genuine virtue, 73, 152; necessary for
    human flourishing, 80–81
SUVs (sport utility vehicles), 198, 206–7,
    209–10
synergism, environmental, 11, 197,
    209–10

Taliaferro, Charles, 10
Taylor, Paul, 219–20, 229n18
Taylor, Prudence, 87
temperance, 184–85, 206–8

Thoreau, Henry, 32–33, 34, 37–39,
    43n40, 74–75, 143, 151

utilitarianism, 107–10

Vandermel, Bud, 146
vegetarianism, 164–65, 211
vice: consumerism promotes, 205–7;
    defined, 136–37; environmental, 10,
    21, 23, 94, 129–32, 135–58, 138–40,
    197; intellectual, 131–32; a neglected
    topic, 153–54n1; theistic
    environmental, 163–64
virtue, 6–7, 69, 99, 151–52;
    environmental, 3–6, 10, 152
virtue ethics: and action guidance, 216–17,
    228n7; defined, 6–7, 31, 216–17. See
    also environmental virtue ethics
virtues: active vs. passive, 151–52,
    157–58n78, 158n80; aesthetic, 56–57,
    63–64; of attunement, 177, 187;
    Buddhist, 166; business, 20; cardinal,
    10–11, 22, 23, 173–80, 186–88, 189n4,
    194n67; of care, 176, 187; Christian,
    190n23; civic, 62; and consumerism,
    207–9; defined, 99; dirty, 15; of
    endurance, 177, 187–88;
    environmental, 2–7, 197; and GMOs,
    223–26; intellectual, 51–54, 63–64,
    65–66; natural, 61–62; naturalist's, 34,
    127; nonhuman, 34–35, 42–43n26, 69;
    physical, 42n24; pictured, 180–86; of
    position, 176, 186–87; theistic, 163–69

Walzer, Michael, 161
Welchman, Jennifer, 122–23, 176, 177, 219
Wensveen, Louke van, 7, 10–11, 73, 138,
    144, 152, 218, 229n17
Wenz, Peter, 11
Westra, Laura, 8–9
White, Lynn, 19, 26–27, 162
Whitman, Walt, 63
wilderness protection, 38, 40, 43–44n42,
    62–63, 74

Yao, Xingzhong, 161

Zwolinski, Matthew, 9